EUROPE:
a brief history

VOLUME ONE

EUROPE:
a brief history

Revised and Expanded Second Edition

VOLUME ONE
Prehistory to 1815

GEORGE A. ROTHROCK
University of Alberta

TOM B. JONES
University of Minnesota

Copyright © 1975, 1971 by **Rand McNally College Publishing Company**

University Press of America,® Inc.

4720 Boston Way
Lanham, MD 20706

3 Henrietta Street
London WC2E 8LU England

All rights reserved

Printed in the United States of America

Library of Congress Cataloging in Publication Data

Rothrock, George A.
  Europe: a brief history.

  Reprint. Originally published: Chicago: Rand McNally
College Pub. Co., 1975. (Rand McNally history series)
  Includes bibliographies and indexes.
  Contents: v. 1. Prehistory to 1815—V. 2. Renaissance to the present.
  1. Europe—History. I. Jones, Tom Bard, 1909-
II. Title.
D103.R7   1982   940   81-43503
ISBN 0-8191-2069-3 (v. 1)   AACR2
ISBN 0-8191-2070-7 (pbk. : v. 1)
ISBN 0-8191-2071-5 (v. 2)
ISBN 0-8191-2072-3 (pbk. : v. 2)

Reprinted by arrangement with

Houghton Mifflin Company, Boston

All University Press of America books are produced on acid-free
paper which exceeds the minimum standards set by the National
Historical Publications and Records Commission.

Preface

Confronted with the rich mosaic of national societies that comprise the world of the twentieth century, universities now are offering studies of the histories of many peoples and areas. Despite this wholly commendable trend, however, European history and its antecedents always must occupy a special place for the western student, for it is the background and foundation of his own past. It can claim consideration from non-western peoples, too, for many of the ideas and attitudes deeply affecting non-western societies in the modern world are products of western culture, from Christianity to communism. Thus, the broader range of historical studies now available may be expected to complement and enrich rather than displace European history.

There are several texts on the market that present the course of European history or western civilization in one form or another, and it may be useful to suggest why the authors were moved to write yet another. In general, the nature of introductory history courses has changed rather markedly in the last decade or two and textbooks have failed to keep pace with the change; perhaps a fondness for traditional patterns is the occupational hazard of the historian. We are persuaded that the courses now being presented to beginning students are much more sophisticated than was the case not very long ago. We think this development stems partly from the fact that our students are more sophisticated today and partly from two innovations: discussion groups and supplementary readings. In the recent past, reliance upon insufficient staff time resulted in courses depending almost wholly upon lectures, for few graduate students were available to cope with quantities of junior students in small groups; and supplementary readings usually entailed a chapter here and there from books placed on reserve shelves in the library, a system unsatisfactory to all concerned but unavoidable because of the cost of books. In recent years, however, the expansion of graduate study and the growth of the paperback book market have made both discussion groups and supplemental book purchase almost standard for introductory courses.

Despite these changes, textbooks today are little different in concept from those written long ago. There are undeniable improvements, such as broadened perspectives, which include social and economic history, and interpretive rather than purely factual approaches; but almost without exception texts still assume that a student's whole course must be subsumed between two covers, and that the instructor will lecture and examine from the text. This assumption and the attempt to bring a more sophisticated distillation of recent scholarly erudition to the beginning student result in rather formidable bulk and cost; a discouraging consequence is that an instructor must limit severely the number of paperback supplements that he can ask a student to buy and use if he has any regard for the limitations of the student's time and money.

In an attempt to avoid these frustrations, from time to time some of us have tried to run a course without a text, using a list of paperbacks instead, but the results have not been very satisfactory. The student emerges with several bits of fragmentary expertise and weak perspectives. There seems still to be a consensus among instructors of history that a summary text is highly desirable, and it was with this idea that the present book was conceived.

Another consideration that has influenced the writing of this book is our impression that the role as well as the level of sophistication of introductory history courses has changed rather radically since World War II. It once was fair to assume that most liberal arts students would take several history courses and that few other students would take any. Both of these assumptions now are open to serious challenge. On the one hand, the growth of new approaches to the study of human experience—in sociology, psychology and anthropology, for example—has provided meaningful competition to historical study, and working within systems of "options," many students now take only one or two history courses and sometimes none. On the other hand, more and more students from other degree programs are turning up in history courses. Some rather haphazard surveys made in several universities during recent years, have shown that over half the enrollment in introductory history courses came from outside the arts faculty. In part this trend is attributable to the shift in emphasis from method to content study in education faculties; in part it reflects a developing pattern of increased study of humanities and social sciences on the part of science students. Whatever the reasons, many students will take only one history course, and they will come from a variety of areas of study, facts that should make us pause to reflect upon what the course should accomplish.

In one way historians are singularly fortunate. A teaching department must provide its students with both scope and depth, broad views and methodological precision. In contrast to the student in the sciences, who must learn methodology and laboratory technique before proceeding, the history student can begin his study with either aspect of his discipline, scope or depth, so long as he learns both synthesis and criticism in the course of his total program. Future history majors do not suffer by beginning with a broad view which they will fill in with more intensive studies of particular periods and societies, acquiring research methodology as they proceed.

An introductory history course can—and these days must—serve many roles. For the history major it must provide a broad overview that will allow him to make meaningful choices of the areas in which he wishes to concentrate and it must give perspective to his later studies. For other students in the humanities and social sciences it should offer a frame of reference that will add depth and understanding to studies of literature or economics or art. For the non-arts student it should provide a background that can aid his comprehension of his own world and at the same time can challenge his ethnocentrism by showing the validity of other societies based upon values quite different from his own. And for the undecided student, who might contemplate further historical studies, it should show how the historian works, his tools and methods and material, so the student may judge realistically whether this is the sort of endeavor that he would wish to pursue.

A course conscientiously structured achieves success in most of these roles, however, if sufficient flexibility can be maintained, and flexibility and variety are achieved best through the use of several different kinds of paperbacks. Paperback supplements can provide documentary collections to be analyzed, monographic studies to illustrate the complexity of the past, biographies to lend human perspective and "problems" books to show how interpretive theories vary. A prime goal of this book is to provide some perspectives on the European background in sufficiently small bulk and cost as to allow great flexibility in the assignment of paperbacks.

This approach offers several advantages. It should increase the utility of discussion groups, since assignments in the text will be sufficiently brief to permit the assignment of supplementary readings as the basis for group discussion. The use of several outside readings instead of just a few will make it possible to avoid overemphasizing the easy generalizations that are part of any text and to demonstrate how sharply historians disagree on the meaning of the past.

And such an approach should increase the instructor's freedom to determine the nature of the course, for the text presents only general perspectives, and areas of emphasis will depend upon the supplements selected. In Volume I, for instance, when a class comes to discuss Chapter 11, which deals with the period of the Viking depredations, it might go in any of a number of directions. Instructors who consider the Vikings interesting only for their effects upon the more southerly regions of Europe may find the material presented here quite enough about the raiders themselves, but others might wish to assign a supplemental book on the Vikings. Those whose major interests lie in the British Isles may find the sketch of developments on the European continent sufficient and want to add a book on Anglo-Saxon England. Someone else may feel that western Europe is overemphasized and add readings on Kiev Rus, while yet another instructor might prefer a book on the Carolingian Empire. By the same token, in connection with Chapter 15, which concerns itself with tensions and conflicts in medieval society, choices might range widely over heresy, economic development, the apogee of the papacy or the court of Frederick II.

Thus, a course can be shaped around those elements of our ancient and European past that particular instructors find most interesting or most important, and the student can be exposed to the viewpoints of several authors. We hope this book provides the basic background while allowing whatever national or period or topical emphasis an instructor may wish to use. To this end, we have included some rather brief "suggestions for further reading." To discover which of these selections are available in any given year reference should be made to the full listings of *Paperbacks in Print* (dealing with the offerings of American publishers) and *Paperbound Books in Print* (British publishers). Fuller critical lists also can be found in Lyon, Rowen and Hamerow, *A History of the Western World* (Rand McNally, 2nd ed., 1974).

GEORGE A. ROTHROCK
TOM B. JONES

Contents

Introduction	1
1. Historians, History, and Prehistory	6
2. The First Civilizations	15
3. The Early Empires	29
4. The Greek City States	43
5. The Great Empires	56
6. The Decline and Fall of the Roman Republic	73
7. Imperial Rome	89
8. The Twilight of the Roman Empire	101
9. The Heirs of Rome	116
10. Early Carolingian Europe	131
11. A Time of Trial	146
12. The Birth of Feudal Monarchy	159
13. Merchants, Money, and Social Change	178
14. The Apogee of Medieval Christianity	191
15. Challenge and Conflict in Later Medieval Europe	204
16. The Hundred Years War	219
17. The Disintegration of Medieval Europe	233
18. The Renaissance	253
19. Religious Reaction and Reform	269
20. Habsburg Hegemony	284
21. The Scientific Revolution	299
22. The Rise of the National State	312
23. The Birth of the Balance of Power	326
24. Man, God, and Reason	340
25. A Harvest of Violence	353
Suggestions for Further Reading	369
Index	381

Maps

Ancient Egypt	13
Ancient Mesopotamia	14
The Near East and Greece	28
The Ancient World in the Seventh Century B.C.	42
Persian Empire and Greece	49
Alexander's Empire	64–65
Roman Republic in the Time of Caesar and Cicero	86–87
Roman Empire about 120 A.D.	98–99
Roman Empire about 400 A.D.	112–113
Germanic Kingdoms at Death of Theodoric (526 A.D.)	129
Eastern Roman Empire in the Reign of Justinian	129
The Caliphate (750 A.D.)	130
The Growth of the Carolingian Empire	144
Carolingian Empire in 870	145
Carolingian Empire 876–911	145
Germany under the Saxon and Franconian Kings (10th–12th centuries)	174
The Crusader States	175
Europe about 1200	176–177
France in 1483	240
The Burgundian State in 1475	241
Europe in the Middle of the Fifteenth Century	244–245
The Age of Discovery	250–251
The Empire of Charles V (1519–1556)	264
Italy in the Late Fifteenth Century	265
Established Churches and Religious Minorities about 1600	281
Europe in 1810	366
Europe in 1815	367

Charts

Comparative Chronologies, 3000–1000 B.C.	27
Comparative Chronologies, 1000–500 B.C.	41
The Early Carolingians	157
The Saxon and Franconian Kings	157
The Norman and Angevin Kings	158
The Capetian Kings	172
The Hohenstaufen Kings	173
The Valois Kings	173
The Lancastrian and Yorkist Kings	217
The Luxemburg and Habsburg Dynasties	217
The House of Habsburg	218
The House of Valois	218
The House of Tudor	280
The House of Stuart	280
The Austrian Habsburgs	297
The Spanish Habsburgs	297
The House of Bourbon	298

Introduction

The beginning student often is tempted to assume that history is a dead record of the past, and unfortunately a great deal of traditional instruction—emphasizing names and dates and battles and treaties—has tended to confirm that view. But new historical works continue to pour from the presses, and historians argue among themselves constantly. There is a dynamic, a process of continuous change in the understanding of the meaning of events.

No wholly satisfactory definition of history ever has been recorded. Descriptions have ranged all the way from Lord Acton's optimistic opinion that "history is the progress of liberty" to Henry Ford's observation that "history is bunk." Whatever else it might be, however, history is not a dead record but a living tradition, a collective memory offering some roots and a sense of continuity to men and women in any age, people who must confront the challenges and choices of their own times.

Several sorts of variables operate more or less constantly in historical scholarship. First, we continue to learn about what actually happened in the past, and new data often force changes of interpretation. For instance, the discovery and study of the famous Dead Sea Scrolls in the middle of this century have expanded greatly our understanding of life and customs and beliefs in early Palestine, with important consequences for Biblical history. The deciphering of an early Greek script some years ago added new perspectives to the study of early eastern Mediterranean societies.

Moreover, other sources of knowledge have been added to the traditional basis of written records. The excavations undertaken by archeologists and the resultant analysis of physical artifacts—tools, weapons, ornaments and buildings—give us information about preliterate peoples for whom we have no written records and reinforce our studies of other peoples for whom the written record is meager. Related to these studies is the development of technical tools of great advantage; for instance, the carbon 14 dating process and other newer but similar approaches can be immeasurably valuable in helping to confirm estimates of dates on ancient sites. By no means do we know all that we would like to know about what happened in the past, and new knowledge may confirm or may invalidate what we long have thought we knew.

But more significant to the dynamics of historical interpretation is the transformation of our understanding of what events mean, changes that occur for a great variety of reasons. One obvious influence upon historical interpretation has been the development, during the last hundred years, of new techniques of analysis. In the late nineteenth century, Marxism, with its emphasis upon economic causation, produced more than political controversy; it forced historians to a more minute and more sophisticated analysis of the impact of economic factors upon social and political development. The psychological studies of Sigmund Freud early in this century have added enormous depth to our understanding of the complexities of personality and character, so that today one finds little of the "heroes and villains" interpretation that runs through a great deal of older work. New scholarly dimensions have been added by the work of anthropologists in comparative cultures and of sociologists in statistical analysis. So changes in historical interpretations sometimes are motivated by perspectives developed by scholars in related fields of study.

Perhaps the greatest stimulus to changing historical interpretation is the fact that we continually ask different questions of our past. It is remarked sometimes that every generation rewrites history for itself, and the remark carries a subtle implication that because history can be used to prove anything, it really proves nothing. Yet without the cynicism, the observation is valid. To a certain extent every generation *must* rewrite history, because every generation seeks perspective upon its own problems and, therefore, wants to know different things about its past. Certainly circumstances never repeat themselves sufficiently for one to be able to find in the past a definitive prescription for the ills of the present; but categories of problems recur, and at the lowest level of commonality all problems in history are problems of men in conflict with their environment and/or their fellow men. In the process of attempting to choose between competing courses of action—say between concession and repression in the face of political violence—the experience of our predecessors may aid us in making decisions.

The easiest illustration of this phenomenon is a theme that became extremely prominent in historical writing during the last two generations, the multinational approach. It is no coincidence that many-volume integrated studies of European and world history were launched in three languages and in three different countries at roughly the same time—the years between the first and second world wars. Most histories written during the nineteenth and early twentieth centuries tended to have a distinctly national orientation, reflecting the great strength of nationalism in most European countries at that time. While conceding certain commonalities of a classical and Christian background and of modern alliances and trade, historians tended to stress the individuality and uniqueness of their own nations and to write histories of the development of national institutions and national cultures that helped to explain this individuality and uniqueness. Then the cataclysm of the Great War demonstrated irrefutably the close interconnection of the several national societies of Europe, showing clearly that whatever their differences of organization and aspiration their fates were interwoven inextricably. The need to understand better the development of Europe as a whole, the relationships among its various components, produced three new historical series: in France, *Peuples et Civilizations,* in Germany, *Propylaen Weltgeschichte,* and in the United States, *The Rise of Modern Europe.* All of these turned back to material often studied before, but they asked different questions of the material, and consequently they were able to offer new and different understandings of modern European history.

Another question that one must confront in any study of mankind, historical or contemporary, is the problem of free will and determinism. The problem is particularly acute when dealing with prominent or great men and women. Do individuals change the direction of their society and impose their will upon it, or are they but products of inexorable processes, puppets of economic, political and social forces? The ancients believed in the unreasoning vagaries of the gods and the fates, granting one man happiness and condemning another to tragedy quite haphazardly. Early Christians had to confront the problem too, for if they asserted the existence of an all-powerful God, how could they maintain that man had free will and, hence, the responsibility of choosing good instead of evil? (In general terms the rather complicated solution was to assert that God refrained from exercising his potentially all-determining power so as to leave mankind choice, offering the strength to choose goodness to all who sought it sincerely.) To the later medieval world the problem appeared in yet another guise. Astrology, a belief that the future could be read in the stars, was largely an import from the Near East and won wide support in Europe. The implications of determinism, and hence of lack of responsibility, were dangerous, but the church found a compromise, conceding that events in the physical world might be determined and their pattern revealed by God in the heavens, but asserting that man remained responsible for his moral and spiritual choices.

In more recent times determinist arguments have arisen most often from the development of the social sciences. A number of relatively recent approaches to the study of man have been quite disturbing to the supporters of free will. Psychology has demonstrated, for instance, that some human behavior is conditioned by sexual attitudes, parental relationships, and early experiences. And sociologists have been able to establish fairly accurate estimates of crowd behavior, suggesting that when a group of certain composition is confronted with a particular situation, given percentages will react in predictable ways. The proponents of free will reply, however, that psychology can predict only how an individual *is likely to* behave in certain categories of situations and cannot predict how a person *will* behave in every particular situation. By the same token, sociology can predict patterns of crowd behavior, but it cannot predict how particular individuals will behave.

Most modern students of human behavior tend to compromise between the extremes of absolute free will and complete determinism, asserting that man exercises free will within generally definable limits. In this context the social sciences may be regarded as helping to define the limits of the range of choice. Thus one might suggest that on the eve of the French Revolution the king could not have chosen to study and estimate popular discontent by holding a plebiscite and tabulating the results. This idea was wholly foreign to the structure of his society and the tools required to implement such an idea did not exist. On the other hand, he did have to make significant choices—absolute repression, some combination of resistance and concession, sweeping reform. Or one may observe that in struggles for equal rights, where prejudice operates against blacks or Asians or Jews or Catholics, only some men can choose consciously to reject their prejudices as a result of rational persuasion, while others cannot make that choice because years of conditioning or deep-rooted psychological compulsions persuade them unshakably that the objects of their prejudice are inferior or evil or whatever.

Among these many problems and pitfalls the historian must walk cautiously. Probably it is impossible to avoid bias and preconception entirely, but we must at least try to be aware of them. Probably there will always be exaggerated enthusiasm for "new insights" and "revisionist" interpretation, but we must not allow a disdain for fads to render historical methodology inflexible. In any case, among so many variables and challenges history cannot be a "dead record."

Chapter 1

Historians, History, and Prehistory

A very clever French gentleman once said that history is a fable upon which all have agreed. There is some truth in this—man's knowledge of the past is far from perfect—but fabulous or not, there is no consensus. If there were, historical research would cease, and, contrary to fact, it would be impossible to overturn or modify concepts of former events and developments, either by the discovery of new bits of evidence or by the reinterpretation of older material.

The study of history requires access to many different kinds of sources. In general, these fall into three major categories. The first encompasses the record of nature: the geologic, zoological, botanical, and other types of evidence needed to reconstruct the physical story of this planet from its beginning to the present time. The second comprises the archaeological evidence, the material cultural remains of mankind's sojourn on earth: tools, utensils, machines, varieties of construction, and a large assortment of other artifacts fashioned by human beings. In the third category are man's own records—written, taped, filmed, etc. From all these sources, properly arranged and correctly interpreted, one might aspire to outline the history of man and his planet: what the human race has done, what it has thought about the world and itself, what it has hoped and believed, and what it has striven to accomplish. For any detailed study of human society the last category of source material is the most important, for without man's own records the greater part of the story of the last five thousand years would be inaccessible. But however abundant the evidence in any category may be, there are inevitable gaps: missing links in the chain of nature, artifacts that have perished, and the thoughts and deeds of men and women never recorded or those that were recorded but later suppressed or destroyed. All these factors complicate the task of the historian, deny him completeness and absolute conviction of accuracy, and often leave him to assemble pitiful little scraps of evidence and construct hypotheses, some of which may be correct and others wide of the mark.

It was about 3000 B.C., approximately five millennia ago, that writing and record-keeping first began. Although scattered narratives of events do not appear much before 2500 B.C. and formal histories come along even later, most people would agree that the *historic* period, characterized by written records, begins with the introduction of writing. This would coincide with one of the great watersheds in human cultural achievement because at the same time (*c.* 3000 B.C.) the first civilizations, those of Egypt and Mesopotamia, were founded. Defining the historic period in this way permits one to follow the common practice of denoting earlier times as *prehistoric*, although it is not easy to decide where prehistory begins. For a long time there was no life on earth, and even after the first living things appeared there were no animals; moreover, it was millions of years later that the earliest human or manlike creatures evolved, and still more time elapsed before these newest denizens of the earth came into the possession of that unique attribute, *culture*, that would henceforth distinguish them from all other animals.

A useful definition of culture is "the sum total of ways of living built up by a group of human beings, which is transmitted from one generation to another," or one may say that "culture is the aggregate of all that the hands and brains of humanity have produced." In short, a person may literally inherit physical characteristics from his forebears, but cultural inheritance is only figurative, acquired bit by bit from the society in which one lives. Culture includes not only art, music, and literature, for example, but also customs and traditions, all concepts and institutions, and all the materials and material objects fashioned by human hands. The earliest cultures were, of course, much less complex than the later supercultures or *civilizations* generated during the historic period, and, although the chief concern of this book is with developments from 3000 B.C. to the present, a few words must be said about prehistory, especially in regard to the process of cultural evolution leading to the establishment of the first civilizations.

Although it may have been preceded by something else, the first indication that man, the animal, has become man, the animal with culture, is given by the appearance of the most primitive stone tools. These suggest that he has become the habitual user and manufacturer of these implements, and one can follow through the ages the elaboration of such tools and weapons and the invention of others. A progressive series tells the story of the development of hunting skills and the beginning of the manufacture of clothing. Charred remains attest that people had learned to make fire. When humans began to dispose of their dead through burial or other means, it can be assumed that they had evolved a belief in the supernatural; ultimately, this evidence is buttressed by cave paintings which, in addition, suggest the invention of magic to achieve, as they must have supposed, some control over the forces of nature.

It can only be guessed that after becoming a tool-user, but before the time of the cave paintings, man began to communicate by means of symbols—gestures, vocal sounds, and then articulate speech; the last step in this development of communication was taken very late—when writing was invented.

Enough has been said to establish the nature of the basic differences between humans and the other animals: the habitual use and manufacture of tools and the ability to create and use symbols as a means of communication. These capacities in turn stem from attributes attained by mankind in the process of physical evolution. The gradual assumption of an erect posture freed the hands for grasping and handling and furthered the use of that built-in set of pliers known as the "opposable thumb." The erect posture also allowed changes in the shape of the head, which paved the way for binocular or stereoscopic vision and promoted an increasing cranial capacity; this in turn permitted not only the growth of a larger brain but also the development of important areas within the brain, aided and strengthened by the use and manufacture of tools. The larger and more complex brain made possible a more retentive memory and the capacity to imitate more easily, to conceptualize, and to communicate through a variety of symbols. In addition, physical changes permitted articulate speech which, combined with the capacity for symbolization, facilitated more precise communication as well as the exchange and perpetuation of ideas.

Culture was born more than two million years ago. Its earliest known users and possible inventors were not of our species (*homo sapiens*) and perhaps not even our physical ancestors. Even down to about 30,000 years ago, culture was the possession of the various types of "fossil men" as well as *homo sapiens*, but because of greater mental capacity, greater potential for adaptation to different or changing environments, or just luck, our species alone survived.

By combining the record of nature with the archaeological evidence, one can sketch in broad outline the developments in that last phase of prehistory from the beginnings of culture to the advent of the historic period. Although very little can be said about specific events and nothing at all about individuals in prehistory, it is possible to describe or delineate cultures, discuss their technology and economy, and make some educated guesses about social and political institutions and beliefs. In some cases, it is useful to employ analogies drawn from what is known about contemporary primitive peoples to explain certain aspects of prehistoric behaviour, customs, and concepts. With regard to the main sources of information, the record of nature not only relates to human physical evolution but also reveals environmental situations and changes, while the archaeological record shows the cultural response to these things, how men and women developed and altered their culture in order to survive under changing and often adverse conditions.

Three facts of special importance stand out: (1) in terms of population size, humans became more numerous as time passed, mainly because culture increased their chances of survival; (2) by 10,000 B.C. and possibly earlier, our species was to be found in the New World as well as the Old; and (3) shortly after 10,000 B.C. an economic revolution began that increased the human population and paved the way for the rise of the first civilizations.

From the very beginning, men and women, whether they hunted, fished, or gathered, had been food collectors. The introduction of culture did not at first change this condition. Tools and weapons only increased the efficiency of the collectors, while the use of fire for cooking enlarged the menu of edible foods. Hunting and gathering necessitated mobility. Hunters must follow the game, and they must fish or collect foods in certain places at specific seasons. Permanent camp sites and dwelling places were the exception rather than the rule. Even the caves were ordinarily occupied only during the cold weather; people moved out in milder periods of the year to pursue their collecting activities. With an economy of this sort one can hardly speak of population density. Hunters and collectors needed a large territory to support even a small group of people. Under optimum conditions an average of one person per square mile might be attained; by modern standards such a region would be designated as uninhabited.

About 10,000–12,000 years ago in the grassy uplands of the area where Turkey, Syria, and Iraq now share common borders, the inhabitants began systematically to harvest wild grains and to capture young wild animals that were kept in pens until they were big enough to eat. From these activities it was only a step, though a long and important one, to the domestication of plants and animals. Specifically, the cereals (wheat and barley) and the herd animals (cattle, sheep, and goats) played the most significant role in this process. By domesticating plants and animals man became a food producer instead of a collector. This was the so-called Agricultural Revolution, a major turning point in the story of mankind.

The consequences of the domestication of plants and animals were many and varied. Food supply was greatly increased and could be anticipated with more certainty than formerly. This factor led to a spectacular increase in the human population. The adoption of an agricultural economy also changed the way of life of the human family. In general, a farmer must settle in one place to tend his crops. Permanent dwellings were built, clustered in little villages. Agriculture brought new beliefs and practices in religion and magic; village life produced a new political and social organization. In addition, there was a growing specialization of labor. In a typical village, most inhabitants might be farmers, but there would also be herdsmen, artisans, traders, and some who were primarily hunters and fishermen. In other words, as the farmer became virtually immobile, tied to his crops, other members of the community had to tend the animals, make the tools, seek out the materials and products not locally available, or supplement the food supply by hunting and fishing.

These changes did not take place overnight. Plants and animals were not domesticated simultaneously, and for a long time agriculture and herding were peripheral rather than basic activities. Two thousand years elapsed between the start of the domestication process (c. 8000 B.C.) and the appearance of large "peasant villages" with agriculture as their mainstay (c. 6000 B.C.). By the latter date, moreover, the Agricultural Revolution had spread to adjacent regions in Europe, Asia, and Africa, and this diffusion was to continue for many centuries to come.

Naturally, in some environments that lacked suitable climates or soils, agriculture would never be an essential element in the economy; and, of course, some of the first domesticated plants could not be grown everywhere so that other varieties had to be domesticated to take their place. People who had learned a set of methods adequate for agriculture in one region found that when they migrated to a new area changes in procedures were necessary. This was particularly true of the farmers who moved into the great river valleys of the lower Tigris-Euphrates and the Nile. The soil in these regions was immensely fertile but rainfall was inadequate, so that agriculture was possible only with irrigation. Once this essential lesson had been learned, however, levels of production far above those realized elsewhere were attained. Because more food was available, there was an increase in population; villages in the river valleys grew into large towns, almost cities. Cultural growth was luxuriant and increasingly complex. Civilization was born.

Looking backward from this point, it is immediately apparent that culture had grown at an accelerated pace. For two million years men and women had been food gatherers, but the Agricultural Revolution was accomplished in two millennia, and only about 1500 years elapsed between the arrival of the first farmers in the river valleys and the completion of their journey to the threshold of civilization. This phenomenon can be explained in part by the fact that new culture traits frequently result from the combination of two or more older ones; thus, while the store of culture accumulated during the ages, opportunities for cultural innovation increased in a geometric proportion as the possibilities for new combinations and permutations of culture traits expanded. Another factor in creativity, however, is stimulus, or, as some would have it, "challenge and response." The peasant villagers, for example, who had attained a certain equilibrium and were living comfortably off the fruits of the Agricultural Revolution might have perpetuated their way of life with little change for thousands of years; those who moved into the river valleys, however, found themselves in a different situation, one that demanded change and the exercise of ingenuity. They took the store of culture which they had brought with them and made such modifications as would serve them in the new environment. Variations of this process may be observed in the rise of Greek civilization or in the great renaissance that marked the beginning of the modern era. In these two cases, the rediscovery of an older civilization provided the stimulus for growth; by testing, adapting, and modifying the older elements, foundations were provided upon which something new could be built. In the history of culture amazing results have been achieved by pouring old wine into new bottles.

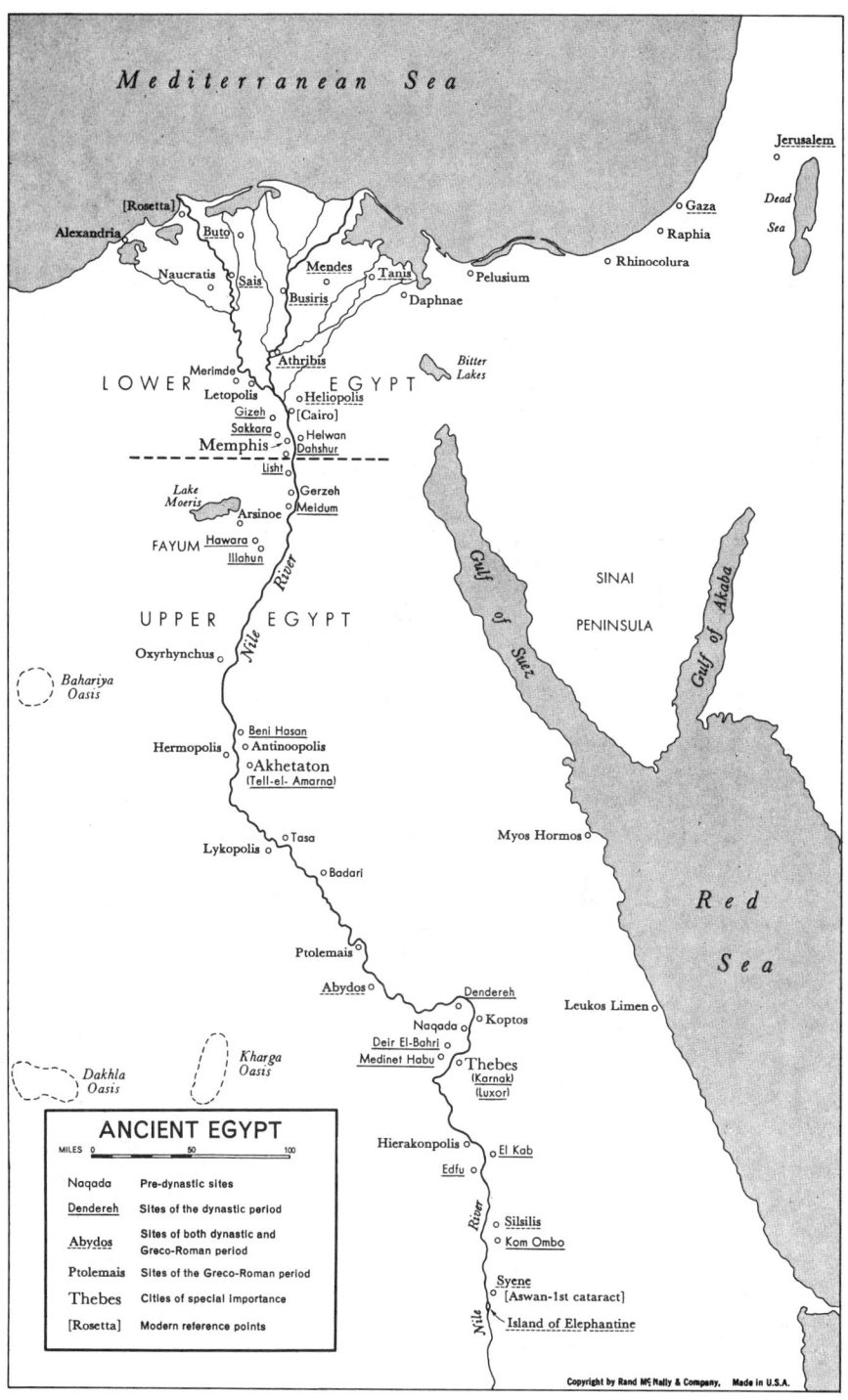

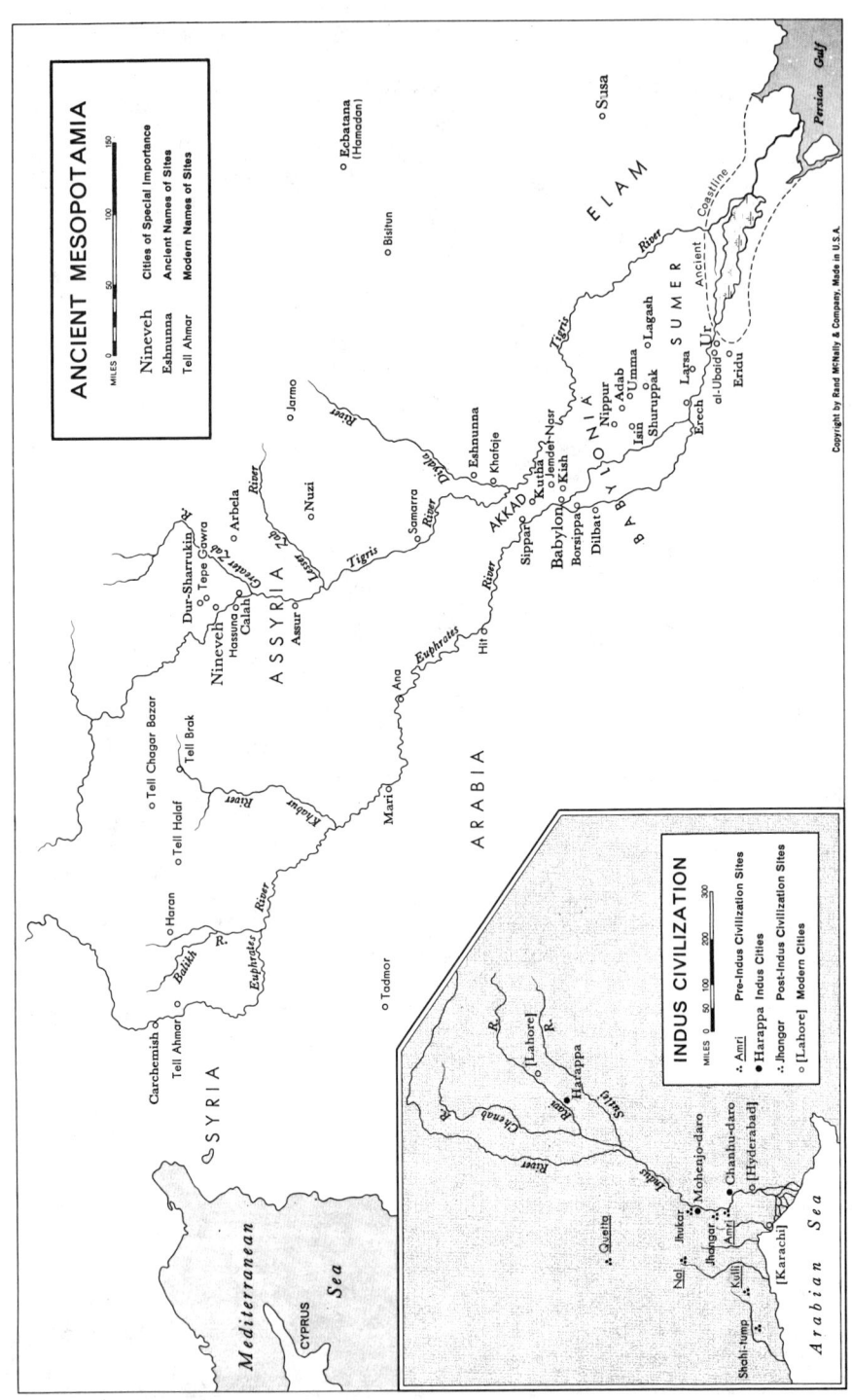

Chapter 2

The First Civilizations

"Western civilization" is not all western. It presently contains many elements from East Asia, Africa, and the pre-Columbian cultures of the New World. In addition, while its principal roots are bedded in the classical Mediterranean civilization of the Greeks and Romans, still others can be traced back to the even more ancient riverine civilizations of the Near East. Viewing the matter in this light, it can be maintained that "western civilization" originated not in Europe but in Asia and Africa and that a survey of its historical development might properly begin with the great river valleys in Egypt and Mesopotamia.

Indeed, it was along the Nile in Egypt and in the lower Tigris-Euphrates valley of Mesopotamia that civilization first appeared. The process of evolution from culture to superculture was virtually complete before 3000 B.C., and the Indus civilization came into existence shortly after this. In the course of time a composite civilization of the Ancient Near East developed from these foundations, and ultimately the civilizations of India, Greece and Rome, and Islam as well as the "western" variety would owe much to the accomplishments of those ancients who created the first civilizations.

The three primary supercultures had much in common. They were all located in river valleys in approximately the same latitude, and each evolved a way of life suited to its own environmental circumstances. Their basic patterns would be maintained by the later inhabitants of the same areas; each became a center for the origin and diffusion of culture traits to surrounding regions—thus fostering the geographical spread of civilization; in addition, there was a remarkable similarity in many aspects of their political and economic organization as well as in certain of their cultural achievements. The economy of each rested upon a massive agricultural base to which trade and industry, although extensive, were subsidiary. All three had to develop large-scale irrigation and to solve difficult problems of flood control. Irrigation and flood control were managed in Egypt and Mesopotamia, and probably in the Indus as well, by the establishment of a centralized government, theocratic (god-ruled) in theory, which by virtue of a combination of "church and state" (temple and palace) wielded a ponderous authority that could mobilize the national work force to construct and maintain irrigation works, accomplish flood control, bring agricultural production to a peak of volume and efficiency, and erect those monumental works of architecture—temples, palaces, pyramids, ziggurats—that were the object of awe and envy for countless generations to come.

In seeking the roots of western civilization it is best to concentrate on Egypt and Mesopotamia, leaving the Indus civilization out of the discussion. The two principal reasons for this are: first, the Indus civilization does not appear to be so directly ancestral to the western; and second, outside of the archaeological remains from the Indus, very little is known about this obviously important superculture. For Egypt and Mesopotamia there are not only the archaeological materials but also such information about these countries as was included in the Old Testament and the Greek and Latin authors of classical times. There is, as well, a wealth of documents written by the Egyptians and Mesopotamians themselves and preserved on stone, metal, papyrus, clay, and other materials used to receive writing. It has already been mentioned that writing is one of the culture traits commonly associated with civilization, and while it is true that the Indus people had invented a script, examples of it are relatively limited in number and the script itself has not yet been deciphered.

In both Egypt and Mesopotamia the primary phase of civilization began before 3000 B.C. and ended shortly after 1600. Both were declining in political strength by the latter date, and in each case the finishing touches were provided by barbarian invasions. Although Egypt soon recovered from this blow and rose to new glories, a thousand years passed before Babylonia (lower Mesopotamia) could once again be counted among the first-rate powers of the ancient world.

In its primary phase Egypt enjoyed two main periods of progress and prosperity during which the country was unified under a central administration directed by the pharaoh, in theory a god-king, all wise and all powerful. The first of these periods was the Old Kingdom, or Pyramid Age (*c.* 2700–2200 B.C.); the second was the Middle Kingdom, which flourished *c.* 2000–1800 and then slowly declined. Throughout most of the Old Kingdom period the pharaoh was never stronger or more secure. Symbolic of all this majesty are the pyramids, the largest structures ever erected in antiquity. These were the royal tombs of the pharaohs, begun during the lifetime of each ruler and requiring the labor of thousands of his subjects over a period of many years. The pyramid would be the dwelling place of the god-king after he retired from this life; surrounded by temples and shrines, the area was a cult center staffed by a corps of priests whose mission was to serve the god forever. Perhaps, as some have claimed, the pharaohs did bankrupt Egypt and themselves with the expense of pyramid building and posthumous ceremonies, but it is certain that the Old Kingdom declined gradually as the authority of the ruler was progressively challenged by the nobles who ruled the nomes, the states or provinces into which Egypt was divided. Decentralization and even anarchy ensued (2200–2000 B.C.) until the rise of the Middle Kingdom.

The Old Kingdom was, nevertheless, a time of splendid accomplishment. It produced not only the pyramids but also fine sculpture and painting, the beginnings of a great literature, a calendar more accurate than any to be devised for hundreds of years, and an efficient economic administration that brought agricultural planning and production to high levels. Largely isolated from the rest of the world, Egypt had developed in her own way using her own resources.

The Middle Kingdom brought the reunification of Egypt, but the new era differed from the old in several ways. The Middle Kingdom pharaohs, for example, were never able to control firmly the nobles who ruled the nomes, and the many professions of goodness and piety by these pharaohs give an impression of nervous insecurity. Some modern historians have referred to the governmental system of the Middle Kingdom as feudal because the pharaoh was not absolute as in the Old Kingdom, but rather a great lord who ruled by virtue of the uncertain fealty of his nobles. Also, in this new period Egypt was less isolated than before. There were more frequent and positive contacts with Palestine and Syria, and Egyptian control was extended southward into Nubia far below the traditional boundary at the first cataract of the Nile. Architecture, sculpture, and painting attained new heights, although pyramid building was curtailed in the sense that these structures of the Middle Kingdom were smaller than those of the great Pyramid Age and built of brick instead of stone. Egyptian literature increased in volume; both poetry and prose flourished, and several medical and mathematical treatises have survived from this period. In general, it can be said that much of what is commonly regarded as typically Egyptian attained its classic form under the Middle Kingdom.

Like the Old Kingdom, the Middle Kingdom eventually declined, but for different reasons. Although the strong warrior kings who had conquered Nubia or invaded Sinai to carry off copper and turquoise had no counterparts among the last pharaohs of the Middle Kingdom, the period was brought to an end not so much by internal weakness as from the external pressure exerted by barbarians from the northeast. Sweeping down from Palestine into the Egyptian Delta, the intruders brought new anarchy to Egypt; the climax came between 1670–1570 B.C. when a foreign dynasty, that of the Hyksos, ruled Lower Egypt (the Delta) and did battle with the feeble kings of the Nile valley who still claimed for themselves the title of pharaoh.

The Hyksos invasion and conquest not only terminated the Middle Kingdom but also ended the primary phase of Egyptian civilization. When Egypt recovered, expelled the Hyksos, and launched into a new and glorious period, that of the New Kingdom (c. 1570–1100 B.C.), many aspects of Egyptian life were to be changed by larger contacts with an outside world that itself had undergone many alterations since Middle Kingdom times.

Unlike Egypt, where from the beginning of the pharaonic era to the Hyksos invasion the population had remained reasonably homogeneous and stable in composition, Mesopotamia was subject to many invasions that affected the makeup of the populace and also produced cultural changes. Not the earliest inhabitants of the lower Tigris-Euphrates valley, but certainly the founders of civilization there, were the Sumerians, a people of unknown origin who spoke a language unrelated to any other known, either ancient or modern. Exactly when the Sumerians came to Mesopotamia is a matter of dispute, although it was undoubtedly before 3500 B.C. At the end of the fourth millennium, if not earlier, they were politically dominant and had managed to organize the lower valley into a dozen or more city states, each independent and controlled by rulers believed to be divinely chosen and commissioned by the gods to rule. By 2500 B.C. frequent intercity disputes had led to the formation of little empires of short duration as one state or another might hold its defeated neighbors in subjection. The general tendency was thus in the direction of the political unification of the whole lower valley, and the inevitable was at last accomplished by the famous Sargon of Akkad about 2350 B.C. He founded a dynasty that exercised a tenuous hold over the other city states for more than a century.

Sargon, sometimes called the "first personality in history," was long remembered as a great conqueror. In time he became a legendary figure credited with many improbable and some impossible deeds. Besides the fact that he was the first to unify the lower valley, however, perhaps the most important thing about Sargon was that he was not a Sumerian but a Semitic-speaking Akkadian whose ancestors had come from Arabia into Mesopotamia, settled in the northern part of the lower valley, and adopted many elements of Sumerian civilization. The Akkadians were very numerous by the time Sargon usurped the throne of a Sumerian ruler and went on to conquer the valley. Eventually, as will be seen, other Semitic groups would come to Mesopotamia. Overwhelmed, the Sumerians would disappear, and their territory as well as the whole of Mesopotamia would have a predominantly Semitic-speaking population for many centuries.

But this is getting ahead of the story. The Sargonid dynasty was unseated as the result of a brief foreign invasion from the north. When the invaders withdrew, the Sumerians got back into power in the city states once more. The climax came when the Sumerian kings of Ur in the extreme south became masters of the lower valley and created a new empire organized with more thoroughness and sophistication than that of Sargon. This new era of the so-called Third Dynasty of Ur began probably in the twenty-first century B.C. and lasted for something over one hundred years. It is the best known of all the subdivisions of the Sumerian epoch and the best documented, but it was also the last. The Ur III dynasty fell when it was attacked simultaneously by a new group of Semites, the Amorites, who came down the Euphrates from Syria, and by a non-Sumerian, non-Semitic people, the Elamites, who swept down from the mountains to the northeast. For a time thereafter the former realm of Ur III was divided into three kingdoms: Babylon in the north, Isin in the center, and Elamite-dominated Larsa in the south. By the eighteenth century B.C., however, unity had been restored in the following manner:

It was the Semitic-speaking Amorites who had taken Babylon as their capital and established there the so-called Old Babylonian Kingdom, which began late in the twentieth century B.C. and endured until about 1550 B.C. The sixth king of the Old Babylonian dynasty was the great Hammurabi, a master of diplomacy and military strategy, who outwitted the Elamites as well as his other enemies, the Assyrians, a Semitic people located up the Tigris in northern Mesopotamia. As a consequence, Hammurabi was able to bring the lower valley under his control and also to make a great campaign westward up the Euphrates that humbled numerous kingdoms almost to the shores of the Mediterranean.

The forty-three year reign of Hammurabi was a high point in early Mesopotamian history. Although his famous law code, for which he is best known today, was neither the first nor the most novel of such compilations, and although he was a most efficient and careful administrator, it was rather the stimulus provided by his combined successes that was in the long run the most important feature of Hammurabi's period. He sparked an age of brilliant creativity in literature, mathematics, and astronomy. A new poetry now evolved, employing the Semitic language of the Amorites and traditional Semitic metres combined with subjects drawn from Sumerian and Semitic mythology and legend. Of the new creations the most notable was the *Epic of Gilgamesh* based on a judicious selection and combination of material from Sumerian ballads relating the numerous adventures of a bygone Sumerian king. In the epic, Gilgamesh, after a series of spectacularly successful exploits, failed, as it was felt human beings must, in his quest for immortality. Like the *Iliad* and the *Odyssey* for the Greeks and Romans, the *Epic of Gilgamesh* was a treasured possession of the Mesopotamians for centuries to come. In mathematics and astronomy, too, the men of the Old Babylonian period were to build on Sumerian foundations in arithmetic and astronomical observation to evolve a mature algebra and a much more sophisticated astronomy. All in all, the achievements of the Old Babylonian era provide a good example of how an older culture that has lost its momentum may yet stimulate creativity in a group hitherto unacquainted with it.

The successors of Hammurabi lacked either his ability or perhaps his good fortune in reigning at an opportune time. Progressive but gradual decline ensued. Finally, Babylon itself was captured and sacked about 1600 B.C. by raiding Hittites who came all the way from Asia Minor just to hit and run. The weakness that resulted from this disaster enabled another group of barbarians from the north, the Kassites, to seize control of the lower valley and to hold it for nearly five centuries. Thus ended the primary period in Mesopotamia. Babylonian supremacy was destroyed, although much that the Sumerians and Babylonians had created lived on and not only determined the pattern of Mesopotamian civilization but also affected the evolution of culture among many adjacent and even faraway peoples in the years to come.

Egypt and Babylonia were alike in some ways, different in others. The habitable area in lower Mesopotamia was roughly rectangular in shape, while that of Egypt consisted of the long narrow valley of the Nile and the fan-shaped Delta, yet both regions comprised an area of some 10,000 square miles, and each had a population of about one million at the end of the primary period. Egypt was isolated, and Mesopotamia was open to invasion, so Egypt could evolve its own culture in its own way while Mesopotamian civilization underwent some changes as invaders introduced new culture traits. Egypt, as the ancients said, was fortified by nature. With the desert on the east and west, the Mediterranean on the north, and the cataracts of the Nile to the south, the only easy access was from Palestine to the northeast, the route of the Hyksos and other Semites. With a minimum of effort the Egyptians could keep foreigners out as compared to the maximum effort required in Mesopotamia. The vulnerability of the latter and the natural seclusion of the former were responsible not only for a different manner of cultural evolution but also for dissimilar political and economic systems. It is interesting to observe that Egypt always had god-kings, while in Mesopotamia only the Semitic Sargonid dynasty and the half-Semitic, half-Sumerian Ur III rulers experimented with this form; even Hammurabi and his people preferred the traditional theory that the ruler was not a god but a mortal chosen by the gods to rule. From the very beginning of the pharaonic period Egypt had devised a planned economy to which subsequent rulers adhered. In Mesopotamia, on the other hand, economic direction in Sumerian times was mostly on a local basis except for the thoroughly regimented national economy of the Ur III dynasty. Before Ur III, in the Old Babylonian period, Sargon's people in the northern part of the lower valley had a free enterprise system. In Mesopotamia during the early Sumerian phase a large proportion of the land was in the hands of the temple authorities while the lands of the ruler were somewhat limited. Then the amount of temple land was reduced by the Ur III kings, and the process was accelerated by the Amorite conquerors who expanded both private ownership and the royal domain at the expense of the temples. The experience of Egypt in this regard was quite different; at first the crown land was the most extensive, while later more and more passed into the hands of the priests as the cost increased for maintaining the cults of the dead pharaohs.

With regard to natural resources, both Egypt and Babylonia lacked wood; Egypt did have some inferior woods for domestic construction and fuel, but in Babylonia the shortage was so severe that reeds had to be used for fuel, even in metal working. The abundance of stone in Egypt naturally promoted the column and lintel type of construction, and, understandably, the Egyptians very early became proficient in stone sculpture. In Babylonia, on the other hand, stone was lacking so that people had to learn to build with mud brick (baked brick was scarce because of the dearth of fuel). The Sumerians, because they did not have stone, had little proficiency in sculpture, and the marked improvement evident in the Old Babylonian period was due to the tradition of stone working that the Semitic invaders brought with them. The difficulty of securing wooden beams suitable for roofing large structures meant that Egyptian rooms in temple and palace construction would be long and narrow because the building material was stone, while the mud brick architecture of Mesopotamia dictated the construction of small square or rectangular rooms arranged in a complex around a central court. In order to construct a tall building under these circumstances both the Egyptians and Mesopotamians had little choice but to pile one platform on top of another, as was done with the pyramid in Egypt or the ziggurat (temple tower) in Mesopotamia.

In addition to wood, neither of the great riverine kingdoms had gold, silver, copper, or tin within its bounds. These had to be secured from the outside world. The Mesopotamians solved this problem by promoting trade, since the regions from which the metals came were either far away or controlled by tribes too powerful to be conquered. The Egyptians, on the other hand, could raid thinly populated Sinai for copper or the eastern desert or Nubia for gold. Without large-scale trade Egypt during the primary phase was always short of silver and produced little bronze because of the difficulty of securing tin. The Mesopotamians had to trade for these necessities and others, so they developed rather large manufacturing establishments to produce the metal work, textiles, and vegetable oils that could be exchanged for the metals and occasionally for wood and stone. In contrast to the growth of industry in Mesopotamia, Egyptian production was on a small scale and intended only for local consumption.

These differences in economic organization and development in the two primary civilizations affected their social and cultural history as well. Mesopotamia came to have a fairly large trading class which had wealth and political influence. Far-flung trade resulted in the wide diffusion of Mesopotamian culture including not only business methods, weights and measures, and law but also religion, language, and literature. Throughout most of the second millennium B.C., to cite only one example, the Old Babylonian (Akkadian) tongue was the almost universal language of diplomacy as well as trade.

The Egyptians and Mesopotamians differed greatly in matters of religious belief and in their general attitudes toward life and death. The stability and isolation of Egypt seems to have contributed to an optimistic view of life after death. By Middle Kingdom times it was assumed that a person who was morally deserving would pass on after death to another world that was a carbon copy of Egypt itself. If a man did his job and behaved himself, he had nothing to worry about. In Mesopotamia, on the other hand, with its many changes of fortune, there was apprehension and only one certainty: immortality was for gods alone. A man must obey the gods and work for them, and he must also accept with resignation whatever evils came his way. The underworld was a dark, damp, cheerless place where the souls of the departed existed but could not be said to live.

There were also differences in the ways in which the two peoples conceived of their gods. In Egypt there was a prevailing totemism: the deities in the nomes had the form of animals—cats, birds, cows, crocodiles, and so on. In Mesopotamia the gods were endowed with the physical appearance and the manners of men. They were capricious, naughty, even wicked, but they were powerful and had to be endured. Perhaps because there was so much that was irrational and contradictory and much need for some kind of explanation, Mesopotamia seems to have had a richer and more elaborate mythology than Egypt. Moreover, theological speculation appears to have been more highly organized and consistent in Mesopotamia. The Sumerian priests evolved an elaborate cosmology that arranged their deities in a complex hierarchy. The father of the gods, An, delegated executive authority to his son, Enlil, who created and ordered the world and its creatures. Enlil also directed the activities of the other major deities: the moon god, patron of wisdom and astronomy; the sun god who was the god of justice; and so on. In the Old Babylonian and successive periods this hierarchy was preserved, but the gods were given the names of their Semitic equivalents: Enlil became Marduk, or Baal; the sun god, Shamash; the moon god, Sin; and Sumerian Inanna, goddess of fertility, love and war, became Ishtar. Perhaps a single example will suffice as an illustration of the way in which the gods were believed to function. When a new ruler came to the throne, it was said that Enlil (or Marduk) had selected him to rule and had directed the sun god to present the nominee with the ceremonial rod and cord which were the symbols of sovereignty. By these tokens also the new ruler was authorized to promulgate a law code which would establish right and justice in the land. Thus, on the great stone stele that bears the Code of Hammurabi one may see a sculptured representation of Shamash presenting the king with the rod and cord.

The importance of and the necessity for writing in the great primary civilizations can hardly be overemphasized. Record-keeping and record-keepers were essential to accomplish the enormous tasks of economic management. There had to be a bureaucracy, and no bureaucracy could function without writing and trained scribes. The earliest writing consisted of simple records of so many cattle, so much grain, etc. Soon writing was used for official communications: orders, reports, letters, and the like; later it was employed for the composition and preservation of religious, "scientific," and general literary materials. Basically, the Egyptian and Mesopotamian systems were alike in origin and mode of operation. Beginning with simple pictographs and signs for numbers, they added ideographs and characters for phonetic values. The characters assumed a different physical appearance in the course of time mainly because the Mesopotamians impressed their symbols on clay with a stylus (the cuneiform script) and the Egyptians wrote on papyrus with pen and ink. In both societies literacy was generally limited to persons trained as scribes by a long and arduous routine. Scribes learned to keep records, take dictation, write letters properly, draw up legal documents, and perform all kinds of mathematical computation. The more proficient scribes copied and even composed religious and literary materials or recorded astronomical observations. Still others who showed administrative ability might advance to important positions in the bureaucracy. In Mesopotamia scribes generally were required to know both Sumerian and Old Babylonian, and before long some had to study the "foreign" languages used by the neighbors of Babylonia. An equal versatility became necessary in Egypt when that country came more into contact with the outside world.

The primary civilizations bequeathed a rich legacy to posterity, the full extent of which is still in the process of discovery by modern scholars. Egypt, though for a long time more isolated, nevertheless exerted a considerable influence on other groups in the ancient world. One can see examples of this in the Old Testament. Numerous maxims from the wisdom literature of Egypt were incorporated into the Book of Proverbs; Egyptian hymns have their echoes in the Book of Psalms. Between 750–500 B.C. Greek contacts with Egypt influenced Greek sculpture, painting, and architecture. Greek arithmetical procedures were indebted to Egyptian methods of computation, and a number of Egyptian stories found their way into Greek literature. From Mesopotamia many peoples of the Near East, including those of the Old Testament, borrowed religious concepts and myths—the creation epic and the flood story are outstanding examples. The cuneiform system of writing was adopted and adapted for writing many languages. The Mesopotamian form of the law code was widely used as were the business methods, legal agreements, and the like which had been developed in the lower valley. Words like mina, shekel, and sesame passed into other languages along with innumerable names for plants, herbs, and stones. Some of these words were used in Greece as early as the middle of the second millennium B.C., and one finds them still in use in the classical period of Greece and Rome. Not directly, but through the agency of the Phoenicians and others in the Near East with whom the Greeks came in contact, Babylonian astronomy and algebra were also slowly diffused westward.

The beacon of Near Eastern civilization continued to shed its light long after the Sumerians and its other creators had been forgotten. Algebra, to cite one example, is an Arabic word, but it goes back to a Babylonian original of the same meaning. The algebraic knowledge which the Greeks acquired from Babylonia was lost to Europeans after the fall of Rome, but the study of algebra continued to flourish in Babylonia in Islamic times, and through the agency of the Arabs was reintroduced into Europe at the end of the medieval period.

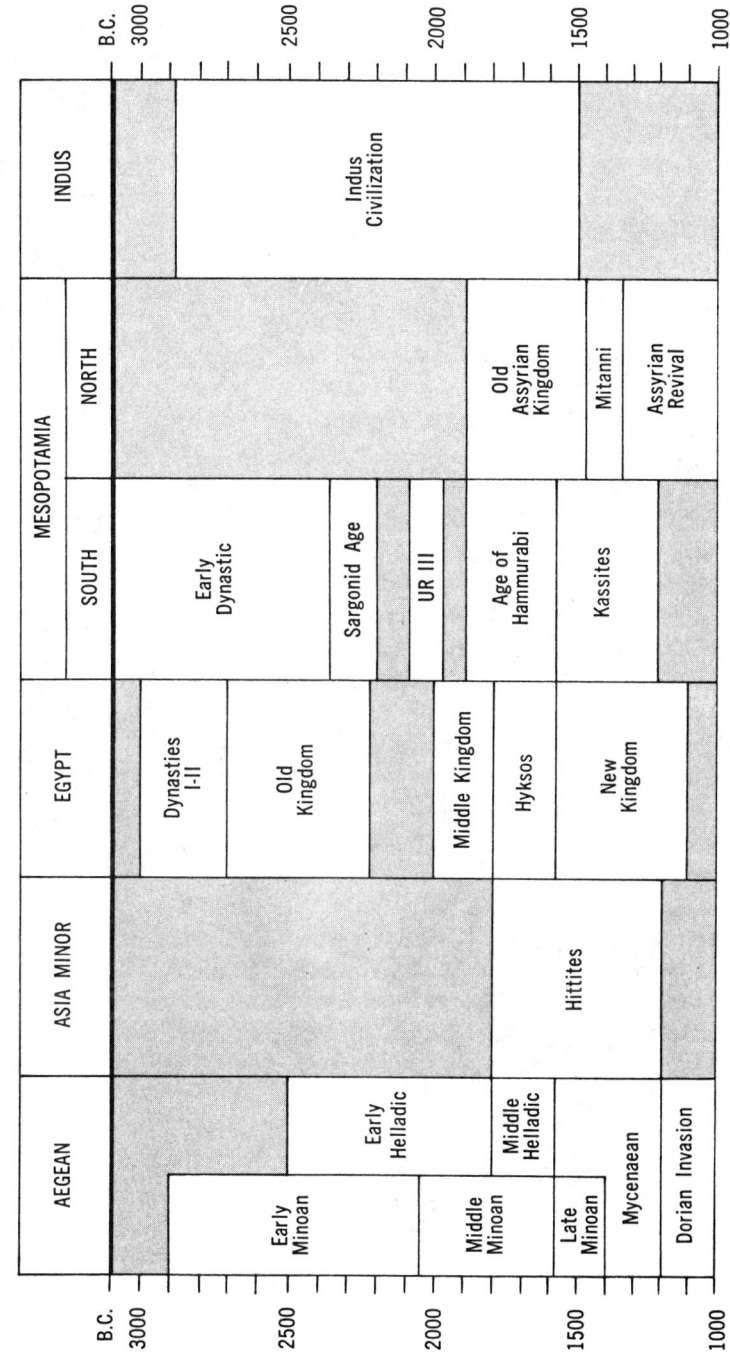

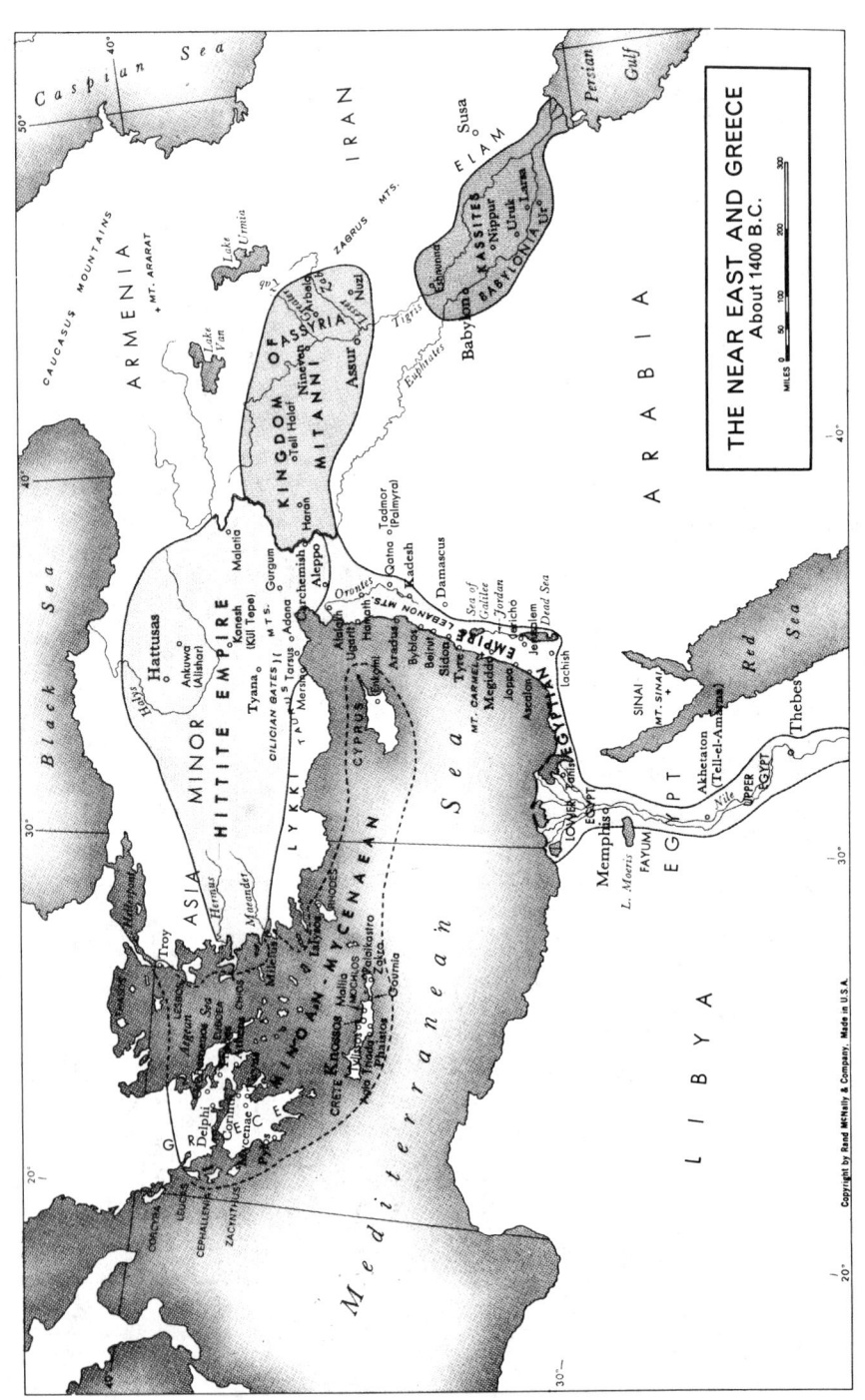

Chapter 3

The Early Empires

In the ten centuries between 1500 and 500 B.C. historical currents moved slowly but surely in one direction: toward the cultural, economic, and political unification of the Ancient Near East. There would always be regional differences due to environmental and ethnic variations throughout this vast territory, but as elements of civilization were diffused from Egypt and Babylonia to adjacent and peripheral areas a universal, homogeneous culture was spread like a mantle from Iran to the Mediterranean and from the Black Sea to Egypt. A network of trade routes fostered an economic interdependence that linked together widely separated parts of the total area so that the prosperity of one region might be adversely affected if it lost contact with another, even though the pair were hundreds of miles apart. As the centuries passed, political units tended to become larger and larger until the whole of the Near East was enveloped in a single empire, that of the Persians which came into existence in the sixth century B.C.

Chronologically, this thousand years of Near Eastern history can be divided into several subperiods. From the middle of the second millennium to about 1200 B.C. three large kingdoms and several smaller ones dominated the scene. This was the era of the New Kingdom, or Empire, in Egypt, the Mitannian kingdom in northern Mesopotamia, and the Hittite Empire, which had its capital in

Anatolia. Lesser contemporaries were the Kassites in Babylonia, the Minoans in Crete, and the Mycenaeans in Greece. Around 1200 the whole picture was changed by massive folk migrations that destroyed Hittite and Mycenaean power and confined the Egyptians once more to Egypt itself; the Minoans and Mitannians had fallen earlier to pressure from the Mycenaeans and Hittites, respectively, and the Kassite dynasty would soon be overthrown by a new Semitic invasion. Between 1200 and 750 B.C. the pall of a dark age settled over the Near East and Greece. Although trade revived as the first millennium began, this subperiod was one in which many small states flourished; no major powers loomed on the horizon until the gradual rise of Assyria in the ninth century. After 750 B.C. the march of destiny was accelerated. Between 750 and 612 B.C. the Assyrian Empire expanded until it included all of Mesopotamia, Syria, Palestine, and briefly, Egypt. In the period after the fall of Assyria in 612 B.C. and until the rapid growth of the Persian Empire (550–525 B.C.), the Near East did not lose its cultural and economic unity, but was divided politically among four major kingdoms, the Saite dynasty in Egypt, the Neo-Babylonians in Mesopotamia, the Medes in Iran, and the Lydians in western Anatolia. The climax came, however, as the Persians overran these states one after another and welded the entire region into a single realm which endured until its conquest by Alexander the Great in the decade after 334 B.C.

It is worth noting that the creation of the empires that dominated at the beginning of this major period (c. 1600 B.C.), was due in no small part to a revolution in transportation and communication resulting from the introduction of the horse and the construction of large, truly seagoing, ships. Suddenly the ancient world had become a little smaller because movement from place to place had been speeded up; it was less difficult to hold a large area in subjection.

The New Kingdom in Egypt began in 1570 B.C. when Ahmose, the founder of the Eighteenth Dynasty, drove the Hyksos from the Delta and reunited his nation. Utilizing the new military organization and the popularity of the throne that Ahmose had created, his successors launched a kind of crusade against the hated "Asiatics" that led Egyptian forces into Palestine and then Syria. By the middle of the fifteenth century both these areas were held securely, and the Egyptians organized a system of imperial government that would assure the collection of tribute and provide for the defense of their empire. The conquest of Syria had been more difficult than that of Palestine because the former was in possession of the Mitannians when the Egyptians arrived. By dint of repeated efforts and an alliance with the Hittites, Egypt finally expelled the Mitannians from Syria only to discover that the Hittites were potentially more dangerous than the Mitannians. In a move that was to have fateful consequences, the Egyptians then broke off with the Hittites and allied themselves with the Mitannians instead. In the fourteenth century the enraged Hittites drove a wedge between the allies by annexing Syria; by playing one faction against another in Mitanniland, they helped the Assyrians to gain their independence on the upper Tigris and then made the western half of the Mitannian kingdom into a Hittite vassal state. The final logical step, however, could not be taken because a plague struck the Hittite army as it was about to invade Palestine and Egypt shortly after 1350 B.C. These last events coincided with the fall of the Eighteenth Dynasty and although the pharaohs of the Nineteenth, especially Rameses II, tried hard to win back Syria, the contest ended in a draw. Recognizing the stalemate, the Hittites and Egyptians became allies once more with the Hittites continuing to hold Syria while the Egyptians retained Palestine. Within a half-century of this friendly settlement, however, the Hittites—racked by a dynastic quarrel—had fallen easy prey to a barbarian invasion, and Egypt was too far away to be of any assistance. In fact, the Egyptians already were girding themselves to repel the attacks of the so-called Sea Raiders, who after several forays came in a body about 1190; they were beaten off by a herculean effort, but the struggle left Egypt so exhausted that it did not recover from the ensuing decline for more than four centuries.

The New Kingdom was memorable in Egyptian history not only for the empire, but also because it was a period of cultural change and achievement stimulated in part by the unaccustomed exposure of the Egyptians to the outside world. The empire brought wealth and with it ostentation. Temples and palaces, as well as the dwellings of high officials, were far more elaborate than before. Captives from foreign conquests increased the number of slaves in Egypt many times over. In painting and in sculpture the Egyptian artist delighted in portraying the foreigners in their strange costumes (bearing tribute, of course). The pyramids were replaced by rock-cut tombs, although the pyramidal form crowned the great monolithic obelisks of the Eighteenth Dynasty pharaohs, and the Egyptian predilection for the monumental was largely transferred from architecture to sculpture: the Colossi of Memnon and the gigantic Ramessid statues at Abu Simbel provide good examples of this tendency.

The most familiar figure of the New Kingdom is that of Ikhnaton, the "heretic pharaoh," who reigned at the end of the Eighteenth Dynasty in the mid-fourteenth century. Blotted from human memory until his capital at Tell-el-Amarna was discovered less than a hundred years ago, the various and contradictory modern assessments of Ikhnaton and his religion of Atonism only serve as a warning that very little is positively known of this unconventional pharaoh and the tangled internal politics of his reign. Even the cuneiform tablets, the remnants of the diplomatic correspondence presumably from the "in-coming" basket of the Egyptian foreign office found at Tell-el-Amarna, need more careful study since it is apparent that some of the letters are not genuine but a group of sample letters written by apprentice scribes.

While Egypt represented the continuation and elaboration of an old tradition, the case of the Hittites and several other groups prominent during this period was quite different. The Hittites, Mitannians, and Mycenaeans came as invaders of the civilized world and established themselves as ruling minorities over large native populations. Another characteristic they shared was that they were Indo-Europeans whose ancestral home was north central Europe; these three groups were participants in a great Indo-European migration in the second millennium that also brought the Aryans to India and the ancestors of the Romans to Italy.

The Hittites entered Anatolia from the Caucasus shortly after 2000 B.C. Individual leaders seized control of various native kingdoms which ultimately were consolidated into a single state with its capital in central Anatolia at Hattusas (Boghazkoy). Here lived the Great King of the Hittites who, it was believed, did not die but became a god when he departed this life. His city covered a vast area ringed with walls constructed of huge stones pierced by mighty gates wide enough to accommodate the passage of Hittite war chariots. The Hittites adopted the cuneiform script for writing their own language, and the discovery of thousands of clay tablets and inscribed stones at Boghazkoy is the principal source for what is known about Hittite history, government, law, and religion. With forests furnishing abundant fuel for smelting, the working of iron originated in Hittite territory about 1400 B.C. By 1200 knowledge of iron-working had become widely diffused, and iron itself was an important commodity in international trade.

Little is known about the Mitannians save that they were Indo-Europeans linguistically related to the Aryans, Medes, and Persians. Their capital, still undiscovered, was located in northwestern Mesopotamia. The Assyrians and other Semitic-speaking groups constituted one large segment of the Mitannian subject population but another subject people were the Hurrians, whose language was neither Semitic nor Indo-European and is still imperfectly understood by modern scholars. Like the Hittites, the Mitannians employed the cuneiform script, but the Mitannian documents that have been found are either in Akkadian (Old Babylonian) or Hurrian, and it is uncertain whether anything was written in the language of the Mitannians themselves.

Thanks to the decipherment of the Linear B (Mycenaean) script by Michael Ventris in 1951, it definitely has been established that the Mycenaeans were Greeks. They may have arrived in Greece as early as the nineteenth century B.C. or as late as the mid-sixteenth. Definitely a ruling minority, Mycenaean kings lived in elaborate palaces situated on fortified hilltops. Their documents reveal a theocratic governmental organization, and an economy based on farming and pastoral pursuits with some industry within the palace complex. Archaeological evidence shows extensive trade with the Near East and the west coast of Italy as well as a connecting link with the amber trade of central Europe; there also is evidence that Mycenaean colonists settled along the coast of western Asia Minor and on the island of Cyprus. Nothing certain is known about Mycenaean diplomatic relations with the Near East, nor can it be established that there was a Mycenaean empire under a single ruler or a great confederacy headed by the king of Mycenae. It is not even clear what the Mycenaeans called themselves, but it was certainly not Mycenaeans or Greeks, and probably not Achaeans. In the course of the widespread disturbances of the thirteenth and twelfth centuries B.C. the Mycenaean kingdoms were destroyed, and a power vacuum was created that allowed other Greeks who had been lurking in the north to move into Greece in large numbers.

In addition to their eastward movement of settlement, the Mycenaeans also occupied central and eastern Crete. This had been the realm of the Minoans, the founders of the brilliant civilization discovered by Sir Arthur Evans three-quarters of a century ago. The Minoans, whose language and place of origin cannot be established definitely, arrived in Crete some time between 2000 and 1800 B.C. They brought with them a culture already well developed, including a style of palace architecture so firmly set in their tradition that all the Minoan palaces discovered thus far on Crete are built on the same plan: a complex of small rooms around the four sides of a great rectangular court and above these small rooms a second floor with much larger rooms probably used for audiences and banquets. The walls of rooms and corridors were decorated with colorful painted frescoes. Many Egyptian conventions were used for colors and poses, but the Minoan style was freer and less traditional than the Egyptian. Exceptional craftsmanship was displayed in sculpture and jewelry in stone, metal, and ivory, and the styles of painted pottery had no rivals in the second millennium.

The Minoans brought with them to Crete a script now called Hieroglyphic Minoan, which closely resembled the Hieroglyphic Hittite script used by the Hittites on their seals, but for ordinary record-keeping the Minoans developed a simpler script usually incised on clay tablets. This is known as Linear A, and the Mycenaean Linear B appears to be derived from it. Even though the values of most of the Linear A characters or signs are known, it is not possible to read these documents because the language of the Minoans has not been identified.

The Minoans traded with Syria, Palestine, and Egypt. They also had settlements or colonies on islands of the south Aegean, some very near Greece. The island of Thera was the site of one such settlement; destroyed by a volcanic eruption in the sixteenth or fifteenth century B.C., the Minoan town is now being excavated, and its importance for Aegean archaeology can be likened to that of Pompeii and Herculaneum in the Roman field.

Although the origin of the Minoans remains a mystery, the bulk of the evidence suggests that they came from southern Asia Minor. The same thing is true of the so-called Sea Raiders—Lycians, Philistines, and others—who, after terrorizing the eastern Mediterranean for a half-century, finally engaged in a mass migration by land and sea (c. 1200 B.C.) that destroyed towns in Cyprus, Syria, and Palestine but was stopped at last by the Egyptians under Rameses III about 1190 B.C. One group of raiders, the Philistines, who settled on the Palestinian coast, gave their name to the whole country; Palestine means the "Land of the Philistines."

During the "dark age" induced by the Sea Raiders, historical interest shifts from the great river valleys, Anatolia, and the Aegean shores to the Syria-Palestine area. This was the age of David and Solomon, when David defeated the Philistines and made Jerusalem his capital, and when Solomon created an important kingdom which had trade relations with Syria, Cilicia, and the Red Sea coast of Arabia. Although the kingdom of Solomon soon split into the rival states of Judah and Israel, forces had been set in motion which would lead to the evolution of a precious heritage still cherished in the Near East and the western world today. In the midst of adversity and all the trials and tribulations of the next four centuries, the Old Testament began to take shape and Judaism, the religion of the Hebrews, went through a formative stage vital to its future.

Among the many groups that flourished in this period were two of great importance in the commercial life of the Near East: the Aramaeans and the Phoenicians. The former, who had come out of Arabia about 1400 B.C. and controlled a number of city states from Damascus northward to the great bend of the Euphrates, dominated the caravan trade connecting Egypt with Mesopotamia and the Mediterranean coast with the Tigris-Euphrates valley. So ubiquitous were the Aramaean traders that their language became the one most commonly used on an international basis. The Phoenicians were Semites who arrived on the Mediterranean coast probably after the great raid of 1200. They established themselves in independent city states whose capitals were Tyre, Sidon, Byblos, Beirut, and Aradus. These were port cities and from them the Phoenicians began to trade around the Mediterranean, first with Cyprus, then Greece, then North Africa, and finally with Spain. The Phoenicians also colonized: Cyprus in the tenth century and North Africa and Spain in the eighth. In addition to being great traders, navigators, and explorers, the Phoenicians were manufacturers of jewelry, bronze work, textiles, and ivories; historically, however, they were most significant as carriers of Near Eastern civilization. Weights and measures, business methods, law codes, technology, and art motifs, as well as the elements of mathematics and science, were diffused to the west. Most conspicuous among the culture traits carried westward by the Phoenicians was their alphabet, which became the parent of early Greek alphabets in the eighth century B.C.

By 750 B.C. a new era was dawning for the Near East and the eastern Mediterranean in general. Prosperity was returning, contacts among peoples were becoming more common, and the increasing military strength of the Assyrians was beginning to make itself felt in Mesopotamia and Syria. The Assyrians, whose ancestors had arrived on the upper Tigris about the time that the forefathers of Hammurabi settled in Babylon, had once had a powerful kingdom in northern Mesopotamia just before the rise of Hammurabi's empire. Later, the Assyrians had been subject to the Mitannians but had revolted and regained their independence in the fourteenth century B.C. Surrounded by enemies on all sides, the Assyrians began a long struggle to retain their freedom. One result was that in the ninth century they became wholly united and militarized, with a citizen militia led by warrior kings. By attacking and raiding their neighbors as part of a policy of self-defense they became stronger and more skilled in the art of warfare. Raids to the west, in particular, increased in range and intensity until the Assyrians on occasion reached the Mediterranean coast. They also got involved in the politics of the Aramaean and Phoenician city states and the rivalry between Judah and Israel. After a time of internal trouble in the early eighth century caused by a declining royal family, intercity rivalries, and the eclipse of 763 B.C., which precipitated a decade of anarchy, the Assyrians emerged stronger than ever, convinced that mere raids were insufficient for national security: instead of raiding and getting their enemies off balance, they must conquer them and hold them in subjection. With this change of policy after 750 B.C., the Assyrians began to build an empire. They annexed the Aramaean and Phoenician city states, and Babylonia, and then captured Samaria, the capital of Israel, about 722. In the seventh century Judah, the other Hebrew kingdom, was reduced from the status of an Assyrian ally to a tributary state; Egypt was invaded and Assyria dominated the Delta for two decades. Great and famous kings, often mentioned in the Old Testament, ruled Assyria in this period: Tiglath

Pileser, Sargon II, Sennacherib, and Esarhaddon. The last of the line was Ashurbanipal, son of Esarhaddon, whose rule of four decades ended in 626 B.C.

At the beginning of Ashurbanipal's reign the empire had never been larger or seemingly more secure, but when the king had to give his full attention to quelling a Babylonian revolt led by his own brother, the subject peoples on the periphery of the empire began to slip away. The Egyptians became independent, the Medes ceased to pay their tribute, and others followed suit. None of these losses could be recovered, and in 625 B.C., the year after Ashurbanipal's death, the Babylonians revolted again, successfully this time. They commenced a long war of aggression against the Assyrians in which the Medes joined, and in 612 B.C. the Assyrian capital of Nineveh was captured. When the remnants of the Assyrian army were wiped out in a final battle six years later, the Assyrians themselves disappeared from the scene.

The Assyrians were gone, but not forgotten. The memory of their ferocity was enshrined forever in the pages of the Old Testament. In the future other empires would build upon and refine the system of imperial government that the Assyrians had created. The marvelous narrative style of their great display inscriptions, telling the story of many campaigns, and the construction of huge and elaborate palaces would be copied by their successors. Elements of the Assyrian style of sculpture were adopted by the faraway Greeks, and the magnificent library of Mesopotamian religious and literary documents collected by Ashurbanipal at Nineveh and rediscovered by Layard in the nineteenth century A.D. would provide the foundation for the modern scholarly discipline of Assyriology.

Of all the periods of Near Eastern history the century following the fall of the Assyrians was the most familiar to ancients and early moderns because it had received considerable attention from the writers of the Old Testament and the fifth-century Greek historian, Herodotus. People knew something of the history of the successive kingdoms—the deeds of Nebuchadnezzar and Nabonidus in Babylon, of Psammetichus and Amasis in Egypt, of Gyges and Croesus in Lydia, and of the kings of Media. After initial contests of strength, the four great kingdoms settled down in an atmosphere that was relatively peaceful and characterized by an unusual balance of power. As the horizons of international trade expanded, the Greeks came in large numbers to buy and sell in Syria, Palestine, and Egypt. As a result, more cultural diffusion from east to west occurred. In this period also the Greek cities grew in size and wealth. Some of these eastern Greeks hired out as mercenaries to fight in the armies of Babylonia and Egypt; others migrated to settle permanently in Syria and Egypt or southern Asia Minor.

Then came the rise of Persia. It all began when relations between the Babylonians and Medes were deteriorating. The Babylonian king, Nabonidus, hoped to make trouble for the Medes by supporting a revolt among the Persians who were Median subjects. Under the Persian leader, Cyrus the Great, the uprising was so successful that by 550 B.C. the Medes had become subject to the Persians, and Nabonidus soon discovered that the Persians were more dangerous than the Medes. When Croesus, the Lydian king who was an ally of both Medes and Babylonians, invaded the new Persian holdings in Asia Minor, he was defeated by Cyrus and chased back to his capital, Sardis, in western Anatolia. Cyrus then captured both Sardis and King Croesus in 547, adding the Lydian kingdom and also the Greek towns in western Asia Minor to his growing empire. By 539 B.C., taking advantage of internal opposition to Nabonidus, he was able to annex the Neo-Babylonian kingdom. Although Cyrus died fighting in Bactria (Turkestan) in 530, the empire continued to expand when his son Cambyses overran Egypt in 525 B.C. Cambyses died three years later as a faction of his own Persians turned against him, but order was restored by the Persian nobility who supported the accession of Darius the Great. He was a distant relative of Cyrus and Cambyses descended, as they were, from a long dead Persian kinglet named Achaemenes. Darius pulled the empire back together and added to it new conquests in the east and in Thrace (now European Turkey). In his long reign (c. 522–486 B.C.) he also was to venture against the mainland Greeks but without success.

Cyrus created the Persian Empire by his far-flung conquests, but Darius organized and gave a permanence to the empire that enabled it to endure for three centuries. Darius divided the empire into about thirty satrapies, or provinces, and provided a system of transportation and rapid communication that helped to hold the empire together. He promulgated a law code, established imperial weights and measures and a uniform coinage, and introduced a new system of writing, a cuneiform script used mainly for display inscriptions on palaces and monuments. There was no single capital or administrative center for the Persian Empire: Darius had palaces in Babylon, Susa (the Elamite capital), Ecbatana (Hamadan, the old Median capital), Pasargadae (the capital of Cyrus the Great), and the new cult center of Persepolis. At various times of the year, Darius and his successors might be found at one or another of these centers.

Despite the efforts of Darius, real unity was impossible. The empire was too far-flung and subject to all kinds of separatist tendencies. The Persians were too few to garrison their empire, and when they went to war they had to pad their forces with unreliable subject levies and equally unreliable mercenaries. For a Mediterranean fleet they depended mainly on the Phoenicians and a few ships from subject Greeks. In order to hold the empire together, the Persians had to favor some of their subjects over others since they could not hope to please them all. Thus, Phoenicians were given preference over Greeks and Egyptians because of the fleet. This made the Greeks and Egyptians prone to revolt on the slightest pretext. Among others, preference was given to the Jews. They were given the opportunity to resettle Jerusalem, which had been captured and depopulated by Nebuchadnezzar, and some individuals who remained behind in Babylonia seem to have had influence in the Persian government. The Babylonian priesthood which had backed Cyrus against Nabonidus also enjoyed special privileges. Among the subject Greeks the Persians took their support wherever they could find it, and there was no dearth of collaborators willing to exchange liberty for personal advancement. One suspects that this was true of others besides the Greeks.

The Persians, like the Greeks, were Indo-Europeans, but in their proximity to the flourishing civilization of Mesopotamia they had little choice but to adopt it on a grand scale. In sculpture and architecture there was a "Persian" style, but it is uncertain how much of this originated with the Persians since their artists and builders are known to have been Egyptians, Babylonians, Greeks, and others. The Persians could claim as their own, however, the prophet Zoroaster who flourished in the sixth century as a contemporary of Cyrus and Cambyses and who was said to have converted the father of Darius. Very little is known about the original Zoroastrianism because most surviving evidence dates from about eight hundred years later when the religion underwent a revival in Iran and had been altered by contacts with Judaism, Christianity, and certain old

Iranian beliefs. It seems safe to say that Zoroaster preached monotheism, or monolatry at least, forbade graven images, and adhered to a morality of the most admirable kind. Purity, truth, humility, and compassion seem to have been the watchwords of his creed.

By 500 B.C. the civilized world encompassed much more than the area of the Near East. As the seedbed of civilization this region had fulfilled its function and for the time run its course. The next important developments would occur in Greece, a barren unpromising land, yet one in which the fruits of civilization transplanted into a new environment could produce new and hardy varieties.

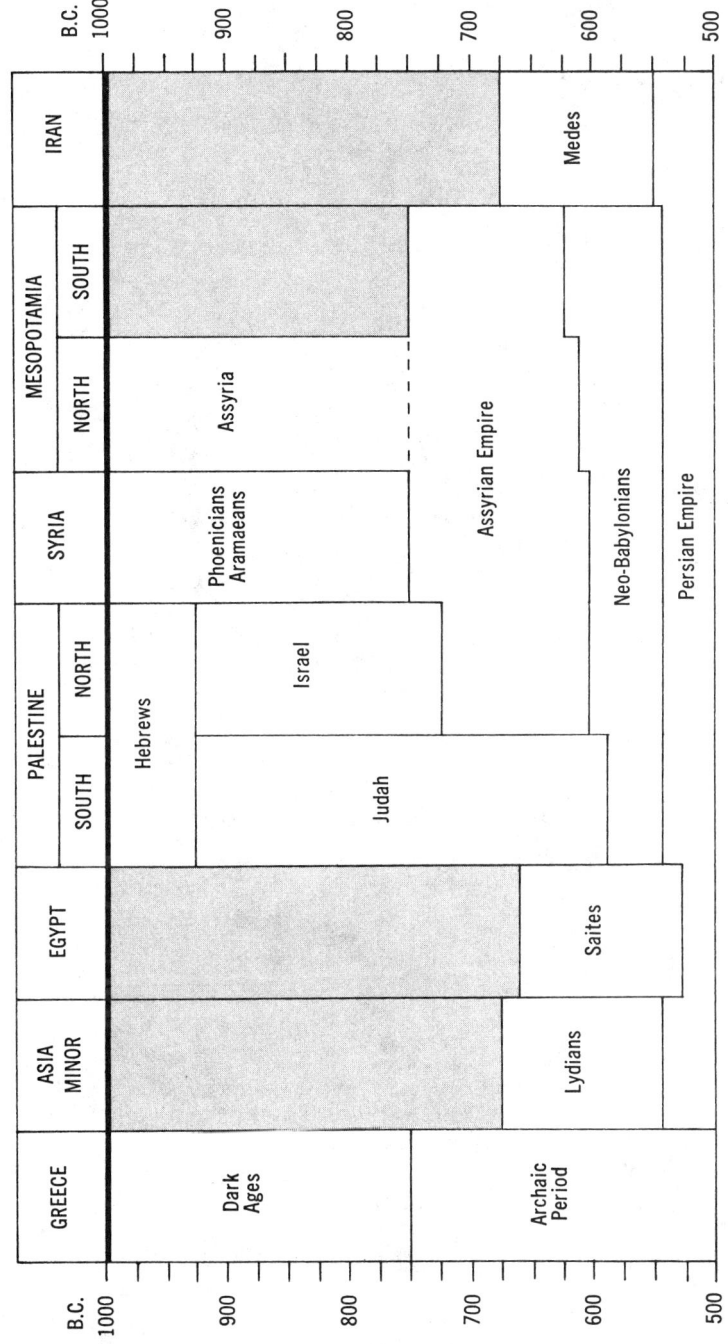

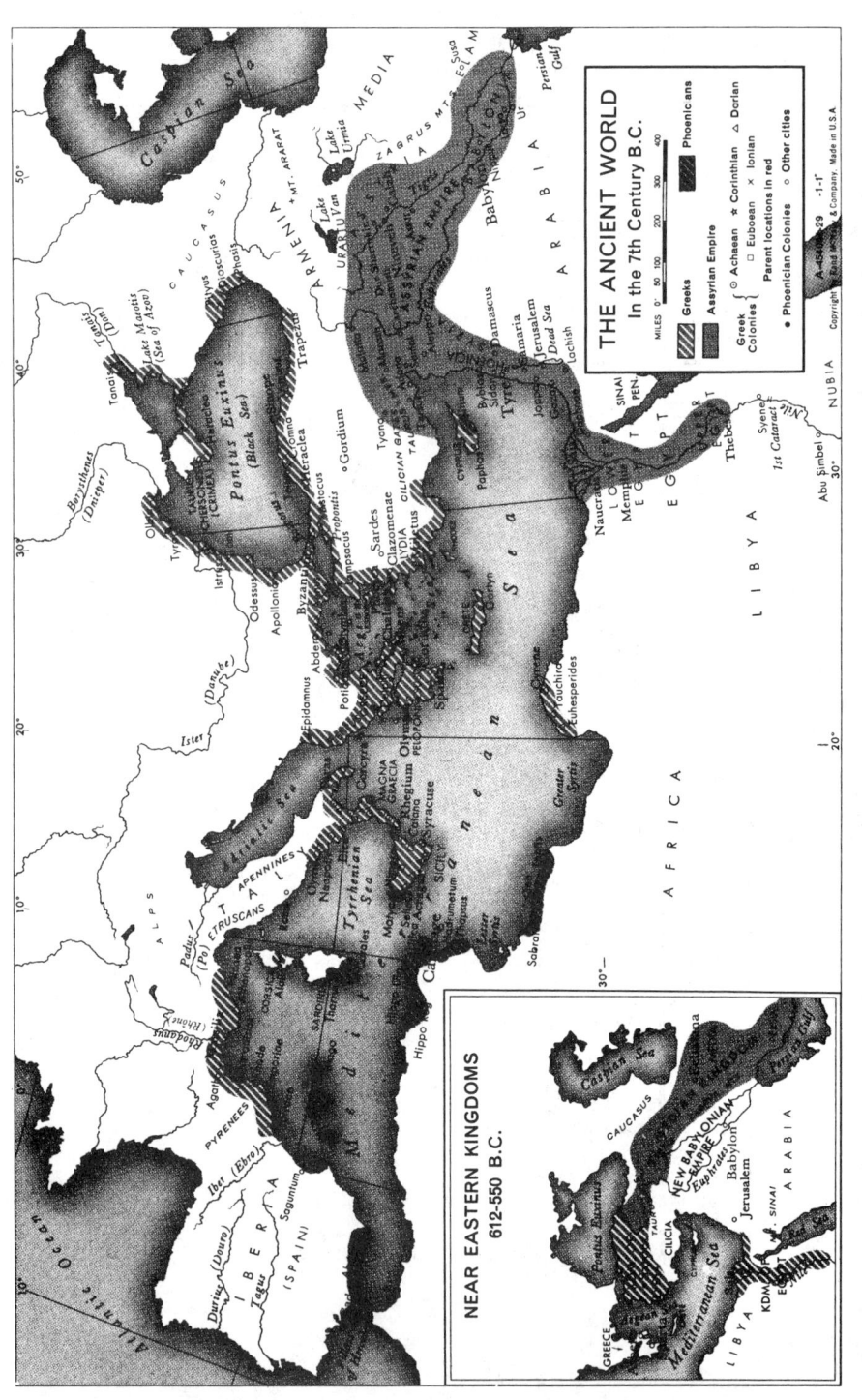

Chapter 4

The Greek City States

There is always a temptation to oversell the Greeks despite the fact that the Greek achievement speaks for itself. In order to understand the Greeks and to appreciate what they accomplished, it is probably best to state the matter simply and avoid submerging the subject in a flood of superlatives. It has been said, for example, that we are all Greeks. In the sense that the Greeks established what is still the traditional "western" approach to things intellectual and aesthetic, this statement is undeniably factual. It also can be said that we are all Greeks since, being members of the human race, we do not differ from them in physical form, psychological makeup, or potential creativity. In addition, there are other aspects that merit consideration. An early Greek philosopher maintained that it is not possible to make something out of nothing, and today it is becoming more and more apparent that the ancient Near East furnished much of the cultural clay from which the Greeks fashioned the European, or western, tradition. Even now, civilization tends to be an urban phenomenon. This was certainly the case in ancient times. In Greece itself there were extensive areas especially in the north and west that had scarcely been touched by civilization at the very end of classical antiquity, and the centers of cultural activity and creativity were confined to a limited number of Greek cities in east-central Greece, along the shores of western Asia Minor, on some of the Aegean islands, and in Sicily and southern Italy. The distribution was wider in the period after Alexander the Great, but the centers were still urban. Finally, it was just as true of the Greeks as it is of those living in the twentieth century A.D. that the originators and leaders in cultural innovation are very few in proportion to the bulk of the population. In ancient Greece there was no plethora of Platos, playwrights, or poets; there were more stonemasons than sculptors; and, of course, there were more politicians than statesmen.

After 1200 B.C. Greece entered a dark age, even darker than that which had settled over the Near East. Contact with the civilized world was cut off, trading activities were limited in scope, most people were farmers and herdsmen, and there does not seem to have been much communication between even the small geographic areas into which Greece is naturally divided by its rugged topography. In the period between 1200–750 B.C. the new wave of Greek invaders spread out over the land, settled down, and gradually learned how to exist in a new environment. This required considerable technological, economic, and political adjustment. By 750 B.C. the Greek *polis* or city state had made its appearance along the shores and on the islands of the southern Aegean. The city state was a small political unit with its boundaries defined by nature. Its citizens might live either in the principal town, quite often both the political and religious capital of the region, or they might be scattered over the countryside. In any event, the capital was the scene of governmental activity; there the executive branch was located, the council deliberated, and the assembly of all qualified citizens convened. By this time the aristocrats, large land-holders who naturally identified themselves as the "best" people, had abolished the traditional monarchy in which the king was essentially a war leader and replaced him with several magistrates elected from the ranks of the aristocracy to serve terms generally one year in length; the council, instead of being composed of the elders, was now monopolized by the aristocrats; and the assembly, which was basically the army, comprised of citizens who had performed military service or were capable of providing themselves with arms and armor, was now dominated by the aristocrats and small farmers who could still qualify for military service. Many other citizens, by reason of poverty, had lost their right to participate in the assembly. The aristocratic control of government was a source of bitter dissatisfaction for all but the aristocrats, but even worse was the land hunger. With the best land concentrated in the hands of a few people and with many Greeks without land or with holdings too small to support them, either the economy had to be diversified so that agriculture would no longer be the main activity, or many Greeks would have to migrate to more fertile territory. After 750 and down to about 500 B.C., the problems of land hunger were solved by extensive colonization around the Mediterranean and by the development of trade and industry at home in Greece, the latter either to supply the colonies or to exchange products with the Near East. Again, it should be emphasized that it was mainly along the shores of the south Aegean and on the islands that colonization and diversification occurred.

Diversification brought many important results. The growth of trade pushed Greece once more into contact with the Near East where prosperity had been reborn; the Greeks shared in this prosperity, but they also began to import culture as well as commodities from Egypt, Palestine, and Syria. Trade and industry brought an accumulation of capital, some of which was used by cities and individuals in the form of patronage to support artists, philosophers, and literary persons. As a result of this support and with the inspiration of the Near Eastern civilization newly discovered by the Greeks, literature, the arts, and philosophy burst into bloom in the sixth century B.C. The Greek temple began to take shape; Greek sculpture and painting went through a formative stage; the Ionian philosopher-scientists flourished; and new kinds of poetry—the elegy and the lyric—began to challenge the earlier epic forms used by Homer and Hesiod. The new economy, moreover, brought political change. Land was no longer the only basis for wealth, and a new socioeconomic class of traders and businessmen was able to challenge the aristocratic monopoly of the government. Sometimes peacefully, sometimes by revolution, aristocracy was replaced by timocracy, in which the extent of an individual's participation in government was based upon his wealth. Often instrumental in the downfall of the aristocrats were the tyrants, usually aristocrats themselves, who led the oppressed classes in revolt and sometimes dominated the new governments for a time. The tyrants not only helped to alter the political scene but they were in many cases outstanding patrons of culture.

It is worth remembering that more is known about Athens and Sparta than about a number of other city states of potentially equal importance in the history of Greek culture. If more information were available about Corinth, Argos, Miletus, Ephesus, and Thebes, for example, many current ideas regarding Greek history and cultural growth might be changed. Neither Athens nor Sparta followed the ordinary pattern of development in Greece in the period before 500 B.C. For example, Athens did not colonize to any significant extent. Through the reforms of Solon (*c.* 570 B.C.) she attained timocracy and diversification and only knew tyranny under Peisistratus and his sons (546–510). Sparta, for its part, never abandoned the monarchy and did not participate in colonization in any significant way. She solved her problems by a redistribution of wealth that equalized commons and nobles and provided a kind of social security in which every citizen by lifelong service to the state knew discipline but not poverty. Because they possessed some of the richest agricultural land in Greece, the Spartans could maintain their system and forego trade and industry, but they had to control their serfs (the helots), and their locally independent subjects, the *perioeci*. This required eternal vigilance and perpetual military service. It made the Spartans the best soldiers in Greece, but even that was not enough. In order to protect themselves from external attacks the Spartans in the sixth century organized a series of defensive alliances with neighboring states. This was the Peloponnesian League, the most formidable military force in Greece. Fortunately for the other Greeks, the Spartans did not practice aggression but instead were committed to an isolationist policy that sent them to war only when they felt their own security endangered.

It was inevitable that as trade came to play a larger role in the economy of some Greek states, the competition for markets would bring rivalry to the point of hostility. This was certainly the case between Athens and Corinth by the latter part of the sixth century, and it did not bode well for Athens that Corinth was a member of the Peloponnesian League. In the western Mediterranean, particularly, the Greek traders found themselves in competition with the Phoenicians. Again, this spelled trouble because the Phoenicians soon were to become valued and pampered subjects of Persia. It was unavoidable, moreover, that as the Greeks established trade relations they should become embroiled in the international politics of the day. Although relations with Egypt were friendly enough because the Egyptians were too far away to exert much influence on Greek affairs, the situation with the Lydians was quite different. Some Asianic Greeks were subject to Lydia, with the result that within such states there were pro- and anti-Lydian factions. On the Aegean islands and even on the Greek mainland similar divisions were occasionally to be found. The Spartans, for example, were allied with Croesus, the Lydian king; Athens and Argos were not. Hence, when the Persians annexed Lydia, the Athenians and the Argives—the bitterest enemies of the Spartans—were inclined to regard with favor the rise of this great new power to the east. Later on, however, when the Persians conquered Egypt, thus limiting Greek trade with that country, the Athenian attitude changed. Further animosity was generated not only by the favoritism shown the Phoenicians but also by the Persian control of Cyprus, which diminished Greek supplies of copper.

Before the end of the sixth century pro- and anti-Persian factions existed in every major Greek city state. Some states wanted Persian support against their enemies; within some city states warring political factions courted Persian intervention so that they could triumph over their rivals. The situation was most dangerously explosive among the Asianic Greeks who were now subject to Persia. These city states were ruled by pro-Persian collaborators appointed by the imperial government. Many people had fled from these towns to the islands or to mainland Greece. Both the exiles and the anti-Persians who had remained behind constantly agitated for Greek intervention to free their states from Persia. At the same time, heavy taxation and declining revenues added to the misery of those Greeks under Persian rule.

The fifth century B.C. began with the Ionian Revolt, which plunged the Greeks into a war with Persia; it ended with the disastrous Peloponnesian War, which ruined Athens and severely damaged the economy of mainland Greece. The rise and fall of the Athenian Empire and the Athenian democracy took place during this century, but it was also the period of Athenian leadership in art, philosophy, and literature. Athens became the cultural capital of the civilized world, a position she was to enjoy for centuries to come. However the Athenians felt about it, one must conclude that they were fortunate to have saved their most precious possession from the wreckage of imperial greed and tarnished democracy.

The Ionian Revolt began in 499 and lasted about five years. It promised success at first because the Persians were caught off guard. The Ionians called for aid from Greece, but Sparta would not stir, and only the Athenians and a single state in Euboea sent troops. As

Persian resistance stiffened, the Athenians ran for home and left the Ionians to be defeated and more downtrodden than ever. Darius the Great was not a man to be trifled with. He was determined to punish the Athenians, but a first expedition to Greece in 492 B.C. was called off because the supporting Persian fleet was destroyed in a storm, and a second attempt in 490 was blunted by the Athenian victory at Marathon. Darius died soon afterwards, giving the Greeks a ten-year respite until Xerxes picked up the gauntlet in 480 B.C. A large-scale attack by land and sea was launched upon mainland Greece, but the new Athenian navy destroyed the Persian fleet in the Battle of Salamis (480), and the combined Greek armies commanded by the Spartans forced the evacuation of Greece by the Persian land force after the Greek victory at Plataea (479 B.C.). Greece was saved. The Persians did not come back, although they continued to meddle, keeping the Greeks off balance until the time of Alexander the Great.

After the Battle of Plataea the Greeks went on the offensive under Spartan leadership. Their plan was to free the Greek isles and Asianic Greek states from Persian rule. After two years, however, the Spartans withdrew from the war, returning to their usual policy of isolation. The command of the allied forces then fell to the Athenians, who organized the so-called Delian League to carry on annual campaigns against the Persians. Allies might contribute ships and men or make a money contribution to foot the bill for each year's operations. Because most allies preferred the latter course, the Athenian fleet became the main weapon of attack, financed and kept in readiness by the funds provided by the allies. After about ten years of fighting, during which most of the Greeks subject to Persia had been freed, some allies felt that the Delian League had accomplished its purpose and should be disbanded. The Athenians, however, maintained that the pacts concluded with the allies were perpetual and could not be dissolved. When member states of the League then attempted to withdraw, they were set upon by the Athenians and reduced to the status of tributary subjects. Thus began the Athenian Empire, and, despite some setbacks, it continued to grow past mid-century.

When Pericles came to power in Athens in 461 he adopted an aggressive policy aimed at adding a land empire to the already extensive maritime holdings of Athens. Since his designs encompassed Megara and central Greece, this precipitated a long war with Thebes

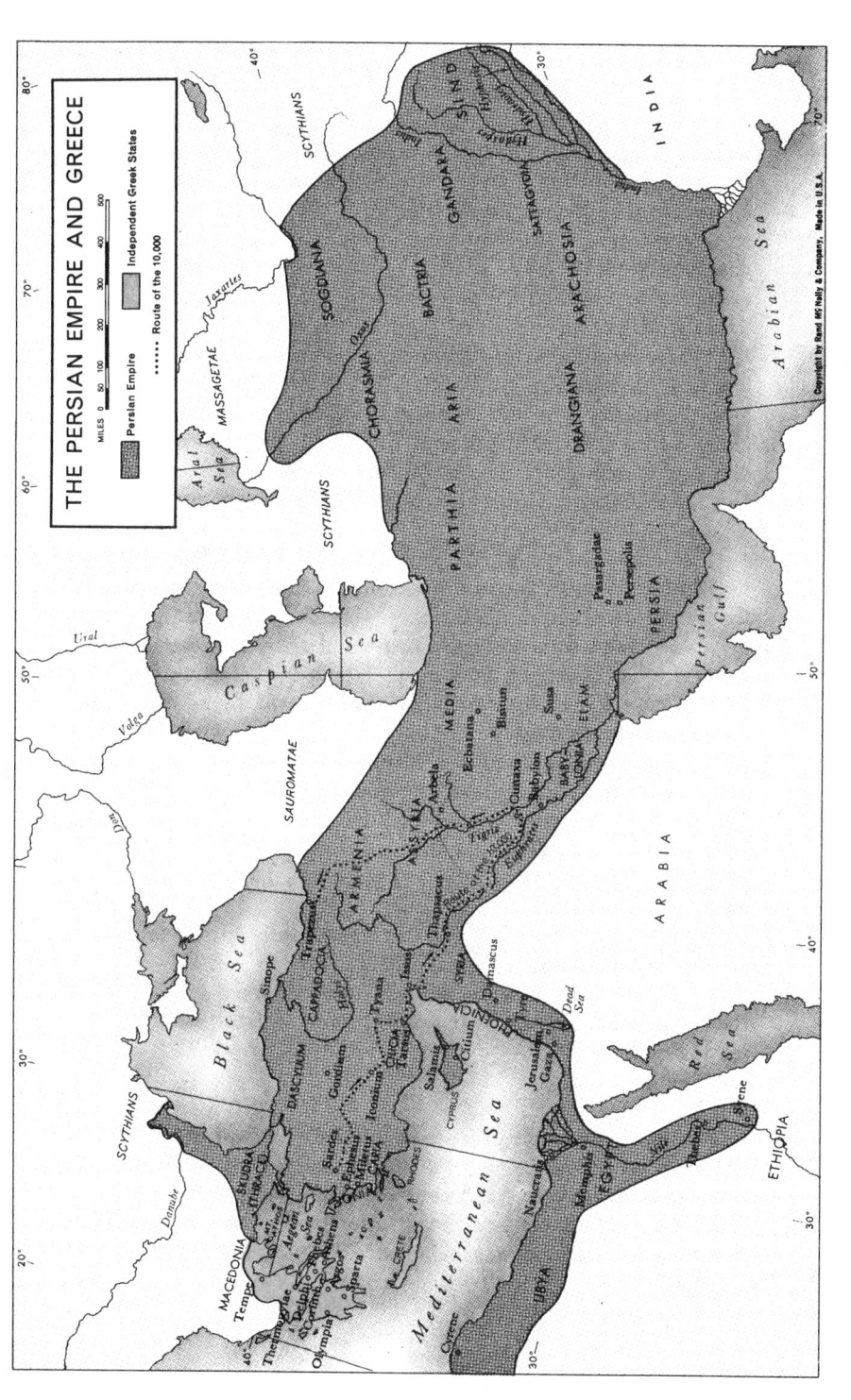

and the Peloponnesian League which ended in 445 with heavy losses for the Athenians. It is doubtful whether Athens could have been victorious in any case, but Pericles made the mistake of supporting anti-Persian revolts in Egypt and Cyprus while fighting against such dangerous odds in Greece itself. It proved to be too much; the consequence was renewed Persian wariness along with bitter rancor towards Athens among other Greek states, eventually leading to a fight to the finish between Athens on one side and the Peloponnesians and their Theban allies on the other. The showdown came in 431 B.C. with the beginning of the long and destructive Peloponnesian War. When Pericles died of the plague in 429 B.C., the Athenians lost the one determined leader who might have saved them from utter defeat, even though a clear-cut victory for Athens was next to impossible.

After the end of the Peloponnesian War in 404 B.C., the Spartans embarked on an imperialist venture. Because they had promised to free the Greeks from Athens, they were also committed to liberating those Greeks who had again come under the domination of Persia, which had become a Spartan ally late in the Peloponnesian War. The Spartans, like the Athenians earlier, soon found themselves simultaneously fighting the Persians as well as their own dissatisfied former allies in Greece. These included Thebes and Corinth who had formed an unusual quadruple alliance with Argos and Athens. The Thebans finally broke the back of Spartan imperialism at the Battle of Leuctra in 371; and after a decade of fruitless imperialism by Thebes, the end came in 362 at Mantinea. There the last of the great Theban leaders, Epaminondas, expired on the battlefield and with his dying breath advised his countrymen to abandon their dreams of superiority and make peace. Greece was ruined. As if that were not enough, while the Persians still lurked and plotted in the background, an even more deadly enemy was gathering strength in Macedonia.

So far as the ancients were concerned, the least noteworthy of Athenian achievements was their democracy. Modern opinion has been quite the reverse, and one can hardly discuss Athens of the fifth century B.C. without some reference to this subject. The governmental form of Athens began with the primitive Indo-European monarchy in which there was an hereditary king, primarily a war leader, a council of elders who advised the king, and an assembly of the warriors. The monarchy gave way to aristocracy, as it did elsewhere in Greece at the end of the dark age. At Athens the king was replaced by three annually elected aristocratic officials called archons. One was something like a mayor of Athens, another commanded the army, and a third was the religious head of the state. The council was, as elsewhere, monopolized by the aristocrats, and the assembly (ecclesia) became more limited in size and composition because many citizens were prevented from participating in it by their poverty. Early in the second quarter of the sixth century the reforms of Solon created a timocracy at Athens. The wealthiest citizens had full civic rights and could hold any office; those of the next highest census class, mainly small farmers and artisans, were eligible for the council and could fill minor offices; but most important of all, every citizen, regardless of wealth, was able to participate in the assembly. This was the first step in the direction of democracy, and it should be noted that while timocracy did become the normal form of government elsewhere in Greece, few timocracies were as liberal as that of Athens.

At any rate, the timocratic form was continued at Athens until the fifth century when a series of changes occurred. One of the most significant of these was the introduction of ostracism (c. 487 B.C.) by means of which the entire citizen body voting in the ecclesia could choose the leader whose policies they favored by voting to ostracize (send into exile for a period) his rival. The next important, but not the only, step was taken (462) when the Areopagus, the oldest of the Athenian councils, composed of ex-archons, was deprived of its power of judicial review. Previously the council had been able to block legislation passed in the assembly by declaring it unconstitutional, and the council had consistently struck down measures aimed at liberalizing the government. After 462 B.C. the assembly, in which the poorer citizens had most of the votes, was supreme. It was the sole electoral body, the main legislative arm of the government, and it possessed the power of ostracism. The only real brake on the activity of the assembly was that it could not initiate legislation: it could ratify, reject, or emend measures submitted to it, but such proposals had to come from the *Boule* (Council of the Five Hundred). This was a relatively new body dating back to the late sixth century and composed of five hundred members chosen annually, with each of the ten tribes into which the Athenian citizen body was divided being represented by fifty tribesmen on the council.

The Council of the Five Hundred had certain features typical of the new Athenian democracy: its members were not elected but chosen by lot (sortition); they could not serve a second term; and they were paid for their services. The underlying theory of sortition was that any citizen could perform the duties of any office just as well as any other citizen. It was also the aim of the democracy that as many citizens as possible should have an opportunity to participate in its government. This was accomplished by rotation and by the use of the committee system. There were innumerable boards or committees—the police commissioners, the prison commissioners, the market commissioners, etc.—each composed of a secretary and ten members, chosen by lot from each of the ten tribes. Even the archons, now increased to nine, were chosen by sortition.

In the case of the jury courts (*dikasteria*), another innovation of the Periclean age, the jurors were paid, but they could repeat as jurors year after year. The jurors were volunteers (six hundred from each tribe), chosen to form a pool of six thousand available for jury duty. The pay was minimal so that ordinarily the juries consisted of senior citizens and the unemployed. Juries were large, ranging from 51, 501, and up in number of members. There were nine courts in which cases were tried; an archon presided over each. The court cases involved not only Athenians but also the subjects of Athens and her remaining allies. The fines and penalties assessed helped to fund the pay of the jurors.

Because of the requirements of the office, the Athenians were forced to reject sortition and rotation in the case of the board of the ten generals who commanded the army and navy, administered the five tribute districts into which the empire was divided, and acted as the diplomatic representatives of Athens in its dealings with foreign nations. The generals were elected annually by the assembly, and they could succeed themselves in office indefinitely. Between 461 and 429 B.C. Pericles was elected general every year except one. The generals were political leaders as well as military men. The composition of the board reflected the waxing or waning strength of various political factions at Athens. In some years the generals would be almost all backers of Pericles; in other years his opponents might be well represented on the board.

With strong leadership, such as that provided by Pericles, the democracy functioned fairly smoothly because the supporters of Pericles were a majority in the assembly, and the assembly in consequence would vote usually in favor of his policies regardless of their merit. After Pericles died, the Athenians were split into many factions. Policy decisions were hard to make, and often a decision made one day would be revoked the next. The hysteria and hardship induced by the bitter, exhausting Peloponnesian War contributed to this wavering and lack of consistency, of course. As far as the rest of the ancient world was concerned, Athenian democracy had failed, and although it was continued at Athens after the Peloponnesian War it could no longer function in its accustomed style because it lacked the wealth of the empire to support it. Also, it should be noted that the democracy had never had the backing of all Athenians. A wealthy conservative faction always had opposed and conspired against its institutions. This group would have preferred the class rule of an aristocracy or a timocracy to a democracy such as the Athenian, in which the commons constituted the ruling class. In short, it was not quite an ideal democracy.

Even in their present ruinous state, the buildings constructed in Periclean Athens echo the glories of the empire that provided the revenues to erect them. Civic pride swelled as the fortified hilltop area of the city, the Acropolis, was adorned with such marvelous edifices as the Propylaea, the Parthenon, the Erechtheum, and the temple of Athena Nike. The Parthenon, with its sculptural decoration and its gold and ivory cult statue by the great Athenian sculptor Phidias, was the greatest marvel of all. Below the Acropolis, down in the Agora (marketplace) were the public buildings of the fifth century: the Royal Stoa where the king archon held forth, the Bouleuterium where the Council of the Five Hundred met, the round Tholos where public records were kept, and many others. Unlike other cities that had to import marble, Athens was blessed with its own quarries, and could use this stone lavishly.

Although tragedy and comedy flourished elsewhere in Greek lands, the works of the Athenian dramatists were judged the best by the ancients. Beginning in the sixth century with impromptu plays and mumming in honor of the god Dionysus, the plays attained their definitive character rather early in the fifth century B.C.

Couched in poetic form, the songs of the chorus alternated with the lines of the actors, and the writers of tragedy selected subjects from ancient legends to illustrate the moral issues confronting mankind. Grand in concept, thought-provoking, and deeply moving, the tragedies of Aeschylus, Sophocles, and Euripides are still exciting to read and even more thrilling to view in actual performance. The principal exponent of comedy was Aristophanes, whose bawdy burlesques pilloried politicians, the jury courts, the intellectuals, the warmongers, and even the workings of the democracy at Athens.

Three major Greek historians also lived and wrote in Athens during the fifth and fourth centuries B.C. Thucydides and Xenophon were Athenians, but Herodotus, known as the father of history, came to Athens from Halicarnassus in Asia Minor. Herodotus dealt in epic fashion with the Persian Wars; Thucydides took his inspiration from Greek tragedy as he told the story of the Peloponnesian War; and Xenophon described the March of the Ten Thousand in his *Anabasis* and also continued the history of Thucydides from the closing years of the Peloponnesian War to the Battle of Mantinea. Of lesser stature than the earlier two historians, Xenophon was typical of a new breed of writers: essayists, political and economic commentators, and biographers.

There were other notable trends and developments. Oratory had always been important in political life. In the timocracies and even more in the Athenian democracy, ability to speak well was required to command the attention of one's fellows, as was the art of persuasion; such skills became necessities with the growth of the law courts, too. The study of oratory became an organized discipline; professional orators who taught the subject and wrote speeches for other people were able to make a very comfortable living. Moreover, in the fifth century B.C. intellectual developments embarked on a new tack. The concern of the sixth-century philosopher-scientists had been with cosmology primarily, but the new trends were away from theoretical science toward utility. The techniques of persuasion in oratory had brought logic to the fore as well as argumentation. The Sophists appeared. These were itinerant, professional teachers and lecturers who went from city to city expounding on every conceivable subject: oratory, logic, politics, religion, science, mathematics, and so on. Some of the Sophists were brilliant and talented; others were charlatans. Nearly all, however, were able to attract large audiences and earn huge fees. Many of the topics treated by the Sophists were controversial, and they created both excitement and resentment when they called the sun a burning stone, or questioned the existence of the gods, or denied the possibility of ascertaining absolute truth. At best, they shook traditional complacency and got some people to think along new lines; at worst, their arrogance produced a violent anti-intellectual reaction during the difficult war years at the end of the century that threatened to undo all the good they had accomplished. One important result of the Sophistic movement was that serious philosophers—Socrates and Plato, for example—turned away from the study of cosmology and natural phenomena to the contemplation of human affairs. They were interested in morality, ethics, and political systems and sought to divine and define the nature of such things as justice, piety, virtue, knowledge, and the like. Socrates wrote nothing, but Plato ranged widely over the whole field. His philosophy not only endured, but also engendered many later brands of philosophy. These were the glories of Greece, and they were not inconsiderable.

Chapter 5

The Great Empires

When Epaminondas died on the battlefield at Mantinea, so did the Greek city state. Reckless imperialism had ruined Athens, Sparta, and Thebes, leaving Greece at the mercy of the first powerful enemy to come along. This, however, was more an immediate than a fundamental cause of the decline of the *polis*. In Europe the day of empires was at hand, and the consolidation that the Greek imperialists had tried to impose upon Greece was consonant with the trend of the times. A similar process had taken place long before in the Near East, which had known city states, then larger combinations, and finally real empires. The Persians, who had created the last and greatest of these empires, were at the outset a barbarian people who had just begun to taste the fruits of civilization. Warlike, fortunate in their leaders Cyrus and Darius, and fired with a kind of nationalism, the Persians had easily overrun states that were tired and divided among themselves. Now in like manner the semi-barbarian Macedonians, northern neighbors of the Greeks, who were inspired by the leadership of their king, Philip II, and proud of being Macedonians, would have little trouble in overcoming the weary and disorganized Greeks. What Philip began, his son Alexander completed by creating an empire that encompassed both Greece and Persia. It should occasion no surprise, therefore, that two centuries later the Romans, newly arrived at the threshold of civilization, should first conquer the west and then add to their domains the kingdoms founded by Alexander's successors.

Philip became king of Macedonia in 359 B.C., three years after the Battle of Mantinea. His people were farmers and herdsmen, economically and politically just emerging from a dark age of the sort that had ended in Greece four hundred years earlier. The nobles were starting to challenge the position of the king and might have succeeded in establishing an aristocratic form of government if Philip had not appeared on the scene to give the monarchy new vigor. By Macedonian standards, Philip was a man of the world. He had spent some time in Thebes as a hostage when he was a boy, and there he had learned about the new military tactics and organization that had replaced the phalanx. He also learned all he needed to know about Greek politics, including the fact that any Greek statesman could be bribed. Philip was ambitious. He wanted to elevate Macedonia from a satellite position to one of major importance in world affairs. This would not be easy, but Philip was determined and was able to advance methodically step by step until he attained his goal.

Macedonia was landlocked because long ago the Greeks had colonized the coast and cut off Macedonian access to the sea. Consequently, little trade and no industry had developed. Philip had to get control of the coast, but before he could do that he would have to secure the landward frontiers of his country against the attacks of savage tribes, unite his people, modernize the army, and somehow fill his empty war chest for the military and diplomatic maneuvering that would come when at last he was ready to deal with the Greeks as a whole. A series of brilliant campaigns pushed back the threatening tribes, seasoned the new army, and generated enthusiastic support for Philip as the leader of his people. A foray to the east brought the annexation of the mines of Mount Pangaeus so that Philip had not only instant wealth but also an assured income. Turning next to the coast, he played one city state against another. In the end he controlled them all, but the major states of Greece had interests in the north Aegean and tried to thwart Philip's advance. For his part he continued his game of setting one against another, exploiting their rivalries. For example, his gold bought the support of some politicians who argued vigorously in Philip's defense when Demosthenes tried to warn the Athenians of the Macedonian menace. Philip's trump card was that many people in the Greek states wanted peace and stability more than liberty itself and thought that Philip could unite the Greeks in some way and put an end to intercity warfare.

A quarrel broke out in central Greece involving the trusteeship of the shrine of Apollo at Delphi and the management of its finances. Philip was asked to intervene and came out of the affair with a position on the governing board of the shrine. This official standing in Greek affairs was resented bitterly by Thebes and Athens, which combined against him. Philip defeated the allies at the Battle of Chaeronea in 338 B.C. He then forced the major Greek states to join together in a league of which he was commander-in-chief and announced that he would go to war with Persia to free the Asiatic Greek states still under Persian control. His advance force already had invaded Asia Minor in 336 when Philip was assassinated. Although his assassin was apprehended and executed, it was never known whether the deed had been planned by jealous Macedonian nobles, his son Alexander, his enemies in Greece, or the Persians.

Alexander, although estranged from his father, was made king within a short time after Philip's death. Only twenty, handsome, popular, and well remembered for leading the cavalry charge that had won the Battle of Chaeronea two years earlier, Alexander immediately went to work. He chastised the northern tribes, put down with severity an uprising in Greece, and in 334 B.C. resurrected his father's plan to free the Greeks in Asia. The results exceeded his fondest expectations. In one year he drove the Persians from the western coast of Asia Minor; during the next he crossed through central Anatolia and invaded Cilicia by passing through the famous Cilician Gates; then driving on into Syria he defeated the Persian king, Darius III, at the Battle of Issus. By 332 B.C. Alexander had overrun Phoenicia and annexed Egypt. Returning to Asia the following year, he invaded Mesopotamia and defeated Darius for the second time. This was the Battle of Gaugamela, which opened the way to Babylon and then into Persia, where Alexander spent the winter in the great palace complex at Persepolis. In 330 B.C. the victorious march was resumed, this time northward into Media where Darius had taken refuge. As Alexander approached, Darius fled in the hope of escaping to faraway Bactria (Turkestan), but he was murdered by his own generals on the way. Instead of turning back to consolidate his conquests, Alexander pressed on, vowing to avenge the murder of Darius. He arrived in Bactria in 329 and spent two years in that remote area before invading the Indus valley. How much farther he would have attempted to go is uncertain, but wounds, illness, and a near mutiny of his army forced a halt. Alexander sailed down the Indus to its mouth and returned at last to Babylon in 325. After contracting a fever, he died there in June 323 B.C.

Alexander was a military genius, but it is not clear whether he possessed the talent and knowledge to fashion an imperial government adequate for the needs of his vast empire. Perhaps he could have found ways of reconciling the various theories of sovereignty that prevailed among the Greeks, Egyptians, Persians, and other heterogeneous groups among his subjects. He could have ruled by force, but eventually his subjects would have had to feel some loyalty or be persuaded that it was in their interest to support the new regime. His own Macedonians were becoming dissatisfied with him; the Greeks were ready to revolt; and the disposition of the Indus people was uncertain. One guesses that he might have been able to hold on to most of what had been the Persian Empire, but he would have had difficulty in retaining the rest.

Alexander died without naming a successor. Although a weak regency was created to rule for the benefit of Alexander's posthumous son, and for Philip, Alexander's mentally retarded half-brother, such an arrangement could not possibly work. Alexander had left behind too many able and ambitious generals, each of whom wanted part or all of the empire for himself. Within ten years all pretence of allegiance to the regency had been abandoned, and during the next forty years the generals, their sons, and even their grandsons fought over the heritage of Alexander. No one of these was able to get all of it, and by 275 B.C. three major kingdoms had been created. The first, consisting mostly of Egypt, Palestine, and Syria, was founded by Ptolemy, one of Alexander's young generals who had seized control of Egypt as early as 323. He established a dynasty that would rule Egypt until the suicide of Cleopatra in 30 B.C. The second kingdom was established by another of Alexander's companions in arms, Seleucus, who took Babylon and at one time held most of the Asian possessions of Alexander all the way from Asia Minor to the Indus; this Seleucid dynasty dated its foundation from 312 B.C. and continued to exist until 63 B.C. The third kingdom had its seat in Macedonia and more or less controlled Greece until just after 200 B.C. Its rulers, the Antigonids, traced their descent from Antigonos the One-Eyed, one of Alexander's older generals, but the Antigonid kingdom was not founded until 277 B.C. when Antigonos II (Gonatas), grandson of the old general, finally gained the Macedonian throne. The dynasty survived until 167 B.C. when it was extinguished by the Romans.

The three kingdoms were at their height from 275 to 200 B.C. A kind of balance of power prevailed, although the Ptolemies and Seleucids engaged in a series of "Syrian" wars that ended in victory for the latter kingdom. The cause was the Seleucid need for an outlet to the Mediterranean to ensure their prosperity, which was based on trade, and the Ptolemies' need for naval stores from Lebanon and the warships of Phoenicia to protect Egypt from invasion by sea. Fortunately for the Ptolemies, the Seleucids had other problems to engage their attention. A band of Gauls coming down the Danube all the way from what is now the territory of France invaded Asia Minor, and attempts to cope with the Gauls led to the virtual independence of the western part of that region and ultimately to its alliance with the Ptolemies in Egypt. Another problem for the Seleucids was posed by the rise of the Parthians (c. 250 B.C.) who led a nationalist movement in Iran and drove a wedge between the eastern and western Seleucid provinces. By 160 B.C. the Parthians had annexed Babylon; then they took all of Mesopotamia and confined the Seleucids to the Syrian and Palestinian territory which they had wrested from the Ptolemies towards the end of the third century. The Antigonids of Macedonia, although they controlled a smaller territory than the Seleucids or the Ptolemies, were nevertheless a power to be reckoned with because of their military potential. But their difficulty in subjugating the Greeks kept them from being even more dangerous. Two Greek leagues, the Achaean and the Aetolian, proved difficult for the Macedonians to manage. The Achaean League, a combination of city states in the Peloponnesus, gained control of the key city of Corinth and held the Macedonians at bay from 250–225 B.C.; later, the Aetolian League, an alliance of rural cantons in central Greece, performed the same function. About 220 B.C., however, the balance of power in the eastern Mediterranean was destroyed as the Antigonids under Philip V and the Seleucids under Antiochus III began to work together to dominate that part of the world and bring the Ptolemies to their knees. Antiochus nearly overran Egypt in 217 B.C., but was stopped by an all-out

Ptolemaic effort that achieved its purpose, although it left Egypt exhausted and forced to look to Rome for help. At the same time Philip seemed on the verge of conquering all of Greece; he would have done so if it had not been for the stout resistance of the Aetolian League, which had some Roman backing. As the year 200 B.C. approached, the situation was very tense, and the future seemed to depend on whether Rome, by then the major state in Europe, could redress the balance of power by coping with both Philip and Antiochus. The Romans proved themselves more than equal to the occasion, and the states that had appealed to Rome for help found the cure worse than the disease; but that is another story which must be preceded by a discussion of the general aspects of the period 350–200 B.C. and a description of the rise of Rome from obscurity to the position of a world power.

The period from the death of Alexander the Great in 323 to 146 or 133 B.C. is known as the Hellenistic Age and is usually defined as an era in which Greek civilization became the possession of Greeks and non-Greeks as well. During this time many thousands of Greeks left the Aegean area to settle in the Ptolemaic and Seleucid empires, and untold numbers of non-Greeks either migrated of their own accord or were transported as slaves from the Near East to Greece and the western Mediterranean. Consequently, just as elements of Greek culture were diffused eastward and adopted in many urban areas, there was a comparable flow of eastern culture to the west. Hellenistic civilization was thus actually Greco-Oriental, yet it is important to recognize that some of its features on the Greek side had already begun to appear before 323 B.C., in the transitional period between the Battle of Mantinea and the death of Alexander.

The Hellenistic Age gives the impression of having been bigger if not better in every way than the "classical" period that preceded it. There were more cities and larger ones than ever before. Alexandria, the Ptolemaic capital in Egypt, had a population of several hundred thousand; Antioch in Syria, the Seleucid capital, was nearly as populous; and there were many more cities larger than any of the fifth century. Urbanization was truly one of the outstanding characteristics of the age, as was the existence of a world-wide trade. Not only was there an all-encompassing Mediterranean commerce, but trade lines to southern Asia included direct trade with India and more than slight contacts with China. Manufacturing under private and state auspices was on a larger scale than formerly. There came to be a middle class possessed of great wealth and exercising considerable political influence. For the "haves" it was an age of great prosperity, but for the "have-nots" one of extreme poverty. Prices rose; wages did not. The free worker had to compete with slave labor, and in the cities even a day's labor was hard to get.

Individualism was another major characteristic of the Hellenistic age. It pervaded sculpture, painting, and literature and made its way into religion and philosophy. The old city-state cults declined into mere formality while the mystery religions, mostly eastern imports, were immensely popular with their promises of salvation and eternal life. Philosophy became "personal," too. Epicureanism and Stoicism, both products of the late fourth century B.C., offered a way of life for intellectuals and pseudo-intellectuals who could not believe in the old gods or accept the extravagant promises of the mystery religions. Stripped of its "scientific" justification, dialectic, and elaborate ethic, Epicureanism preached: "Do not fear the gods because they are not concerned with human affairs, and do not fear death because it is only eternal sleep." The essence of Stoicism was withdrawal: "Forsake the world, compose yourself, accept whatever good or evil comes your way, create a solitude and call it peace."

The Hellenistic age was also noted for its science and scholarship. Aristotle (384–322 B.C.) was more than a forerunner of the new period. In dialectic, political theory, physics, astronomy, natural science, and literary criticism he gave it its start. His insistence on logical classification proved an invaluable scientific method. He founded the science of zoology just as his pupil, Theophrastus, became the "father of botany." This same period also saw the publication of Euclid's *Elements*, which in translation is still the basic textbook on geometry in many schools. Euclid, the tutor of Ptolemy II, was only one of many scholars who enjoyed the patronage of the Ptolemies in Alexandria. Greater than Euclid was Eratosthenes who measured the circumference of the earth and came out, by a fortunate combination of errors, very close to the true figure. Given his assumption that the earth is a perfect sphere, there was nothing wrong with his method, but he simply did not have the facilities for accurate measurement. Then there was Aristarchus, whose careful editing improved the text of Homer and whose mathematical and astronomical studies led him to evolve the heliocentric theory which, though correct, was rejected by most other astronomers because it did not "save the phenomena," i.e., explain the available data as well as Aristotelian geocentrism. None of these scientists of the third century B.C., however, could match the genius and versatility of Archimedes of Syracuse whose contributions to mathematics, astronomy, mechanics, optics, and hydrostatics were nothing short of phenomenal. The study of medicine also advanced at Alexandria and other major centers by anatomical and physiological research which enhanced the physicians' understanding of the brain, the nervous system and the circulation of the blood.

Never had there been more schools nor a higher rate of literacy. The larger reading public and the increased availability of papyrus, the ancient equivalent of paper, augmented literary production. Historical works, treatises on economics, political science, geography, and military strategy, as well as works of fiction and little essays on a variety of inconsequential subjects abounded. Among the authors of the age were Polybius the Achaean, soldier, statesman, and historian; Apollonius of Rhodes whose full-length epic, the *Argonautica*, told the story of Jason and the Golden Fleece and Medea; and Menander, the greatest playwright of the New Comedy.

Some of the so-called Wonders of the World and some of the most familiar works of ancient sculpture were products of the Hellenistic age. In the first category were the Pharos—the great lighthouse at Alexandria—the Mausoleum at Halicarnassus, the huge temple of Artemis at Ephesus, and the Colossus of Rhodes. The Colossus also belongs in the second category along with the Winged Victory, the Dying Gaul, and the Laocoön. Distinctive schools of sculpture flourished at Alexandria, Antioch, and Pergamum, all imperial capitals noted for their patronage of the arts.

The great empires were not the only novelties in the field of government, although it should be noted that the authority of the ruler in each state rested on a different foundation. In Egypt, particularly, there was a centralization of administration and a proliferation of bureaucracy that went beyond anything known in pharaonic times; the reigning Ptolemy was the pharaoh and thus a god-king. In the Seleucid kingdom the monarch, somewhat like the Persian kings of old, ruled by divine right; in Macedonia the Antigonids had a position only slightly different from the traditional one that had characterized the old Indo-European monarchy. Old-line city states—

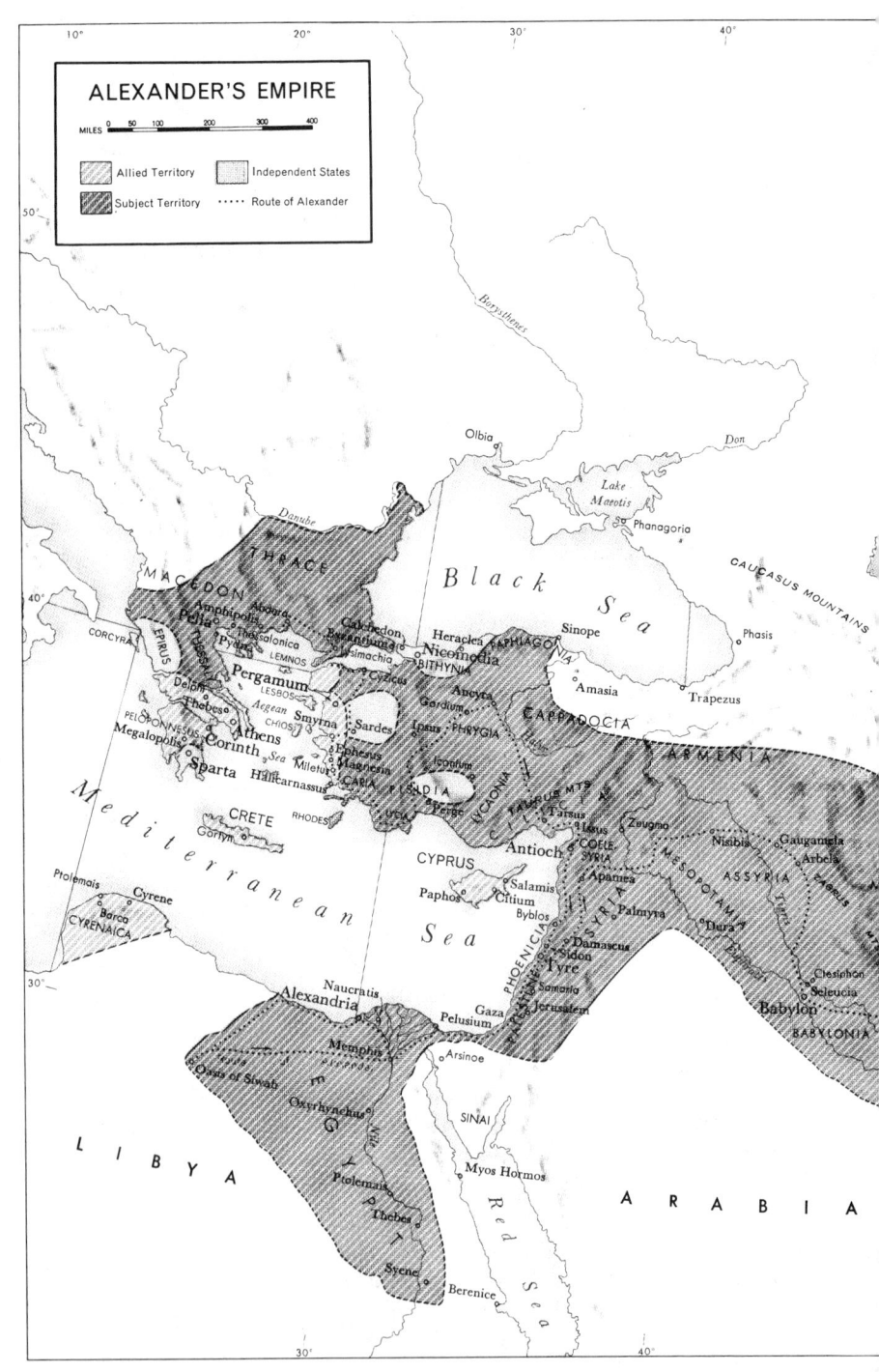

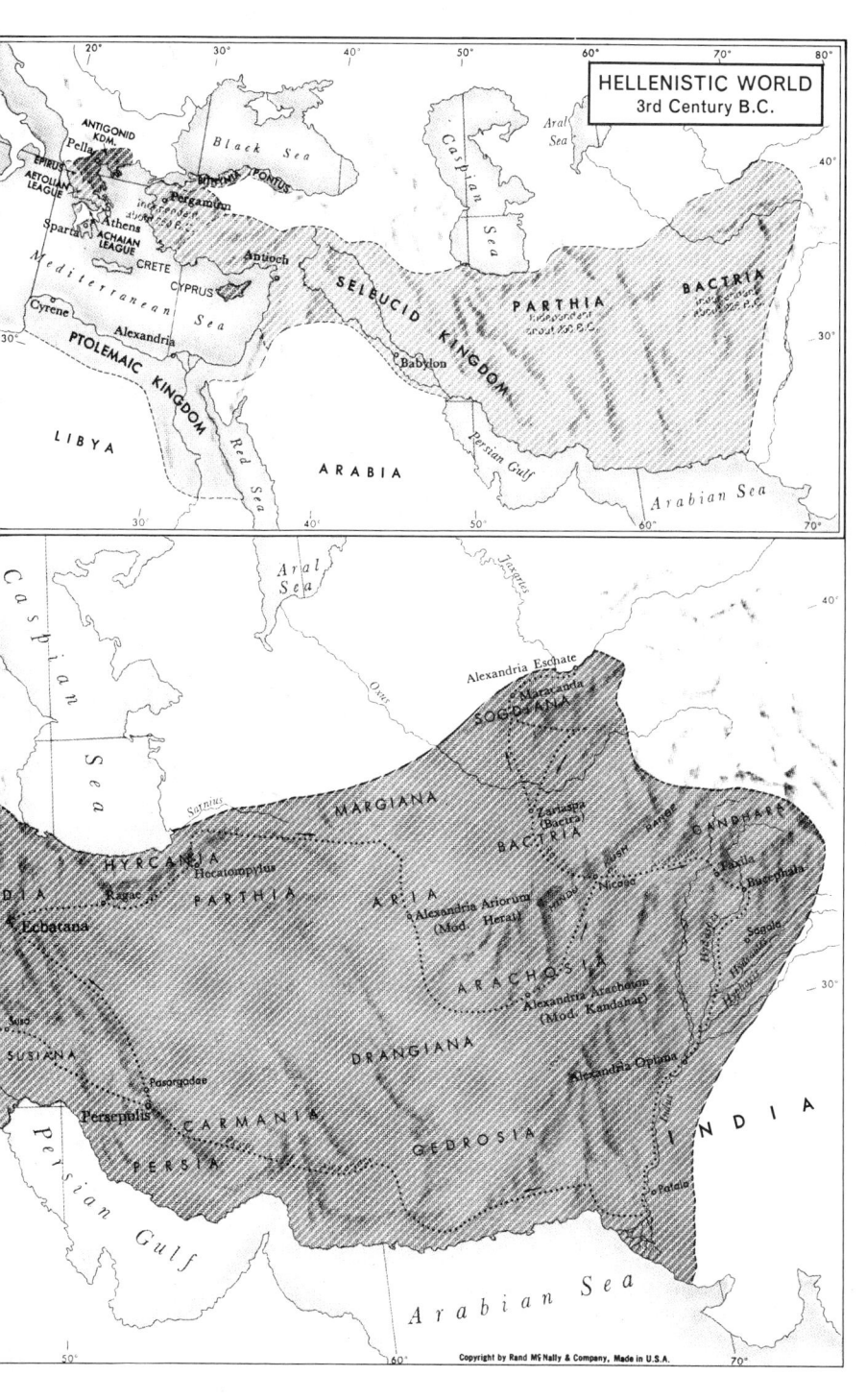

Athens, Rhodes, and others—continued to function; but in the great kingdoms, although municipal government was often of the *polis* type, it was obviously employed as a subordinate unit lower down the scale than the imperial or provincial establishments. The Greeks were in agreement by the end of the fifth century B.C. that the city-state system involving the direct participation of all citizens in the government only functioned properly when the citizen body was relatively small. A solution to this problem was provided by the new Achaean and Aetolian leagues, which turned to representative government and even went so far as to use proportional representation based on the population or military strength of the member units. Unfortunately, the idea of representative government never really caught on in antiquity. It might have saved democracy for the Romans who came out in the end with that other "novelty" of the Hellenistic Age, the Oriental monarchy.

Rome, destined to "rule the world," got off to a very slow and inauspicious start. The forefathers of the Romans belonged to an Indo-European linguistic group called the Latins, who had invaded Italy from the north late in the second millennium B.C. They finally settled in a region called Latium situated on the south bank of the Tiber River near the west coast of the Italian peninsula. In the eighth or possibly the ninth century B.C. a tiny settlement was established at a ford in the river. Here, cradled in the famous seven hills, Rome began.

The Latins—and hence the early Romans—were close relatives of the Greeks. They shared a common origin; Latin and Greek belonged to the same Indo-European linguistic subgroup; and both peoples entered the Mediterranean world about the same time, bringing with them essentially the same political and social institutions. Moreover, during the early centuries of residence in new homelands their cultural evolution proceeded along paths remarkably similar. When they finally came in contact with cultures more complex than their own, however, the divergence between Greek and Roman began. The earlier civilization of the ancient Near East had a profound effect upon the Greeks, while the Romans felt first of all the influence of the Etruscans, and, then, from the late fourth century B.C. onward, the Greco-Oriental culture of the Hellenistic age, which engulfed Rome like a tidal wave.

The Etruscans were apparently an Asian people, related to the Lydians, living originally on the west coast of Asia Minor or on islands off-shore. In the ninth century B.C. groups of Etruscans had migrated to Italy and occupied Tuscany (ancient Etruria), where there were valuable mineral resources. Establishing independent and often warring city states, they exploited their new territory and its native population, maintained trade relations with the Near East, and kept up their nautical skills by piratical forays in the western Mediterranean. In the seventh century the Etruscans began to expand their holdings in Italy by moving both north and south. Before 600 B.C. they occupied Rome and made that little hamlet into a stone-walled city with paved streets. The Capitoline Hill became the citadel of the new town and was crowned by a triple temple dedicated to Etruscan deities called by the Romans Jupiter, Juno, and Minerva. Although the Etruscans were expelled from Rome by a revolution, probably shortly after 500 B.C., they had left their mark on the Romans. There were many religious concepts and ceremonials of Etruscan origin that the Romans retained, and various Etruscan words were incorporated into the vocabulary of the Latin tongue. Included among these were the Latinized forms of the names of Etruscan deities: for example, Juno, Neptune, Vulcan, and Mars.

Although the legend of Romulus and Remus and the founding of Rome on April 15, 753 B.C. is not historically admissible, the tradition that Rome was first ruled by kings is sound, and what was dimly remembered of that early period suggests that the monarchy was of the primitive Indo-European type, such as that of the Greeks in the dark age. Even the fact that the last kings of Rome may have been Etruscans does not seem to have affected the monarchical constitution. In that time there was a king, a council of the elders called the senate, and an assembly of the warriors known as the *comitia*. As in Greece, there evolved an aristocracy of large landholders that came to dominate the council of the elders and the assembly and finally challenged the monarchy itself. When the revolution expelled the Etruscans, the monarchy was abolished and replaced by the Roman Republic. This government began as a thoroughgoing aristocracy of the same type that had succeeded the monarchy in Greece, or might have won out in Macedonia if it had not been for Philip II.

As the Republic began (traditionally in 509 B.C., but certainly later) the operation of the government was little different from that of the monarchy. There was still the senate, though now composed entirely of the landed aristocrats (the patricians) and the assembly (*comitia*) of the warriors, which included the patricians and those commoners (plebeians) who could equip themselves for military service. By this time there were many plebeians so poor that they could not serve in the army and as a result had been deprived of their public rights as Roman citizens. In fact, under the aristocracy, even those plebeians eligible for military service and so admitted to the assembly did not have the *ius honoris,* the right to hold office, which was restricted to patricians. This had been the situation, too, in the closing years of the monarchy. The difference under the early Republic was that the hereditary king who had held office for life was replaced by two magistrates called consuls. These were elected annually by the assembly from the ranks of the patricians. The consuls were military leaders, embryonic judicial officers, and administrators of the city of Rome. They were empowered to call and preside over meetings of the senate and the assembly. Both consuls had equal authority, so that one consul, if he wished, could block actions of the other. This short-term magistracy combined with the veto power of one magistrate over the other was designed to prevent a revival of the monarchy or the institution of a tyranny. The patrician monopoly of the government was naturally a source of dissatisfaction to the plebeians, and during the first two centuries of the Republic a long struggle ensued between these two groups. A survey of the early history of republican Rome will show that a combination of external and internal developments led at last to the establishment of political equality.

For a hundred and fifty years after the expulsion of the kings, it was touch and go for the Romans. Against the Etruscans and hostile Italian native tribes, the Romans and their allies, the Latins, fought desperately to survive. A really low point came about 390 B.C. when a band of Gauls, related to those who invaded Asia Minor a century later, captured and sacked Rome. This disaster, however, was not without its redeeming features. Not only were the Romans forced to reorganize their army and government, and rebuild their city, but it turned out that the Gauls had hurt the Etruscans more than the Romans—so much so that the Etruscans ceased to be dangerous to Rome. Henceforth, things went better. The Romans adopted a new policy of subjugating their enemies rather than beating them off, and as a result they began to control more and more territory. By 272 B.C., when they captured the Greek city of Tarentum, a port town located in the instep of the Italian boot, the Romans were supreme in peninsular Italy, and a short time later they acquired the Po valley in the north.

In the meantime, as a consequence of internal and external crises and sheer necessity, the Roman government had been changing. Some of the changes came as the plebeians found ways to bring pressure on the patricians; others were the result of growing governmental responsibilities that exceeded the ability of consuls alone to manage. Each consul was given a subordinate, named a *quaestor,* who acted as a treasury official in Rome and a quartermaster on military campaigns. The direct management of the grain supply and the marketplace of Rome was turned over to four officials called *aediles.* Judicial matters became the responsibility of a *praetor.* All the officials were annually elected and were subordinate to the consuls. The assembly was revised to include all citizens, whether or not they could afford to equip themselves for military duty. The new assembly, meeting under the presidency of the consuls, passed laws, elected the officials, and acted as a court of appeal from sentences involving the death penalty, heavy fines, or exile; but the votes of the citizens were weighted in a way that made it possible for a limited number of wealthy persons to outvote the majority who were poor or of modest means. By the middle of the fifth century B.C., the patricians had made concessions that gave the plebeians the *ius honoris;* in theory, a plebeian could hold any office, even the consulship, but the catch was that he had to muster enough votes to be elected. Before this happened, however, the plebeians had organized their own government, a state within a state, which had an assembly composed solely of plebeians that elected annually four (later ten) officials, the plebeian tribunes, who called and presided over the plebeian assembly. The assembly passed measures called plebiscites. In effect, these were laws binding on all plebeians, and the patricians conceded that a plebiscite approved by the senate would also be binding on patricians. The long patrician-plebeian struggle was finally resolved in 287 B.C. when the plebeians threatened to secede entirely from the state. The patricians capitulated, and the upshot of the matter was that the plebeian assembly, henceforth known as the Assembly of the Tribes, was enlarged to include patricians as well as plebeians. The plebiscites passed by this assembly were to have the same force of law as measures passed by the other assembly, the Assembly of the Centuries, presided over by the consuls. The Assembly of the Centuries was unchanged; it continued to elect the various officials, to legislate, and to act as a court of appeal; and it was still presided over by the consuls. The new Assembly of the Tribes, under the presidency of the tribunes, could legislate; it elected the plebeian tribunes (no patrician could hold this office); and, of course, in this assembly the votes were not weighted—the will of the majority (who were plebeians) always would prevail. The implications of this dual system were not immediately apparent. For the moment, the plebeians were satisfied with what seemed to be equality with the patricians, and during the next century and a half the Romans were so engrossed in foreign affairs that domestic problems received little attention. It was only after 133 B.C., as will be seen, that the democracy represented by the tribal assembly and the tribunes came into conflict with the oligarchy entrenched in the Assembly of the Centuries, the senate, and the consulate.

As late as 265 B.C. no one could have accused the Romans of deliberate and conscious imperialism. They themselves certainly would have defined their conquest of Italy as a policy of self-defense. After that year, however, it was a different story. Gaining control of the western Mediterranean in the Punic Wars against Carthage, the Romans found their new possessions in Sicily and Spain very profitable and concluded that if a little empire was so advantageous, a big one would be even better. This was certainly a potent factor in their decision to confront the Antigonids and the Seleucids after 200 B.C. Capable of infinite self-deception, the Roman man in the street and even some of the policymakers in the senate would have argued that Rome's very existence was threatened by the Carthaginians, or the Antigonids, or the Seleucids, or that Rome's mission was to protect the Greeks.

The Carthaginians were descendants of Phoenician colonists who had settled in north Africa in the eighth century B.C. With the fall of the Phoenician city states first to Assyria, then to Babylonia, and finally to Persia, Carthage had become independent. Extending its control over other Phoenician settlements in Africa, Spain, Sicily, and the western islands, it had created a commercial and territorial empire of considerable expanse. This aggravated old trade rivalries with the Greeks. In Sicily the Greeks and Carthaginians engaged in a long and almost continuous struggle, in the course of which the Carthaginians came very close to conquering the whole island on several occasions. The Romans had allied themselves with Carthage when the war with Tarentum was in progress (281-272 B.C.). The agreement was that if the Carthaginians would attack and pin down the Greeks in Sicily so that they could not aid the Greeks in Tarentum, the Romans would give the Carthaginians a free hand in Sicily. This proved to be no better than other promises the Romans had made to former allies, including the people of Tarentum. In 264 the Romans intervened in a dispute in Sicily and so precipitated the First Punic War (264-241 B.C.), in which the Carthaginians were driven out of Sicily. The Romans not only acquired control of the island but soon afterward got Sardinia and Corsica as well. Two decades later the Carthaginians were goaded into the Second Punic War (218-201 B.C.), in which they gave a somewhat better account of themselves. Their great military leader, Hannibal, ravaged Italy for more than fifteen years. If the Carthaginian fleet had supported him with reinforcements and supplies, and if Philip V of Macedonia, his ally, had been able to come to his aid, Hannibal might have written *finis* to the story of Rome. As it was, the Romans won again and acquired profitable territory in Spain as a result.

The treaty ending the Second Punic War had scarcely been ratified when Rome received an urgent appeal from Athens, Pergamum, and Egypt for protection against Philip V of Macedonia and Antiochus III, the Seleucid king, who were alleged to have combined to conquer the eastern Mediterranean. When the Romans defeated Philip and drove him out of Greece (197 B.C.), they proclaimed the "freedom" of the Greeks in the following year. It soon became apparent, however, that this freedom meant that Rome instead of the Antigonids or the Seleucids would dictate to the Greeks, and so the Aetolian League promptly invited Antiochus to come back to Greece and free the land from the Romans. This occasioned another war, which drove Antiochus from Greece and Asia Minor (192-188 B.C.). In still another conflict (171-168), the Macedonian monarchy was abolished and the Seleucids expelled from Egypt. Finally, between 149-146 B.C. simultaneous Roman operations in Macedonia, Greece, and Africa destroyed Carthage (Third Punic War), and Corinth (the Achaean capital), and made Macedonia a Roman province. The territory of Carthage became the Roman province of Africa, and the climax came when Attalus III, last king of Pergamum in Asia Minor, willed his kingdom to Rome (133 B.C.) because he knew the Romans would get it anyway. This rich territory was then organized as the province of Asia.

The Roman success was not without its drawbacks, and subsequent developments must have given some measure of solace to the conquered peoples. The greed of the Romans for the spoils of their empire eventually destroyed the Roman Republic and brought the people of Rome under the heel of autocrats as unfeeling as the Romans themselves had been toward the well-being of the people they had conquered. The close association with Hellenistic civilization that began with the Punic Wars and continued as the Romans advanced eastward undermined traditional Roman culture; indeed, "captive Greece" finally did capture her captor, Rome. Moreover, in order to explain to the Greeks the meteoric rise of Rome that "had conquered the world in the space of fifty years," Polybius the Achaean was inspired to write one of the great historical works of antiquity.

Chapter 6

The Decline and Fall of the Roman Republic

In 333 B.C. when Alexander the Great won the Battle of Issus, the most decisive of all his victories, the Romans at the other end of the ancient world were just beginning the aggressive defensive moves that would give them control of Italy within the next half century. Two hundred years after Issus the Romans had destroyed Carthage, made Macedonia a Roman province, humbled the Seleucids, "inherited" the kingdom of Pergamum, dissolved the Aetolian and Achaean Leagues, and emerged as the sole great power in the entire Mediterranean area. Related to, and no less important than, Rome's rise to a position of international dominance were the internal changes that had taken place in Roman government, economy, society, and culture. A makeshift apparatus for imperial government had been tacked onto the city-state frame; the farmers—patrician and plebeian—of the fourth century had been replaced by three socioeconomic classes: senatorial, equestrian, and proletarian; and the language, literature, art, religion, and intellectual life of the Romans had been subjected to such massive Greek influence that traditional Roman culture was in decay.

    The close contact with the Greeks and the changes in economics, society, and government had begun with the Punic Wars. The ruin of the small farmer in Italy commenced at the end of the First Punic War when he could not compete with the low-priced Sicilian grain that came in great volume as tribute from the new province. The devastation wrought in Italy itself by the Second Punic War led to the abandonment of many farms, and the pattern of land use changed. The traditional small farm was replaced by great estates (*latifundia*) devoted to cattle raising and to the production of wine and olive oil. Worked by slave labor, managed by bailiffs, and belonging to absentee landlords of the senatorial class, these large holdings provided their owners with great wealth. Prohibited by law from engaging in commerce, the senatorial class from which the senators, officialdom, and provincial governors were recruited was the ruling class. Not only did it staff the government, but it also constituted a political faction, interested in agriculture as opposed to trade and industry, and extremely eager to gouge what wealth it could from the empire by fair means or foul.

The Punic Wars had also produced the equestrians; originally they were contractors supplying the military with food and material. Amassing capital by war profiteering, the equestrians invested in trade and industry, but the bulk of their income continued to be derived from government contracts. They bid for the right to collect taxes in the overseas provinces and obtained leases to exploit the mines, forests, and fisheries, which were state-owned. Ultimately, the equestrians became money lenders. They were the creditors of ambitious senators who needed greater and greater sums to campaign for public office. They also made loans to city states, kingdoms, and even whole provinces when these subject peoples needed help in raising the money to pay their taxes which, of course, the equestrians were going to collect. Little control was exercised over interest rates, so that in many cases the interest due exceeded the principal within a short time. As with the senatorial class, the main target of the equestrians was the wealth of the empire, and it was inevitable that the two groups often clashed at home and abroad.

The proletarians were in large part descendants of the small farmers ruined by the Punic Wars. They had drifted to Rome, where there was little work for unskilled labor, but where life was exciting. The poverty-stricken proletarians had one marketable commodity: their votes. Anyone seeking election to office or enough votes to pass some cherished measure had to court the proletarians and give or promise them something in return. The political weight of the proletarians was not altogether a matter of numbers. There were many Roman citizens scattered throughout Italy who were artisans, farmers, and tradesmen, but in order to vote in elections or on bills presented to the assemblies they had to be physically present in Rome, and this was seldom possible for them. Consequently, the votes of the proletarians were usually decisive.

All in all, it was an unsatisfactory situation. Rome was being run by a minority of its citizens, divided into three groups, each with a different axe to grind and with little or no concern for the welfare of the state or its citizens. The democracy that the plebeians had fought to achieve was virtually forgotten. There were, in fact, large numbers of Roman citizens, the descendants of slaves and non-Romans, who knew nothing of the ancient traditions or the workings of the Roman constitution. Worst of all was the plight of the subjects of Rome who had no one to defend them against the injustice of senatorial administration or the rapacity of the equestrians.

In 133 B.C. Rome was generally at peace with the rest of the world, a condition that had seldom prevailed over the previous two hundred years. Unfortunately, the external calm was not accompanied by internal peace and quiet. The cessation of war had focused attention on affairs at home which were found to be quite unsatisfactory. The proletarians had long been unhappy because the lion's share of the profits of empire had gone to the senators and equestrians; their bitterness was increased by the mounting postwar depression that the government had failed to alleviate, even while initiating public works programs and a minting policy that put a substantial volume of money in circulation.

At this time Rome came close to a revolution that might have culminated in the establishment of a tyranny of the Greek type. Two young men of the senatorial class chose to forsake assured political careers of the conventional kind to become leaders of the proletarians. These were the brothers Gracchi, Tiberius and Gaius. They were the sons of a famous general, Sempronius Gracchus, and a highly cultured Roman matron, Cornelia, daughter of Scipio Africanus, the conqueror of Hannibal. The motives of the Gracchi are obscure. Modern opinion is divided as to which of the brothers was the idealist and which was the ambitious, pragmatic realist. The fact is that Tiberius Gracchus, the elder brother, discovered what seemed to be a shortcut to instant and perennial power. Instead of following the *cursus honorum,* the sequence of officeholding that would lead him from the post of quaestor or aedile to that of praetor and finally to the consulship (at which point he could propose the legislation he had in mind), Tiberius sought and won the office of plebeian tribune. Once elected to preside over the tribal assembly and identified as one devoted to the well-being of the Roman people, he could introduce the measures that he thought would correct a bad situation. Tiberius said that he wanted to revive the small farm, manned by the sturdy yeomen who in former days had been the backbone of the army and the republic itself. He proposed to reclaim state lands that had been occupied illegally by the senatorial landlords and to distribute the land in small plots to landless citizens. The proletarians supported what seemed to be a gigantic giveaway, but senatorial opposition materialized and managed to delay the project by various means until Tiberius' year of office was running out. When he sought a second year as tribune, his opponents objected on the grounds of unconstitutionality. There was a law that forbade successive consulships, for example, but the question of multiple tribunates had never been raised. In the disorder that followed, Tiberius was killed by a mob, and the revolution was halted temporarily. The opposition to Tiberius was not based on his program of land reform; rather, it stemmed from the fear of the senators that the revived tribunate might bypass and render obsolete the whole system of senatorial government.

Ten years after the death of Tiberius, his brother Gaius took up the battle. Although he started where Tiberius had left off by election to the tribunate, he then revived and enlarged the land bill by coupling it with a program of overseas colonization. Thus, the schemes of Gaius were much more elaborate than those of his brother. Gaius introduced a bill to provide cheap grain for the needy, and this along with the land act gave him solid proletarian support. Then he went a step further by forming a coalition of equestrians and proletarians to oppose the senatorial faction. He wooed the equestrians by bills that gave them the right to collect the taxes of the new province of Asia and put equestrians instead of senators on the juries (*quaestiones*) that tried senatorial officials accused of misgovernment in the provinces. These juries, established twenty-five years before, had not worked satisfactorily, for the senators were hesitant, understandably, to convict their peers of offences which they themselves had already committed or hoped to commit in the future. The equestrians were indifferent to good government for Rome's subjects, but they saw their own participation on the juries as a club to force provincial governors to overlook the gouging of equestrian tax collectors. Justice was served in neither case. With a senatorial jury, acquittal was a foregone conclusion; with an equestrian jury, condemnation was the rule.

Gaius was so successful that he was elected to a second year as tribune. Then he overreached himself by promoting a bill to give citizenship to the so-called Italian allies. These were Italian communities bound by treaty to Rome. They were locally independent, but their foreign affairs were handled by Rome, and they had to furnish troops to fight alongside the Roman forces in time of war. The allies were slowly coming to the conclusion that these arrangements did not operate to their advantage, and they wanted either complete independence or full Roman citizenship. If Gaius could have managed this coup—citizenship for the allies—he would have won the support of thousands of new voters; it would have been necessary to confer the rank of senators and equestrians on some of them, but all the new citizens, even those who did not qualify for the higher census classes, would have had full civic rights and would have been eligible to vote in the assemblies. It was an ambitious scheme. If it had succeeded, Gaius could have headed the government of Rome for years, and the senatorial machinery would have been rendered useless. Few Roman citizens of any class, however, wanted to share their privileges with the allies, and Gaius lost most of his old followers. Rioting broke out. In street fighting many of the remaining supporters of Gaius were killed. He himself was hunted through the streets of Rome and finally committed suicide to foil his pursuers. Thus, the Gracchi failed, but they had introduced new moves into the game of politics that were to be used by ambitious politicians henceforward: the land giveaway, cheap grain soon to be followed by a grain dole, a coalition of proletarians and equestrians, and the dream of enfranchising the allies to gain additional voter strength.

Although the senators had won the first round, the fight was not over. Two decades after the death of Gaius Gracchus the senatorial faction had its collective back to the wall because of the scandals arising out of a war in Africa against King Jugurtha of Numidia. Jugurtha not only had defeated the senatorial commanders sent against him, but in some cases, he had bribed the Romans to surrender or to make disgraceful settlements. It was at this point that Gaius Marius came to the fore. Marius, an equestrian by birth, had served many years in the army and was noted for his bravery and skill. By no means adept as a politician, Marius had managed with some effort to go through the *cursus honorum* to the stage at which he was eligible for the consulship. After serving under a senatorial commander in some of the campaigns against Jugurtha, Marius returned to Rome to run for election. Criticizing the conduct of the war by his former chief and maintaining that he himself could achieve victory, Marius was elected consul and given the command against Jugurtha. Within two years he returned victorious, dragging Jugurtha in chains through the streets of Rome. As he celebrated his triumph (105 B.C.), a new assignment awaited him. Italy was threatened by an invasion from the north that promised to repeat the disastrous Gallic sack of Rome in the fourth century B.C. The barbarians, two tribes from central Europe known as the Cimbri and Teutones, had defeated a succession of senatorial commanders and destroyed several Roman armies. Marius rose to the challenge. He defeated one tribe in Gaul, the other in northern Italy, and returned to Rome to be hailed as the saviour of his countrymen.

At the end of the second century B.C. Marius was again consul, for the sixth time in less than a decade. His successive consulships violated the law that ten years must elapse between one consulship and the next, but since Marius was indispensable the voters had been willing to overlook this regulation. In his new consulship Marius had to cope with domestic rather than foreign enemies. He was the standard-bearer of the new coalition of equestrians and proletarians, but his already demonstrated political ineptitude worked to the advantage of his opponents. His chief political advisors were two demagogues, Saturninus and Glaucia, who had a long record of skullduggery and criminal actions. Their behaviour in this year was so outrageous that the senate was able to maneuvre Marius into a position where he had to lead a police action against his own supporters. Saturninus and Glaucia were killed; Marius was disgraced; and the senate was back in control again.

Marius may have served his country well on the battlefield, but in many ways he, like Gaius Gracchus, had contributed to the destruction of the Roman Republic. Not only had Marius been encouraged to flout the law in the instance of his many consulships, but he had created a professional army which would come to be used as a weapon in future political struggles. The military reforms instituted by Marius in both organization and tactics had made the legions almost unbeatable for generations to come, but more important still, by abandoning the traditional policy of conscription and accepting long-term voluntary enlistments, he had made the army a career. The tendency was for the soldiers to put loyalty to their commanders above allegiance to the state and to have the usual contempt of the military man for mere civilians, even if these civilians were heads of state.

Following the lead of Gaius Gracchus, a number of politicians had schemed to gain citizenship for the allies, but time after time the schemer failed. The allies finally lost patience and began a revolt. This was the so-called Social War (War with the Allies) of 90–88 B.C. For some months it appeared that the allies might be successful in breaking the power of Rome forever, but the Romans pulled themselves together. They kept the revolt from spreading by granting citizenship to those who had not taken up arms or would stop fighting, and then finally defeated the remaining allied forces in the field. The result of the whole affair, however, was that all the allies, whether belligerents or not, gained full Roman citizenship.

At the end of the war the consulship was dominated by Lucius Cornelius Sulla, a reactionary senator of patrician ancestry, who had been the most successful general on the Roman side. Long a rival of Marius, it was actually Sulla who had captured Jugurtha, and Sulla also claimed some responsibility for the defeat of the Cimbri. Marius, for his part, had come out of obscurity to fight in the Social War and was near to making a political comeback. Thus, the battle line between the senatorial class and equestrian-proletarian coalition was drawn again, and disorder followed. First, Sulla was expelled from Rome, but he swiftly returned and drove Marius and his faction into exile. Then Sulla sponsored a series of reactionary reforms intended to make the senate supreme in the governmental process. This was the beginning of a new round of trouble.

At this same time the Romans were already engaged in a new foreign war against a king far more dangerous than Jugurtha. Mithridates VI of Pontus was the ruler of a kingdom on the south shore of the Black Sea. In twenty years on the throne Mithridates had built an empire that stretched round the Black Sea to the Crimea, and he had threatened Roman allies in Asia Minor on several occasions. When it appeared that the Romans might lose the Social War, Mithridates thought he saw his opportunity; he engineered a revolt among the unhappy Roman subjects in the province of Asia, which culminated in the massacre of 80,000 Romans there. Then, when he was invited to free Greece from the Romans, Mithridates sent his armies across the Aegean to support a Greek revolt already in progress.

Sulla, feeling that affairs in Rome were under control, set off to fight Mithridates and drove the latter's forces from Greece and out of the province of Asia. By 84 B.C. Mithridates was confined to his own kingdom and might have been destroyed by Sulla, but the Roman general was so anxious to get back to Rome where things had gotten completely out of hand that he signed a peace treaty with Mithridates, leaving the wily king to fight another day. During Sulla's absence, there had been a considerable upheaval in Rome. The Marians had regained power and had instituted a blood bath that eliminated many of Sulla's friends. Marius became consul for the seventh time in 87 B.C., and although he died almost immediately, the other leaders of his faction remained in power until Sulla's return in 83. In the meantime, they had rescinded Sulla's legislation, had declared Sulla himself an outlaw, and even had sent their own army (which subsequently deserted to Sulla) to fight Mithridates.

On his return to Italy Sulla soon disposed of his enemies. Those who survived fled to Africa and Spain, only to be pursued by Sulla's generals. The problem, however, was to reestablish legitimate, constitutional government, and the solution was to appoint Sulla dictator with full power to restore order and revise the constitution. Sulla held the dictatorship from 82–79 B.C. when he finally retired because of ill health. His regime was marked by repression and bloodshed, and his extensive reforms were aimed at recreating the senatorial monopoly of government that had prevailed at the beginning of the republic. Among other things, the senate was given the right to veto legislation passed by the assemblies; the senators replaced the equestrians as jurors in the *quaestiones;* the competence of these courts was enlarged to include many criminal offences; and the power of the plebeian tribunes was curtailed greatly.

Because they were no more than a backlash, Sulla's reforms could not survive his death. The pendulum had swung so far to the right that it inevitably reversed its direction. By 70 B.C. all of Sulla's legislation had been repealed, but, like Gaius Gracchus and

Marius, he, too, had set precedents that would help to bring down the Roman Republic. Sulla's tampering with the constitution was bad enough, but his greatest disservice to the state was his revival and new interpretation of the dictatorship. In the early days of the republic and down to the end of the Second Punic War the Romans had frequently found it necessary in times of military or domestic crisis to replace the two consuls with a single chief executive. He would possess supreme power, not only as commander-in-chief of the army, but also as law-giver with the right to change the constitution. It was, for example, a dictator who in 287 B.C. changed the plebeian assembly into the Assembly of the Tribes. In its original form, however, the dictatorship had a limited life span. A dictator had to resign as soon as the crisis had passed; even if it had not, his power ended with the beginning of a new year or at the end of six months within the year of his appointment. Sulla not only had revived this institution, dormant for over a century, but also had given it a new and dangerous form: the long-term or indefinite, even perpetual, dictatorship. This indeed boded ill for the future.

During the thirty years following the retirement of Sulla, the contest between the senatorial faction (now known as the Optimates) and the equestrian-proletarian coalition (the Populares) was renewed, but both groups and the army as well became pawns in the hands of power-hungry individuals. There was a progressive breakdown of constitutional practice until the political game was played with almost no rules at all. Democracy was long since dead; the republic was doomed; and the "liberal" equestrian-proletarian coalition lost its influence. Through all this, however, the essentially reactionary yet cohesive senatorial faction, though basically impotent, managed to outlive the republic itself.

The four Romans who figured prominently in the events of the generation after Sulla were Pompey and Crassus, who as young men had joined Sulla in 83 against the Marians, Julius Caesar and Cicero, in the beginning attached to the Marian faction but too young to be much involved in the civil strife of the eighties. Pompey, thought to be Rome's greatest general, and Crassus, the richest man in Rome, became bitter rivals. Neither, despite their original adherence to Sulla, had any permanent political affiliations. Over the years they shifted from one faction to the other when it suited their immediate purposes. Caesar, who had been outlawed by Sulla for his Marian connections and sympathies and later pardoned by the dictator, never changed sides. His aunt had been the wife of Marius, and during Sulla's dictatorship Caesar was married to the daughter of one of Marius' principal successors. In contrast to Caesar, whose patrician family was one of the oldest and most distinguished in Rome, Cicero was an equestrian whose ancestors had never been involved in politics to the extent of holding important offices. He came from Arpinum in Latium, the home town of Marius, and his family were staunch Marians. As a youth Cicero himself had written a poem in praise of Marius, and although when he reached maturity and gained political stature of his own he was known for a while as an independent, he ended his career among the Optimates.

Mithridates of Pontus was active once more just after Sulla's death. He threatened Roman hegemony in Asia Minor and allied himself not only with the pirate bands who now controlled the eastern Mediterranean but also with the Marian forces still holding out in Spain. At this time Lucius Lucullus, who had been Sulla's second in command in the earlier war against Mithridates, was governor of Asia. By a series of successful moves he drove Mithridates back, expelled him from Pontus, and chased him into the neighboring kingdom of Armenia. As Lucullus was on the verge of annexing Armenia, however, his troops mutinied and Mithridates slipped back into Pontus to resume the war. Lucullus, who represented the senatorial faction, was disgraced. In the meantime Pompey had overcome the Marians in Spain, participated in putting down the famous revolt of Spartacus and the gladiators, and in 67 B.C. was given an "extraordinary command" against the pirates. With authority that embraced the whole Mediterranean and extended fifty miles inland, with tens of thousands of troops and hundreds of ships, and with twenty-five legates or subordinates to assist him in command, Pompey's power was to endure for three years. Nothing quite like this had ever been granted to an individual commander before, and when Pompey wiped out the pirates in three months, people began to worry about his next move. It was at this juncture, however, that Lucullus' troops mutinied, so it was with some relief that the Romans decided to send Pompey after Mithridates. By 65 B.C. Mithridates had fled to the Crimea where he died two years later. Pompey settled affairs in Asia Minor and then annexed the Seleucid kingdom in Syria in 63 B.C.

The Decline and Fall of the Roman Republic 83

With his share of the spoils as commanding general Pompey returned to Rome a richer man than Crassus. The latter, who had always been jealous of Pompey's military success and was still smarting over having to share with his rival the credit for ending the War of the Gladiators, now had another reason for hating Pompey. All during the sixties Crassus had schemed futilely against Pompey, but as his enemy returned home the prospects for revenge seemed a little brighter. Pompey anticipated that the senate would ratify the diplomatic arrangements and territorial settlements he had made in the east and also provide benefits for his veterans. Crassus was determined to block this, as were Lucullus and the senatorial faction. Pompey himself had some supporters, headed by Cicero, the ex-consul of 63 B.C., who claimed to have put down the conspiracy of Catiline virtually single-handed. Even so, the odds were against Pompey, but fortunately the senatorial faction was opposed to Crassus as well as Pompey. The consequence was a three-way draw in the political contest. Nothing could be accomplished because of the stalemate, although Pompey was in less danger than he might have been if his enemies had agreed to work together.

The deadlock finally was broken when Caesar returned from his governorship in Spain to seek election to the consulate for 59 B.C. Sizing up the situation, Caesar persuaded Pompey and Crassus to pool their resources and support his consular campaign, in return for which he would oversee the passage of various measures desired by his two allies. This unofficial coalition of Pompey, Crassus, and Caesar became known as the First Triumvirate. Caesar was as good as his word. After he became consul, he fought successfully for the legislation desired by Pompey and Crassus. His reward was a five-year command in northern Italy and southern Gaul, which eventually led to his conquest of Gaul as described later in his famous *Commentaries*. In 56 B.C. it was agreed to extend Caesar's command another five years, while at the same time Crassus was given a similar mandate in the East so that he could try to win the military glory he had always wanted; Pompey was to remain in Italy to manage affairs in the capital. Caesar continued successfully in his conquest of Gaul, but Crassus provoked a war with the Parthians, suffered a costly defeat at Carrhae in Mesopotamia, and was captured, tortured, and killed by the enemy (53 B.C.). The death of Crassus ended the triumvirate. Pompey drifted into the senatorial ranks and so became Caesar's enemy. After several years of negotiations, Caesar was forced into rebellion (49 B.C.). In the civil war that spread over the whole empire, Pompey was driven from Italy and defeated at Pharsalus in Greece. When he tried to take refuge in Egypt he was assassinated by Ptolemy XII. Caesar arrived in Alexandria shortly afterward, criticized Ptolemy for killing a Roman citizen, and joined Cleopatra, Ptolemy's sister and queen, in a successful civil war against her brother. With Ptolemy dead and Cleopatra as official ruler of Egypt, Caesar was in control of Egypt for all practical purposes. He could have annexed the country had he so wished, but there were many other things to be done. The Pompeian forces still held Africa and Spain, and many reforms were needed in Rome itself. Only after 45 B.C., when the last Pompeians had been routed, could Caesar give his full attention to the needs of Rome.

Caesar had been made dictator when he overran Italy in 49 B.C.; later he was given the dictatorship for five years, and then for life. As dictator, he was the supreme authority in military and civil affairs and could, of course, make changes in the constitution. At the same time he held the consulship year after year. He was accorded the power of a plebeian tribune so that he could veto legislation or the acts of other officials; as *pontifex maximus* since 63 B.C. he was not only the head of the state religion but also had the power to undertake criminal proceedings; and he also filled the newly created post of Prefect of Morals, a perpetual censorship, which gave him the right to appoint new people to the senate and to equestrian rank as well as to grant citizenship to foreign individuals and communities. In addition, by virtue of special legislation he could nominate or even appoint state officials including the consuls, and all bills passed by the assemblies had to have his approval before they became law. Finally, he was given control of the coinage. In this way, Caesar became supreme in every branch of government and created a thoroughgoing autocracy. As a Marian, Caesar was in theory the champion of the Populares in the style of Gaius Gracchus. As a great general, he had the charisma of Marius and thus the loyalty of the army. As dictator, he widened the breach made by Sulla in the constitutional framework.

A master of political strategy and a military genius, Caesar now demonstrated his extraordinary capacities as an administrator. He inaugurated an imperial program of colonization which settled veterans and proletarians in many provinces; he revised the administration of the city of Rome and standardized the municipal government of the Italian towns; and he began the codification of Roman law—a process not completed until six centuries later. The most lasting of all his reforms, however, was the introduction of a new Roman calendar, called the Julian, which was used in Europe until the sixteenth century A.D. when it finally began to be replaced by the Gregorian calendar used today.

On March 15, 44 B.C., Caesar was assassinated by a senatorial conspiracy, and the empire was plunged into civil war once again. At first, it seemed that the senatorial faction would be victorious, but its ineptitude allowed a new coalition to be formed. The leaders of this new faction were Mark Antony, Caesar's right-hand man, Lepidus, one of Caesar's generals, and Octavian, Caesar's grandnephew and legal heir according to the dictator's will. Ill-assorted and distrustful of one another, the three leaders were forced by circumstances to band together. They took over Rome in 43 B.C. and were given a kind of triple dictatorship, known as the Second Triumvirate, which differed from the earlier triumvirate in that it constituted an official board of three rather than an unofficial behind-the-scene alliance. Only scattered opposition to the triumvirate remained after the senatorial forces had been defeated in the Battle of Philippi in 42 B.C. No longer faced with the imperious necessity of working together, the triumvirs began to quarrel among themselves. Lepidus was put aside, and Octavian and Antony ultimately battled for supremacy. Antony had gone to the East where he had become the consort of Cleopatra and warred unsuccessfully against the Parthians; but as Antony seemed to assume the role of an Oriental potentate, the popularity of Octavian grew. Finally, Antony and Cleopatra massed their forces in west-central Greece for an invasion of Italy. Opposed by Octavian and his general Agrippa, Antony was defeated in a sea battle at Actium in 31 B.C. Pursued to Egypt and besieged in Alexandria, Antony and then Cleopatra committed suicide (30 B.C.), and the victorious Octavian came back to Rome to initiate the reforms that would end the Roman Republic and replace it with the Empire.

Paradoxically, as the Republic went crashing to its death, as thousands of Romans, soldiers and civilians alike, perished in the

civil wars, and as the whole economy of Rome was threatened by chaos, Latin literature entered upon its most brilliant period. During the half century preceding the Battle of Actium, two great Latin poets flourished: Catullus, whose lyrics are imperishable, and Lucretius, the author of the philosophical epic, *De Rerum Natura*, which constitutes an important source not only for the doctrine of Epicureanism, but also for the scientific thinking of the first century B.C. Before the period ended, both Virgil and Horace had come to prominence, too. The immortal *Commentaries* of Caesar had appeared, as well as the works of the historian Sallust. From the pen of the latter two interesting works, one on the *Jugurthine War* and the other on the conspiracy of Catiline, still survive.

Above all, however, this was the Ciceronian Age. Cicero lifted Latin prose to its highest stylistic point. In his orations, letters, discourses and dialogues on rhetoric and oratory, and his philosophical treatises, Cicero became the model and the teacher of future generations in western Europe almost to the present time. Brilliant as an orator and trial lawyer, a charming letter writer, although not always understanding of either philosophy or politics, Cicero was cursed with a colossal ego and a vituperative tongue which made enemies and often repelled friends. Despite achievements that should have satisfied even a Cicero, he could not reconcile himself to failures and misfortunes, often of his own making. Cicero was not a brave man, though much given to bluster, but he redeemed himself in the end as he stood forth against Antony and Octavian. He earned their undying hatred, prompting his execution in 43 B.C. Caesar, rather than Cicero, was probably the genius of the age. He could do everything—many contemporaries preferred his oratorical style to that of Cicero, and his free-swinging disregard of convention was what one ordinarily expects of a genius. Cicero, on the other hand, was an overachiever. He had his great moments, countered by other occasions when his actions were mean and indefensible, yet one can see in him the quintessence of humanity with its promise and nobility tempered by all the frailty to which mankind is subject.

Chapter 7

Imperial Rome

The term "Roman Empire" is employed in two ways: it may designate the vast territory acquired and controlled by Rome, or it may be used to refer to the governmental form that replaced the Roman Republic near the end of the first century B.C. The empire of Rome had its beginnings with the Punic Wars, and by 30 B.C., with the annexation of Egypt by Octavian, most of the land around the Mediterranean was under Roman rule. On the other hand, the Empire as opposed to the Republic is generally agreed to have begun in 27 B.C. It had two phases: the first is called the Principate; and the second is variously known as the Dominate, the Autocracy, or the Later Roman Empire. The founder of the Principate was the Emperor Augustus (Octavian) who reigned from 27 B.C. to 14 A.D., while the architect of the Dominate was the emperor Diocletian (284-305 A.D.).

The Roman Republic did not become the Roman Empire overnight, nor was the metamorphosis a foregone conclusion. After the defeat of Antony and Cleopatra, which ended the civil wars, a brief restoration of normal republican government might have taken place, followed by new civil strife culminating in a dictatorship; or a division of the Roman domain into two separate states, East and West, might have occurred if Antony and Octavian had agreed upon some peaceful settlement instead of fighting it out to the bitter end. The least likely result was that the Republic would have been given a new lease on life, since the protective wall of constitutional practice had been breached so often that little of it remained.

But none of these things happened, and the reason was that Octavian, the sole major survivor of the civil wars, the strong man thought by many Romans to be the only person capable of preserving peace and accomplishing postwar reconstruction, lived on for forty-five years after the Battle of Actium. His longevity, unexpected in view of his chronic poor health, was an historical accident that changed the course of history itself.

After Octavian returned to Rome in 29 B.C., he spent two years mustering out his soldiers and keeping a watchful eye on the situation to see that no further disorder occurred. Then, in 27 B.C., he proposed the restoration of the Republic; that is, he offered to return to the Senate and the Roman people the extraordinary powers which he had acquired as triumvir and as commander-in-chief in the war against Antony and Cleopatra. The Romans, however, dared not cut themselves adrift from the leader whom they regarded as their saviour. Instead, Octavian was retained as commander-in-chief of the army and was given the responsibility for the government of Egypt as well as a number of other provinces, especially those on the frontiers or in which large military contingents were stationed. At this time also he was given the honorary title of Augustus (Revered); later generations were to refer to him as Augustus rather than Octavian, and this practice has continued to the present time.

In the years following 27 B.C. several crises resulted in the augmentation of Augustus' powers: to deal with the Parthians the conduct of all foreign affairs was turned over to him, and during a famine he was placed in control of the grain supply for the city of Rome. He became *pontifex maximus,* virtual head of the state religion, and he was the permanent *princeps senatus,* a post reserved for the most distinguished member of the Senate, who was always asked to speak first on any matter under consideration by that body. Eventually, a new title came into use with reference to Augustus and his successors: *princeps,* First Citizen, from which comes the term Principate.

The *princeps*, the emperor, was a permanent chief magistrate who theoretically governed in partnership with the Senate, but in reality his broad powers made him something more than the senior partner in this arrangement. This, along with the progressive failure of the Senate to discharge its full responsibilities, brought the government step by step to its final autocratic form. The Senate had once directed the foreign relations of Rome and controlled state finances; the first function now had passed to the emperor, and the others would soon do so. The emperor could indirectly, or directly if he chose, control the membership of the Senate; he also could see that individuals whom he favored held governorships in the senatorial provinces or were chosen to fill the offices of consul, praetor, quaestor, or other posts reserved for senators. In addition, the emperor came to hold the purse strings. His provinces produced greater revenues than the senatorial ones, and the emperor himself had personal resources so vast that he often replenished the senatorial treasury when it was empty, or embarked on great building projects which he himself financed.

Because of the division of responsibility for the government of the provinces and because of the special functions given to the emperor, a new arm of the state was developed to assist him. In the provinces assigned to him, the emperor not only had to have his own governors and financial officers, but he also needed loyal and able assistants in Rome. The top echelon of these aides had the title of prefect, and they were appointed by the emperor from persons of equestrian rather than senatorial status. In this way, the dream of Cicero for a "concord of the orders" was partially realized, since both senators and equestrians were joined in the governmental process. At any rate, under the new system there was an equestrian praetorian prefect, who commanded the imperial bodyguard; another prefect headed the combined police and fire department for the city of Rome; still another was in charge of the grain supply; ultimately there was a prefect of the city who governed Rome in the emperor's absence. Just below the praetorian prefect in rank was the Prefect of Egypt, for all intents and purposes a viceroy, the emperor's other self in that country. In connection with all these responsibilities, the emperor also had to issue directives and make judicial decisions. These came to have the force of law and were cited as precedents. Ultimately, because the emperor often was asked to make rulings and decisions about matters even within the domain of the Senate, he tended to become not merely a source of law, but the principal one.

In the early part of the reign of Augustus, the Principate was not seen by contemporaries—and probably not by Augustus himself—as anything more than a short-term expedient to tide Rome over a crucial period. As the years passed, however, the emperor came to feel that the new regime must be continued for reasons of stability, and that some provision must be made for an orderly succession to power after his death. Since he himself owed some of his prestige to the fact that he was the heir and adopted son of Julius Caesar, it seemed imperative that a member of the family, either by blood or marriage, should succeed. Augustus' first choice was his friend and principal general, Agrippa, who married his daughter Julia. But Agrippa died, and Julia then married Tiberius, the stepson of the emperor. When Gaius and Lucius, the sons of Agrippa and Julia and thus the grandsons of Augustus, approached manhood, they were groomed for the succession instead of Tiberius. By 4 A.D., however, both grandsons were dead, Augustus was forced to turn once more to Tiberius, and the two shared power for the next decade. When Augustus died, Tiberius was in possession of imperial authority, and the Senate, which might have terminated the arrangement as Tiberius indeed seems to have hoped, then decided to continue the Principate instead of restoring the Republic. Thus, patterns and precedents were established, and henceforth, except in those instances in which a dynasty was terminated by revolution, the successor of an emperor was his son by blood, marriage or adoption.

The subsequent history of the Principate was far from peaceful and orderly. The Julio-Claudian dynasty, in which the emperors were members of the family of Augustus or his wife Livia, or both, managed to hang on until 68 A.D. Tiberius may have been smothered by a pillow in the hands of his grandnephew Gaius (Caligula), who in turn fell victim to a senatorial conspiracy in 41. Claudius, the uncle of Caligula, was murdered in 54 by his wife, Agrippina, sister of Gaius. Apparently, she could wait no longer to assure the throne for Nero, her son by a former marriage, even though Nero was married to the daughter of Claudius and had been adopted by Claudius as his son. The dynasty ended with Nero's suicide in 68, when he despaired of quelling a military revolt that was spreading from province to province in the west.

The War of the Legions or the Year of the Four Emperors, as it sometimes is called, lasted for twelve months or so during 68–69 A.D. The legions of the west, the praetorian guard, and finally the Danubian and eastern legions made and unmade three emperors before the Flavian dynasty was established by Vespasian, the candidate of the east. Vespasian was succeeded by his two sons, Titus and then Domitian. The former died in 81, and the latter perished in a palace conspiracy in 96.

The assassination of Domitian caught the military, even the praetorian guard, by surprise. As a result, the Senate was given the rare opportunity of choosing the next emperor. In a decision that was something less than wise and savored of the academic in its worst sense, the Senate picked an elderly senator named Nerva, a legal pundit who just happened to be *princeps senatus* in consequence of the death of Domitian. Within a few months the legions had begun to murmur against Nerva, while people at Rome were complaining of the senility of the emperor and his associates and about the fact that many of Domitian's hated supporters were not merely still alive but even on good terms with the emperor. A new war of the legions was avoided only when Nerva adopted as his son, heir, and co-emperor, Trajan, Rome's best general.

Nerva died in 98, and the era of the "good emperors" began. Trajan, Hadrian, Antoninus Pius, and Marcus Aurelius were related by ties of marriage, sometimes strengthened by adoption. Superficially, affairs were peaceful enough, although Hadrian was not universally popular, and Marcus Aurelius faced a revolt by one of his own generals. But when Marcus was succeeded by his son Commodus in 180, troubles began to surface. Economic decline, barbarian pressure on the frontiers, unrest among the legions, and finally the insanity of Commodus himself spelled disaster. When Commodus was assassinated on the last day of 192, a second war of the legions ensued. After two ephemeral emperors were eliminated, the commander of the eastern legions, Septimius Severus, founded a new dynasty that lasted with only one brief interruption from 193 until 235. Although the empire, which had threatened to split into three parts, was pulled back together by Septimius, his chief accomplishment was an elevation of the status of the military in government and a temporary delay of the inevitable chaos. Twenty-six emperors, not counting mere pretenders to the throne, graced or disgraced the period 235–285 A.D., and only one died a natural death. During this grim fifty years the empire did indeed split into three parts, although it was finally reunited again by the herculean efforts of the so-called Illyrian soldier-emperors of the period 268–284, beginning with Claudius Gothicus and ending with Diocletian, the founder of the Autocracy.

All things considered, the Principate in its heyday had been a viable form of government. It had worked reasonably well during its first two centuries; the troubles of the final period of its existence were not of a nature that could have been controlled easily. Perhaps the most severe criticism that might be made of the Principate is that it was not responsive to regional needs. Also it seems likely that the emperor and his advisors frequently were told only what they wanted to hear rather than what they needed to know.

In the course of time the Principate had matured in organization. Instead of relying on the emperor's household servants for clerical and other governmental housekeeping as under Augustus, a more professional kind of civil service staff gradually had emerged. Claudius (41–54) established bureaus or departments for the treasury, judicial affairs, the royal correspondence, and so on. At first these were headed, it is true, by freedmen (ex-slaves), the next to lowest social class. Many, however, were competent people, even if greedy for power. At any rate, the bureaucracy grew in efficiency and importance until, under Hadrian, the departmental chiefs were equestrians instead of freedmen and the holding of such a position became a stepping stone to the great prefectures. It was also under Hadrian that the long process of codifying Roman law was begun in earnest; this had been one of the unrealized dreams of Julius Caesar, two centuries before, and it was not to be finished until the reign of Justinian, three hundred years after Hadrian.

Beginning with Augustus the Romans had sought to discover sharply defined and easily defensible frontiers for their empire. In Africa the desert was a good stopping place for expansion to the south as was the Atlantic Ocean for the west, but northern and eastern boundaries were more difficult to find. In the north Augustus nearly completed the establishment of a Rhine-Danube frontier, but it was overly long and expensive to defend. He tried to shorten it by German conquests that would set an Elbe-Danube line, but a military disaster in 9 A.D. forced him to fall back to the Rhine. In the east, part of a frontier was provided by the Arabian desert and the great bend of the Euphrates; though both were useful for demarcation, they had little value for defense. Farther north, in eastern Anatolia, Augustus relied upon client kingdoms as buffers. The real problem, however, was that the Romans needed Armenia as a defense against the Parthians. In possession of that country they could invade western Parthia (Mesopotamia) if necessary or simply use Armenia as a threat to deter Parthian invasions of Syria. The Parthians were just as anxious to control Armenia for the same reasons, so it became a battleground, alternately won and lost by Romans and Parthians. Thus, the problem never was solved, even after the Parthians were overthrown and replaced by the Sassanian Persians in the third century A.D.

The wisdom of Augustus was demonstrated by the experiences of the Romans when they decided to extend the empire beyond the frontiers he had identified. The conquest of Britain was unprofitable and expensive and something of a failure because a truly defensible frontier could not be found; even Hadrian's wall did little more than keep off raiding parties. The British conquest was a political move that brought a temporary popularity to the Emperor Claudius. Trajan's conquest of Dacia was motivated in part by political considerations, but it was also undertaken to stop Dacian raids across the Danube into Roman territory; Dacia, moreover, was a rich agricultural area that could be colonized. The success of the Dacian Wars emboldened Trajan to try the same tactics in Mesopotamia. Both Armenia and Mesopotamia were overrun and proclaimed Roman provinces, but neither could be held and were soon abandoned. Subsequently, Dacia and Britain were given up as indefensible when the Roman Empire fell upon evil times.

Often it is said that the ancient world reached its culmination in the first two centuries of the Christian era. Certainly, this was the highest point of ancient urbanization and the period during which the Roman Empire was most populous. Ancient civilization was never more widespread geographically, never more complex, and never more voluminous in the gross number of its individual culture traits. Finally, this age coincided with the apogee of the Roman

Empire, when this largest of all ancient empires was most far-flung and possessed its greatest power and influence. All this quantification, however, must be tempered by qualification.

Bits and pieces of Greco-Roman culture, it is true, were scattered from the Atlantic to the Indus and from the Baltic to the Sahara, but, although political frontiers did not inhibit cultural diffusion, the main concentration was within the boundaries of the Roman Empire. Civilization, moreover, was an urban phenomenon; even inside the domain of Rome, country people were little affected by it. Finally, despite the territorial extent of the civilized area and the complexity and bulk of civilization itself, the most important climax in the history of ancient civilization had already come and gone; the high point of ancient creativity seems to have been reached in the first part of the Hellenistic Age or even earlier. Culturally, then, the Roman Empire had many flowers but little fruit; fully mature, ancient civilization soon began to decay.

The Roman Empire was grand, colossal, and even great in comparison with the lesser kingdoms and empires that were its heirs and immediate successors. The teeming Roman cities with their huge and magnificent public buildings, the great roads, bridges and aqueducts, the commodious harbors would have no rivals for centuries to come. Trade and manufacturing existed on a larger scale than formerly. Though the poor were numerous, ill-fed and ill-housed, there were many individuals at the top of the economic pyramid who possessed great wealth, and the Roman middle class was large and comfortable by ancient standards. Schools were everywhere and literacy reached a new high; even by modern standards teachers were well-paid.

It was a glittering facade that, for a time, masked many serious problems, some of them insoluble. Given the available means of transportation and communication, the empire was too vast; it was simply unmanageable. Spending—imperial and municipal—soon outstripped declining revenues. Before the end of the first century A.D. the economy had ceased to expand, and already a number of the older provinces were deep into an irreparable depression. An educational system that taught people to orate brilliantly about inconsequentials or to meditate about the impractical did not prepare them to tackle the problems of the real world. It made little difference that the government was not representative, not directly responsible to the people. The officials in charge of the conduct of affairs (not necessarily the emperors) were for the most part fully aware of the most serious problems and eager to solve them; moreover, they were probably better informed and better equipped to deal with the situation than the masses whom they did not consult.

One of the major difficulties of the Romans was that they could no longer make imperialism pay. In the days of the republic, when they had acquired most of the richest and most valuable parts of their empire, the plunder from conquest and the tribute from newly organized provinces had filled the coffers of the government and the purses of victorious generals and their soldiers—not to mention the profits that accrued to Roman tax collectors and other equestrian entrepreneurs who gorged themselves on the new wealth. At first, the provinces of Sicily, Spain, Africa, Asia, Syria, and even Macedonia yielded considerable revenues, but these steadily diminished through mismanagement and overexploitation; later, there was a further cut in payments to Rome as the imperial government adopted a more moderate and responsible policy that curbed rapacity and lowered taxes. With the exception of Trajan's conquest of Dacia at the beginning of the second century A.D., the Romans made no really valuable additions to their territory after Caesar overran Gaul and Octavian annexed Egypt. There simply were no more great prizes to be won. An occasional victory over barbarians beyond the frontier might yield an ephemeral profit, but the continuous expansion that piled riches upon riches had ended. The imperialism that had once been deemed a necessity had left the Romans finally with an empire they could not afford.

If the Romans were saddled with an empire, they also had an albatross hung about their necks: the army. Originally an instrument of conquest, the army could neither be disbanded nor reduced when there were no more conquests to be made. Instead, it had to be maintained to keep some areas in subjection and to defend the empire from invasion. Every year military spending was a big, if not the biggest, item in the imperial budget. The soldiers not only had to be well paid in an attempt to insure their loyalty, but they also had to receive frequent bonuses. In later republican times the army often had been a tool in the hands of ambitious politicians; in the imperial period the situation frequently was reversed, with the soldiers forcing their commanders to revolt in order to make and unmake emperors at will. Eventually only those with long and successful military records, who enjoyed the respect of the troops, were

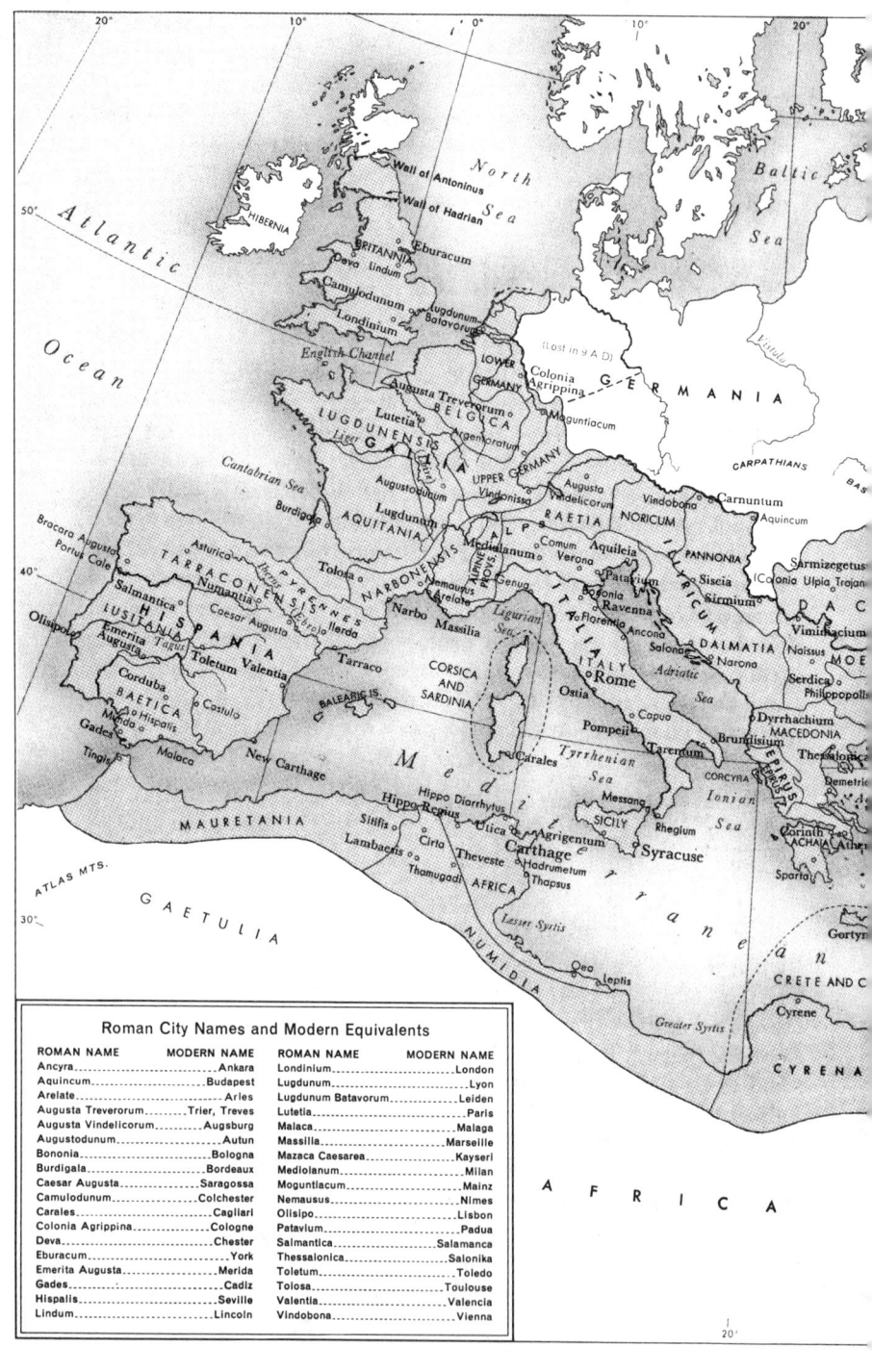

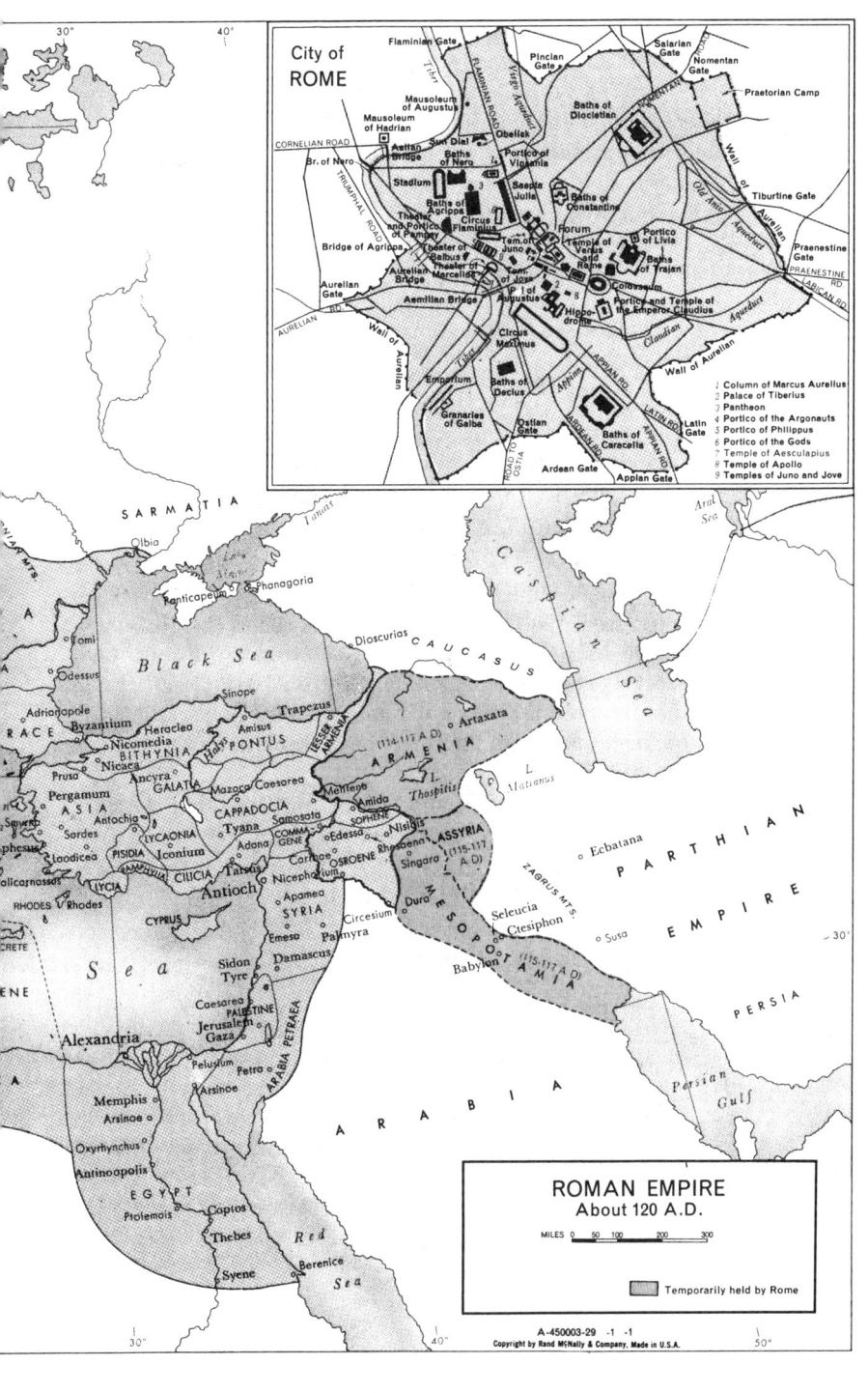

considered suitable candidates for the throne. The end product was the militarization of the government itself.

In addition to declining provincial revenues, the unprofitability of imperialism, and the cost of defense, there were other factors causing the downward trends within the Roman domain. An unfavorable balance of trade with the Far East and with northern Europe drew off gold and, more particularly, silver at a time when the productivity of the Roman mines was falling sharply. Equally distressing was the fact that the Parthians, whose menace to Rome had abated somewhat, were overthrown and replaced by the Sassanian Persians, newly arrived and bursting with expansionist vigor. Within a generation of their appearance on the scene, the Sassanians handed the Romans their worst defeat since the Battle of Carrhae against the Parthians in 53 B.C. Simultaneously, the barbarians on the northern frontiers became relatively stronger and certainly much bolder. The Goths ravaged the Balkans and Asia Minor during the second half of the third century and would remain dangerous for more than a hundred years to come. Political unity was threatened further by the growing regionalism within the empire, in which geographic components—North Africa, Gaul, Egypt, Syria, and so on—each desiring a different imperial policy beneficial to itself, sought to dominate the whole or to break away to enjoy an independent existence.

Despite these strictures, it must not be forgotten that the epoch of imperial Rome was an important one in human history and particularly in the heritage passed on to medieval and modern Europe. Virgil and Horace, Seneca and Quintilian, Celsus and Pliny the Elder would not be forgotten even during the darkest of dark ages. In early modern times other authors of the Roman Empire would be rediscovered and provide new inspiration: Tacitus, Plutarch, Galen, Frontinus, and many others. These literary monuments, together with the fallen ruins of Roman buildings, bridges and aqueducts, and the many legends that amplified the glories of the Roman past, were to inspire future generations not only with awe but also with a desire to emulate or surpass these achievements.

Chapter 8

The Twilight of the Roman Empire

The Autocracy, that second phase of the Roman Empire, which succeeded the Principate, coincided with what well might be called the twilight of Rome. Close to extinction in the mid-third century A.D. but pulled back together by the Illyrian soldier-emperors, Rome was reinvigorated temporarily at the end of the third and beginning of the fourth century by two able emperors, Diocletian and Constantine. The magnitude of their achievement is best understood if one considers the situation in which they had to operate.

First of all, it must be recognized that the empire never was united wholly, never was integrated into a socioeconomic entity. Its only really unified aspects were military and, to a lesser extent, political. Roman armies had conquered a vast territory that centered on the Mediterranean Sea, but most of the time the Romans demanded only two things of subjected peoples: that they pay their taxes and keep the peace. One well-known example will serve for illustration. Roman troops were stationed in conquered Palestine, but the country was administered by the puppet king of the Jews. When Jesus stirred controversy and was arrested, the Romans lent enforcement officers, but he was charged under Jewish law and tried in a Jewish court. Because the Jews were restive under Roman rule and prone to riot, the Romans reserved the right to review all capital sentences, so the prisoner was sent before Pontius Pilate. It is significant that even confronted with what he personally considered a gross miscarriage of justice, the Roman governor refused to interfere with local authorities and ceremonially washed his hands of the whole affair. Only a threat to Roman interests in policy or taxation would have justified intervention.

Nor did economic development ever progress very far. The Mediterranean basin was largely homogeneous, and consequently there was no great regional variation in products; meats, grains, wines and olive oil were produced throughout the Roman world. Trade tended toward luxury goods of small bulk and high value, such as gems and fine cloth, with the consequence that by modern standards the empire had only a small middle class between its governing landed aristocracy and its mass of small proprietors, landless sharecroppers and slaves, however large that class might appear when compared to earlier counterparts. Roman government sat atop enormous social diversity, and it was not reinforced by any significant economic integration.

The vicious civil wars of the third century gave final form to the Roman Empire until its collapse in the west—the form of a military despotism in which the whole populace and every political institution existed only to maintain the army, and the army had little purpose except to maintain itself.

The basic factor was instability. Until the beginning of the reign of Diocletian in A.D. 284, no third century emperor ruled as long as twenty years; only two ruled more than ten years; fifteen ruled for periods of one to six years; and almost every succession was disputed. With government so confused, supply and pay of the army became chaotic; mutinies were not uncommon, and troops often intervened in politics to support the ambitions of a would-be emperor who promised to pay them. Taxation became increasingly heavy in the face of so many problems, but because of poor administration little was accomplished. Then an economic recession worsened, due in part at least to the combination of civil war and oppressive taxation.

At this low point in Rome's fortune, Diocletian and then Constantine achieved a total administrative reorganization that practically turned the empire into one great military camp. Recognizing that it was too large for effective management by one man, Diocletian divided it into eastern and western portions and chose a co-emperor; then he took up residence in the east while his co-emperor governed in the west. It should be emphasized, however, that the new arrangement was only a division of responsibility, not a partition. In theory the two emperors enjoyed equal authority throughout the empire, and edicts appeared over both names. In an attempt to ease the critical succession problem, both emperors chose assistants, called Caesars, who were to succeed them; this was appealing in theory, but it did not take into account those impatient Caesars who might try to hasten the succession, or rivals who might not wish to share authority. Thus Constantine, who was not a Caesar, came to the throne through hereditary claims and civil war and appointed no co-emperor. After Constantine's death, Diocletian's system was practiced again from time to time but with indifferent results, and Rome never found a way to regularize the imperial succession.

To implement the imperial will, Diocletian and Constantine organized two great bureaucracies, one military and one civil; to meet the pressing necessities of frontier defense they increased the military establishment by several expedients. It was not possible to recruit or pay enough professional soldiers from the population of the empire, so the old legions were supplemented by small permanent garrisons of soldier-farmers established along the frontiers; these troops were backed up by mobile forces which could be rushed to threatened points while the permanent garrisons tried to blunt an attack and delay an invasion. In this context, heavily armed cavalry became ever more important, and many bands of foreign mercenaries were hired, a practice for which there were many precedents since traditionally the Roman forces were primarily heavy infantry. By these innovations Diocletian and Constantine succeeded in raising Rome's armies to about half a million men. This was a considerable increase over the three hundred thousand that they had averaged before the third century civil wars, but Rome paid a heavy price for increased numbers.

Although the empire long had welcomed foreign recruits in its armies, usually they had come as individuals or in small groups, and slowly they had been Romanized. The employment of large groups of undisciplined tribesmen in separate units and of part-time soldiers, Roman or foreign, lowered the overall standards of training in the army and gave military importance, with implicit political influence, to unassimilated mercenary chieftains. Contrary to popular impressions, it is unlikely that the new arrangements had a very great effect upon the morale and the loyalty of the army. The pattern of the revolts and civil wars of the legionaries of the third century suggests that, like mercenaries, they responded more to their paymasters than to any patriotism or dedication to the Roman Empire. But there is little doubt that the increased size and diversity of the army meant reduced military efficiency and discipline.

A fundamental reorganization, not only of civil administration but of society itself, was required in order to pay for this large army in the declining economy of the time. Only high officials of the imperial government, who rapidly came to constitute a land-owning, tax-exempt aristocratic class, escaped crushing burdens. The rest of the society was organized along military lines and was governed by a civil administration whose chief purpose was to extract the taxes necessary to support the army. The currency had collapsed, so taxes were taken mostly in kind (goods) and were assessed upon both property and labor; small property owners and tradesmen bore most of the burden. Since municipal officials were most susceptible to legal processes, they were made responsible for collecting from their neighbors, and they had to make up deficits personally. As a result of unrealistic assessments and collective responsibility, small owners, tradesmen and town officials tried to abandon their farms, businesses and offices to become soldiers or monks, or bondsmen on aristocratic estates. Imperial response was swift and harsh: Men were forbidden under heavy penalties to leave their crafts and trades and offices, and these obligations were made hereditary. The result was a rigid caste system supervised by an elaborate bureaucracy, all existing to support the army and the imperial government.

Constantine introduced another major innovation to the empire when he was converted to Christianity and gave imperial support to the spread of the new faith. Historical judgments of his policy have ranged from acceptance of his sincerity to cynical estimates of the advantages he may have anticipated. Probably his personal conversion was a matter of faith and his encouragement of Christianity proceeded from his convictions and from his hope that a dynamic and idealistic religion could help to bind the empire together. If this be true, it suggests that the emperor recognized that some moral force was necessary to undergird the governmental reorganization.

During the next century and a half the organization of the empire changed little, but the contrasts between the Greek-speaking eastern regions and the Latin West—in which lay Europe—became more pronounced. Most often, historians have looked to two great sources for the background of European history: the Greco-Roman and the Judeo-Christian traditions. There were many reasons for this, some of them excellent. First, it was for these traditions that the fullest record existed—the classical heritage on the one hand and Scripture and church records on the other. Secondly, most European historians have been Christians, and for many generations a modern education meant study of the classics: thus, by their faith and their early training they were prejudiced in favor of Christianity and classicism. These interests, however, have resulted in the Celtic and Germanic antecedents of European history being seriously underestimated. Nationalistic enthusiasms in the nineteenth century did evoke some assertions—often exaggerated—of the importance of Germanic traditions, but on the whole it is still true that the contributions of the northern European peoples have been ignored systematically. In all fairness it should be noted that before the Roman conquest both the Celts and the Germans were preliterate peoples, and archeology is a relatively young discipline (and the historian's interest in its results even younger). Until very recently it has been next to impossible for the historian, who normally relies upon written records, to glean more than vague impressions of these peoples from the few comments about them left by their Roman neighbors. Of earlier peoples absorbed by the Celts, their names alone remain, such as Ligurians and Iberians.

The only very extensive Roman description of the Celts is Caesar's *Commentaries on the Gallic Wars* in the middle of the first century B.C., and as a source this book presents serious problems. In the first place, it describes Celtic society in the last years of its independence, but by that time many of the Celtic peoples had had long contact with the Romans and had been influenced by them considerably. The only Celts among whom Caesar moved very freely were allies of Rome, those most likely to show Roman influence. Secondly, there were problems of bias. Caesar obviously liked the Celts as people, but he arrived as a conqueror, hardly a role best suited to objective analysis. And Caesar had his own interests to advance; he was politically ambitious, and his book was intended to serve that ambition. For his own political credit he wanted to emphasize the warlike qualities of the Celts to enhance his victories. And to magnify the value to Rome of his conquests, he was eager to stress the potential contribution of these people to the empire. Thus, he tended to portray them as noble savages—primitive and ferocious, but clever, brave and honorable. His work is very valuable for its uniqueness, but it must be used cautiously.

Two Roman sources exist for the early Germans, but again they present a problem. Once more Caesar is prominent; his *Commentaries* give brief descriptions of the Germans whom he met in battle, whom he captured, and whose lands he visited on brief reconnaissance patrols. But his observations are sketchy, and in these, also, his bias is important. The German pressure on the Celts was one of the excuses for Roman intervention and eventual conquest. To both the Romans and the Celts, Caesar wished to show himself as the protector. So the Germans were the enemy. He stressed their primitivism and savagery and exaggerated their differences from the peoples whom he wished to incorporate into the empire. The other Roman source for the Germans is equally difficult to use, the *Germania* of Tacitus, written about a century after Caesar. First, Tacitus was not an observer; he compiled his account from information supplied by travelers back from the north. Second, he was a social critic of what he considered the degeneracy of the Romans, so he tended to idealize the bravery and the warriors' code of his Germans to heighten the contrast. Thus the written record offers no very reliable account of these early peoples.

The consequences of these historiographic patterns have been unfortunate. A general impression seems to exist that Europe was a land of extremely primitive barbarians called Celts, who were finally conquered and civilized by the Romans. Then the Germans, even more fierce and primitive, swept in and destroyed this civilization, so that all reverted to barbarism until the influence of the church again produced a civilizing effect. Nothing could be farther from the truth.

It was the Celts whose culture dominated Europe while the Greeks and Romans were building their civilizations in the Mediterranean basin, and they also contributed to the cultural patterns of the great matrix that was to become European tradition. The usage by the Greeks and Romans of the word "barbarian" has had unfortunate effects for the modern student, for the connotations of the word have changed. To the Greeks and Romans the word simply designated the "they" in a pattern of "we and they," and the word certainly was no insult; those who were not of the Greco-Roman cultural tradition were barbarians. But between the two civilizations, Celtic and classical, the differences were less significant than usually is assumed.

But for the single feature of a written language, and the important consequence of a surviving literature, the Mediterranean peoples enjoyed no great advantages over the Celts. The former excelled in their use of stone for building, while the Celts built mostly of wood (often richly carved, one should note), but on the other hand Celtic metalwork clearly was superior and found a large Mediterranean market for products ranging from swords to bronze and gold jewelry. The Mediterranean peoples introduced the grape and wine to Europe, but it appears to have been Celtic carpenters who first built wooden barrels to store it, replacing the excessively fragile pottery amphoras of the Mediterranean. Celtic religion, a polytheistic cult, was presided over by Druid priests who were also educators and judges and seems no more primitive than that of the Greeks and Romans. And the Celts appear to have been as great travelers as their Mediterranean neighbors, trading tin and lead from the British Isles and metalwork, timber and smoked meats from Europe into the Mediterranean basin. Some hired out as mercenary soldiers, fighting in places as far from their northern forests as the Greek islands and Egypt. They never developed the effective military discipline of the Greeks and Romans, but as individual soldiers they had a high reputation, and their weapons were much admired. Celtic social structure greatly resembled that of the southern peoples, with an aristocracy of priests and warriors, a lesser class of free farmers and a social base of masses of slaves. Towns of considerable size existed, sited defensively and enclosed by strong walls that evoked even Caesar's admiration, though the Celtic nobility seems to have preferred living on country estates as did many Roman aristocrats.

That such a people, who settled most of Europe two to five thousand years before the Romans came into the area, should have left no significant influence is beyond belief, but their contribution is only beginning to be understood. After the Roman conquest of Gaul, in the middle of the first century B.C., the Celts on the European continent adapted quickly to Roman culture in government, language and religion—eventually adopting Christianity along with the rest of the Roman world. In England, Celtic civilization was little touched by the later rather superficial Roman occupation and endured until displaced by German (Anglo-Saxon) invaders several centuries later, and Ireland continued as a Christian Celtic society into modern times.

As war, diplomacy, government and religion long have been the major interests of historians, the inattention to Celtic contributions to European culture-is perhaps understandable, for it is in the folkways that Celtic traditions seem to have survived, in such things as wearing trousers and boots rather than tunics and sandals, in the use of butter instead of olive oil for cooking, in love of country life. Simple festivals also seem to have old roots—such as maypole dances, which appear to trace to some sort of phallic worship associated with spring fertility rites, and barbecues and beer. These things seem a minor counterpoint to such themes as war and religion, but until quite recently, at least, they influenced profoundly the way western peoples ate and drank and dressed and lived, and they should not be ignored.

In the period of about the third to fifth centuries, then, western Europe was populated by a mixture of Celts and Mediterranean peoples governed under the authority of the Roman Empire. Its civilization was a mixture of Celtic folkways and classical formal culture. It was reasonably prosperous, with an economy based upon flourishing agriculture, some manufactures and some exports. And in this society, a primitive Christian church was developing a channel through which a Judaic tradition would be added to the rich cultural mix. But troubles were developing which would rip apart the seemingly invincible empire, and western Europe as part of the empire was to experience its full share of those troubles. The more or less constant struggle with the Sassanian Persians necessitated the concentration of the empire's best military forces on the eastern borders, while at the same time economic recovery progressed more rapidly in the area of the eastern Mediterranean than it did in the west. Thus, slowly the Greek-speaking eastern part of the empire became relatively more important, and when Germanic invaders began to cross the frontiers to plunder the northern and western Roman lands late in the fourth century, little help could be spared from the east. The only solution was to employ bands of tribesmen as mercenary allies. As a consequence, barbarian chieftains with the titles of Roman generals came to fight other barbarian chieftains for control of Rome's western provinces—and while those provinces were pillaged the victors made and unmade emperors.

Perhaps the most salient feature of the new military expedients was that they were not very effective. Late in the fourth century a Germanic people called the Visigoths defeated a Roman army and ravaged the Balkans; early in the fifth century they crossed into Italy, where they sacked the city of Rome in 410, following which they wandered into southern Gaul. About the same time Gaul was overrun by other tribes, of whom the Vandals and the Burgundians were the most notable. Behind them, pressing westward, were the fierce Asiatic people known as the Huns, who fell upon the western empire in the middle of the fifth century. Rome's few successes in repulsing these raiders were won mostly by Germanic commanders in her service. Thus the empire's most successful defender at the end of the fourth and beginning of the fifth century was the Vandal Stilicho, and in the middle of the fifth century the Visigothic leader Theodoric played a major part in defeating the Huns. But despite occasional successes the western empire suffered grievously. Rome was sacked again in 455, this time by the Vandals, and all through the fifth century ill-disciplined armies wandered back and forth. By and large, the population of the Roman empire met the invaders with indifference. Since the oppressive imperial government benefitted no one but the politico-military aristocracy, the mass of the populace had no motive to defend it.

Some of the Germanic tribes settled and established kingdoms within the old boundaries of the empire, and the emperors—helpless to do otherwise—legitimatized their rule by giving them imperial titles. Clearly the west was in serious trouble, but the deposition of Emperor Romulus Augustus in 476, traditionally considered the end of the Roman Empire, probably had no particular significance for contemporaries. Another emperor, Zeno, ruled in the east, and there was no reason to assume that the western title would not be restored. Such things had happened many times. Roman civilization did not so much "fall" as crumble away, and many historical arguments have turned around the questions of what it was that disappeared, and when, and why.

The first modern students to take very serious interest in the history of the ancient world were scholars of the Italian Renaissance, beginning in the fourteenth century, and their interest turned mostly to classical literature. The Renaissance scholars were rather hostile toward supernatural religion, so they tended to identify the waning of classical philosophy and literature with the rise of Christianity. Even though they had to admit a weak revival of classical literature under the restored empire of the fourth century, they tended at least implicitly to equate the decline of Rome with the growth of Christianity; and they saw in the later empire only an increasingly barbarized remnant of a once great classical civilization. In this context, the Germanic invasions and the deposition of Romulus Augustus only finished off a culture long on its deathbed.

By the eighteenth century, admiration of classical civilization had grown into adulation. Moreover, the eighteenth century witnessed the growth of an enormous interest in politics, producing Voltaire, Rousseau, and Jefferson and the American and French revolutions. This different intellectual climate resulted in different evaluations of Rome. Most admired were her law, her government and her writers on duty and civic virtue. Hence, eighteenth-century thinkers found tragic grandeur in the efforts of Diocletian and Constantine to revive the empire, wondered at the failure of the populace to rally to the defense of its government and identified disaster with the establishment of Germanic kingdoms in the place of the imperial government. By these standards, Germanic invasions brought about the fall of the empire, and the deposition of the last emperor in the west marked its final collapse.

The outstanding exponent of this view is Edward Gibbon in his *Decline and Fall of the Roman Empire,* based on a painstaking review of surviving Roman literature. Gibbon concluded that the cause of Rome's fall was a many-sided moral problem. He mustered evidence showing widespread corruption in both private and public life. He pointed to the use of mercenary troops as an indicator of the breakdown of any sense of patriotism and civic obligation. And he repeated the indictment of Christianity, both because the gentleness it taught undermined military ruthlessness and because the church attracted some of the later empire's best minds to its service, minds that otherwise might have served the state. Gibbon's arguments often are summed up superficially as a contention that all that interested later Romans was "bread and games"—material support and daily distraction.

Gibbon's moral arguments have proved attractive both to his contemporaries and to later generations, for they express noble sentiments and they tend to equate virtue and success; fundamentally, however, they are rather simplistic. Most of Gibbon's charges against the Romans of the later empire are valid, but they would be valid also in earlier periods when Rome was at the height of her power, so they are not very persuasive as arguments accounting for her decline. Gibbon proved that not all Romans were models of virtue, but he did not prove that this fact had any particular effect upon the empire.

The experience of the late nineteenth and early twentieth centuries forced western intellectuals to recognize that there were factors other than culture and politics that had to be considered in evaluating social evolution. Industrialization, urbanization and global imperialism accentuated the enormous complexity of administrative problems that governments face when they rule over vast areas and large populations. And the contentions of new theorists, especially socialists with their arguments of economic determinism, forced historians to consider the possible influence of economic factors upon the development of historical societies. Applied to the decline of Rome, these modern considerations provide yet more arguments that must be weighed.

The most fully researched and carefully argued analysis of Roman administration was produced by a French scholar, Ferdinand Lot, in *The End of the Roman Empire and the Beginning of the Middle Ages*. Lot presents case after case in which orders were disobeyed, tax moneys misappropriated and problems allowed to become chronic because the imperial government learned of them too late, and he concludes that the Roman administration became "a worn-out machine that creaked slowly to a halt." In this context, of course, the end of the Roman Empire is to be found when the administrative machinery ceased to function adequately, which occurred at different times in various parts of the empire, and in some instances long after the coming of the Germans. Lot's arguments must be taken seriously, for he demonstrated that often the German kings did not attempt to destroy Roman administration but to make themselves its beneficiaries and that only over a long time did failures of

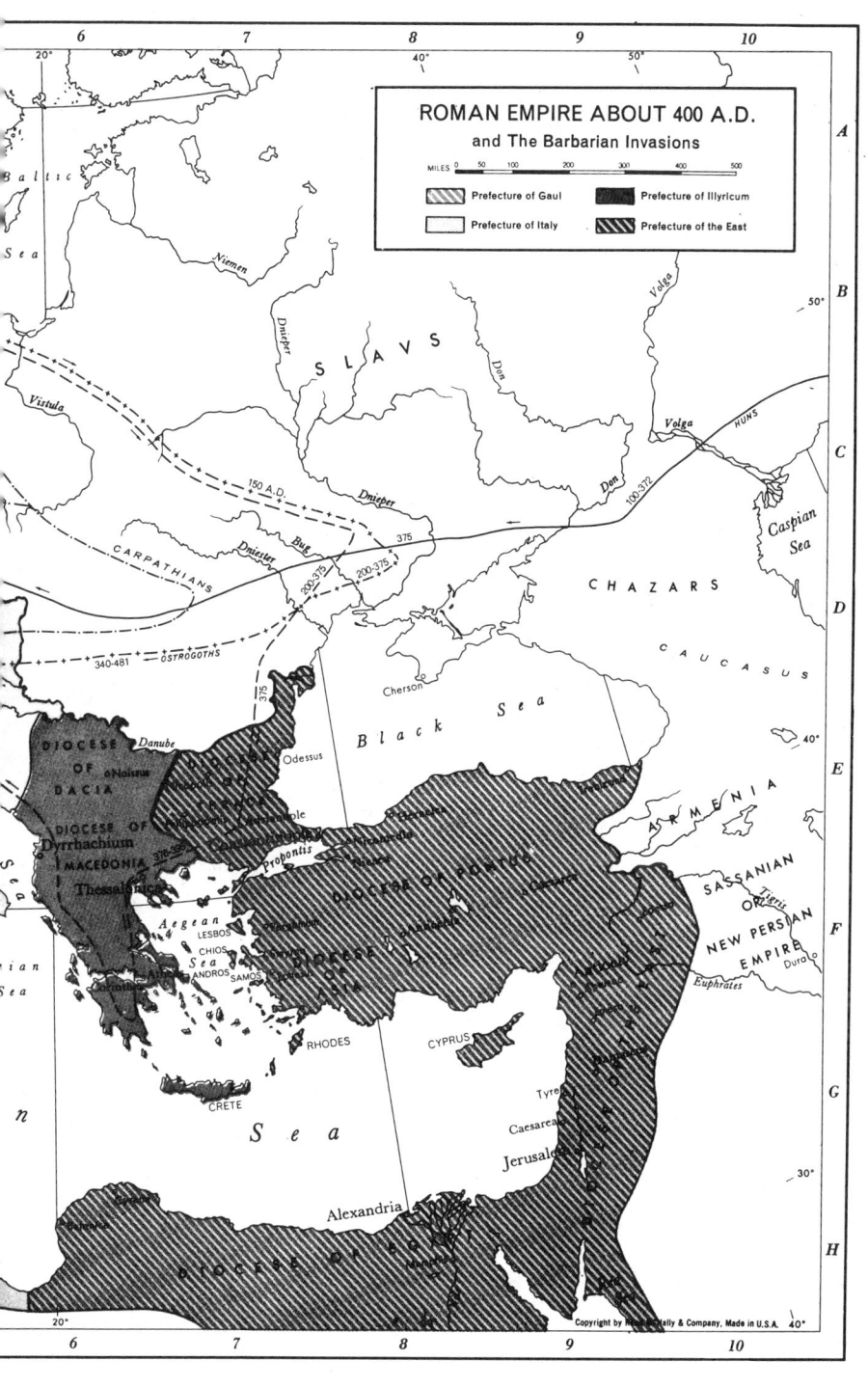

administrative machinery become so common as to justify the judgment that it had broken down. But until someone can prove that there is something inherently biological or mechanical about government, the argument that "it grew old and wore out" is less than compelling. The question remains, why did a government that had functioned for centuries and had survived many crises finally break down?

Economic arguments were advanced most forcefully by the Belgian scholar, Henri Pirenne, whose thesis still is disputed hotly. To Pirenne, the "heart" of the Roman Empire was not a cultural product, not a political process, and not an administrative structure but rather the economic organization of the lands lying around the Mediterranean Sea. He contended that the economic patterns established under Roman rule continued long after the cultural decline of the third century, long after the end of the western imperial title in the fifth century and even long after the administrative breakdown of about the sixth century. Pirenne asserted that the economic patterns survived so long as the Mediterranean remained a relatively open highway of communications and trade, until Islamic expansion turned the Mediterranean into a battleground between two hostile worlds, and he pushes the "end" of the Roman Empire forward into the seventh and eighth centuries. While most historians find this latter part of Pirenne's argument overextended, his insistence upon considering the economic organization of the later empire has proved a great contribution and has put analysis of the decline of Rome's domination of the western Mediterranean regions upon a much sounder basis.

The impossibility of definitive answers to the causes of Rome's decline does not impede an attempt to evaluate her contribution to medieval society. The Roman Empire provided a common classical background to much of southern and western Europe, and the recovery of the classical heritage over many centuries was a frequent stimulus to the intellectual vigor of medieval culture. The Latin language affected profoundly the speech of Germanic settlers and must be credited with much of the richness of expression of modern western languages. The Roman Empire provided a vague and idealized memory of peoples united under one government in peace and prosperity, a confused recollection of a sort of golden age in the past; and the desire to achieve again that happy condition—which in truth never existed—but served as an inspiration to the growth of medieval civilization.

Above all else the Roman Empire, by uniting the lands around the Mediterranean, facilitated the spread of Christianity, despite persecutions, and the patronage of Constantine and most of his successors upon the imperial throne contributed enormously to the institutional growth of the church. The Christian Church served as a channel through which some part of the classical heritage was transmitted to the future, while most was lost temporarily in the confusion of the early middle ages. The church was the major civilizing influence upon the newly settled and rather primitive Germanic peoples in the west; with some fragments and memories of classical civilization, the Christian-Germanic fusion gave birth to medieval European society.

Chapter 9

The Heirs of Rome

Thus far, both Christianity and the Germanic peoples who emigrated into the western Roman Empire have been mentioned only cursorily, but as important foundations of medieval European civilization they must be considered in more detail.

Unfortunately the origins of Christianity are obscure for a number of reasons. Jesus was born and reared in a province far from Rome, and neither his life nor his death attracted the serious attention of chroniclers in the imperial capital. Such local records as might have been useful largely were destroyed between A.D. 66 and A.D. 70 during Rome's suppression of a great Jewish revolt, when Jerusalem was levelled and the great Jewish temple destroyed. As a result, until rather recently it has been necessary to depend upon the accounts of Jesus' early followers, and these present serious problems: such accounts were written with the intention of inspiring and teaching early Christians rather than recording cold fact with strict accuracy, and in addition most were written many years after the events they purport to describe, depending upon recollection and word of mouth repetition. In consequence, they are less than wholly reliable as historical sources. In the twentieth century the discovery of the famous Dead Sea Scrolls, records carefully hidden away by the Jewish people during the Roman repression, have provided some alternatives to total reliance upon the Christian gospels for the history of the Jewish peoples in Jesus' time, and the origins of Christianity are understood somewhat better.

It is clear that Jesus was an inspired preacher and teacher, a humanitarian who preached compassion, tolerance and love in an environment little congenial to such thought. Certainly he offended and threatened the establishment in pointing out the hypocrisy in Jewish religious practice (for example, driving the money-changers from the temple) and in attacking the narrow exclusiveness of Jewish thought ("not all my sheep are of this fold"). Implicitly, too, he threatened the stability of Roman rule, for though he preached peace and said one should "render unto Caesar what is Caesar's," his followers accepted him as the messiah, the saviour long awaited by the Jews: while some saw this as an expectation of religious salvation, others—in the context of their times—thought it would mean deliverance from the Romans. Since he was viewed as a threat by both the Jewish and Roman establishments, it is not surprising that Jesus was seized and executed, but what is more important than the facts of his life and death is the interpretation that was put upon them afterwards. During his lifetime Jesus usually had been regarded as the leader of a dissenting Jewish sect, and such sects were not rare, but soon after his death the belief in his divine role spread to non-Jews and became a movement of considerable proportions.

In Jesus' time many otherworldly religions were widespread in the Roman Empire, particularly in the eastern Mediterranean, most of them derived from Egypt or southwest Asia which had long traditions of such belief. The nature of Roman society at the time encouraged the growth of such sects; while there was great luxury for those at the top of the social scale, life for most was hard and insecure, unending drudgery with no prospect for improvement. In such circumstances it is understandable that many turned to cults that promised another life in which goodness and simplicity would be rewarded rather than wealth and ruthlessness, a life in which "the first will be last and the last will be first."

The otherworldly religions, which Romans generally called mystery cults, shared a surprising number of characteristics, but despite this, early Christianity enjoyed several advantages in competition with the others. Many included some "washing away" of sin, often in blood. This usually demanded the sacrifice of a valuable animal, as in the cult of Mithras wherein a bull was slaughtered on a sort of a trestle and everyone passed beneath to be drenched in the blood.

Such procedures required the participation of someone wealthy enough to provide the animal, but the Christian substitution of bread and wine as the body and blood made this symbolic cleansing available to the poor themselves. Almost all the cults were wracked by divisions and quarrels among their priests and by the disqualification of priests through immorality, but the Christians early agreed that the priest was only the channel or vessel of divine power and that the sacraments he had administered were valid despite human weaknesses. While certainly these factors were less important than the appeal of the central core of Christian teaching, they greatly strengthened early Christianity in the struggle with its competitors. No less important was the Christian belief that salvation was assured to those who died as martyrs for the faith; during the vicious persecutions that early Christians suffered at many hands, they faced death with a certain equanimity, confident of a heavenly reward.

But if early Christianity enjoyed certain advantages, it also confronted many problems. Perhaps foremost among these was the necessity to meet scornful criticism and attack from educated members of Roman society who brought Greek logic to bear upon the early faith and found it simply ridiculous. What was a Trinity, three in one? How could the Son be equal with the Father, since the latter presumably was necessary for the procreation of the former? How could God or a part of him be born of woman in human flesh? How could the crucifixion be considered a triumph if the Son of God were taken by his enemies and killed? In an attempt to meet these criticisms and to resolve the contradictions within their belief, the Christians turned to logic themselves and developed a group of theologians who, reasoning in the Greek manner, explained vague principles of the faith more fully and extrapolated rules of conduct from basic principles. St. Paul was one of the foremost of these early theologians. But Jesus had taught in nonspecific parables, and extrapolations could reach different conclusions, so the early church soon was torn by internal dissension while at the same time being persecuted sporadically by the civil authorities. In addition, as the new faith spread, rivalries developed among the larger Christian centers; in the west a certain limited supremacy had been conceded to Rome from the early fourth century, but in the east similar authority was claimed by Alexandria, Jerusalem and Antioch, and a bit later by Constantinople. Hence, in the spread of Christianity and in its development into an organized church there were many problems to be overcome.

The legalization of Christianity by Constantine at the end of the first quarter of the fourth century had an enormous impact upon the early church. The most positive result was that the church was freed from persecutions and was able to conduct its services publicly and to proselytize openly. But legal status and protection also meant that being a Christian was no longer a dangerous commitment requiring courage and deep conviction, and as the church became larger it attracted careerists who saw in it a road to security and power outside the army or the bureaucracy of the empire. Inevitably legality brought institutional growth and formalization, and the followers of Christianity were transformed slowly from small, persecuted communities into powerful congregations organized around their bishops. Paganism remained widespread, especially outside the cities, but during and after the fourth century the church grew rapidly into one of the important institutions of Roman society, patterning its organization and its law upon Roman governmental models.

Recognition and legality also brought to the fore the problem of the church's relations with the state. In legalizing Christianity, Constantine had no intention of creating an institution independent of his own authority, and indeed Roman tradition long had assumed some sort of fusion of civil and religious authority under the emperor. In the mid-320s an attempt to resolve a religious quarrel made this point quite clear. Once again the Greek love of hair-splitting argument precipitated a crisis. A priest named Arius taught that Jesus had to be of different substance than God the Father, thus undermining the whole structure of the Trinity; his views were called Arianism. The opponents of Arianism were called Athanasians, taking their name from one of their chief exponents; they taught that the Father and Son were of the same substance. As the quarrel rent the church, Constantine convened a council of bishops at Nicaea over which he presided himself, and the Athanasian views were pronounced orthodox, or true, while Arianism was declared heretical, or false religious teaching. The quarrel was not resolved easily, however, especially since the Greek east and, even later, Roman emperors showed considerable sympathy for Arian views, and argument and violence continued for several decades. But the most important aspect of the quarrel may have been that in calling the council and presiding over it Constantine established in Christianity the basis for caesaropapism, the unity of civil and religious authority, which was to continue in the east and was to provide grounds for enormous conflict in the west.

Shortly after the legalization of Christianity, the Roman Empire began to experience serious difficulties with the Germanic peoples who lived beyond its northern frontiers. These were preliterate tribal peoples, but their primitivism ought not to be exaggerated simply because the Romans called them barbarians. They had a well-defined social structure comprising nobility, freemen and slaves, and a rather elaborate body of tribal law. Though ill-disciplined, their military prowess was to be respected, and they were also respected for their metalwork and, among some tribes, for their skill with horses. In addition, many of the tribes had been Christianized by missionaries, though unfortunately they were committed almost universally to Arian Christianity, which had been declared heretical. They long had been neighbors of the Romans, traded with them, and served as volunteers in Roman armies. They certainly were not savages who suddenly erupted out of nowhere.

The Germanic tribes became exceptionally restive toward the late fourth century, and for the next two centuries their movements were a major influence upon European development. Fiercer and more primitive people from central Asia were moving into Europe, and their pressures upon the eastern Germans sent a ripple of unrest westward. Population growth made old German lands overcrowded, and tribal movements were at least partly a search for new land; in such a situation, the relative prosperity of Roman lands was a temptation too great to be ignored. A remarkable series of Germanic movements resulted, not so much military invasions as migrations in which whole peoples moved, men, women and children.

The first serious confrontation of Romans and Germans over the issue of German entry into Roman lands occurred in 378 with the Visigoths (West Goths). It should be recognized that in this and most ensuing struggles between Romans and Germans the question was not so much land as security and authority. Most parts of the Roman Empire were rather lightly populated, and there was much undeveloped land to be taken up; what mattered was whether the Germans could be integrated into Roman society and bound by imperial authority. In fact the Visigoths first entered the empire with Roman permission, but they soon protested that the Romans had not fulfilled their agreements (which included promises of some supplies) and they revolted. In the ensuing battle at Adrianople in 378 the Germanic cavalry proved its worth; the Roman armies were cut up, and Emperor Valens was killed. After that the sporadic fighting with the Germans became more frequent and more serious, and the Romans could not devote their best efforts to it because of the danger from the Persian Empire to the east. Despite retaliatory raids and such innovations as settling some bands as allies, called *foederati*, to keep out other bands, the frontiers were breached more and more frequently, and by the late fifth century many groups of Germanic peoples were wandering all over the western empire.

Shortly after the battle of Adrianople, the Visigoths were pacified temporarily and settled as *foederati* in the Balkans, but soon they were again hostile; they ravaged Greece, and when they were driven out of there they invaded Italy, sacking Rome in 410. About the same time an Asiatic people called Huns overran western Asia and parts of eastern Europe, setting other Germanic peoples in motion. Fleeing before the Hunnish onslaught, the Burgundians and the Vandals crossed the Rhine into Gaul; the former settled there, while the latter drifted toward Spain. Pressed by these attacks and still torn by civil strife, the Romans evacuated Britain in 407, and the undefended islands soon were subjected to invasions by Saxons and Angles. By about the middle of the fifth century Britain was gone from the Roman orbit and was being Germanized rapidly. After sacking Italy, the Visigoths wandered across southern Gaul and into Spain, driving the Vandals before them into Africa, and the empire recognized a Visigothic kingdom in southern Gaul and Spain in 419 and a Vandal kingdom in Africa in 435; these peoples were at least partially Romanized, and though they were quite uncontrollable, theoretically they became part of the Roman Empire, and their leaders were granted Roman titles and dignities. Italy seemed more stable, the Germans having passed on, and in the 430s imperial authority appeared secure when a Roman general of Germanic origin, Aëtius, succeeded in pacifying Gaul. Except for the loss of Britain, the empire seemed to be reviving.

The new stability was short-lived, however. In 450 the Huns, under their famous leader Attila, invaded Gaul. Repulsed there, they turned next to Italy but gave up the attack, probably because they were bought off and plague was spreading in their ranks. It was clear that imperial frontiers were still insecure, and when Aëtius fell victim to political assassination in 454 the military situation deteriorated rapidly. The following year Vandals crossed from Africa and sacked Rome with a roughness that has made "vandalism" a permanent part of western languages. The next quarter century was very confused with many military and political figures rising to brief prominence, even to the imperial title in the west, and then falling as quickly through deposition or murder. In 476 the deposition of Romulus Augustus, last titular emperor of the west, was only one of many incidents of this kind as Italy and Gaul fell into chaos once again. Effective imperial authority was limited to a small area around Ravenna on Italy's east coast, which had been made the capital because its communications with Constantinople could be assured easily, and in Ravenna imperial authority was wielded as often as not by Romanized Germans. Only toward the end of the fifth century did it again appear that the situation was stabilizing. In the 480s the emperor recognized the power of the leader of yet another Germanic tribe, the Ostrogoths (East Goths). With imperial military titles, this Germanic king, Theodoric, invaded Italy and took Ravenna; he suppressed rival factions and ostensibly as the emperor's general established the Ostrogothic Kingdom of Italy, which was recognized by Constantinople in 497.

About the same time, a stable state was being built in Gaul by another Germanic people, the Franks. These were tribes settled around the lower reaches of the Rhine, divided broadly into two groups, the Salians who lived near the sea and the Ripuarians who lived farther up-river. The Franks had served as allies of the Romans on occasion, but they were more primitive and less Romanized than the other Germanic peoples already considered; they differed from them in another way, too, in that they did not abandon their old homelands to migrate but rather spread southward into Gaul in a steady expansion. In the 480s an extraordinary Salian king, Clovis, crushed the last Roman military power in upper Gaul and united all the Frankish people under his rule. In the 490s he defeated others of his Germanic neighbors, and then shortly after 500 he conquered both the Burgundians on the upper Rhone and the Visigoths in southern Gaul, creating an enormous kingdom. Like Theodoric the Ostrogoth, Clovis was recognized by Constantinople and given Roman titles, but despite these superficial similarities of military conquest and imperial acceptance, the Frankish and Ostrogothic kingdoms were very different from one another.

Though a Goth, Theodoric was quite Romanized, and he tried hard to fuse the vigor and military strength of his people with Roman culture and civilization. He kept close contacts with Constantinople, negotiated alliances with his Germanic neighbors and tried to keep the peace. He employed learned Italians in his government, and he based his edicts upon Roman law. He also was something of a patron of the arts. Clovis, on the other hand, was a simple barbarian chieftain, though very astute. He governed on the basis of tribal law and ruled through subchiefs, though the latter often were given Roman titles such as count or duke. He was a ruthless expansionist and was almost constantly at war.

But the most important difference among the late fifth and early sixth century kingdoms was in the matter of religion. Most of the Germanic peoples were Arian Christians, and this made serious problems in the Ostrogothic, Visigothic and Vandal kingdoms, for the populations and clergy upon whom these conquerors had imposed themselves were of Catholic (Athanasian) belief. At this time, theological quarrels were pursued with a ferocity almost incomprehensible to the modern student, for to the orthodox Christians the Arian was a heretic, a corrupter of religious truth, and the most detestable object on earth. By contrast, the Franks escaped this religious controversy.

The problem of heresy was particularly severe in Italy because of the growing power of the pope and of Rome as the western center of Catholic Christianity. It is clear that the bishop of Rome exercised no special authority in the very early church (in fact, the Latin *papa*, pope, was applied to bishops generally), but nonetheless Rome enjoyed considerable prestige. It was the old imperial capital, the site of the martyrdom of St. Peter and the keeper of the tombs of two apostles, Peter and Paul; and with the removal of the imperial capital to the east (330), the Bishop of Rome often found himself the only remaining political authority in Italy. All of these factors contributed to the growth of prestige and power, and early in the fifth century Roman primacy was set upon a scriptural basis by Pope

Celestine I who asserted the Petrine Doctrine drawn from St. Matthew's Gospel, that Christ had designated St. Peter the founder of the church and had conferred upon him "the power of the keys," which then had passed in succession to all the Roman bishops. A successor, Pope Innocent I, claimed universal jurisdiction over the church, and then in the mid-fifth century the first great pope, Leo I, brought all of these developments to a synthesis. He extracted from the emperor an edict declaring that papal decisions had the force of law; he proclaimed the mystical unity of St. Peter and his successors; he dictated a solution to another heretical quarrel; and he repudiated an attempt by a council of bishops to declare the patriarch of Constantinople supreme in the church. In addition, it was he who confronted Attila and his Huns (as an imperial representative) and turned them back; probably he pointed to spreading plague and the arrival of Roman reinforcements and negotiated a price for withdrawal, but as it was believed popularly that only a miracle spared Italy, he won tremendous prestige from the success. It was only some twenty years after Pope Leo's death that Theodoric and his Ostrogoths conquered Italy, and compromise between the aggressive and powerful leadership of the western church and the detested heretics proved impossible. Theodoric was a tolerant man, but he never was accepted by his Italian subjects and their Latin-Catholic clergy, and Pope Gelasius (492–496) even pronounced the formal independence of the church from civil authority (Gelasian Doctrine).

The Franks, on the other hand, enjoyed a much happier religious situation. When they began their conquest of Gaul they were still pagans, not having been reached by serious missionary efforts. As pagans they were much more acceptable to Catholics, for the church regarded pagans as untaught innocents and hoped for their conversion, while heretics were foul perverters of truth. Clovis became even more acceptable in 496 when he had himself and many of his warriors baptized as Catholic Christians. His motives can only be guessed at: he had married a Catholic girl; he had had several years' experience of the power and position of the Catholic clergy in Gaul; he claimed to have found strength in battle through prayer to the Christian God. Whatever his motive, his conversion was enormously important. Though a pretense of imperial authority endured, military and political power in the western empire was in the hands of Germanic kings, and of them all Clovis was the only one who was religiously acceptable to the indigenous population and its clergy. He was regarded as the sword of God, the deliverer from the heretic, and he enjoyed wide support.

Other circumstances also conspired to give stability to the Frankish kingdom while the apparently more civilized Ostrogothic kingdom proved short-lived. The emperors in the east had by no means abandoned hope of reasserting real authority in the west, and an imperial resurgence in the second quarter of the sixth century altered the balance of power drastically. The Emperor Justinian (527-565) dreamed of the reestablishment of a universal Christian empire under his authority, and after making peace with the Persians and crushing rival forces in the capital, he embarked upon the reconquest of the west. Because Justinian increased the bureaucratization of the government and the professionalism of the army, and because he gave definitive preference to Greek over Latin, the empire that he left to his successors was rather different from anything that preceded it; his reign usually is considered to mark the transition from the Roman Empire in the east to the medieval Byzantine Empire. His interests were manifold, and he also lent his authority to the last great codification of Roman laws, known as the Justinian Code. But while Justinian is important historically for many reasons, his immediate significance to western development lies in the campaigns of conquest that he launched. In the 530s and 540s Byzantine armies landed in North Africa and crushed completely the Vandal kingdom there, bringing the whole area back under the rule of Constantinople. From the mid-530s to the mid-550s Byzantine armies fought over the length and breadth of Italy, finally destroying the Ostrogothic kingdom and reestablishing imperial rule. In the mid-550s the fighting was extended to Spain, of which the southeastern part was reconquered.

Thus patterns changed rapidly from the beginning to the middle of the sixth century. The Vandal and Ostrogothic kingdoms were destroyed by Justinian's armies; the Visigothic kingdom, reduced by the Franks in the early part of the century, was further weakened by Byzantine forces. Arian rule over Catholic Christians, which had caused so many problems, was abolished through Italy and Africa and a part of Spain (and in 587 conversion of the Visigoths from

Arianism to Catholicism completed the process). Except for the British Isles, Gaul and part of Spain, the lands of the old Roman Empire were again under imperial rule.

Justinian's great conquests did not long survive his death, however. In 568 another Germanic people, the Lombards, invaded and conquered much of Italy while Constantinople was distracted by new political troubles and renewed war with the Persians. Thereafter Italy was a strange mosaic of jurisdictions with Byzantine rule (with its capital at Ravenna still) in parts of the east and south, papal rule (nominally under imperial authority) in Rome and adjacent territories, and Lombard rule (with its capital at Pavia) in most inland regions. Already torn by the Gothic and Byzantine wars and wracked with plague and famine, Italy largely was barbarized by the Lombard invasion. Though the Lombards gradually were absorbed to the extent of adopting the language and the religion of their subjects, they established governmental patterns resembling those of the Franks, personal rule of dukes and counts who usually were large land-holders and were responsible to the king. At the same time the grant of episcopal immunities (from government jurisdiction) made bishops virtually the temporal rulers of the remaining towns, and the elevation of another strong pope, Gregory the Great, advanced the independence of the church from secular authority.

Yet one more important influence was to be felt before a new pattern in the west emerged fully. This was the rise and rapid expansion of Moslem power. Mohammed, the prophet of the new faith, came from the Arabian town of Mecca, which was an important center of trade and culture. Deeply interested in religion, he had studied Christian and Jewish religious ideas, and in 612, when he was in his early 40s, he began preaching. His chief themes were the oneness of God, the importance of charity and prayer, divine judgment, and submission to God's will (Islam). Ill-received by the populace of Mecca, he fled with a handful of followers to Medina in 622 where he had great success with surrounding tribesmen. War with Mecca followed, but the Moslems, as the followers of Islam were called, eventually won, and by the time of Mohammed's death in 632 a great many Arab tribes had been won over or subjugated.

After Mohammed's death the direction of the faith was undertaken by a caliph, the vicegerent of the prophet, and rapid expansion continued, with the conquest of Persia, Syria and Egypt accomplished by the early 640s. In the latter half of the seventh century the pace of conquest was slowed by internal political and religious quarrels, but still the Moslem expansion pushed on, eastward to India and central Asia and westward along the north African coast where an alliance was made with the Berbers. Then, in 711 the armies spilled across into Spain where the Visigothic forces were defeated utterly, and by 715 all of Spain was taken, with resistance continuing only in the wild mountains of the north. Moslem armies moved into southern Gaul, taking Narbonne, and at the same time other forces advanced far enough in Asia Minor that in 717 and 718 they besieged Constantinople, though they failed to take the city.

In the next decade or two, however, a number of factors combined to halt the seemingly inexorable advance of Islam which was threatening to engulf Europe from both east and west. In the east, Byzantine defenses held; within the Islamic empire there erupted a great struggle for control of the caliphate, which ended by dividing Spain and the western parts of north Africa from the rest of the Moslem world; and in Gaul the Franks managed to defeat and contain the Islamic advance in a great battle at Tours in 732. While the struggle for Constantinople was to continue for centuries, the Frankish victory in the west proved decisive; a quarter century later the Moslems had been pushed back over the Pyrenees, and Frankish Gaul survived as a Germano-Christian synthesis on a Roman foundation.

Thus, by the early eighth century the destruction of the Roman Empire was complete, and in its place stood three distinct entities. Around the eastern, southern and western shores of the Mediterranean lay the Moslem world, strong, dynamic, and alien in religion and culture. East of Italy the northern parts of the Mediterranean basin belonged to the Byzantine Empire, the most direct heir of Rome perhaps, but by now Greek, bureaucratized and defensive. And in western Europe there stood the raw new Kingdom of the Franks, Germanic with a faint Roman tradition, still turbulent but with strength proved against the Moslems. Amidst these competing powers stood the Italy of the Lombards and the Pope and weak imperial pretensions, a power vacuum to which all looked hungrily. In the mid-eighth century a papal alliance with the Franks, provoked by the dangers of the Italian situation, proved a catalyst that completed the Germano-Christian fusion and launched medieval society in western Europe.

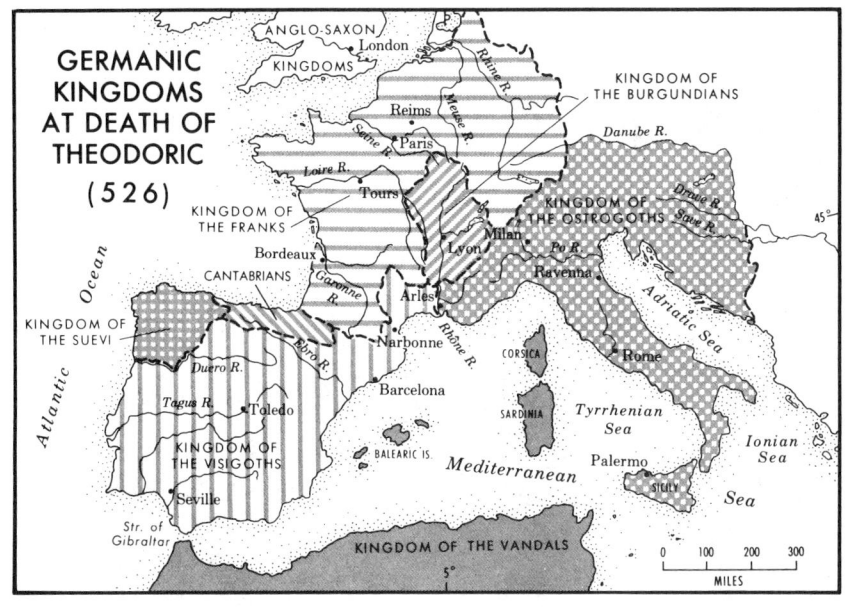
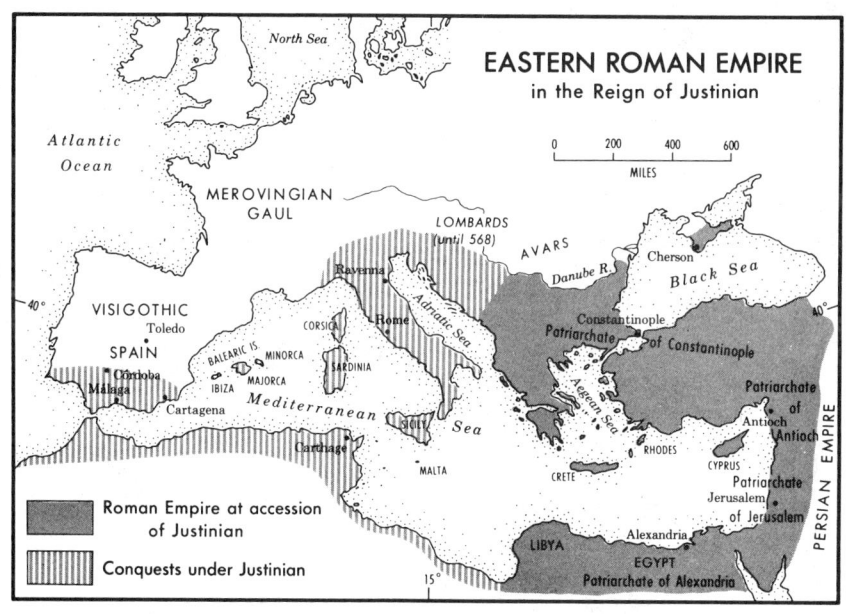

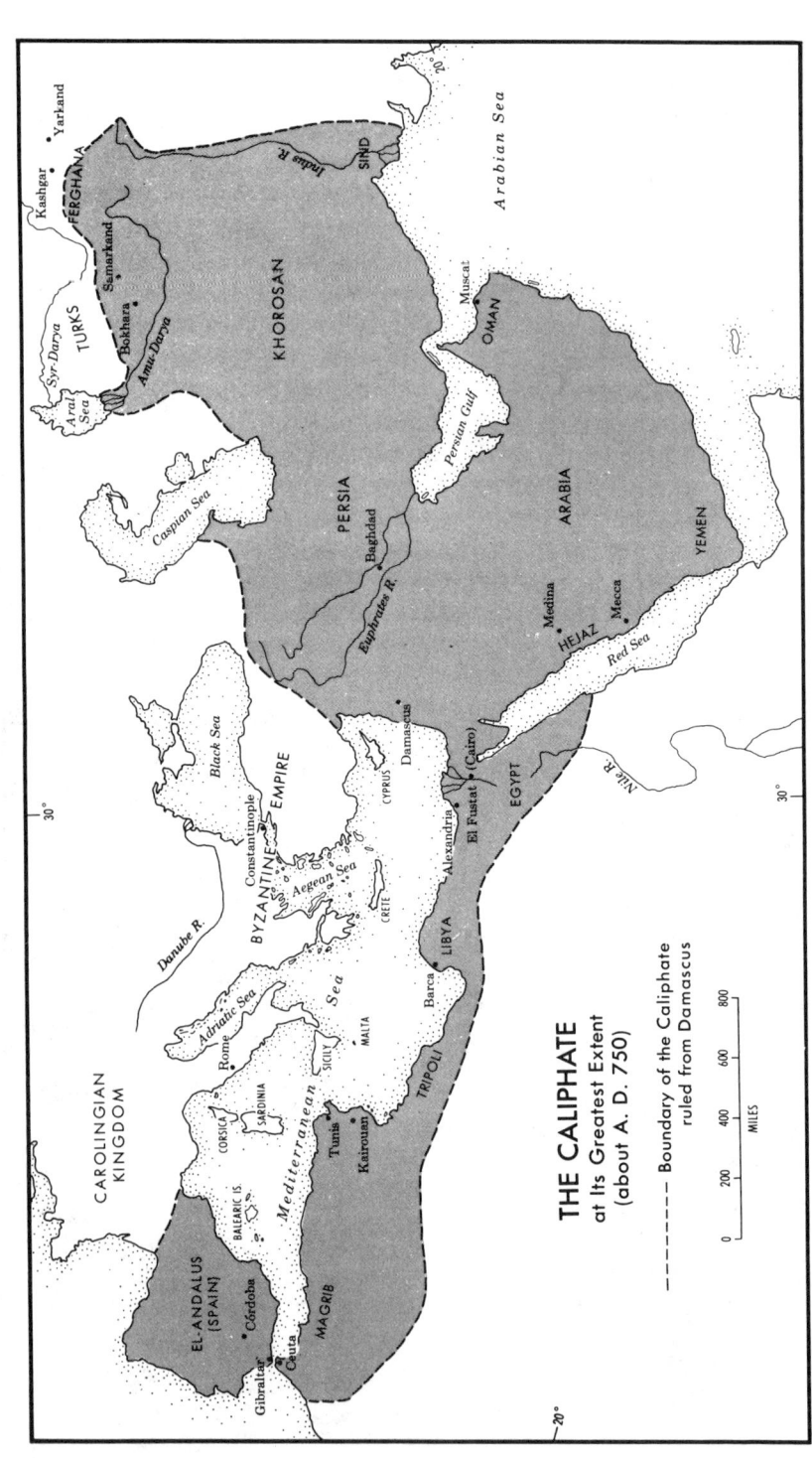

Chapter 10

Early Carolingian Europe

By the eighth century the focus of political and social development in western Europe was Frankish Gaul, but there had been no steady progress from the promising beginnings made by Clovis. Indeed, Clovis' family, called Merovingians after a semilegendary ancestor named Meroveg, produced singularly few competent kings. Except for the reign of Dagobert in the second quarter of the seventh century, Merovingian history is a sad tale of civil war and fratricide. In fact, royal authority deteriorated so far that after the mid-seventh century the Merovingian kings were no more than figureheads, and real power gravitated into the hands of great nobles, the dukes and counts. Merovingian power had been weakened further by territorial divisions to provide crowns for royal sons, and four more or less distinct kingdoms became generally recognizable: Austrasia, lying farthest to the east, was basically Frankish; Neustria, to the west, was essentially Gallo-Roman; Aquitania, in the south, was Gallo-Roman and Visigothic; and Burgundy, in the southeast, had a mixture of Burgundians, Franks, and lesser Germanic peoples. Had nothing happened to arrest this decline, it is likely that the Moslems would have overrun Gaul easily, but fortunately for the independence of Europe and of western Christianity, a revival of sorts took place in the early eighth century. The revival owed nothing to the Merovingians but turned rather on the ambitions and abilities of one of the great Frankish noble families, later called the Carolingians.

The growth of noble power that paralleled the degeneracy of the Merovingian kings had favored particularly the officials of the royal households who had access to the king's person and his treasury. In this situation the Mayors of the Palace, originally menials of the household, had grown to be important figures, representatives of the landed nobility controlling the reality if not the titles of royal power. To preserve their positions, the mayors developed the practice of proclaiming Merovingian infants as kings and then deposing them and locking them away in monasteries when they had grown to adolescence. With such practices it was the mayors, of course, who actually governed. Mayors occasionally tried to usurp the royal title, but until the eighth century they were unsuccessful, for the delicate balance of pretense and reality served the interests of the great landowners who had no desire to see governing power joined to legitimacy in a potent combination that might curb their personal ambitions. Early in the eighth century, however, an able and ambitious mayor of Austrasia found a way to consolidate his power without an overt attempt upon the Merovingian crowns. In the civil wars endemic in Gaul, Charles, called Martel "The Hammer," defeated his rivals and forced his acceptance as mayor in all four of the kingdoms. In the course of these struggles Charles Martel also developed an unusually competent military force, preferring a small band of well-armed heavy cavalry to the traditionally numerous but ill-equipped Frankish footmen. It was with this elite force that he led the Frankish armies that stopped the Moslems at Tours in 732, and after that victory, his prestige and the strength of his army assured his power. Still Martel did not attempt to usurp the royal titles, but contented himself with the title *dux francorum,* Duke of the Franks.

The revival of Frankish power under Charles Martel entailed far-reaching social and political developments, which are understood more easily if it is remembered that at the root of all of them was Martel's desire to improve his military force. Traditionally all Frankish freemen owed military service, but when the levies were called up, they often shuffled into camp with no equipment other than a spear. In place of this rabble Martel sought to develop a cavalry, well-mounted and equipped with spear, sword, shield and armor, but this was a costly program. In the eighth century, the major form of wealth was land, tenanted productive land, and it was this that would have to be "spent" to build the new army. Martel held considerable land, both his own family possessions and the royal estates he controlled as mayor, but he had no intention of impoverishing himself *vis-à-vis* the other great landowners of the kingdom, so he sought an alternative source, the church.

Through gifts and endowments the church had become a very large land-holder, and Martel determined to make use of church lands to support his army. This was a very delicate question, for churchmen always insisted that the holdings they "managed" were God's property and immune from governmental interference, and usually they had royal charters confirming this view. However, through a combination of persuasion and pressure, and the proposal of some very complicated arrangements, Martel finally got the church to agree to support his soldiers. Essentially, each of the new cavalrymen received the use of (but not the title to) some church land for his support; he held the land so long as he rendered the requisite service to Martel, but he also paid a token rent to the church, symbolic of his recognition of the church's continuing ownership. With this arrangement Martel stripped the church of vast tracts of land and built his army. (Fully cognizant of the potential advantages of the good will of the church and of the dangers of consolidated opposition, he tried hard to mollify the clergy, most notably by encouraging and supporting the work of the great missionary St. Boniface, who was trying to convert the German tribes beyond the Rhine.)

These innovations in land tenure were of great importance, for the creation of a class of propertied small nobility all over the kingdom who depended upon Martel strengthened his position with the great landowners. But even more significantly, Martel's practice of granting the use of land in return for military service, though not without precedents, was the first large-scale use of this arrangement; if on the one hand it symbolized the decline of a commercial monetized society in which it was possible to hire service, on the other it demonstrated a viable alternative that was to become the basis of medieval European feudalism.

Despite his many achievements, there was a real danger that Martel's work would not long survive his death in 741, for in keeping with Germanic tradition he considered his titles and powers personal property, and at the end of his life he divided them between his two sons, Pepin and Carloman. For a half-dozen years the two brothers shared power, but in 747 Carloman retired to a monastery (apparently voluntarily), and Pepin ruled alone until his death in 768. Though overshadowed by his son Charles, called Charlemagne, Pepin made great strides in the development of Frankish Gaul, and his achievements must not be passed over lightly.

Although Charles Martel tried to avoid any open quarrel with the church, despite his seizure of church lands, he seems never to have been moved by any deep personal convictions. By contrast, both Pepin and Carloman were influenced profoundly in their youth by the zeal of the missionary St. Boniface, and both appear to have been sincerely religious. In Carloman's case this sentiment resulted in his withdrawal into monastic life; Pepin, on the other hand, gave expression to his convictions through a total reform and revitalization of the church in Gaul and a close alliance with the papacy.

The condition of the church in Gaul and its relations with the Frankish government before Pepin's reforms defy the usual stereotypes of pious early Christians. Under the Merovingians the Franks had treated the church respectfully, almost as a tribal totem, had protected it and endowed it with lands, but had not taken its attempts to interfere in private life very seriously. Kings and nobles practiced polygamy, and in addition to several wives often kept concubines. Moreover, they murdered with equanimity, repudiated wives of whom they tired and generally treated Christian moral teachings casually. And the church was not much better. Bishops often were appointed through political influence before even being ordained as priests. Clerics often tried to steal church lands for their families, clerical marriage and concubinage were common and many instances were recorded of priests rebuked for drunkenness or brawling. Monasteries were ill-disciplined communities more noted for sloth and drunkenness than for religious practices. Hence, Pepin's ambitions for reform faced formidable problems.

Nonetheless, there were some bright spots in this generally gloomy picture. There were able and dedicated churchmen such as St. Boniface and those who followed him into the wilderness in Germany; and there was a reform movement within monasteries that sought to establish discipline and piety as the foundations of monastic life. By persuasion and command, through clerical appointments that he made and by convening councils of bishops, Pepin sought to strengthen these wholesome trends and to reduce abuses. To give the church a sound economic basis he restored some of the lands that his father had taken away, though not enough to undermine Martel's work, and he instituted tithing of the laity. To reestablish some sort of discipline within the clergy, he prescribed that priests must wear distinctive dress, setting them off from the populace at large, and he lent his support to the monastic reform movement and prescribed its practices for all the monasteries in Gaul.

The reformed monks who attracted Pepin's favorable attention were known as Benedictines, after their founder St. Benedict of Nursia, an early sixth century Italian. Monasticism in the early church usually meant hermits who dressed in tatters, begged food, engaged in long fasts and vigils and generally sought solitude in the wilderness. While this program offered the solace of years of contemplation to many in the eastern Mediterranean, in the harsher climate of western Europe it was simply a prescription for an early death. Consequently, European monks tended to gather in communities, but too often these were infamous for laxity and immorality. As an improvement over both earlier forms of monasticism, St. Benedict formed a community of monks and established a discipline for them that included a regular schedule of prayer, study and manual labor, so that they might remain sincere in their dedication, might become more learned in their faith and might feed themselves by their own efforts. With the motto "a sound mind in a sound body" St. Benedict prescribed normal rest and simple but adequate diet, and he forbade exaggerated fasting and excessively harsh physical disciplines. St. Benedict's own monastery of Monte Casino was a notable success, and his principles, or Rule, soon became the inspiration of other monastic communities. It was this Benedictine Rule that Pepin commanded be accepted by all the monasteries in Gaul, and not only did this command reform existing monasteries, it also stimulated considerable expansion of the monastic movement. Until the mid-eighth century Christianity was chiefly an urban faith, a congregation of townsmen governed by their bishop. Rural folk still were wedded to traditional primitive beliefs, a situation illustrated by the fact that the word for "countrymen" also meant "non-believers" (Latin *pagani*). As reformed monasteries sprang up all over Gaul, they carried the faith into the countryside and completed the internal missionary work that had been begun several centuries earlier.

The other great achievement of Pepin's rule was the establishment of a close alliance with the papacy. The papacy had sought such an alliance earlier, but Charles Martel had rejected it. By contrast, when the opportunity presented itself to Pepin early in the 750s, he welcomed it. In a sense, Pepin and the pope were both aiming at usurpations, and they needed each other; Pepin had ambitions for the Frankish crown, while the pope was seeking to wrest political control of Italy from the emperor at Constantinople. Pepin had the power to seize the crown from the enfeebled Merovingians, but he sought some legitimation, some religious sanction for taking what Germanic law regarded as property. When the pope asked for help against the Lombards and sought an alliance in 751, Pepin discreetly inquired "whether it would not be better that he who exercises the power of the kingdom wear its crown," and the pope answered in the affirmative; the last Merovingian promptly was packed off to a monastery, and Pepin was crowned and anointed by St. Boniface, who was acting as the pope's representative. Thus the crown of the Franks became more significantly Christian, dependent for its legitimacy less upon Germanic traditions than upon the religious sanctions of the church. Thereafter the ties that linked the Frankish monarchy and the papacy could not be broken easily, and the new relationship was strengthened three years later when the pope travelled to Gaul and anointed and blessed Pepin personally.

In fulfilment of his responsibilities under the new alliance, Pepin led his army into Italy in 754 and 756, defeating the Lombards and confirming the authority of the pope over disputed lands in a document called the Donation of Pepin; since technically these lands belonged to the emperor in Constantinople, Pepin's action amounted to recognition of claims that the pope was the heir of the Roman Empire in Italy and a major achievement for papal policy. The Donation founded the Papal States, lands governed directly by the pope, which were to endure until the late nineteenth century and which survive vestigially in the independent Vatican State.

In keeping with Frankish tradition, Pepin divided his lands and titles between his two sons, Charles and Carloman, before his death in 768, but again the state that the Carolingians were building survived intact; in 771 Carloman died, and Charles ruled alone until his death in 814. The astonishing achievements in many fields during

Charles's reign earned him the title "the great" in his own lifetime, and it is thus he is remembered—Charlemagne.

Most of Charlemagne's reign was filled with warfare, Frankish armies conquering in all directions. A series of campaigns southward pushed the frontier across the Pyrenees, establishing against the Moslems a buffer known as the Spanish March or March of Barcelona; it was during these campaigns that the mountain Basques annihilated the Frankish rear guard, an action commemorated in the famous *Song of Roland*. War with the Saxons to the north and northeast lasted over thirty years, through eighteen separate campaigns, before they submitted to Charlemagne. The struggle with the Lombards was renewed, and Charlemagne destroyed their kingdom and pushed to the Adriatic coast and around the north end of that sea into Dalmatia, the coast of modern Yugoslavia. Campaigns eastward absorbed Germans and Slavs and finally defeated the Avars, an Asian people on the lower Danube. By the end of his life, Charlemagne ruled most of western and central Europe and considerable parts of eastern Europe.

Yet Charlemagne's fame rests on far more than conquest, for he developed complicated mechanisms to pacify and integrate new areas into his government. For instance, he defeated the Saxons several times, only to see them rise in rebellion again. He determined to force Christianity upon them as a civilizing influence that he hoped would develop moral bonds between them and his other peoples. To this end, he supported the establishment of churches and monasteries among the Saxons and insisted that they accept baptism; then if they were found gathering again in war bands and celebrating ancient pagan rites, they were guilty of heresy, which ecclesiastical crime Charlemagne made punishable by death. His ruthlessness extended even to large transfers of population, moving thousands of Saxons into Gaul for resettlement and displacing many Franks into Saxony, to break up the cohesiveness of Saxon resentment of the conqueror. After thirty years of struggle, these policies of forced conversion and deportations were successful.

In areas that were less troublesome, Charlemagne behaved less harshly. After defeating the Bavarians, he forced the Bavarian chieftain, Tassilo, to swear an oath of loyalty and obedience and then allowed him to retain his rule over his people, making him a Carolingian duke; ultimately Tassilo violated his oath and revolted, whereupon Charlemagne deposed him, but he seemed willing to try moderate measures before resorting to extremes.

To govern his far-flung territories, Charlemagne developed an administrative system of some sophistication. The land was divided into districts ruled by counts, officers theoretically appointed for life but often removed. Begun in old Frankish lands, this system gradually was extended into Italy, Saxony, and Bavaria, and the tribal dukes largely were curbed. The counts had viscounts and vicars to assist them, and they appointed landowners as judges, called *scabini*, to oversee local justice. To limit the ambition of the tumultuous noblemen upon whom his administration depended, Charlemagne created two control systems. The first of these was his practice of establishing all through his domains loyal retainers whom he trusted; these men, called *vassi dominici* (vassals of the lord), were given land grants in return for oaths of loyalty and obedience to Charlemagne personally. The other control mechanism was a roving inspectorate of men called *missi dominici* (those sent by the lord). These officers travelled in pairs, usually a count and a bishop; they held their own courts, heard complaints and inspected financial, judicial and clerical administration. When they found abuses or corruption, they had wide discretionary powers for corrective and punitive action. They were the chief connection between central and local administration.

To provide for frontier defense, Charlemagne created special border districts called *marches* or *marks*, governed by a margrave (*mark graf*). These were highly autonomous counties whose administrators had wide military and financial powers so they could meet emergencies quickly. Among the more famous marches protecting Charlemagne's frontiers were the Spanish March against the Moslems and the Dane Mark against the Danes.

Charlemagne continued the good relations with the church established by his father, but like Constantine he expected the church to serve him too, as in the pacification of the Saxons. In the same way, he fought the Lombards to defend the papacy, and he confirmed the Donation of Pepin; but he expected the pope to crown and bless Frankish kings, and he considered himself sovereign in papal lands. Nor did Charlemagne limit his personal role in the church to worldly matters. When a new doctrinal quarrel arose, Charlemagne convened a council of bishops in 794, presided over it himself and dictated a solution. He was quite as much a caesaropapist as any Roman emperor.

Perhaps the most dramatic aspect of Charlemagne's relations with the church was the imperial coronation which took place on Christmas Day of the year 800. After further campaigns against the Lombards, the Frankish king went to Rome for the Christmas festivities, and after Christmas mass the pope set a crown upon his head and proclaimed him Roman Emperor, a title that offered Charlemagne many advantages. The German royal crowns were essentially tribal and ethnic, but Charlemagne ruled Lombards, Saxons, Bavarians and others in addition to his own Franks. By conquering and annexing royal crowns he could not bind these people to him, but the imperial title implied universality, and allowed him to stress the common Christianity of all his subject peoples, a tie that might hold them together. However, the imperial coronation raised serious problems. The Byzantine Empire resented it deeply, for it still considered itself the only empire and believed itself the legitimate claimant to all the western lands of the Roman Empire. To the Byzantines, Charlemagne was a German upstart and the pope a rebel for usurping the powers and functions of the empire. It required a dozen years before a compromise was achieved and Byzantium recognized Charlemagne's title as a sort of revival of the old Roman practice of eastern and western emperors.

An historical controversy long turned around the matter of the imperial coronation. Some years after the emperor's death, Charlemagne's biographer, Einhard, wrote that Charlemagne had regretted it. It has been suggested that he was unaware of the pope's intentions, but this is hardly credible, for the pope was in a weak position and utterly dependent upon the Frankish king; he could not have dared so important an act without Charlemagne's knowledge and consent, nor could the elaborate arrangements have been carried out in secret. Rather it would seem that Charlemagne had second thoughts on the matter. Considering the complications with the Byzantine Empire and reflecting upon the dangerous precedent implicit in having the imperial crown bestowed by the pope, he probably wondered later if it had been worth it.

Charlemagne also is remembered as a patron of learning, for he presided over a cultural reawakening usually called the Carolingian renaissance. Personally he could speak Latin in addition to his Frankish tongue, and he understood some Greek, but that was as far as his scholastic achievements went; he never learned to write. But he established a school in his palace and made himself a patron of scholars whom he brought from all over Europe. The foremost of them, Alcuin, came from York, in the north of England; Einhard, who wrote Charlemagne's biography, came from Fulda, deep in Germany; and Paul the Deacon and Peter of Pisa came from Italy.

The importance of the Carolingian renaissance is exaggerated easily, but it should not be underestimated either. The Palace School produced little that was original, though Einhard did his biography of the emperor and Paul the Deacon wrote a *History of the Lombards*, but it was a center for the recovery, copying and preservation of ancient writings culled largely from scattered monastic collections. But for the patient transcribing of ninth-century scholars, the surviving body of ancient literature would be much smaller than it is today. Also, the Palace School developed a smaller and much more legible handwriting, called Carolingian miniscule (upon which most modern typefaces are based), which replaced the older large cursive scrawl. Nor did the impact of Charlemagne's patronage of learning stop at the Palace School, for many who had been associated with it established schools of their own, and Tours, Rheims, Cologne and Fulda became famous centers of learning. So though its achievements were limited, the Carolingian renaissance was very significant. As it sometimes is expressed, "In the darkness of the ninth century the light of a single candle is important."

Under the rule of the early Carolingians, European society began to assume patterns, manorialism and feudalism, that were to be its foundation for many centuries. Manorialism was a socioeconomic pattern based upon self-sufficient estates which eventually included most people in Europe. There are precedents at least as early as the later Roman Empire, aristocratic estates called *latifundia,* but by the ninth-century towns nearly had disappeared and almost everyone was involved in manorialism in some capacity. Probably the reasons for this economic regression never will be explained to every historian's satisfaction, but the decline is indisputable and is attested to by a new silver coinage introduced by Charlemagne; gold was simply too expensive and could not serve as a medium of exchange for the petty transactions that survived. Hence, manorialism was a pattern of an essentially agrarian society.

Though there were many superficial differences from one manor to another, there were certain basic features that were common to all: a water source, fields for growing grain and vegetables, pasturage and some sort of fuel source—usually a wood lot though in some areas a peat bog. Dwellings clustered together in a village, often dominated by the castle of the lord of the manor; a powerful lord, however, would hold several manors, and of course he would not build a castle on each one. The distribution of manor lands was very complex. Usually the pasture and wood lot were "common," shared by everyone, but the arable lands were divided into a maze of strips worked by different farmers rather than into consolidated blocks of individual proprietorship. Division of lands among sons and multiple inheritance tended to make most manor lands a crazy quilt, and in addition, when new lands were cleared, it was common to distribute in strips so everyone shared equally in rich bottom lands, steep slopes and poor hilltops.

Since manors were largely self-sufficient, a wide variety of people lived on them: farmers, blacksmiths, carpenters, wheelwrights, etc. In early medieval Europe most of these people were serfs, neither slaves nor freemen. A serf was bound to his land, and certain of his actions were restricted; typically, the lord could not sell the land from under the man nor sell the man off the land (though he could sell land and man together), and the serf could not leave his land or marry without the lord's permission. It was a harsh existence, but many freemen entered into serfdom voluntarily to escape the crushing burdens of taxes and military obligations which they could not afford to meet.

The charges and obligations upon the tenants of a manor were heavy. Typically they would pay land rent, a share of the crop, for lands they worked for themselves, would have to work some days on the lord's own land, would have to render some personal service in the lord's stables or kitchens and would have to offer special "presents" at Christmas, Easter and other holidays. But the system did offer some security on both the personal and the collective level. It made the individual part of a closely interconnected community in times when war, famine and plague were more than a family could cope with alone, and it supported a professional military and governing class that could defend the whole society.

Feudalism concerned only the military and governing class of medieval society, ten or fifteen per cent of Europe's inhabitants. It was based upon a pattern of personal relationships in a society that had no concept of service to the state, and it provided a means of reimbursing for service in a nonmonetized society. The foundations of feudalism were the two institutions of benefice and vassalage, and these in turn depended upon the idea of granting not land but the products of it, in Latin *usufruct*, the right to the fruits of the land. Benefice was land granted in this way for service, with the grantor retaining title but the grantee enjoying the income. This was the way Charles Martel used church lands to support his soldiers, adding yet another complexity; the church retained title, Martel was given the right of disposition of usage, and the soldiers received the income of the land assigned them, rendering military service to Martel and token payment to the church. Vassalage was the practice of one man "commending" himself to another, swearing an oath of loyalty and promising service. There are precedents for benefice and vassalage in Roman and Germanic tradition, but in Carolingian times the two institutions came to be connected. The overlord would grant the *usufruct* of land to those who pronounced their oaths and became his vassals; in return they would promise to bear him military service with an agreed number of soldiers and to serve as advisors in his council when he required it. Often these vassals then would subdivide the lands granted to them so as to take vassals of their own, a process call subinfeudation. (One of the very delicate issues in medieval society was the question whether subinfeudated vassals owed primary allegiance to their lord or to his overlord if the two should quarrel.)

In a sense, every member of the feudal elite had a part in manorialism, for each was the lord of a manor or manors from which he drew his support, but that was the only point of contact between the two systems. Manorialism organized the great mass of commoners, providing them some security in return for their support of the politico-military elite. Feudalism organized the elite within itself, providing some means of ranking and of remunerating service. Under the early Carolingians, both of these patterns emerged rather clearly and produced a society that was expansive, more secure than Europe had seen for three or four centuries, and capable of sustaining a modest cultural renaissance.

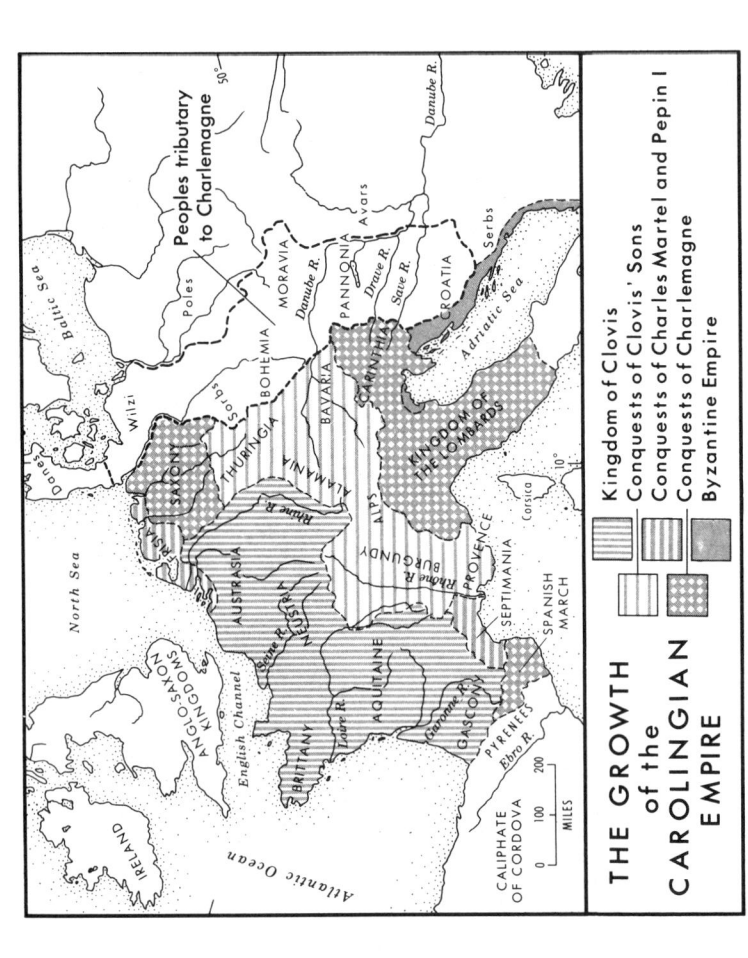

CAROLINGIAN EMPIRE IN 870

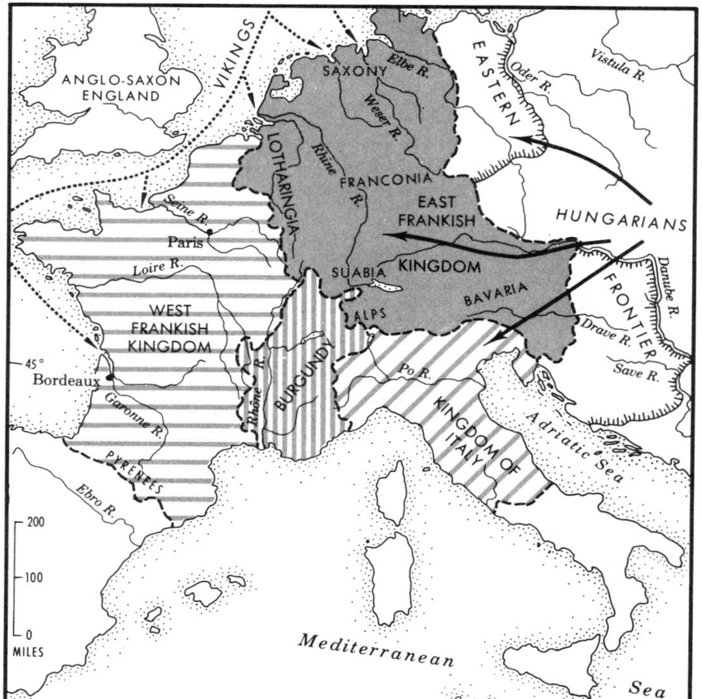

CAROLINGIAN EMPIRE 876-911

Chapter 11

A Time of Trial

By the time of Charlemagne, European society had developed rather elaborately, and it presented an appearance of considerable strength. In the south, the Islamic invasions had been stopped, and though raiding along the Mediterranean coast continued to inflict costly destruction, there was little threat of Europe's being overwhelmed. In the east and north, hordes of tribal peoples moved along the borders of the Carolingian Empire, and conflict with them was more or less constant, but the empire stood secure behind its shell of "marches." And most of the west enjoyed the security of a seacoast.

Within the Carolingian Empire it is possible to suggest a comparably optimistic picture of stability and progress. The cultural revival flourished. An administrative system focussed on the emperor was designed to enforce general peace, provide military forces in time of danger and offer justice through various levels of judgment. Men closely tied to the emperor were scattered throughout the land to guard against usurpation and rebellion while others roved, inspecting and checking the whole operation. Despite private quarrels, border raids, subsistence agriculture and massive illiteracy, European society in the early ninth century seemed to demonstrate stability and security and a modest intellectual rebirth.

In the islands off Europe's coast, the situation could be described with comparable optimism. Celtic kingdoms had grown up in Ireland, not without internecine warfare but with enough security to allow a flourishing monastic movement that made Ireland one of the centers of northern Christianity. Scotland and Wales still were peopled by wild tribesmen, but in England proper the Anglo-Saxon kingdoms seemed to be stabilizing somewhat as the larger absorbed the smaller and conquered most of the Celtic remnants in the west country. And the personal suzerainty of Offa of Mercia and Egbert of the West Saxons, roughly contemporaries of Charlemagne, suggested consolidation. In England, as on the continent, there existed cultural centers of note, especially in Northumbria. Churchmen from the British Isles had played no small part in Christianizing the continental peoples and in aiding the cultural revival in Europe. In the islands as on the continent, increased security, political consolidation and cultural revival appeared to be developing trends.

The reality behind the appearances was far less encouraging. Ireland still was divided, while in England the apparent political consolidation was but a personal bond with no institutional supports, and it masked bitter rivalries. No one man actually commanded in the islands, and no one was capable of raising really large military forces. Behind the appearance of growing consolidation lay the old anarchy of many petty rival kingdoms.

The reality on the continent was even more in contrast to appearances. Despite effective leadership and institutional development, there were appalling weaknesses. The military system was clumsy and inflexible. Under Charlemagne the Frankish army accomplished some quite remarkable feats of mobility and demonstrated a notable tenacity in campaign after campaign against the Saxons, but the whole structure depended utterly upon the capacity, the energy and the strength of the emperor—his ability to compel obedience and to lead to victory and glory. Equally the administration turned only upon its apex, the emperor. It was his capitularies that gave initiative, his authority that controlled the counts, his concern that directed the *missi* and the *scabini*. All depended upon him. And by the same token, even the cultural revival owed its main impetus to the rather remarkable Charles whom Europe called "the Great." His patronage of men of learning, the seminal influence of the Palace School, these were the real bases of the Carolingian renaissance.

Charlemagne had created an impressive edifice that rested wholly upon himself, like a new Atlas who upheld the world upon his shoulders. In that lay the seeds of disaster, for the structure of the empire provided no guarantee for the competence of Charlemagne's successors nor even for the stability of the succession. The succession, the problem that had plagued the Roman Empire so greatly, was not resolved clearly among the Carolingians. Pepin had ruled his father's kingdom in its entirety only because his brother preferred the monastic life. Charlemagne himself had acquired the whole Frankish kingdom only because of the fortuitous death of his brother. Even the transformation of a German tribal kingdom into a "universal" empire in the famous ceremony on Christmas Day of 800 had done nothing to modify the basically Germanic and personal conception of Carolingian rule. Charlemagne appears to have planned a partition of his lands, and only the accidents of human mortality preserved the empire intact; Louis the Pious was the only one of his sons to survive him. So behind the facade of Charlemagne's empire there loomed always the potential of division and fratricidal strife.

Nor should it be forgotten that Carolingian power depended upon wealth—the wealth to reward followers, to maintain impressive display and to underwrite innovation (such as Charles Martel's cavalry or Charlemagne's Palace School). But the increasingly agrarian foundations of the economy, reflected in the change from a gold to a silver coinage, meant there was only one real form of wealth in the society, land; and land is a decidedly inflexible sort of treasure. In the face of military necessity, Charles Martel had found an expedient in the expropriation of church lands, permitting large-scale expenditure without diminishing significantly the basis of his own power. But such an expedient could not be repeated very often, and land once granted, even with the technical limitation of granting only its fruits, was very difficult to reclaim. With declining monetary wealth, the successors of Charlemagne faced ever greater competition from the landed nobility.

To old dangers the Carolingians added some new ones. The closer alliance with the church—reflected in government support of St. Boniface's missionary efforts, in permission for tithing, in defense of the papacy—certainly produced advantages, such as help in pacifying the Saxons, a sanction for the exercise of power and an imperial crown. But at the same time this policy encouraged dependence upon clerics for governmental personnel, high military expenditures for expeditions into Italy and an implication of authority superior to the emperor's through papal coronation. So long as the church was weak and threatened and the emperor a forceful person commanding military strength, the danger was only theoretical; but the potential for trouble was enormous.

Finally, one might note with some irony that the Carolingian military establishment had very limited capacities, despite the great conquests of Charlemagne. The weaknesses of organization were many. Border defense pivoted upon local commanders who were allowed enormous autonomy, who were controlled in fact only by the dominant personality of the emperor. Hierarchical organization meant considerable delay in response to a summons, and mustering the entire host depended upon the cooperation and obedience of a horde of lesser commanders. The weaknesses of integration and support are illustrated well by the famous *Song of Roland,* when the rear guard of the army was wiped out in an ambush and its commander was left rather pathetically sounding his horn in a vain appeal for relief. But the greatest weakness of the Carolingian army was its limited fighting capacity. It was definitely an offensive force. Because of clumsy mobilization it had to fight at times of its own choosing. Because of weak organization and indiscipline it was at its best in a grand melée rather than in planned operations. The soldiers were brave, and by the standards of the day their equipment was good; if the enemy chose to stand against them they could give a good account of themselves, as they demonstrated against the Moors and the Avars and the Lombards. But the Saxon wars demonstrated the army's weakness. Problems of supply and responsibilities at home would not allow it to undertake a long-term occupation. Discipline did not permit sending roving units to ferret the Saxons out of their forests. The Saxon war was won by tenacity, and the fact that it lasted thirty years is significant. The Carolingian army burned villages and destroyed crops year after year, took hostages, deported whole populations; and it defeated such Saxon forces as tried to stand against it in open battle. Gradually it ground the Saxons down, but so long as the will to resist endured, the Carolingian army was unable to impose a solution, and it was unable to stop the raiding of Frankish lands or the looting of churches. Only because the Saxons' base areas were vulnerable were they finally defeated.

All of these problems became significant soon after Charlemagne's death early in the ninth century, and it is probably only a slight exaggeration to suggest that the real strength of his empire was his genius, his energy and his impressive qualities of leadership. His son Louis, a gentle man, followed a policy of subservience to the church that earned him the sobriquet "Louis the Pious"; one result was considerable loss of control over the church through the grant of immunities—freedom from governmental jurisdiction over church lands. And Louis proved quite unable to enforce obedience from the turbulent nobles or even from his own sons. His three sons quarreled and fought over the inheritance while their father still lived, and after his death the unity of the empire was broken as it was divided among them. To Charles (called "the Bald") went the western lands, known thereafter as the West Frankish Kingdom. To Louis went the eastern lands, which became the East Frankish Kingdom. The eldest brother, Lothar, received the title of emperor and a long narrow territory known as Lotharingia, which stretched from the mouth of the Rhine southward along the Rhine and Rhone valleys and into northern and central Italy. This last kingdom was destined to be the focal point of bitter conflicts. Geographically difficult to consolidate, it was also militarily indefensible; and in addition it offered great temptations to Lothar's brothers because it contained so much of the personal landed wealth of the Carolingian family, the royal fisc as it was called. Bloody fratricidal struggles ensued, and except for three years of peace in the late 880s, Charlemagne's successors almost constantly were involved in civil wars throughout the latter half of the ninth century.

But the weakness that was to rend most dramatically both the empire that Charlemagne had built and the Anglo-Saxon and Celtic kingdoms of the British Isles was their inability to cope with a new series of raids and invasions. The first of the new raiders arrived in Charlemagne's own lifetime. They came by sea from the north, so the Europeans called them Northmen, but they called themselves Vikings.

Scandinavia was populated by Germanic peoples of rather a primitive nature, peoples of whom little was heard until late in the eighth century when they began the great wave of raids and migrations that lasted through the ninth and tenth centuries. Viking longships from Norway and Denmark swept the coasts of western Europe and the British Isles and probed deep inland along the river systems, while Vikings from Sweden, often called Varangians, sailed east through the Baltic and penetrated the river valleys of Russia, which they soon dominated.

The reasons for the sudden expansion of the Scandinavians still cannot be explained satisfactorily, but a number of contributing factors have been identified. At this period a process of political consolidation was under way, binding tribal groups into the kingdoms of Denmark, Norway and Sweden, and it has been suggested that some of the more turbulent elements of the Scandinavian population left rather than submit to this new authority. In addition the archeological record indicates that there was a considerable increase of population putting severe pressure upon the limited and relatively unproductive northern lands. Why this sudden population explosion should have taken place is unclear, but legends suggest that large families—and particularly many sons—constituted a status symbol, and the practice of polygamy and the maintenance of concubines as well as wives made possible very large families. Larger village sites imply an ample supply of young men, and primogeniture—total inheritance by the eldest son—meant many men were landless and eager to earn, through raids and plunder, the price of a farm or the bride price to buy a wife.

Trade also may have been a factor in the Scandinavian expansion. As the trade of the Mediterranean dwindled under the impact of the Moslems, a much more modest trade in the north seems to have benefitted. Charlemagne's Frisian subjects in the Rhine delta conducted a flourishing small trade with Scandinavia in such things as furs and walrus ivory, and there are grounds to believe that lucrative piracy and a desire to secure control of profitable legitimate trade were also factors in drawing the Scandinavians southward. In any event it is frequently the case in primitive commerce that when there is a parity of strength there is trade, and when there is a disparity the strong take from the weak.

A technological factor also seems to have been operative in the development of the Viking raids. Sails had been known in the Mediterranean for centuries, and in fact as far north as the west coast of Gaul some of the Celtic peoples were using sails in Caesar's time, but the Scandinavians appear to have built only rowboats until the sixth century. Then through the sixth to eighth centuries Scandinavian rowboats evolved into typical Viking longships with large sails and solid keels. They were built in various sizes but to a more or less standard configuration. Long and low, they were rather broad-beamed, which gave them stability in the rough North Sea and in the Atlantic. Their strength was increased further by the method of planking the hulls; boards were overlapped and then nailed or riveted together, rather than simply being butted and nailed to frames as was the case in the south. This technique allowed more solid caulking and produced a vessel more seaworthy in heavy weather. And their shallow draught allowed them to be brought close inshore or to ply quite shallow rivers.

On the other hand there were drawbacks to these ships too. They were open or only partially decked, offering little shelter for the crew. They were guided by a long sweep oar, they had a single square sail and they had a shallow though strong keel; all of this resulted in rather poor steering control. Running before the wind they were sleek and fast, but in a crosswind they drifted off course wildly. (At least part of the credit for the Norse discoveries of Greenland and North America would appear to be due to the inability to hold a course.) In consequence, the long voyages across the open sea must excite great admiration, for the ships really were ill-suited for such uses. But they were ideal as raiders, for they could slip along the coasts close inshore, looking for targets, and they could probe far up the rivers for the plunder of inland cities.

The men are as interesting as the ships. Noble chiefs often commanded while staunch peasant boys made up the crew, though in at least one famous instance some Vikings told the Franks that they were all equals. If the wind died they rowed. And when they happened upon a likely target, they disembarked and leaped to the attack with sword or battleaxe. Actually they seem not to have been particularly redoubtable fighters, as they had little success at first against Europe's professional military caste. Their complete indiscipline on early plundering raids and their relatively primitive weapons were quite surpassed by evolving European political organization and by the mounted knight. Charlemagne built a string of watch towers and beacons that largely protected the coasts of Gaul until well into the reign of his son, and late in the ninth century Alfred the Great organized generally successful campaigns against Scandinavians who had settled in England.

Though the large invading forces of the late Viking period appear to have learned something of planning and discipline, the private raiders seem to have been quite ill-organized. Sometimes they went into battle in a drunken stupor after an all-night drinking bout during which alcohol, songs and epics of great heroes were supposed to arouse their courage to its highest pitch. The seeming paradox of their primitivism and their devastating impact upon Europe and the British Isles is explained by their mobility and their choice of targets. Appearing suddenly, plundering and burning, and then withdrawing, the Viking raiders rarely fought pitched battles with European armies. Usually they were opposed only by the peasants or monks who were their victims, and by the time the noble knights could gather to resist them, they were completing their withdrawal to their ships, in which they sailed away safe from pursuit. If a selected target mounted a stiff resistance, they often abandoned it in favor of a different objective. One source of plunder was as good as another. So they hit the weakest aspect of Europe's military establishment— the slowness of mobilization. In contrast to the tactics that finally crushed the Saxons, it was not possible for European forces to retaliate with strikes at their base areas, destroying their homes and crops.

In the last years of the eighth century and the first half of the ninth century the raiders struck without warning against isolated monasteries and small villages, looted, and then returned to their homelands safely guarded by the sea. But about the middle of the ninth century the nature of the Viking incursions began to change. The men from the north had grown familiar with the lands they preyed upon, and a half-century of raiding had built a large reserve of experienced warriors. They grew bolder, and they learned to act together. Fleets as well as individual ships began to prowl, and they attempted more ambitious targets.

Early in the 840s a Viking fleet entered the Seine and plundered the city of Rouen, and another ascended the Loire and sacked Nantes. The latter force also set another precedent, establishing a winter camp on an island off the river's mouth instead of returning north. Early in the 880s England witnessed the same phenomenon as Danish raiders established a permanent base in the mouth of the Thames. And about the same period Swedish adventurers, called Varangians, founded settlements in Russia, where the East Slavic state was just emerging, first at Novgorod—southeast of the Gulf of Finland—and then at Kiev—to the south on the middle reaches of the Dnieper. Thus the Vikings settled both east and west.

From these new European bases they quickly extended the range of their depredations. Soon they had probed inland along the Loire and the Seine valleys as far as Orleans and Paris, had struck the south through the Garonne and had rounded Gibraltar into the Mediterranean and ascended the Rhone valley—raiding Spain, Morocco and the Balearic Islands along the way. England suffered as severely, for there Danish raids turned into conquest in the last quarter of the ninth century, and before the situation was stabilized by the Anglo-Saxon king of Wessex, the Danes held most of England north of the Thames. In the east the Swedes who were settled in Russia were developing contacts with the Byzantine Empire, sometimes raiding, sometimes trading, sometimes hiring out as mercenaries. So in all quarters the new peoples from the north were becoming ever more intimately associated with the older settlers in Europe.

It was only about the beginning of the tenth century that the northmen began to be assimilated. By the middle of the century the kings of Wessex had succeeded in subjugating the Danish invaders to their rule and to Christianity, and they governed an England that was jointly Anglo-Saxon and Danish. On the continent a sort of stability was achieved in 911 when the West Frankish king, Charles the Simple, granted lands at the mouth of the Seine to the Viking chief Rollo on the conditions that he defend the area and accept Christianity. Thus the nucleus of a new principality was established, which would develop—with later additions—into the powerful duchy of Normandy. Thereafter Rollo's band protected the Seine and Channel coast and helped to protect the Loire, so that during the next two or three decades the Viking raids on the West Frankish Kingdom died out.

Something similar occurred in Russia where the Swedish invaders, always relatively few in number, were absorbed rather quickly into the nascent East Slavic state at the end of the ninth and beginning of the tenth centuries. Western Russia was consolidated around Kiev, and through contacts with Byzantium the prince of Kiev was converted to the Greek form of Christianity just before the end of the tenth century. Thus, large numbers of Scandinavians eventually were settled and Christianized (at least nominally) in more southerly parts of Europe but during the ninth and tenth centuries they spread destruction far and wide, and the first bloom of cultural revival in England and the West Frankish lands was crushed.

The foregoing discussion would seem to suggest that the Eastern Franks were fortunate. While the Anglo-Saxons, Celts and West Franks were being ravaged by the Danes and the Norwegians, and the East Slavs were being invaded by the Swedes, the largely land-locked East Frankish Kingdom was spared the Vikings except for some raiding along the Baltic coast. But the Eastern Franks did not escape the fire and sword. From the east—whence the Goths and the Huns and the Avars had descended upon Europe—appeared a new fierce Turkish people, the Magyars. The devastation of central Europe simply came a bit later than the sacking of the West.

When the Varangians penetrated Russia, the Magyars occupied the northwest coastal area of the Black Sea, and together with the Avars, whom Charlemagne had conquered and confined to the plains of Hungary, constituted a sort of wedge between the southern Slavs of the Balkans and the East Slavs of Russia. At the end of the ninth century, under pressure from the Varangians, the Magyars migrated westward into Hungary where they joined the remaining Avars, to whom they were related. Then through the first half of the tenth century they raided into Germany, reaching as far west as the Rhine valley and on one occasion even probing deep into eastern France and sacking Rheims. Not until the middle of the century were they stopped, when the East Frankish king imposed a crushing defeat upon them, confining them—like their predecessors —to the Hungarian plains. In the year 1000 the Magyars were converted to Christianity by St. Stephen, and from then onward they, too, constituted a permanent element in the population of Christian Europe. Though the Magyar raids had lasted less than half as long as the Viking depredations, they had been terribly destructive.

Finally a word should be said about the southern borders of Europe at the end of the tenth century. In the east the Byzantine emperors had concentrated their attention upon their rich Asian provinces which were threatened first by the Persians and then by the Arabs. The European provinces had been left largely to their own devices, and during the seventh and eighth centuries there was a considerable alteration of population. It was during this period that Slavs and a Turkish people, the Bulgars, moved into the Balkans, and they and the Avars devastated the European provinces to the walls of Byzantium for the next two hundred years, until a Byzantine emperor crushed them and absorbed Bulgaria into the empire about A. D. 1000.

The rise of Mohammedanism and the rapid expansion of the Arabs from the second quarter of the seventh century onward had accomplished a major transformation of the balance of power in the Mediterranean. They held all of the eastern lands bordering that sea south of Asia Minor, and they had spread westward to occupy the whole of the North African coast and Spain, crushing the Visigothic Kingdom in the latter area in 711. In fact the expansion had halted only when the Moslems crossed the Pyrenees into Frankish lands and encountered Charles Martel's force, as was noted previously. Internal dissension sprang up during the attempts to consolidate these vast conquests, and the dynamic of expansion was never regained, but about the year 1000 the power of Islam remained the dominant force in the Mediterranean.

Italy was divided. Most of the peninsula was at least nominally under the control of the Holy Roman Emperor, but the Byzantines held several fortified positions from Venice in the northeast through coastal areas in the extreme south to Naples in the southwest, and the Moslems held Sicily. Fighting among these factions was endemic, and Italy—once the center of Western civilization—was torn and broken.

THE EARLY CAROLINGIANS

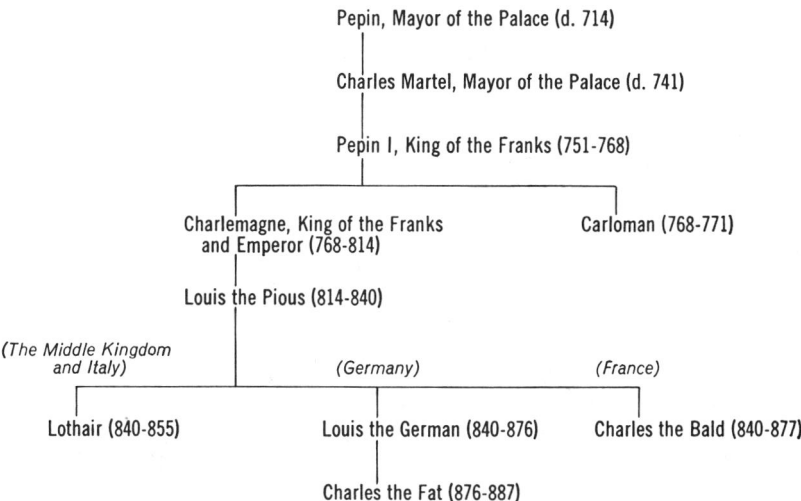

THE SAXON AND FRANCONIAN KINGS

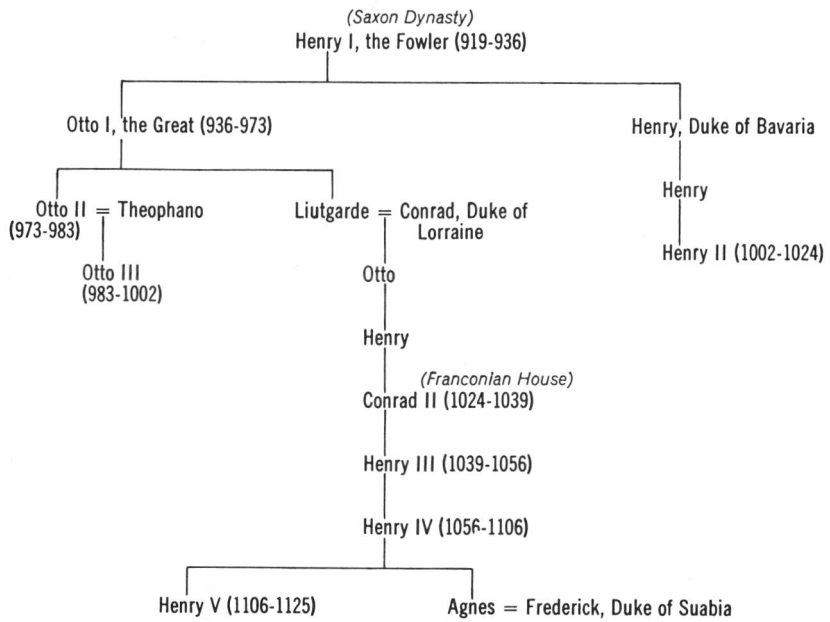

THE NORMAN AND ANGEVIN KINGS

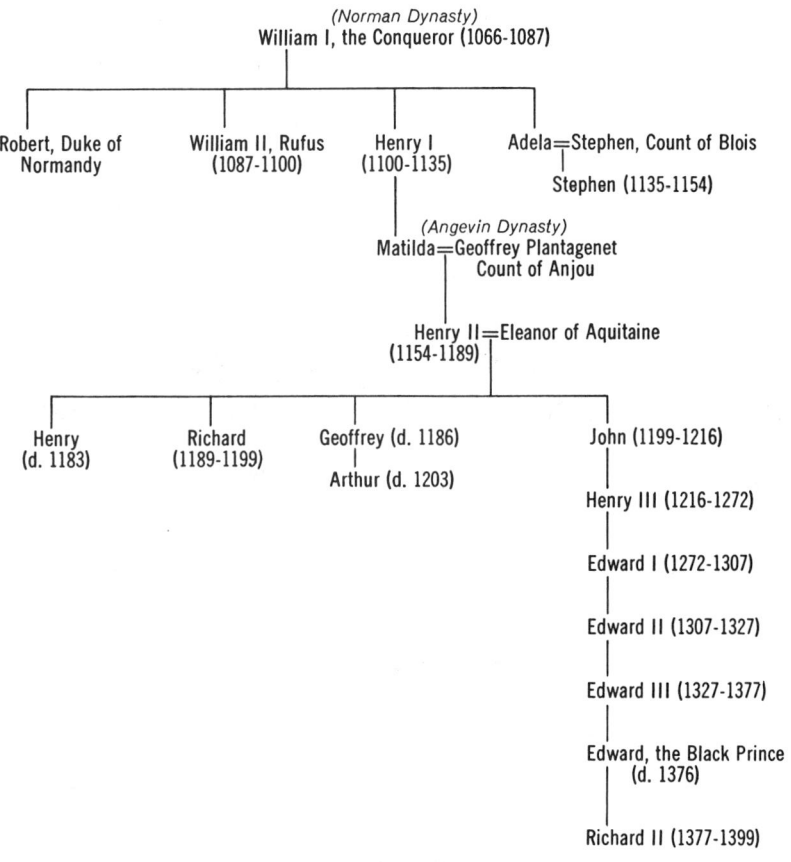

Chapter 12

The Birth of Feudal Monarchy

During the ninth and tenth centuries, domestic quarrels and foreign invasions weakened Carolingian monarchical power to the advantage of the great nobility. Some noblemen succeeded in exacting concessions of land and authority from the kings as the price of their support in civil wars, while others achieved comparable gains as leaders of the defense against the Vikings and Magyars; by the late tenth century these trends had resulted in new ruling families and new patterns of government in both the western and eastern Frankish kingdoms. During the same period in England, the Saxons composed their differences in the face of the Viking threat, establishing a strong monarchy for a time, and then they collapsed completely before an invasion from Normandy in the middle of the eleventh century. Thus, England also developed new governmental patterns.

In the West Frankish Kingdom the decline of the Carolingians was related directly to the effects of the Viking raids. In the late ninth century a nobleman called Robert the Strong was sent by the Carolingian king to defend the Loire Valley against Viking incursions. Though he had only indifferent success in fulfilling this commission, he proved very successful in acquiring new lands for himself, several counties between the Loire and Seine Rivers, emerging as a powerful magnate of the kingdom. In 885 Robert's son Odo commanded the successful defense of Paris against a Viking attack, and a few years later the West Frankish nobility chose Odo as king instead of the Carolingian claimant. During the next century the throne alternated between the two families, four Carolingians and three of Odo's descendants holding it at one time or another, and then in 987 it passed definitively from Carolingian control with the accession of Hugh Capet, from whom the new ruling family derived its name, Capetian.

Hugh Capet (987–996) inaugurated policies so successful that his direct descendants ruled until 1328. Perhaps the most notable of these policies was his decision to associate his son with his rule during his own lifetime, with the consequence that the succession was not disputed. Continued by Hugh Capet's descendants, this practice negated the elective principle of Germanic monarchy so effectively that the French crown became hereditary. In addition, Capet began what usually is called the "domainal policy," concentration upon effective rule of his family's personal lands while avoiding interference with the great nobles who were legally his vassals but were actually his equals or superiors in power; thus he avoided antagonizing dangerous rivals while building a solid foundation for his dynasty.

In consequence of the domainal policy, the Capetian monarchy of the eleventh century was very different from that of Charlemagne. The kings ruled directly only in the Ile de France, their personal lands, contenting themselves in the rest of the kingdom with a vague suzerainty that produced prestige and a small revenue but no effective political control. They did not pretend to legislate for the whole kingdom, nor had they an administrative apparatus of controllable counts and *missi dominici*. Outside the Ile de France, great feudal lords governed their own domains as the king governed his, limited only by a few minor financial and legal obligations of their vassalage. On the other hand, the kings had a few advantages no other feudal lords could claim. They stood at the apex of the feudal pyramid, the only lords in the kingdom who had no overlord. They enjoyed the prestige of being the successors of Clovis and Charlemagne, anointed as God's lieutenants at their coronation. Finally, they benefitted directly from their special relationship to the church, both from the general support of the clergy, who saw the kings as the most viable alternative to the instability and the endemic violence of feudal rivalries, and from their regalian rights over two dozen bishoprics and three dozen monasteries all over the kingdom, rights which provided both revenue and control of appointments. These advantages were enough to maintain the Capetians for a century and a half, and only about the middle of the twelfth century did they embark on an effort to expand their effective political authority more widely in the kingdom.

Political development in the East Frankish Kingdom from the mid-tenth to mid-twelfth centuries followed a course rather different from that in the west, largely because conditions were quite different. Most of Germany never had been part of the Roman Empire, so civilization had come only with the missionary work of the church and with the conquests of Charlemagne. Thus, Germany had not developed so elaborate a pattern of hierarchical feudalism and had remained closer to its tribal origins, a sort of ethnic tradition exemplified by the survival of large regional subdivisions called "Stem Duchies"—Bavaria, Swabia, Saxony and Franconia. In the face of strong traditions and popular support of the Stem Dukes, Carolingian patterns of administration by controllable officials never had been established so strongly as in the west, and under the pressure of Viking and Magyar raids these patterns broke down altogether while the Stem Dukes grew stronger. One result was that the Carolingians were abandoned early in the tenth century, and weak kings were chosen or the throne was left vacant, which left the political power of the Stem Dukes uncontested.

In Germany as in France, however, churchmen favored the authority of a king rather than a number of dukes, and their arguments were accepted when it became evident that only unified leadership could curb the Magyar raids. In 919 the dukes reluctantly chose the strongest of their number, Henry the Fowler, duke of Saxony, as king, and he set to work immediately to rebuild the monarchy. Henry (919–936) tried to reestablish royal control of the counts, aided churchmen in the recovery of lands that had been usurped and gave them the power of counts in their lands, and led effective military campaigns against the Magyars. His son, Otto I (936–973) continued these policies with considerable success. He managed to acquire control of Franconia as well as his own Saxony, so that he held two of the four Stem Duchies; he continued to support bishops and abbots so that several became important secular as well as ecclesiastical lords and constituted an effective check upon the power of rural dukes; and he imposed a crushing defeat upon the Magyars in 955, which confined them to the Hungarian plain. In addition, Otto conquered Burgundy and Lombardy, thus adding important parts of the Frankish Middle Kingdom to his own domains, and as a logical conclusion to these successes he went to Rome and was crowned Holy Roman Emperor in 962. But though Otto I had reunited a vast territory and had revived the imperial title, his authority rested upon weak foundations. Only in Saxony did he have reliable local support; in south Germany the dukes of Bavaria and Swabia were more rivals than vassals, and in the rest of his domains he depended upon ecclesiatical fiefs and his army. His son and grandson proved unable to maintain the personal authority that he had created, and in the second quarter of the eleventh century the German monarchy underwent another transformation when the crown passed to the Franconian House, called Salians.

The first of the Salian emperors, Conrad (1024–1039), did little more than try to recover the authority lost in Germany while the late Ottonians were involved in Italy, but under his successors, Henry III (1039–1056) and Henry IV (1056–1106) the Salians inaugurated contentious new policies, the most controversial of which was the appointment of a class of untitled royal officials called *ministeriales.* These officials, completely dependent upon royal favor and wholly devoted to royal interests, were given command of castles all through the realm and were intended deliberately to undermine the power of the Stem Dukes and the powerful princes who had developed under the Ottonians; naturally they aroused great resentment. In addition Henry III encouraged the work of the monastic reformers known as the Cluniacs, who had support in the papal *curia;* he seems never to have realized that one of the chief aims of the reformers was to free ecclesiastical appointments from secular control, a goal which would undermine the foundations of the German monarchy since it depended so heavily upon the ecclesiastical princes whose powers the Ottonians had expanded. The harvest of these dangerous policies was reaped in the reign of Henry IV, princely revolt and a long-drawn quarrel with the papacy.

This great struggle, which broke the power of the Salian emperors, is called the Investiture Controversy, because the overt issue was the right to invest bishops with the symbols of their spiritual offices; the real issue, however, was the selection and appointment of high churchmen. As a consequence of policies begun by the Ottonians, the

German prelates were one of the most important bases of the imperial administration; the emperor considered this role their first obligation, and naturally he wished to control their appointments. By contrast, the religious reformers wished to free ecclesiastical appointments from secular control; to them, the prelate's first obligation was to the church, and his selection was a matter for the clergy of his diocese. The issue became a crisis with the election to the papacy of the fiery reformer Hildebrand, who took the papal title of Gregory VII (1073–1085).

Pope Gregory did not limit his claims to the empire, but he made his strongest effort there, for Henry IV was the most powerful prince in Europe, and if he surrendered, other princes would be likely to do the same. The quarrel became acrimonious; Gregory excommunicated Henry, while Henry called Gregory a false pope, improperly elected. Generally the German clergy, Henry's appointees, supported the emperor, while the German princes, who opposed Henry politically, supported the papacy. The outcome was a hollow victory for Gregory's successors and disaster for the empire. Compromise early in the twelfth century provided that diocesan clergy should elect bishops in the presence of the monarch or his representative; this provision made elections a farce and left effective control with the secular ruler. The only real gains were made by the German princes who managed to seize imperial lands and authority during the bitter struggle. For one more generation the Salians continued to hold the crown, but the reign of Henry IV's son was wracked by civil wars, and when he died without heirs in 1125, the Salian monarchy died with him.

The violence that marked the last quarter of the eleventh century and the first quarter of the twelfth century changed the whole political structure of Germany. During the turbulence freemen were forced into serfdom, and lesser nobles became the vassals of princes; at the same time the princes usurped royal offices and fiefs, making them hereditary, and built a multitude of castles to defend their recent gains. By the middle of the twelfth century manorialism and vassalage were established firmly in Germany, but they constituted a truncated feudalism, lacking an apex, for the hierarchy culminated in a number of princes, over whom the emperor reigned as no more than a figurehead.

England's political experience from the mid-tenth to mid-twelfth centuries was unique, chiefly because of invasion and conquest. The strong Saxon monarchy that had been built by Alfred the Great

(871–899) continued through the tenth century, and probably was the most effective government in western Europe. While an elective principle survived, the crown tended to remain with Alfred's descendants, the royal house of Wessex. Every able-bodied man owed military service at the king's summons, which provided the basis for an army. And the kings drew revenue from many scattered estates that formed the crown lands, from fines collected in criminal courts and, after 991, from a land tax called *danegeld* which originally was a levy imposed to pay tribute to Danish invaders. In addition the kings enjoyed extensive control of local officials called sheriffs and of prelates of the court.

In the middle of the eleventh century a succession dispute left this attractive kingdom vulnerable to invasion. Upon the death of the Saxon king, Edward the Confessor (1035–1066), the crown was conferred upon Harold Godwin, Wessex magnate. However, there were two other powerful contenders, Duke William of Normandy, who had secured papal blessings for his claims, and Harold's brother Tostig, the latter allied with the king of Norway. In 1066 both launched independent attacks upon Harold, who succeeded in defeating the Norwegians but was defeated and killed by Duke William, who assumed the crown as William I (1066–1087).

Though the Norman conquest had profound consequences for the future of England, its immediate impact ought not to be exaggerated. Though scattered fighting continued for five years, the country did not suffer extensive military operations. As William considered himself Edward the Confessor's rightful successor, he promised to maintain ancient customs; moreover, Saxon landholders who had not opposed him openly retained their property, simply becoming his vassals, though the lands of others who had resisted were expropriated to reward his followers. Perhaps the greatest single impact of the conquest was the establishment of more fully developed continental feudalism and manorialism; both newly settled Normans and surviving Saxon landowners were compelled to accept the military obligations common to feudal relationships in Normandy, providing for an army of about 5,000 knights. Common farmers, most of whom had been freemen in Saxon England, were depressed into serfdom. To record the many obligations owed to him, William inaugurated a great survey of the value and tax assessment of English landholdings, called *Domesday Book*.

In the century following the conquest, the Normans introduced a number of innovations into England. One of the most notable was castle-building, begun by William I to tighten his hold on the country and to assure his route of retreat in case of a successful Saxon rising; his successors continued this construction program, and by 1150 England was defended by a network of about 1200 castles, which made another successful invasion very unlikely. Henry I (1100–1135) added improvements in the fiscal and judicial administration, permanent treasury officials in the exchequer and roving royal judges. After his death, quarrels over the succession plunged England into two decades of civil war during which the barons usurped great authority; by the middle of the twelfth century the English king appeared as helpless before his vassals as did the emperor in Germany, but thanks to the institutional growth encouraged by the early Norman kings, there remained in England the basis for a powerful royal revival.

Political developments between the middle of the twelfth century and the middle of the thirteenth century had enduring effects in the Holy Roman Empire. The crown passed to the House of Hohenstaufen, and a vigorous attempt to revive imperial power ensued. Emperor Frederick Barbarossa (1152–1190) did not attempt to govern Germany outside his own Duchy of Swabia. Instead, he concentrated upon establishing effective control of Burgundy and northern and central Italy. The new policy brought him into conflict with developing Italian towns and with the papacy, but after some military reverses he achieved considerable success through diplomacy. He granted autonomy to the towns in return for revenue, and he neutralized the papacy through a marriage alliance with the Kingdom of Sicily, which established Hohenstaufen positions flanking the Papal States both north and south. By the time of Barbarossa's death, the empire had been transformed totally; Germany had become a feudal monarchy in which the emperor was only the suzerain of the princes, but the House of Hohenstaufen enjoyed extensive revenues outside of Germany, and in Swabia and Italy it had solid political bases.

The short, troubled reign of Barbarossa's son, Henry VI (1190–1197), produced little that was remarkable except the integration of Sicily into Hohenstaufen possessions, but under Henry's son, Frederick II (1215–1250), the great struggle between pope and emperor for control of Italy was renewed. Fortuitously, Frederick's chief rival in Germany was defeated crushingly in a war with the king of France, and relieved of that concern Frederick practically abandoned Germany to its princes so he could concentrate his efforts on

Italy. Although his brilliant court in Sicily and his fascinating personality led his contemporaries to call him "the wonder of the world," Frederick achieved little politically, and after his death the House of Hohenstaufen declined rapidly. The German princes and the north Italian towns maintained their independence; papal fortunes revived in central Italy; and then the last Hohenstaufen lost Sicily to a brother of the king of France. After Frederick II the imperial crown was little more than an empty title, though one much fought over; there were no more revivals of imperial authority as a political force until the sixteenth century.

The period from the middle of the twelfth century to the end of the thirteenth century witnessed extraordinary and closely related developments in the two western monarchies. King Louis VII of France (1137–1180) had married Eleanor of Aquitaine, heiress to vast domains in the western and southwestern parts of the kingdom, but he had drawn little advantage from these lands as the local nobility proved quite ungovernable. Thus, when Louis desired the annulment of his marriage, chiefly because Eleanor had given him no sons, the loss of Aquitaine did not seem very significant. However, no sooner was the annulment pronounced, in 1152, than Eleanor married again, and Aquitaine represented a very important addition to the domains of her new husband, Henry Plantagenet, count of Anjou, duke of Normandy, and two years later, king of England as Henry II (1154–1189). Thus Eleanor's remarriage brought together under a single rule the kingdom of England and most of western France from Normandy to the Pyrenees, creating what often is called the "Angevin Empire." Louis VII protested feebly because as feudal suzerain for Henry's continental lands he should have been consulted, but he could accomplish little against the vigorous Angevin monarch. Henry II and his son Richard the Lionhearted (1189–1199) pursued a policy of integration of their lands, and for the remainder of the twelfth century the French kings faced western vassals far stronger than themselves.

Louis VII did his best to maintain his dynasty, and a new marriage with the House of Blois and Champagne brought powerful support to the French crown and produced the needed heir, Philip II, called Augustus (1180–1223). By his own marriage Philip later assured the alliance of the Count of Flanders and laid the foundations for a French recovery. But as both of the first two Angevins had real military talent, neither Louis VII nor Philip Augustus could accomplish much against them, and it was only when Richard the Lionhearted died and was succeeded by his brother John (1199–1216) that fortune turned in favor of the French crown.

Philip Augustus understood the value of legal position in his struggle with John, and he exploited the possibilities of his role as feudal suzerain to the fullest. When John quarreled with one of his vassals and the latter appealed to Philip as John's overlord, Philip promptly escalated the issue into a major confrontation. He summoned John to appear before him, and when John refused, Philip's court declared him a disobedient vassal within the terms of his feudal contract and pronounced all his fiefs forfeit. Thus Philip acquired a clear legal right to take whatever he was strong enough to seize of John's continental possessions. By a combination of sieges and bribery of castle commanders, he secured one after another of the Angevin fortresses during the next few years, and by 1205 he had taken all of John's northern French lands and had won the support of many of the southern barons. The "Angevin Empire" survived only in the coastal regions of the southwest, Guienne and Gascony. John attempted to recover, attacking Anjou himself while his ally, Otto of Germany, Frederick II's rival, invaded France from the north. However, Philip Augustus smashed the German force at the Battle of Bouvines in 1214, one of the crucial military engagements of medieval Europe. As a result of this victory, John was forced to withdraw to England, the French crown's conquests in the west were secure, and Frederick II was free to embark upon his Italian adventures.

The great struggle between the Capetians and the Angevins stimulated important developments in royal government. Henry II increased the revenues of the English crown considerably by reviewing and raising the assessment of monies his vassals paid him in lieu of military service, by increasing his fees for royal consent on such occasions as the marriage of a vassal or the inheritance of a fief, and by expanding the operations of the royal courts which brought large sums to the treasury through fines. By-products of the last policy were a considerable expansion of the common law and the beginning of the extensive use of juries. Henry II's sons continued his practices, but the growing strength of the crown evoked a baronial reaction. King John, though a competent enough administrator, was never popular with his vassals, and after the humiliating loss of most of his continental possessions to Philip Augustus, his English barons revolted against him. Largely through the influence of the Archbishop of Canterbury, Stephen Langton, the barons pressed for general concessions instead of satisfaction of specific private grievances, and John was forced to agree. The document that embodied the agreements, *Magna Carta,* basically was a statement of the terms of feudal obligations and a definition of the powers of royal government in the early thirteenth century; most of its specific provisions were outdated quickly, but its limitation of the king's right to collect money and its requirement that arrests and punishments follow proper legal action amounted in fact to an admission that the king was bound by law, an admission from which has grown much English legal and constitutional tradition.

John died a year after his assent to the *Magna Carta,* and during the long reign of his weak-willed son, Henry III (1216–1272), the baronial reaction continued to erode the position of the crown. But at the end of the thirteenth century Henry's son, Edward I (1272–1307), again provided vigorous royal leadership, and feudal monarchy in England reached its fullest development. Under Edward I specialization of the royal administration continued, with further elaboration of the exchequer and the courts that had been created by Henry I and Henry II. But perhaps the most important political development of this reign was the growth of parliament in 1295. English kings long had consulted barons, prelates, knights and townsmen concerning various matters for which they felt the need of support; Edward I's innovation was to bring all of these elements together in one assembly, and by the end of his reign such a convocation of the whole realm—the king in parliament—generally was recognized as necessary to decisions regarding legal changes and tax levies.

A comparable governmental development took place in France during this same period. Philip Augustus' conquests increased enormously the revenues of the French crown, finally rendering it stronger than any of its vassals. This sudden increase in the lands governed directly by the king necessitated expansion and improvement of the crown's financial and judicial administration, and Philip created new salaried officials for this purpose, *baillis* and *senechals;* as numerous assistants to these officials were appointed, a rather large bureaucracy developed rapidly.

Philip's son reigned too briefly to be effective, but his grandson, Louis IX (1226–1270), called St. Louis, contributed importantly to the continued growth of the French crown, not so much through institutional developments as through the enormous respect for the royal personage inspired by his piety and his reputation for justice. It must not be assumed that these qualities implied weakness; though personally devout St. Louis staunchly defended the independence of the French church against papal pretensions, though famous for scrupulously honest judgments he vigorously enforced his jurisdictional rights when they were contested by his vassals, and throughout his reign he contended with considerable success against the private warfare that was endemic to feudal society.

Under St. Louis' son and grandson, Philip III (1270–1285) and Philip IV (1285–1314), these policies continued, though a baronial reaction forced Philip IV to grant charters resembling *Magna Carta* except that they were regional rather than national. The elaboration of the royal government, with specialized sections, also paralleled English developments. Philip Augustus had improved treasury procedures considerably, and under Philip IV this effort came to fruition with the establishment of the *chambre des comptes,* which resembled the exchequer. St. Louis had established his chief law court as a more or less permanent body called the *parlement* of Paris, and under Philip IV this court developed specialized sections. Like Edward I, King Philip IV recognized the advantage to the crown of support by a broadly representative body, and he fused several of the assemblies that the crown was in the habit of consulting, convening the first estates general in 1302.

There were, however, some important differences between English and French government. Most notably, France was larger and more populous than England, and the French king never was able to make decisions of the estates general binding in detail upon the whole realm as was the English king; in France, a multitude of regional assemblies continued and had to be dealt with even after general agreement in the estates general. This both reduced the estates general's value to the crown and impeded its capacity to present a unified opposition to the king. In addition, the French government used far more paid professional administrators than did the English government, which continued to rely heavily upon local landowners. Thus, the French bureaucracy developed more of a sense of separateness from the realm, a concept of being over the country rather than of it. This attitude was strengthened by the study of Roman law which contributed to the idea that the king was God's lieutenant on earth and that, consequently, while he had an obligation to rule with justice, he was not bound stringently by custom. Thus, lacking England's compactness, its common law and its dependence upon dedicated amateurism, French government—despite similar institutions—developed along more bureaucratic lines with a consequent alienation of the governing from the governed.

In addition to important governmental development, the thirteenth century also witnessed the growth of a practice in France that was to lead to serious problems for the crown, the designation of large areas as appanages to support younger royal children. That this practice did not lead earlier to considerable alienation of royal domain lands probably was due only to the fact that the royal family was small, for precedents for the establishment of appanages go back at least to Hugh Capet. But the thirteenth and fourteenth century Capetians, and after them the Valois, sired more sons, and providing for them led to the foundation of important new aristocratic houses related to the crown. In one way the creation of appanages probably helped the kings to control the country at last. After the conquests of Philip Augustus the area that owed obedience to the French crown was enormous, and both the state of communications and the rudimentary nature of thirteenth century government precluded direct administration of all of it from Paris. The kings had to trust others to act as their agents. In medieval society only someone of considerable personal stature could command even limited obedience from feudal lords; but most great nobles were more the kings' rivals than their trusted associates, so the use of close relatives probably was a reasonable expedient. The difficulty was that after a generation or two the appanages were held not by the sons or brothers of kings but by cousins, and family ties weakened accordingly. Thus, in late medieval France, while the crown was suppressing the independence of the great fiefs it was creating new princely houses that would prove just as troublesome in the late fourteenth and fifteenth centuries.

Despite the differences noted, certain generalizations are possible about the nature of feudal monarchy. Germany and Italy lie outside the consideration, of course, for in Germany the feudal structure was truncated, without an effective monarchy superior to the princes, and Italy was subdivided into a multitude of jurisdictions. But from the mid-twelfth century to the late thirteenth century feudal monarchy developed along similar lines in France and England, despite differences in detail between the two realms. As conquerors, the English monarchs started from a stronger position, while the foundation of the French monarchy was tribal tradition and election. But both depended originally upon the sanction of the church, and both drew their early revenues largely from the income of personal lands and from irregular fees, known as aids and reliefs, that derived of their positions as feudal overlords. In both realms the development of the monarchy as a dominant institution followed the same course: the exploitation of seigneurial and judicial rights for increased revenues, the specialization of administration for improved efficiency and, finally, the development of representative institutions for more effective consolidation. With the creation of the parliament and the estates general feudal monarchy reached its apogee.

THE CAPETIAN KINGS

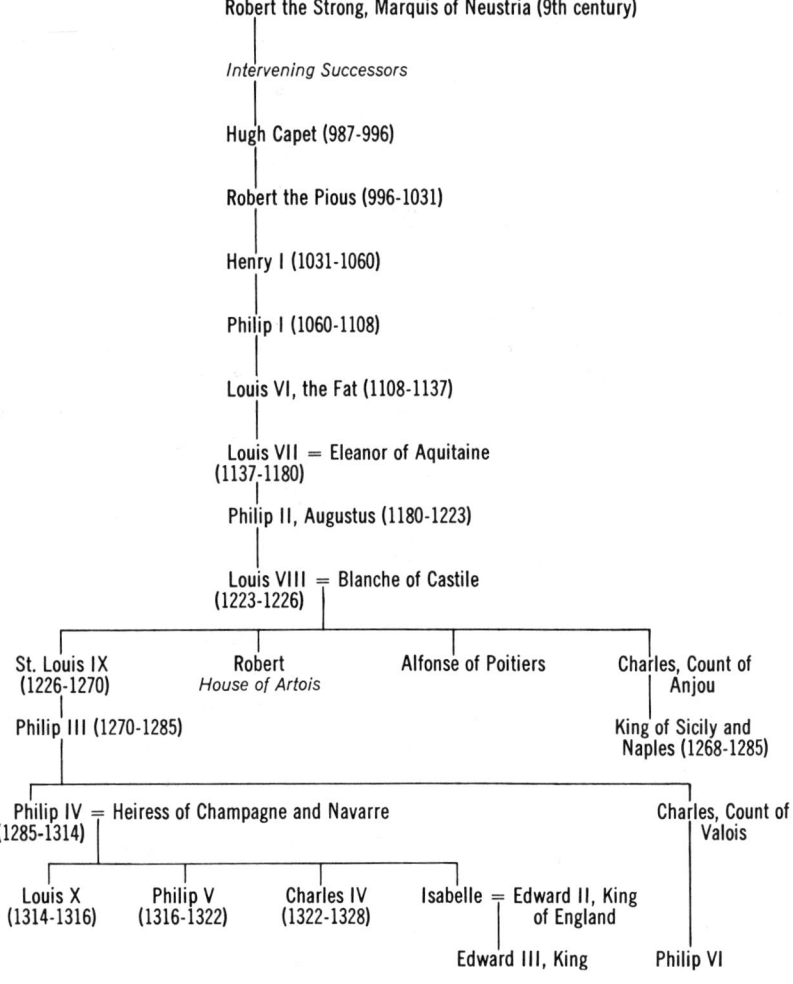

THE HOHENSTAUFEN KINGS

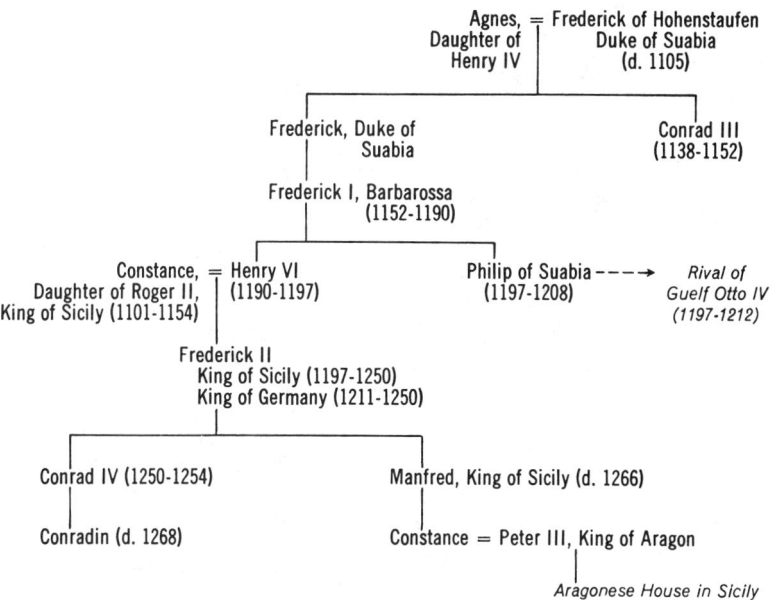

THE VALOIS KINGS

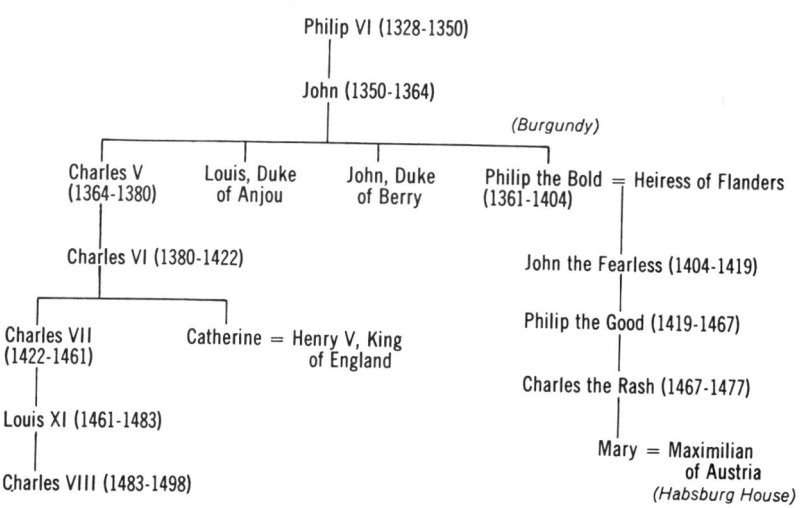

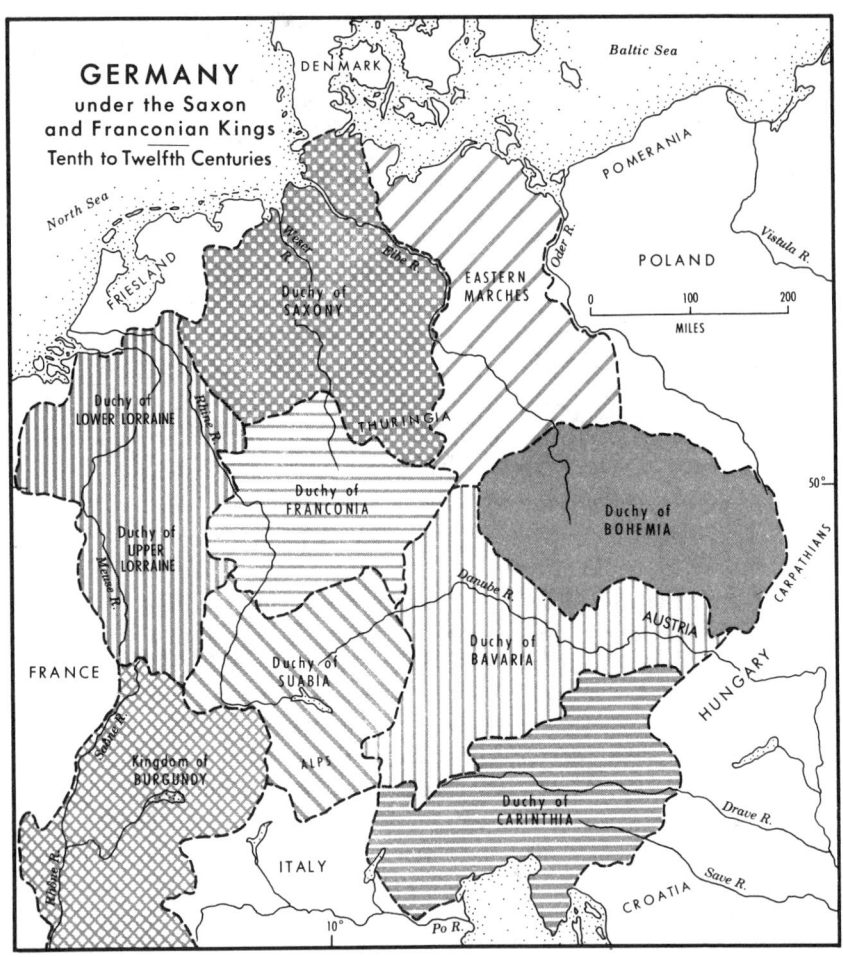

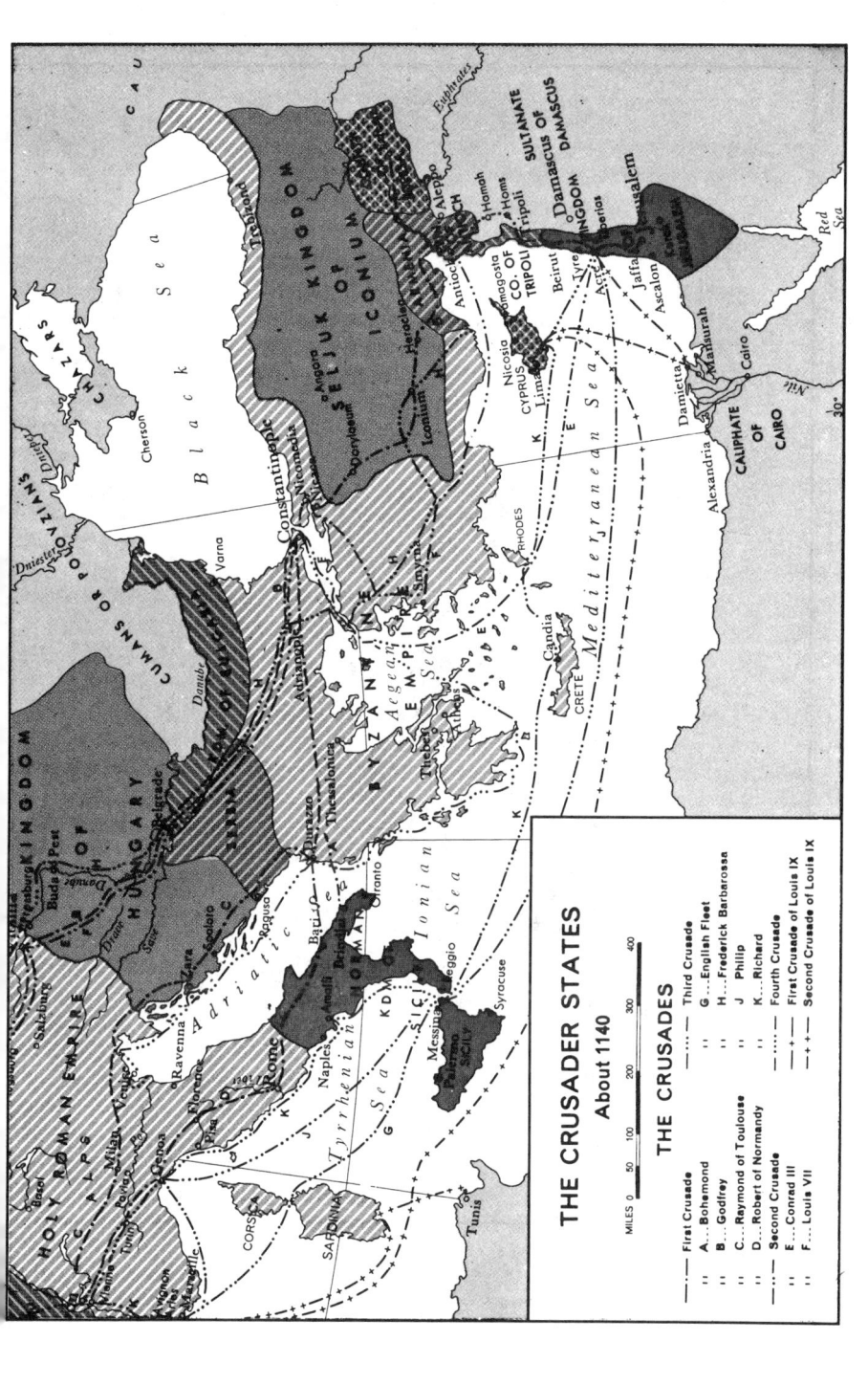

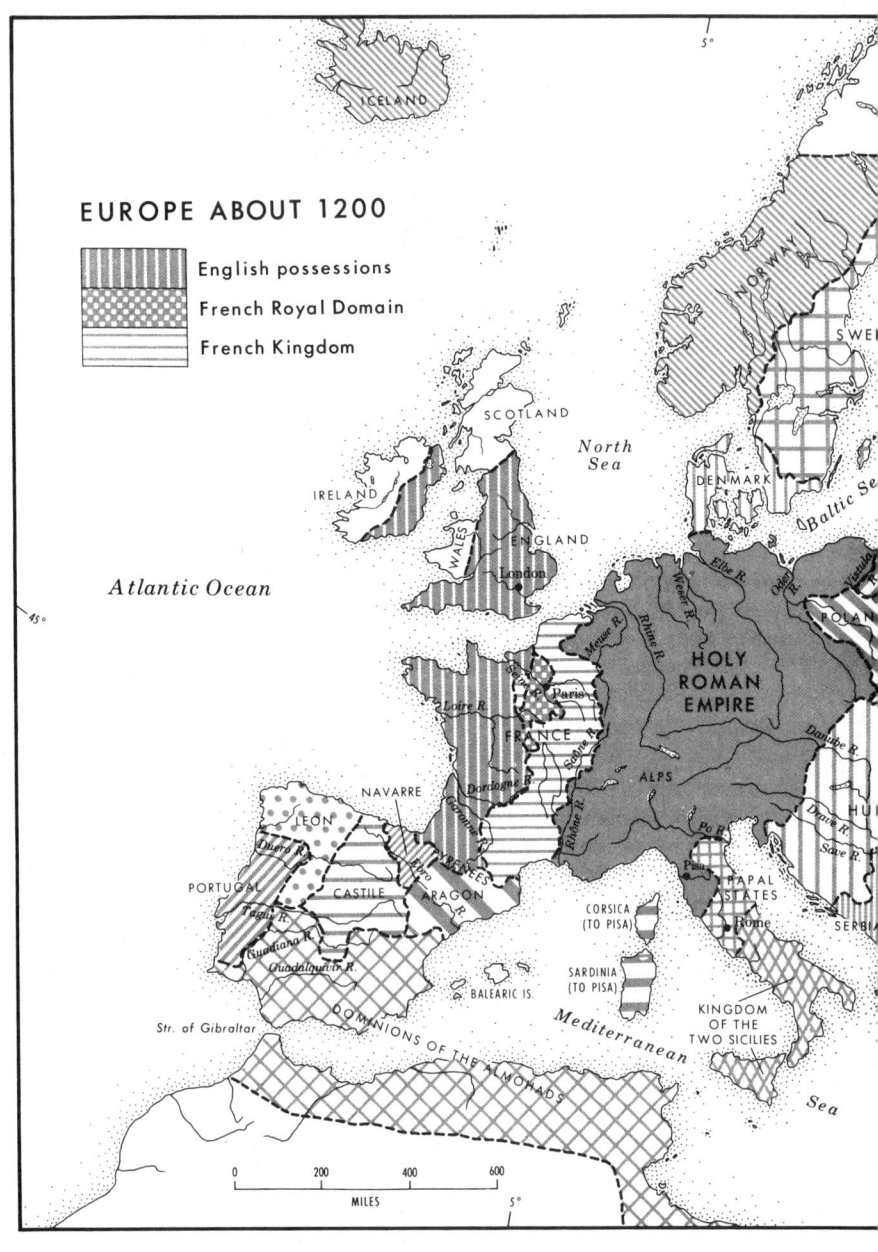

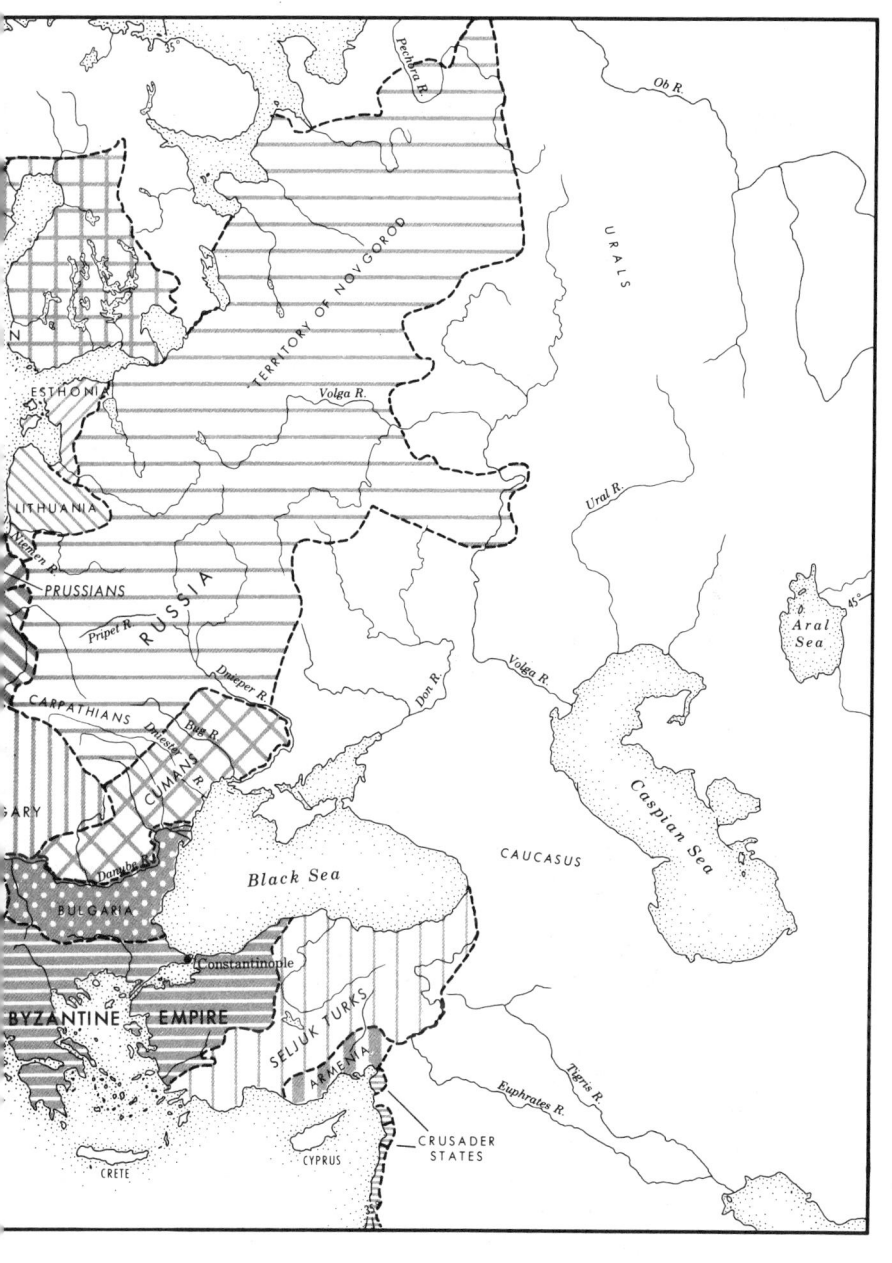

Chapter 13

Merchants, Money, and Social Change

To some extent the political development of Europe between the early eleventh century and the late thirteenth century depended upon important economic and social transformations, of which the most significant were the revival of commerce and the renewal of urban life. These changes created new elements in the old agrarian-aristocratic society and introduced new forms of wealth in money and movable goods rather than in land and rights of *usufruct*.

It should be remembered that the decline of commerce, which began in the late Roman period and reached its nadir in the ninth century, never was absolute. Some universally necessary goods, such as salt and iron, were found only in limited regions, and people outside those regions had to barter to obtain them. Even a trickle of long-distance commerce survived; a few Jewish merchants moved between the Christian and Moslem worlds and carried on a small trade in luxury goods, and the Byzantine navy usually managed to protect the sea route between Constantinople and Venice, along which European grain and lumber were exchanged for the manufactures of eastern craftsmen. But the total commercial activity was of small volume, and it was on a basis of barter rather than money.

Though medieval European trade eventually included such exotic items as Chinese silk and Indonesian spices, the commercial revival began with more mundane goods, such as salt, grain, wine and textiles. The growth of monasticism contributed importantly to this trade, for the monasteries constituted large communities that had to be fed and clothed, and some of the earliest merchants of the European revival were monastic agents called *negotiatores* (negotiators), who offered the wine and wool of their monasteries for salt, iron and other commodities that could not be produced locally. This modest expansion of trade within Europe helped to create the accumulations of capital that made possible a revival of long-distance trade in more luxurious and consequently more costly goods.

In the tenth century, the surviving international trade through Venice had wide repercussions on the north Italian mainland, where the trickle of eastern goods stimulated local manufactures, particularly textiles. In north Italy towns had survived in a modest way, as civil and episcopal administrative centers, and in the tenth century they began manufacturing good cloth. Soon the existence of surplus products, which had little market to the east where it had to compete with the more developed industry of Constantinople, led north Italians to seek markets to the west. Despite the danger from Moslem raiders, ships from Genoa and Pisa began to sail along the coast of southern France in search of trade. When joint expeditions by the two towns succeeded in driving the Moslems from Sardinia and Corsica early in the eleventh century, and Norman knights conquered Sicily in the latter part of the century, the increased security for Christian shipping stimulated the western Mediterranean commerce, and it expanded rapidly.

While north Italy was developing as a focus of revived Mediterranean trade, a smaller but still important commercial center was growing in Flanders, the area that lay generally around the mouths of the Rhine and its tributaries. The region had been famous for its woolen cloth even before the Roman conquest of Gaul, and this industry had continued as one of the few bases of trade in Carolingian times. Though disrupted by the Viking raids, trade had revived as soon as the Counts of Flanders had succeeded in restoring order in the second half of the tenth century, and the area's communications—across the Channel to England, northward to Scandinavia and up the Rhine deep into Germany—soon stimulated a flourishing commerce. In the eleventh century business was so good that the Flemings began importing raw wool from England, and in the twelfth century England became Europe's chief wool producer, mostly for Flemish looms. England's commercial connections with the continent also were stimulated in another way after the conquest of 1066. England's Norman masters refused to abuse their palates with domestic ales, and a very active new trade developed around the importation of wine from France; until the middle of the twelfth century the Seine valley was the chief producer for this trade, shipping through Rouen, and then after the accession of Henry II the Loire valley and the Bordeaux region became important suppliers.

In the twelfth and thirteenth centuries Mediterranean commerce was stimulated considerably by the crusades, chiefly because they provided eastbound cargoes. Until the crusades north Italian merchants confronted the difficult problem that while demand for eastern goods was growing in Europe, there was little that Europeans could sell in the east, and sending ships out in ballast raised costs and reduced profits. The European military expeditions to the Holy Land offered cargoes of men and horses to be transported, and even when the crusaders went overland they expected to be supplied by sea; moreover, the soldiers were followed by hordes of religious pilgrims who wished to visit the Christian holy places, so the transport of passengers continued to be important for rather a long time; and upon returning home these people contributed to the growing demand for fine goods with which they had become familiar while in the East. The once popular notion that the crusades were the basic cause of the revival of commerce in Europe must be considered an exaggeration, for there was an important redevelopment of domestic trade before they began, but it is beyond dispute that the crusades contributed importantly to the expansion of Mediterranean shipping and, hence, to the diversification of the commercial revival throughout Europe.

The opening of a connection between the two trade centers of north Italy and Flanders established the framework for a fuller development of medieval European commerce. Storms, distance, and the threat of Moslem pirates around the Straits of Gibraltar precluded any extensive use of a sea route, so the connection was made overland along the French river valleys that the Romans had traveled long before. From north Italy, merchants sailed to Marseilles, then followed the Rhone and Saône into Champagne, where they could cross easily to rivers that flowed north and west—the Rhine, the Moselle, the Seine and the Loire. This route also presented serious problems in the form of poor roads, bandits and the exactions of feudal lords who charged tolls for the rights of passage across their lands, but nonetheless it was cheaper and more secure than the sea passage; in the twelfth century, merchants began moving silks, spices and Italian horses along this route to be exchanged for the furs, metals and hunting hawks of the north.

Inevitably, the revival of commerce affected the noble elite of European society, and the reactions of its members varied widely. Some noblemen saw merchants simply as focal points of mobile wealth which presented opportunities for pillage, and these robber barons had to be accepted as one of the hazards of trade, necessitating such precautions as armed guards for caravans. Other noblemen considered merchants a source of welcome cash income, for they would pay for the hire of some of the lord's men-at-arms as caravan guards, and their commerce provided tolls from charges on roads and bridges and market taxes from sales. Some few lords, the exceptions, studied the new developments, came to understand the economics involved and used their social position and resources to participate actively for enormous profit; the most notable examples of this latter group were the counts of Champagne.

Located at the junction of routes leading to the great areas of trade and manufacture in north Italy and Flanders, Champagne was situated ideally to develop as a center of exchange for all of Europe, and the counts of Champagne were astute enough to recognize and exploit this potential by sponsoring fairs. The counts established fair grounds at several points in their lands and made a fortune through the services they provided and through taxes on the trade. Probably their most famous fair was the one at Troyes, from which derive the Troy weights still used in the measurement of precious metals and gems. They built and rented out booths, set up police to keep order and judges to settle disputes, and provided money changers to handle the varied coinage that appeared at the fairs—all for a price. They collected tolls as goods were shipped in and out of Champagne and market taxes on sales. The fairs provided a veritable gold mine and the counts made every effort to encourage and protect them, using some of their large income in a new institution called the "money fief" to increase security for those coming to the fairs. Something like this had existed in Merovingian times, before the waning of a monetary economy had tended to equate benefices with grants of land; money fiefs were simply grants of cash rather than of land, and the counts of Champagne used them extensively to enlist barons along the main routes to Champagne as protectors of merchants coming to trade. Through the twelfth and thirteenth centuries the fairs of Champagne were among the greatest markets in Europe, but they waned in the fourteenth century; for one thing, the county came into the possession of the French crown which overcharged the merchants, and for another, effective competition was developed further east by a league of German towns called the Hansa and further west by sea-borne convoys of Venetian galleys sailing to England and Flanders.

Participation by nobles in the new commerce on the scale of the counts of Champagne was rare, but no great lord could escape entirely the impact of economic change. Undeniably life was becoming more comfortable—and more costly; the nobles' need for money grew and grew. Instead of rough cloth woven by local women, lords and ladies learned to desire the fine products of great textile centers. Instead of crude weapons made locally, the noble lord hungered for a fine blade from Damascus or Toledo. Instead of a long winter of smoked, salted or tainted meat, noble families desired the variety offered by spices from the distant east. The list was long, and the cost was great.

One of the more obvious results of the revival of trade was the redevelopment of towns as centers of production and commerce. As noted previously, some modest agglomerations of population had survived in Europe, usually around a noble's residence, an episcopal center, a great monastery or some combination of the three. Naturally such communities had resident craftsmen such as blacksmiths, carpenters, millers and weavers, and in some instances increased production projected these communities into the commercial revival, as has been observed in north Italy. In other cases, the location of such towns and the attitude of the local nobleman attracted merchants who settled there and established a base for their operations; generally this development required that the community be on a good route and that its overlord be willing to accept money payments in lieu of personal services and levies of goods. But whatever their origins, the new commercial communities required a degree of personal freedom and possessory rights that had no place in the older feudal and manorial social patterns.

A common arrangement was for a lord to issue a charter which, in effect, made the town a corporate person and made the townsmen collectively responsible for obligations calculated in money rather than goods and services. These charters delegated important powers of internal administration to the town, such as the right to establish a governing council, courts and law codes; such delegation allowed the development of commercial law, called law merchant, which dealt with problems of contracts and trade practices in contrast to older feudal law which concerned itself primarily with the rights and obligations of land tenure and inheritance. A common provision of such charters was that a runaway serf who came to the town and avoided recapture for a year and a day became free; lords granting charters often exempted their own serfs from this provision, but they were happy to receive serfs of other lords, and sometimes they chartered towns near the borders of their lands and deliberately encouraged this form of population growth. An active town could provide good income to its lord, despite his cession of arbitrary rights over persons and goods within it, for he collected fees for the issuance and periodic renewal of the charter, taxes on the trade that the town attracted, and sometimes a portion of fines levied in town courts. Though the initiative for early charters probably came from merchants, ambitious lords soon began issuing them of their own volition in hopes of atttracting commercial growth and its attendant income.

An early development in the new towns was the formation of guilds, associations to serve the common interest of merchants. The guilds had various functions, economic, social, and political; they maintained monopolies of local business, presented a common front to the overlord and looked after dependents of deceased members. Usually they dominated the council allowed by the charter, and commonly town officials were officers of their guilds. Normally a town began with a single guild, but conflicts of interest usually led to craftsmen forming their own guilds, for merchants sought to buy local products cheaply and sell imported goods dearly, while the craftsmen's interests dictated the opposite. Thus the early guilds tended to evolve into merchant guilds, while artisans formed craft guilds; by the thirteenth century the latter had proliferated with enormous variety as every craft organized itself separately. To the traditional functions of the merchant guilds the craft guilds usually added training programs (apprenticeships) and stringent regulation of quality, quantity and the price of products. The proliferation of guilds led to competition for political power in the towns, usually in the form of craft guilds disputing the traditional control of the merchant guild, and the resolution of this issue often was bloody, but by the fourteenth century it was common that representatives of all the guilds participated in town government.

Town charters usually established extensive economic rights and very limited political rights, essentially administrative autonomy within the town, but some towns obtained far greater political rights, amounting to independence, through armed rebellion. About the end of the eleventh century this phenomenon began to be seen in north Italy, where the towns joined nearby country noblemen in associations called communes, and in the twelfth century these communes fought successfully against the authority of bishops, pope and Holy Roman Emperor. Against the Hohenstaufen emperors they formed an alliance of towns called the Lombard League which defeated an imperial army. During the stalemate resulting from the quarrels between popes and emperors, these towns not only attained political independence but also established their authority over the surrounding countryside, re-creating a pattern reminiscent of the Greco-Roman city states. Competition among them was intense, and they hired armies of professional soldiers with which they tried to subject one another. As their commerce flourished, this competition spilled over into cultural matters, and by the late fourteenth century the north Italian towns were being embellished with new public buildings, magnificent private residences and a variety of art works.

Outside of north Italy the pattern of communes rarely developed so fully. From the late eleventh century onward armed uprisings did occur but in conditions so different as to make generalizations difficult. North of the Alps the communes tended to face political authorities that were stronger and more stable, and where such movements enjoyed success it often was more limited and was attained through the sympathy of some other political authority.

Thus, a king or feudal prince eager to see the power of bishops reduced might intervene in a dispute in the name of pacification and render a decision generally favorable to the townsmen. In this manner many towns acquired full political rights—electing all of their officials, exercising high justice, and excluding all other authority from the town, but rarely did anything as independent as the Italian city states appear in the north. More typical was the arrangement in Paris, where local administration was handled by an elected council headed by an official called the Provost of the Merchants, but the king reserved to himself rights of high justice and maintained strong points and soldiers both to defend and to control the town. (High justice referred to serious crimes—as opposed to offenses punishable by fines.)

The need for protection and the Christian character of medieval society led to certain similarities of appearance in the new towns, which were all huddled together on small sites and dominated by their walls, castles and churches. The little communities that preceded the commercial revival were incredibly tiny. Gregory of Tours described the Chateau of Dijon in the sixth century, observing that as it had many towers and housed several hundred people it really should have been called a town rather than a castle. In the south of France, inhabitants of the Roman town of Nimes who survived the barbarian invasions refounded their community *inside* the old Roman amphitheatre, blocking up the outer arches to make a defensive wall; and there remained enough unused space for them to pile earth on some of the spectator benches and make terraced vineyards of them. Even at Paris both the royal and episcopal establishments fit nicely onto the Ile de la Cité, a small island in the Seine River, though the monasteries that enjoyed royal patronage were on the mainland.

The new mercantile settlements clustered around centers such as these, forming little suburbs, and eventually, if they prospered, a new wall would be built around the whole community. But walls were expensive, so the space within them tended to be developed intensively; tall, narrow houses, their upper floors projecting over cramped streets, were typical. Such houses often had a shop or place of business on the ground floor, with residential quarters above it, storage space higher still, and a loft on top where apprentices and household servants slept. Most were built of wood, though in the fourteenth and fifteenth centuries wealthy merchants began building fine stone residences in some quantity.

Most of the more important towns grew up around castles that could offer refuge in time of danger, and these castles long dominated them, as the Tower in London or the Louvre and the Bastille in Paris. In addition, the towns usually had a great many churches, and—with the castle—their towers dominated the skyline, as many old drawings show.

Conditions within the new towns cannot have been pleasant except for the very wealthy. The narrow streets overhung by the upper stories of houses were dank and dark by day and pitch black by night. Until the thirteenth century paved streets were a rarity, and most were dusty in summer and a sea of mud in winter. Garbage and sewage were thrown into a ditch in the middle of the street to be flushed away by rain. And water was drawn from rivers or open wells that must have been polluted most of the time. In these crowded, airless communities contagion spread like wildfire, and when an epidemic struck, as did the Black Death in the middle of the fourteenth century, mortality rates were astronomical. Yet the opportunities that existed in these settlements attracted large numbers of people, and despite all the shortcomings the towns became one of the most creative forces in medieval society.

The expansion of commerce was accompanied by the development of some international banking operations. At first the nature of these operations was dictated by two pressing problems: the need to evaluate and exchange enormous varieties of coins (for many feudal lords coined their own money) and the need to provide for the secure transfer of funds over very unsafe roads. There was profit to be made from both of these operations, and in the twelfth and thirteenth centuries much of this business was in the hands of two establishments of the church, the Knights Templar and the Knights Hospitaler. These were crusading orders of warrior monks who had been endowed heavily all over western Europe. Thus they were in an ideal position to accept deposits in one place and issue payment orders in another, charging for the service, of course; and when it was necessary to transfer funds physically, they could provide strong armed escorts. By the thirteenth century there also were merchant houses extensive enough to practice this business, and these forms of international banking expanded rapidly.

By contrast, lending operations developed slowly, largely because of restrictions imposed by the church. The church had shown itself suspicious of all business endeavor from the beginning of the commercial revival, for its ethics were as deeply rooted in the older agrarian-aristocratic society as were those of any feudal prince, but slowly it had come to admit that those who moved goods or money from one place to another performed a useful service deserving compensation. However, on the issue of lending money for interest, the church remained adamant, for such activity was interpreted as an attempt to profit from one's neighbor's need and hence contrary to the principle of Christian charity; the practice was called usury and was forbidden, with the result that until the thirteenth century money lending remained in the hands of Jews, who were not bound by church law. In most of Europe, Jewish communities of merchants and money-lenders were tolerated within but separate from Christian society; typically, a king or prince would protect Jews, at the price of frequent unrepaid loans, heavy inheritance taxes, and quite arbitrary special levies. The Jew in medieval Europe served a function basic to the revival of commerce and urban life, but he was totally vulnerable, pillaged by the princes who tolerated him and often victim of pogroms by a populace that detested him for his profession and his religion.

Even this tenuous position was undermined in the thirteenth century when Christians learned how to avoid the laws of their church and persuaded governments to eliminate competition by expelling Jews and confiscating their property. Many evasive practices developed, such as writing a long-term loan for a short period and then charging penalties for delayed payment or agreeing to repayment in goods at a predetermined rate below market prices. Thus, collusion between borrower and lender allowed the growth of Christian money-lending and permitted a fuller development of commercial society despite the conservatism of the church. By the fourteenth century a number of great merchant houses, of which the Medici of Florence probably is the most famous, were diversifying their interests into money-lending, credit operations and manufacturing, often with considerable political involvement.

The commercial revival had an enormous and multifaceted impact upon medieval Europe. The towns challenged many of the assumptions of the agrarian-aristocratic society. They possessed obvious and powerful wealth, but the wealth was not related to land. They housed people who were neither lords nor peasants, not only the wealthy new middle class but also the simple laborers who too often are overlooked. Towns and trade posed new problems in law—questions of interest rates and repayment schedules, of disputed ownership of movable and perishable goods, of rights of residence and participation in urban government, of charges and taxes upon commerce by governments. And leagues of towns were powerful political forces outside the old feudal patterns, as the Lombard League and the League of the Hansa demonstrated.

In one way or another most noblemen felt the impact of the commercial revival. The relations of a nobleman with his peasants on the one hand and his lord on the other were influenced massively by the availability of money. The presence of urban markets for foodstuffs meant that surplus agricultural products could be sold for cash. To the serf it could mean money to buy emancipation, to the lord money to buy out of the military obligations of vassalage.

The immediate effects upon the peasant should not be exaggerated, for freedom brought no sudden improvement in his economic condition. Emancipation meant the right to marry or move at will, but he bought the freedom, and usually he had to pay his lord a fee when he exercised his new rights. He might pay annual fees instead of labor services, but the fees were high. In the long run, however, the peasantry gained, for the charters of emancipation usually fixed obligations in perpetuity, and as the economy developed, inflation eroded the value of money. With rising market values the peasant's income increased while his obligations remained fixed. Thus the peasant benefited while his lord was caught with a largely fixed income in a time of rising prices.

The presence of money in the countryside also changed patterns of labor utilization on the land. Traditionally the serf had worked some time on his own land and some time on the lord's land, but with serfs freed and money available lords began to hire labor. In many instances it must have been his own former serfs whom the lord hired, for they constituted the only readily available labor force; many of them must have had plots too small to support their families and would have been eager for extra income.

The next step in the process, and it was common in the thirteenth century, was for the lord to abandon completely the role of agricultural producer and to rent out his land in blocks to individual farmers, so that the lord became simply a collector of rents. The sort of contract made had important long-term effects upon a noble family's economic position. If that contract, too, were drawn in perpetuity, the lord was completely vulnerable to inflation. But if shorter leases were adopted, and they were not uncommon, the lord had some protection since every renegotiation allowed a demand for higher rents and thus a share in the higher market value of the land's product. The feudal baron's world was growing much more complicated.

By the same token, money payments in lieu of personal service (so-called shield money) tended to change the traditional relationship between vassals and overlords, and this commutation of service to money payments had advantages for both sides. The lesser lord did not have to absent himself from his estates for the summer, and the overlord was able to hire soldiers who would fight so long as they were paid instead of a force that would quit at the end of forty days. Moreover, such new forces offered honorable employment to younger sons while leaving heads of families free to manage their estates. This new military pattern became quite significant in the fourteenth century when the Hundred Years War erupted between the kings of England and of France, for in that grinding struggle both kings had need of professional soldiers for long service.

In many ways the crusades reinforced the effects of the commercial revival, for they accentuated the lord's need to get money, making him more susceptible to bargains with his serfs and his vassals. Traditionally the lord who lived on his lands was provided with the substance of existence, but crusading was a different matter. Passages had to be purchased, men and horses outfitted, equipment and mounts transported, men and beasts fed and sheltered. It all took money, so the would-be crusader was the more inclined to sell his serfs their freedom and to commute his vassals' military service.

Even then only the more prosperous lords could go to a crusade independently. The lesser knights had to go in the service of a richer man. Thus the crusades introduced much more marked gradations of status within the nobility—those who went and those who did not, those who travelled independently and those who took service; other status symbols accentuated the differentiation—those who built fine stone castles and those who still lived in a wooden keep on top of a mound of earth, those who simply paid an overlord a fee and those who had to render personal service. And to complicate things further, townsmen were buying land and sometimes the noble titles that went with it. So the traditional notion of a homogeneous class differentiated only by administrative and military arrangements or by personal reputation was breaking down. The nobility became a heterogeneous body of petty knights and great lords, of old families and newly purchased titles, of crusaders and non-crusaders.

If a massive generalization may be risked, one might say that the emergent patterns resulted in advantage for the peasants and the great lords and a terrible squeeze upon the lesser lords, the simple knights. The transformation from labor services to money rents benefited the peasant when inflation depreciated money. Tied to a fixed income, the small lord suffered. On the other hand, great lords did well, for chartering fees and sales taxes from the towns on their lands increased with the development of the economy. At the root of all the turbulence and change lay the power of money.

Chapter 14

The Apogee of Medieval Christianity

During the ninth and tenth centuries, when Europe was being raided from every side, the church suffered severely. The raiders soon learned that cathedrals and monasteries often possessed treasure—gold and silver candlesticks, reliquaries, chalices, crosses and ornaments—and ecclesiastical buildings became favorite targets for pillage. Both in England and on the continent the destruction was frightful. In an endeavor to survive, the clergy was drawn ever more deeply into secular affairs, accepting feudal service and maintaining men-at-arms, so that by the mid-tenth century bishops and abbots differed little from other great feudal lords. The papacy was in an equally sad plight, beset by tumultuous mobs in Rome and attacked frequently by Moslem forces from Sicily. With libraries and schools burned, papal leadership distracted and most high clergy enmeshed in the military and administrative responsibilities of emerging feudal relationships, the church was fragmented, and its spiritual and moral leadership was at a low ebb. Its recovery and its enormous achievements between the eleventh and thirteenth centuries was one of the most dynamic developments of medieval society.

One of the most significant elements in the revival of the church lay in a new monastic movement called the Cluniac Reform. Early in the tenth century some churchmen, fearful of the direction in which the church was developing, prevailed upon the Duke of Aquitaine to establish a new monastery called Cluny in some rugged lands he held in Burgundy; the rules of the new foundation were designed to eliminate some of the dangers that threatened older establishments. Cluny was forbidden to accept gifts that required feudal service. Since most gifts of land included resident labor, the old Benedictine injunction that monks should work in the fields had proved impractical, so the monks of Cluny were required to spend far more time in religious services to avoid idleness. In order to prevent corruption of the intentions of the founders, it was provided that any new monasteries that accepted the Cluniac rules should be governed locally by a prior but should be under the general supervision of the Abbot of Cluny, who would make inspections. Through these provisions the reformers hoped to keep the new monasteries independent of secular entanglements, free of idleness and subject to effective discipline. Moreover, Cluny and its dependents were made directly responsible to the papacy, thus escaping potential corruption through local influences. The Cluniac Reform spread very rapidly in the tenth century both directly through the foundation of associated monasteries and indirectly through imitation by other houses that did not actually join the movement. As a result, the ideas of the Cluniac reformers were a powerful force in the eleventh century church, and they spilled over from the monastic to the secular clergy.

Obviously the reforms that were specifically a part of monastic discipline had little role in the improvement of the secular clergy, but the general principles of independence from feudal responsibility and appointments on the basis of religious qualifications inspired important developments. To free papal elections from the influence of both the Roman mob and the emperor, the College of Cardinals was created, providing for popes to be chosen by a clerical assembly. To extend papal influence across Europe, as a counterpoise to the influence of kings and princes, special agents called legates were created with either general or specific commissions to speak and act in the pope's name, and newly appointed archbishops were required to journey to Rome to confer with the pope before taking up their duties. Like the royal governments, the papacy expanded the scope and number of its courts in the late eleventh and early twelfth centuries, creating new appellate divisions, which increased both papal revenues and papal influence in the development of law. But the greatest effort came with the election of the reformer Hildebrand as Pope Gregory VII (1073–1085), for he initiated the great Investiture Controversy with the Holy Roman Emperors. Thus, the Cluniac reform had very wide repercussions in the church, and despite some failures it made real progress in improving the independence and the spiritual integrity of the clergy.

The eleventh century reformers also contributed importantly to strengthening the theoretical bases of the church by standardizing its practices and beliefs. Much of the standardization of practice was accomplished through the elaboration of canon law, the body of regulation that governed the church both internally and in its relations with the laity. This development was aided considerably by the fact that the zeal of the reformers was reinforced by the rediscovery and restudy of the great law codes of the sixth century emperor Justinian, which provided a model for new legislation. The standardization of belief, or doctrine, was advanced greatly from the early twelfth century onward by theologians who attempted to reconcile the contradictions of the Bible, the writings of the fathers of the church and the decrees of councils and popes, often taking some account, too, of the Greek philosophers. The first of the great theologians, Abelard, simply raised questions and indicated methods that might produce solutions, but successors, such as Gratian and Peter Lombard, wrote great summations that gathered together various ancient authorities and tried to resolve their differences through the application of faith and reason. In the thirteenth century these efforts reached their fruition in the work of St. Thomas Aquinas, whose great *Summa Theologica* embraced every aspect of faith and practice.

The enthusiasm sparked by the Cluniac movement and carried on by papal reformers continued to produce new offshoots within the church. In the late eleventh and early twelfth centuries severely ascetic hermits reappeared in Italy and France, seeking spiritual purification through stringent religious exercises; some of these formed communities famous for their dedication, most notably the Grande Chartreuse or Carthusian Order of France. There also were endeavors to improve the standards of parish priests by organizing them into communities and imposing a semimonastic rule upon them. These semimonastic priests were called canons, and through the twelfth century a number of groups of them developed, of whom the most famous were the Augustinians and the Premonstratensians.

Perhaps the most influential element in the twelfth century wave of monastic reform was the Cistercian Order, which took its name from the monastery of Citeaux. Founded at the very end of the eleventh century, Citeaux came under the influence of a fervent reformer, St. Bernard, in the early twelfth century. While St. Bernard was Abbot of Citeaux, from 1116 to 1153, the order expanded startlingly, from five to over 340 houses, and by the end of the thirteenth century this number had doubled. The rapid growth of the Cistercians is explicable only by the appeal that true religious devotion exercised upon medieval society, for the order enforced a very strict adherence to a narrow interpretation of the Benedictine Rule. The monks were allowed only the most utilitarian clothes and diet; the residences and churches of the order were furnished sparsely; no Cistercian monastery could hold populated lands, so the monks had to do their own labor. Moreover, the Cistercians provided for effective enforcement of this harsh discipline, for the new order adopted an hierarchical organization that resembled a sort of idealized feudalism. Having observed that the rapid growth of the Cluniacs made frequent inspection by the Abbot of Cluny impossible, the Cistercians provided for decentralized but effective control. Each monastery was permitted to found new monasteries, and the abbot of the parental establishment was responsible for overseeing them; when it had matured, the daughter house might colonize new monasteries in its turn, and its abbot was responsible for them. Thus regular and effective inspection was assured by limiting the responsibilities of each abbot to manageable proportions.

In addition to the high religious standard they set, the Cistercians also rendered another important service to medieval society; because the only endowments they could accept were uninhabited lands, and because their strict regulations insisted that they must support themselves, they were responsible for bringing much wasteland into production. Their most notable achievement was turning the wastes of northern England into sheep pastures, which became the foundation of England's great woollen exports, but on a smaller scale they made comparable contributions in several fields of agriculture all over western Europe.

The monastic movement contributed importantly to the growth of the church and of medieval society as a whole. Support by monasteries all over Europe was a major factor in the success of papal reforms. The maintenance of an example of an idealized Christian life helped to salvage the influence of the church at a time when many members of the clergy were enmeshed in secular politics, and such an example provided inspiration to new reforming efforts. To a large extent the development of canon law and theology depended upon monastic libraries and men who had been educated in monasteries. Monks acquired the habit of keeping detailed chronicles of events, and but for their efforts there would be little or no record of that part of the past. Finally, many innovations of medieval society derived from monastic communities—better tools, improved agricultural techniques, schools and the architectural style known as Romanesque.

Aside from the great expansion of monasticism, perhaps the most obvious expression of Christian zeal in medieval society was the crusades, but a great many other motives played a role in them, too. Europe had absorbed many peoples under the Roman Empire, the Germanic Kingdoms, and the Carolingian Empire, but there was little compromise between Christendom and Islam, two societies inspired by exclusive monotheistic faiths; fighting had been more or less continuous since the seventh and eighth centuries, and by the late eleventh century Europeans had made some important gains. In Spain, armies from the mountainous Christian principalities of León and Castile were driving the Moslems southward and had taken nearly half the country, as well as beginning the Christian reconquest of Portugal. During this struggle French influence became strong in Spain through the participation of French knights in search of fiefs and French monks, especially Cluniacs, who established new monasteries; the Spanish wars became something of a European affair with ambition for lands and military fame thoroughly mixed with religious motivation. About the same time fleets from Genoa and Pisa had taken Corsica and Sardinia, and had begun raiding Moslem ports in North Africa, largely in the interest of their growing western Mediterranean commerce, and land hungry Norman knights were conquering Sicily. Thus, by the late eleventh century a number of precedents had been established for Christian campaigns against Moslem positions, but while religious zeal certainly was an important factor, other motives also were prominent. It was against this background that the first crusade was proclaimed.

In the third quarter of the eleventh century, a central Asian people called the Seljuk Turks seized control of the Caliphate in Bagdad and then intensified the old struggle with the Byzantine Empire. After suffering a serious defeat at the Battle of Manzikert in 1071, the Byzantine emperor appealed to Pope Gregory VII to send western troops to his aid, but Gregory was involved in the Investiture Controversy and could not help. However, the request was renewed in the 1090's, and this time it produced results, for papal problems had eased somewhat, and there were many reasons why the papacy was disposed to favor the appeal. After years of bitter quarreling, the eastern church had repudiated the authority of the pope in 1054, and there were grounds to hope that the breach might be healed if papal leadership played an important role in what could be construed as a religious war. The popes were trying to strengthen their position in Europe, and the successes of secular rulers against the Moslems of Spain and Sicily were achievements that the popes desired to equal. All over Europe, churchmen were quarreling with secular rulers and were trying to inhibit the destructive practice of private warfare; any project that might draw large numbers of the feudal class eastward would ease both of these problems. Finally, there were always many Europeans traveling as pilgrims to the Holy Land, and there were inevitable tales of ill-treatment by the Moslems of the area. Thus, for a variety of reasons Pope Urban II proclaimed a crusade at the Council of Clermont in 1095, and preachers all over Europe called upon nobles to set aside their private quarrels and turn their weapons upon the enemies of Christendom.

What the Byzantine Emperor Alexius Comnenus wanted was a body of European volunteers to be incorporated into the Byzantine armies; what Pope Urban II intended to send east was an army of heavily armed nobles under the command of a papal agent, the Bishop of Le Puy, to fight as allies of the Byzantines; the first European host to arrive at Constantinople was neither one nor the other but a motley rabble armed only with their zeal and their faith in God's support. Though Urban had intended raising an effective army of feudal barons, popular preachers had enlisted impoverished knights and peasants. When they arrived at Constantinople in 1096, a hungry mob after a hard overland march, Emperor Alexius promptly sent them to Asia Minor where the Turks annihilated them. Other such ill-organized groups never reached Constantinople; some bands so aroused the areas they passed through by plundering that the Hungarians destroyed them, and others dissipated their fervor in Europe in murderous attacks upon Jews, whom they called the Christ-killers. The whole of this early movement, called the Peasants' Crusade, was tragic.

The baronial crusade that left Europe toward the end of the summer of 1096 also started off with ill omens. Bitter rivalries divided the noble leaders, and some of them were mere adventurers hopeful of conquering new fiefs; they thought the Greeks soft and dissipated, while for their part the Greeks considered the western Europeans barbarians; Emperor Alexius wanted to reconquer the valuable provinces of Asia Minor, but the crusaders wanted to push on to the Holy Land. Under such circumstances relations between the allies were troubled; Alexius offered food and transport in return for oaths of allegiance and then left the crusaders to their own devices. Misunderstandings multiplied, and some of the crusaders plundered Byzantine lands and burned part of Constantinople. Finally Alexius got the troublesome army across the straits to Asia Minor, where it took Nicaea from the Turks for him before marching off toward the Holy Land.

Political divisions among the Moslems had allowed the crusaders an easy victory at Nicaea, but resistance stiffened as they moved on, and Turkish adoption of a scorched earth policy soon left them short of supplies. Moreover, however effective the individual European knight, he had never learned discipline and coordinated action; the army moved in two columns only vaguely in contact with each other, and one of the columns nearly was destroyed before the arrival of the other turned the Battle of Dorylaeum from defeat to victory. Next the crusaders succeeded in taking Antioch, and again they defeated a Turkish army. Their luck was incredible; the lightly armed Moslem bowmen had shown that they could keep away from the heavier and slower European knights and cut them to pieces from a distance, but both at Dorylaeum and at Antioch coincidence and Turkish mismanagement had produced hand-to-hand battles in confined spaces, a situation ideal for the crusaders. Leaving behind some forces to consolidate the positions won, the rest of the host moved on to Jerusalem, which it captured with frightful bloodshed in the summer of 1099. Almost immediately the crusaders had to defend their gains against an army sent from Egypt, but this time the Moslem force was light cavalry without bowmen, and it posed little threat; it had to close with the European heavy cavalry, and the crusaders' victory at Ascalon was complete. The first crusade was over.

The successful crusaders quickly organized a Latin Kingdom of Jerusalem, electing one of their number as king, and they divided their conquests into fiefs in the European manner. Through the early years of the twelfth century they expanded these positions, and with the help of Italian naval forces they took the coastal towns, thus gaining ports through which they had direct communications with western Europe. By the middle of the twelfth century the Kingdom of Jerusalem was a highly developed feudal state, differing from its European counterparts, however, in that the king had only the carefully limited authority of a feudal suzerain. The three Christian domains that the crusaders had carved out in Syria (Antioch, Tripoli and Edessa) maintained only tenuous links with the Kingdom of Jerusalem and with each other, developing into self-contained feudal states themselves. Thus, in the absence of traditions such as those of the Frankish or Anglo-Saxon crowns, the decentralization of authority always latent in feudal organization became dominant.

The Christian states in the east developed some local resources, but a great deal of their support came from the west. Most especially, the great military-monastic orders—the Knights Templar, the Knights Hospitaler and, a bit later, the Teutonic Knights—were endowed heavily all over Europe, and their hundreds of soldier-monks formed one of the chief defenses of the crusaders' states. Replacements for casualties were supplied by a constant stream of pilgrims and soldiers from Europe, some of whom stayed only briefly while others remained permanently. And the vital lines of communication to the west were maintained by the fleets of the Italian commercial cities.

The Apogee of Medieval Christianity 199

Before the final destruction of the Kingdom of Jerusalem at the end of the thirteenth century, several other crusades set out from Europe to fight in the Holy Land. An expedition that started from Europe in 1101 achieved nothing and was cut to pieces by the Turks in Asia Minor. In the middle of the twelfth century, when Edessa fell to the Moslems again, the famous St. Bernard persuaded Europe to raise another crusade; this army was led by the king of France and the Holy Roman Emperor. After losing most of the German force and a large part of the French infantry, the princely leaders finally launched a fruitless attack upon Damascus and then returned home having accomplished nothing.

After the 1170s internal quarrels weakened the Kingdom of Jerusalem just when the great Kurdish general, Saladin, was consolidating Moslem power in Egypt and Syria, and in 1187 Saladin destroyed the Christian army and reoccupied all of the crusaders' conquests except some coastal towns; again the crusade was preached in Europe, and the cause was taken up by the Holy Roman Emperor and the kings of France and England. Emperor Frederick I (1152–1190) was the first to go, in 1189, and he won some victories in Asia Minor, but before he could accomplish any permanent conquest, he drowned while bathing in a river, and most of his army went home. After many delays, Philip Augustus of France (1180–1223) and Richard the Lionhearted of England (1189–1199) set forth, sailing from Sicily in the spring of 1191, but Richard paused again to take the island of Cyprus, which he established as a kingdom and gave to a former king of Jerusalem; finally, in the summer of 1191 the armies of both Philip and Richard joined the remaining Christian forces in the east in besieging Acre. The two kings were too hostile to one another to organize a joint assault, but the garrison was starved into surrender. Then Philip went home, and Richard arranged a truce with Saladin that gave the Christians a few more coastal towns and guaranteed the rights of pilgrims in Jerusalem. Another crusade had ended with very small gains.

The crusades of the thirteenth century accomplished even less than those of the twelfth century. Pope Innocent III (1189–1216) launched an expedition, but as the price of transporting it the Venetians had the crusaders subject the Christian city of Zara (on the Adriatic) to Venetian rule in 1202; then in 1204 the crusaders attacked Constantinople instead of the Turks, setting up a Latin Empire which lasted about a half century until the Greeks took it back. Another crusade in 1218 tried to take Egypt, but after early successes it foundered in the confusion of the Nile delta and had to return to Acre without results. In 1227 Emperor Frederick II (1215–1250) led a long-promised crusade, and after more diplomacy than fighting he acquired Jerusalem and a corridor to it from the coast by signing a truce; a decade later two more crusading armies arrived, skirmished a little, and then confirmed and extended Frederick II's agreement. These were the greatest Christian achievements in the east since the first crusade, but in 1244 an Egyptian army wiped out these gains by recapturing all of Palestine except the coastal towns. A few years later Louis IX of France (1226–1270) made a last great effort to restore the Kingdom of Jerusalem, striking at Egypt once more, but his forces were defeated and its leaders captured; after paying a large ransom the king was freed and spent a few years in Palestine, but he returned home after no greater accomplishment than strengthening the fortifications of the remaining Christian towns. That some remnant of the crusaders' states survived another forty years largely was due to the fact that the Moslems were attacked in the east by the Mongols, an Asiatic people. When the sultan of Egypt had turned back these new raiders, he resumed the reconquest of the Christian positions, and the last one surrendered in 1291.

One of the most enduring achievements of medieval Christendom was the rise of the universities in the twelfth and thirteenth centuries. Most earlier medieval education was intensely practical and included little of a literary or scholarly nature. Young noblemen learned the skills of a knight while young noblewomen were prepared for marriage and the management of extensive baronial households. The guilds developed apprenticeship programs that taught crafts and trades. But education of an academic sort largely was limited to a few schools attached to cathedrals or monasteries, which taught reading and writing and some basic arithmetic, for it was desirable that clerics be able to read sacred works and calculate the dates of movable feasts such as Easter. An important exception to this general lack of academic schooling must be remarked in Italy, where schoolmasters continued to teach in the Roman tradition all through the medieval period; as noted previously, it was these centers of study that rediscovered the law codes of Justinian in the eleventh century.

The first universities appear to have grown naturally out of conflicts in places where schools became sufficiently famous to attract large numbers of students; fundamentally they were academic guilds that sought to deal with internal problems such as irresponsible masters and episcopal censorship and town and gown problems such as gouging landlords and student mischief. Hence, while later universities established under charters of princes or popes can be dated, no one knows exactly when the earliest were formed, though inference suggests the existence of universities at Bologna, Paris and Oxford in the late twelfth century, and others developed rapidly in the thirteenth and fourteenth centuries. In northern Europe it was usually the masters who formed the university, to contest the conservative control of bishops and their agents, but in Italy the students took the initiative, and they developed practices aimed at controlling the masters, too, requiring them to post bonds if they wished to leave town during term and fining them if they missed lectures. Despite these differences in particulars, however, all of the universities shared some general patterns of development. Secular and ecclesiastical authorities gradually granted more and more extensive powers of regulation and discipline to university officers, so that academic communities became largely self-governing. Masters and students slowly organized themselves around their particular interests and developed faculties of arts, law, medicine and theology, and conflicts between masters and university officers tended to reduce the power of the latter to awarding degrees to those presented by the faculties. Thus, the general form of modern universities took shape quite quickly.

The program of undergraduate studies in the early universities was not very rigorous. A student had to know Latin since all instruction was carried on in that language, but standards of proficiency appear to have been quite low; because books had to be produced by hand and were quite costly, most instruction involved listening to a master read a book aloud and comment on it, though a student might be required to read a few books himself. Degrees were granted when the masters affirmed that a student had heard and read the requisite books. Graduate work, on the other hand, especially in theology, was much more demanding. The method of instruction was largely the same, but a student might spend a dozen years at it, and in addition he was expected to engage in public debates, called disputations, before being awarded the title of doctor. In the late thirteenth century two developments worked an important change in the structure of some universities. On the one hand many requirements for degrees were waived by dispensation if a student paid special fees, and soon most students simply fulfilled the residency requirement and bought their undergraduate degrees, so that university lecturing dwindled; on the other hand, sympathetic benefactors founded student residences in the universities, such as Robert de Sorbon at Paris or Walter Merton and John Balliol at Oxford, and they usually provided endowments to support a master who lived with the students. Thus instructional responsibility for those who desired it passed slowly to these new collegial residences, with the university simply controlling general matters and awarding degrees.

Despite their shortcomings, the universities made important contributions to the development of medieval civilization. They supported most of the famous scholars of the society, and as their fame grew, they became authorities to which disputes could be referred, a function important to the growth and elaboration of medieval law and theology. They trained the clerks who served some of the great business houses and the officials who staffed royal bureaucracies and the papal administration. And their interest in the further development of the Latin language and of philosophical and legal studies led to reconsideration of ancient writers and the beginnings of the recovery of the classical heritage, developments that were to undergird the later renaissance.

However, one must not exaggerate the achievements of the medieval scholars, for the postulates of their society imposed limits upon their interests and investigations. The chief support of the universities was the church, and the primary interest of the society, in theory at least, was man's salvation in a Christian sense. Hence, theology was the queen of university studies, and all researches tended to be subordinated to the search for salvation. Ancient authors were revived, but Greek logic became servant to the proof of Christian doctrine, and Latin rhetoric was made a tool of theological exposition. Despite religious prejudice, some aspects of the far more sophisticated Moslem world were studied, and the Europeans borrowed from it the classical sources to which it had fallen heir and the mathematical and astronomical discoveries it had made, but always these borrowings were redefined within the framework of Christian conceptions of the universe. Sometimes these restrictions were formalities, and new concepts discovered in classical writings became extremely influential, but on other occasions the limitations were severe. For instance, new studies of Roman law suggested the concept of a ruler who could legislate with few restrictions, an idea quite different from the tribal king or feudal suzerain who was bound by custom and contract, and all over Europe this notion stimulated royal officers to seek an expansion of monarchical power through citation of Roman precedents. But at the same time the study of Greek philosophers stimulated a quarrel called the realist-nominalist controversy, which limited seriously the investigation of natural phenomena.

The realists, inspired by Plato, maintained that reality was a set of ideals of which individual manifestations were but accidental approximations, while nominalists, deriving from Aristotle, insisted that particulars were the reality and ideals were but generalized conceptions of common characteristics. Largely because of theological implications, the realists tended to dominate the argument, with the result that medieval studies concerned themselves primarily with the search for abstract types and ideals, and research into particular phenomena of the physical world was regarded as ephemeral and unproductive. Moreover, the environment of religious studies conditioned scholars to think in terms of authorities from the past, such as the Bible and the church fathers, and this attitude carried over into other subjects, so that writers such as Plato and Aristotle in philosophy or Galen in medicine tended to be read rather uncritically. Hence, while the medieval universities attained impressive results in the reintegration of the classical heritage and in the advancement of theological and legal studies, natural sciences languished and critical empirical methods did not develop.

Chapter 15

Challenge and Conflict in Later Medieval Society

The thirteenth century often is considered the greatest of the medieval centuries, but if it was the apogee of a brilliant culture, it also saw the beginnings of processes that were to destroy medieval society. All the foundations of the medieval world were shaken badly. Relations between clergy and laity, between church and state, between peasants and lords and between lords and princes all changed considerably, and new military and administrative patterns emerged, still primitive but forerunners of modern forms.

Christianity was transformed massively in many ways. As one example, the church appears to have achieved considerable success in its long, slow battle to control public morality. No doubt it would be easy to exaggerate the church's influence; certainly the regulations of the canon law never were observed wholly, but it is interesting to note the wide range of moral matters that churchmen—even if overoptimistic—thought they could regulate.

Unable to keep the turbulent nobility from fighting, churchmen achieved considerable success in protecting noncombatants and directing the attention of the warriors to the enemies of Christendom. The crusades turned much of Europe's military effort to the service of Christianity (at least in theory), and tournaments introduced formal ritual to knightly combat, to the advantage of noncombatants who thus were spared. Moreover, the church seems to have influenced the warrior's code considerably during this period, and to the old virtues of courage and personal glory were added loyalty, the defense of women and children and the service of God. There were many influences leading to the development of the attitudes usually called chivalry, but the church's insistence that a soldier's efforts must serve some sort of higher purpose certainly was important.

During the early thirteenth century Pope Innocent III (1198–1216) achieved greater control over the church and greater political power in Europe than had been exercised by any of his predecessors. Under Innocent's rule, the papacy developed the most efficient administration in Europe, consolidated its hold on the Papal States and imposed its will upon secular rulers. Innocent was not an innovator, but he was a brilliant organizer, and under his rule the business transacted by the papacy increased greatly, and the machinery of papal government expanded rapidly to deal with it. The central institution of papal government, the curia, developed separate bureaus with rather clearly delineated responsibilities in correspondence, legal matters, finance and administration of ecclesiastical powers, which made papal authority far more effective. (One important consequence was that this rationalized administration soon was copied by several secular governments.) The use of armed force, or the threat of it, tightened the pope's authority over the Papal States. Considerable expansion of the use of legates, officers exercising delegated papal authority, extended enormously the influence of the papacy outside of Italy and facilitated a vast increase in appeals from local ecclesiastical courts to papal jurisdictions. And Innocent's argument that as the vicar of Christ it was his duty to judge any question that might involve sin, which included wars, treaties and royal marriages, justified papal intervention in almost any matter anywhere.

Perhaps the most dramatic demonstration of papal power over the whole church and of papal influence throughout Europe was the convocation of the Fourth Lateran Council in 1215. Attended by more than twelve hundred great prelates from all over Europe, as well as representatives of secular rulers, the council was controlled by Innocent, who guided it through considerations of the doctrine and discipline of the church, political affairs and the reform of morals. Heresies were condemned and the sacraments were clarified. The laity was enjoined to more Christian behavior, and the clergy was commanded to more responsible exercise of the spiritual office. Finally a new crusade was proclaimed, and pronouncements were issued on political quarrels all over Europe. The scope and vigor of papal activity during the pontificate of Innocent III made the papacy one of the most important of the influences that gave shape to medieval Europe.

The stronger authority of the papacy, as exemplified by Innocent III, achieved more efficient imposition of its will through the threat of various ecclesiastical penalties. Ecclesiastical courts could proceed against individuals on the basis of charges laid, assigning penances which had to be fulfilled or the sinner risked excommunication. Excommunication cut the individual off from the community of the faithful and denied him the comfort of the sacraments, falling hard even upon those who took their faith lightly; it cancelled all obligations to him who incurred it, voiding the service that vassals owed their lord and the monies that debtors owed their creditors. Some secular governments took a hand if the sinner did not make his peace with the church within a specified time, prescribing imprisonment in England, confiscation of property in France and death in Sweden.

A penalty that fell more broadly was the interdict, which forbade priests of a whole area to administer sacraments other than baptism and extreme unction. Thus a whole people could be deprived of the church's services until an heretical preacher had been expelled or a wayward king brought to obedience; the effectiveness of this grass roots pressure depended, of course, upon the willingness of the local clergy to obey the ban and upon the sensitivity of a ruler to the discontent of his subjects. With due regard for varying personalities and particular circumstances, however, it is safe to say that these threats were compelling.

For instance, marriage regulations came to be observed much more seriously in the thirteenth century. In earlier times the nobility had treated such regulations quite casually, putting aside wives and taking new ones with little regard for the fulminations of clerics, and the best the church had managed was to have one wife and her children designated legitimate so as to reduce fighting over inheritances. But by the twelfth century, the approval of a church court usually was sought for the termination of a marriage, though annulments were granted on quite thin excuses. Then in the thirteenth century there was a concentrated effort at enforcement of marriage bonds. Innocent III liberalized the calculation of relationships that would bar marriages because consanguinity (too close blood relationship) had become a facile excuse for annulments, and he insisted that a French king take back a wife whom apparently he loathed. The effects should not be exaggerated, but the regulations were clarified, and several attempts at enforcement achieved at least some success.

This period also saw the spread of new ideas concerning the very core of Christianity, the Holy Family. During the early medieval period, emphasis had been upon God the Father, a rather stern and harsh Old Testament concept often portrayed as a sort of omnipotent emperor. During the twelfth and thirteenth centuries emphasis shifted to the mercy of Christ and the compassion of Mary, His mother. The representations of the merciful saviour with arms outstretched, which still adorn many gothic cathedrals, illustrate this new view, and the spread of a new movement called the cult of the Virgin proliferated shrines and prayers for the intercession of the Mother of God. The religion of soldiers was being transformed into the faith of humbler and gentler people.

This adulation of Mary accompanied an improvement in the status of women that strikes another discordant note in the patterns of the old agrarian-aristocratic society. Female saints such as Mary Magdalene enjoyed growing popularity, another sign of a deepening respect for women. It became common practice during the thirteenth century to allow a woman to do homage for lands of her own inheritance, a marked departure from earlier practice in which she had to commit herself to the custody of a man. And noble ladies more and more often were entrusted with the management of estates while their husbands were off crusading. Finally, tightening marriage laws lent more security to a woman's position.

On the other hand the growing importance of women did not imply any weakening in the church's vehemently anti-sexual position. The virginity of Mary was emphasized and the concept of the immaculate conception much stressed. Nuns were upheld as the most holy of women. In consequence, the church's attitude toward women became quite ambivalent. On the one hand it defended their marriages, urged upon warriors an obligation for their protection and even glorified some women such as Mary and Mary Magdalene. On the other hand it failed to modify its obsessive concern with sex, and it continued to view women as the descendants of Eve, the temptress.

Virginity still was considered the ideal state, and marriage was more condoned than endorsed. Procreation remained the only legitimate reason for sexual relations, and many penitentials (guides for confessors) warned against even married couples taking pleasure from it. The church's regulations, if observed, allowed only limited sexual relations between married people and, of course, none outside of marriage. The church would not perform marriage during Lent or Advent; intercourse was prohibited from the discovery of pregnancy until forty days after the birth; it was prohibited on all Wednesdays, Fridays, Sundays and religious holidays; it was prohibited during menstruation, during times of penance, and for three days before taking communion. It is probably safe to assume that the laity did not observe the rules without exception.

The changes taking place in the relations between clergy and laity in general were even more apparent in relations between popes and princes. The reinvigoration of the papacy begun by Gregory VII in the late eleventh century came to fruition later during the pontificate of Innocent III, and for over a hundred years the papacy undoubtedly was the strongest government in Europe. Innocent III persuaded Europe's strongest kings to suspend their quarrels with each other and to go crusading together in the service of the church. He made and broke an emperor of the Holy Roman Empire. He imposed his will upon a strong French king in marital matters. And he forced a humiliating (though not wholly disadvantageous) submission upon a king of England. The papacy's secular power over princes was never greater.

Such worldly power, however, invited too deep an involvement in worldly affairs. Whatever animosities they may have felt, contemporaries of Innocent III could never doubt his own deep convictions and his spirituality; the same was not true of his successors. About the middle of the thirteenth century Pope Innocent IV used all of the massive power of the papacy in a political quarrel with the Holy

Roman Emperor, Frederick II, and though this quarrel contributed in no small way to the collapse of the imperial office after Frederick's death, this cynical use of spiritual power diminished greatly the prestige of the papacy. Then Pope Boniface VIII (1294–1303) brought the medieval papacy to its final disaster.

It was the strong and consolidated monarchy of France that challenged the secular pretensions of the papacy. Boniface VIII was a determined and ambitious man who believed unshakably in the absolute power of the papacy. In the mid-1290s he attempted to forbid taxation of the clergy, but he was opposed by two very strong kings, Edward I of England and Philip IV of France; both impeded the flow of monies from their respective kingdoms to Rome, and as Boniface was involved in costly Italian quarrels, he was forced to back down. But he did not forgive, and in another quarrel in the first years of the fourteenth century he sought to humble the king of France.

In the course of the struggle Boniface made the boldest claims of papal power ever enunciated, but times had changed. The political involvements of the papacy had weakened its prestige, and the secular monarchies enjoyed wide support among their subjects. When Boniface attempted to use ecclesiastical weapons against Philip, he discovered that the French laity and much of the French clergy supported the king; then Philip counterattacked, sending agents to Italy in the autumn of 1303 to kidnap the pope, whom he proposed to try for his crimes. The kidnappers seized the pope, but his supporters rescued him before he could be spirited away. Boniface died shortly thereafter, however, and with him died the medieval papacy.

After the one year pontificate of Benedict XI and another year of haggling, French interest secured the election of Clement V, whose support depended upon the king of France. Clement moved from Rome to Avignon to wait for the turbulence in Italy to die down, and the papacy quickly became a pale shadow of the institution that Innocent III had ruled. It had broken the Holy Roman Empire, but it had collapsed in its struggle with France, and in western Europe the initiative passed to the national monarchies.

The troubles of Christianity went beyond changing social attitudes or church-state quarrels, however. The late twelfth and early thirteenth centuries saw the first great eruptions of popular protest against the hierarchy and doctrines of the church in the west, a movement that was to be more or less endemic in Europe until the Reformation of the sixteenth century finally destroyed even the much frayed theory of the unity of western Christendom.

The popular movements against the church were something rather new. The church had weathered challenges before: challenges to the legitimacy of authority had resulted in schisms, as when the eastern church rejected the authority of the papacy in the mid-eleventh century; and variant doctrines known as heresy had been proposed, such as those concerning the divinity of Christ or the equality of the members of the Trinity. But except for the early difficulties with Arian German settlers, these disputes had touched very few people in western Europe and had been confined largely within the clergy. By contrast the thirteenth century heresies were mass movements.

Never before had conditions in Europe been so favorable to popular religious movements, and a number of converging influences sparked an explosion. On the one hand, there was the contrast between increasing popular piety, as exemplified in the cult of the Virgin, and the wealth, power and worldly involvement of the church. Christians were disturbed by the abandonment of the apostolic poverty and disdain of material goods preached by Christ. The monastic orders had maintained the tradition more or less, but the secular hierarchy had not. Criticism of the seculars had come from the monasteries intermittently, and it was much more bitter in the aftermath of the Cluniac reform and the foundation of the stricter Cistercians and Carthusians. Moreover, it had much greater effect in the late twelfth and early thirteenth centuries as the new towns provided large audiences for troubled monks. Earlier, it had been impossible to reach many people, for the populace was scattered. The rise of the towns created concentrations of population that could be addressed by popular preachers, and such preachers—often monks—appeared in large numbers to exhort the faithful to love and serve God, to extol the Christian virtues of poverty and charity and to damn the worldliness of the bishops.

For many reasons townsmen were singularly susceptible to this preaching. In medieval Europe the church was much more central to life than is the case in modern times. Church buildings were usually the chief public structures of town or village, and they were social centers. There women met to gossip; there village and town meetings were held; there young lovers met in dark corners for a few whispered words. The church doors were bulletin boards where notices were posted, and it was in the church that public announcements were made after mass. A society that was largely poor and illiterate and lacked mass media communications turned to the church for news, for hope in hard times, for expressions of thanks in good times. Religious festivals meant holidays and celebrations, and sermons and religious plays and stories were important public amusements. The noble and ecclesiastical elite had some other interests, but most medieval Europeans poured their hopes and dreams and sorrows and frustrations into their religion.

The new towns brought large numbers of such people together, but the towns could be horrible places. Huddled within walls, the towns grew cramped and crowded. Without adequate water supply or sewage disposal or police systems or welfare programs they squeezed together masses of the poor in dark, disease-ridden slums, and they seethed with potential violence. Added to the frustrations implicit in such conditions was the fact that the lords of many towns were bishops, for it will be remembered that early townsmen often built around the fortified episcopal centers for protection. Thus the bishop was not uncommonly the focus of enormous local resentment for his exactions and his failure to relieve misery.

That the potential violence exploded in religious expression is not at all surprising. In the towns popular preachers, especially critical preachers, could always draw a crowd. When worried bishops refused permission to preach in the churches, they simply moved to the fields outside town and preached in the open air. The arrival of an itinerant preacher was an occasion, an excuse for a break from wearisome routine. His talk of God's love and God's wrath stirred popular piety; his fulminations against worldly clergy gave voice to deep-felt resentment. The labors of such men prepared the way for a harvest of violence, especially in the south of France.

In the town of Lyons a movement grew up in the 1170s around Peter Waldo, a merchant. Inspired by an itinerant minstrel's story of a saint, Waldo gave away his property and undertook a life of begging and preaching. He and his followers soon were reported to be preaching heresy, and first the archbishop of Lyons and then the pope forbade their activities, but they ignored the prohibitions; as

Waldensians, or The Poor Men of Lyons, they quickly became well known, and the penalties of the church began to fall upon them. Early in the 1180s the pope condemned them as heretics and excommunicated them, and the archbishop of Lyon expelled them from his archdioceses. Up to that point their only serious offenses were unlicensed preaching and refusal to obey church authority. Under persecution, however, they became more radical, declaring that Christ's teachings in the New Testament were sufficient for salvation and that the church and its sacraments were superfluous. With their expulsion from Lyons they spread across the south of France, and their fate became entwined with that of an even larger heretical group, the Cathari or Albigensians.

The origins of the Cathari (the pure) probably go back to an eastern sect called Manichaeans during the Roman Empire. Direct survivals of this cult seem to have been limited to the east, but in the eleventh century small groups of its adherents were heard of again in the west, mostly in north Italy and southern France but with small congregations scattered all over France and Germany. The strongest western center of the Cathari developed around the French town of Albi, so that among the many names applied to these people Albigensians is the one best known.

Original Manichaeanism was a pagan alternative to Christianity, but after centuries of uneasy co-existence, competition and borrowing, the faith of the Cathari resembled a distorted Christianity sufficiently for its followers to be considered heretics in Europe. The actual doctrine is known only in outline, for most surviving materials concerning it come from its Christian enemies, whose revulsion colored their reporting. It would appear, though, that the core of the faith was a dualism: two powers, one good and one evil, the former the ruler of spiritual matters and the latter of material things. Thus complete asceticism was desirable, and Cathari were forbidden the possession of any material goods, again a challenge to the worldliness of the Christian church. The Cathari regarded the crucifixion as a triumph for the force of evil, and they called those who corrupted the tragedy into a tale of glory agents of the force of evil, thus condemning the pope and the whole Christian clergy. They believed man was tainted incurably, and their support of complete celibacy may have been rooted in a desire for voluntary genocide; only when corrupted humanity died out could good triumph.

The capacity of such a strict cult to win a large following, particularly in the highly cultured south of France, lay in the distinction it made between the perfects who practiced the hard discipline and the believers who simply endorsed it. The "believers" were quite free to live as they wished so long as they received the one sacrament of the cult, the *consolamentum*, before they died. Since the sacrament could be administered only once, a believer usually took it on his death bed, thereby wiping out all previous sins. The perfects, on the other hand, appear to have taken the *consolamentum* and then relied upon asceticism to preserve them from further sin. This distinction allowed most adherents a rather unfettered existence while encouraging great respect for the uncompromising austerity of the cult's leaders.

By the early thirteenth century the Albigensians and Waldensians had won such wide support that normal ecclesiastical weapons were impotent, and though Pope Innocent III was determined to crush them, his early efforts produced no result. Preachers sent in to attempt conversion by persuasion had no effect. An appeal to local lords was equally ineffectual, for the greatest of them—Count Raymond of Toulouse—though a practicing Catholic, was quite indifferent to religion, and another, the count of Foix, had Waldensians and Albigensians in his own family, though he professed Catholicism personally.

Innocent then turned to the king of France, Philip Augustus, and made a series of appeals for royal action. At first the king refused, for he was embroiled in a struggle with John of England, but in 1207—with his own affairs calmer—he agreed to allow northern knights to participate in a crusade in the south; for political reasons, however, he still declined personally to lead an expedition against his vassal. In the summer of 1209 the crusade began, and soon it left a swath of death and destruction in its wake. Under the able leadership of a baron with lands and titles in both France and England, Simon de Montfort, most of the south was cónquered by 1213, with a large-scale slaughter of everyone suspected of heresy. Although the area remained restive for another generation, both the heresies and the power of the southern nobles who had protected them were broken, and later in the thirteenth century much of the area passed into the control of the French royal family. Courts of inquisition operating under special papal authority continued to seek out and persecute heresy, and such heretics as had survived the crusade went underground, so that the area again became nominally Catholic.

The force of popular piety which was largely responsible for the widespread heresies was not killed by the Albigensian crusade; rather, it found new channels of expression. Driven by the same religious fervor that had inspired the heretics, and moved by desire to restore confidence in the church's teachings, pious men formed new religious groups, called the mendicant friars, at the beginning of the thirteenth century; two of these groups became particularly significant, the Francisican and Dominican Orders, dedicated not to monasticism but to service in the world—preaching and teaching. The activities of the mendicant friars were varied and important. Dominicans and Franciscans staffed the inquisition in southern France after the Albigensian crusade; they became leading scholars in the new universities; they undertook missionary work in lands as far distant as India and China; less dramatically, they preached, heard confessions and buried the dead all over Europe. Their effects were considerable: they provided an outlet for the religious enthusiasm that had fed the great heresies; they carried Christianity to the poor and the isolated; and as papal agents they flooded over Europe and increased the pope's power in the church at the expense of the bishops.

Inevitably, the spiritual fires that burned in the mendicants got some of them into difficulty with the hierarchy, for their enthusiasm encouraged extremism. Some of the followers of St. Francis emphasized his insistence upon apostolic poverty and, like the Waldensians, became very critical of the established clergy. This group, known as Spiritual Franciscans, eventually was condemned. Yet the movement of popular piety went on and on, producing new heretical movements in the fourteenth century, the Lollards and the Hussites, and culminating in the sixteenth century with the development of Protestantism.

About the middle of the fourteenth century Europe was struck by the terrible epidemic called the Black Death, bubonic plague, which seemed to contemporaries a visitation of the wrath of God. When the disease struck, it ran its course very quickly, with horrible symptoms, and it was usually fatal. Victims of the Black Death suffered sudden high fever, accompanied by splitting headaches, nausea and lethargy; then delirium set in, usually within twenty-four hours, followed by the appearance of buboes—large, hard swellings of black or purplish coloration in the armpits and groin—on the second or third day. Sometimes the buboes opened and drained, and the patient recovered, but most often he died less than a week after experiencing the first symptoms.

The Black Death seems to have originated in Central Asia in the 1330s and then spread along the trade routes, reaching the west about a decade later, where it washed back and forth across Europe for many years. Of course a society with almost no concept of sanitation was terribly vulnerable to epidemic; mortality was very high, while the agony of the sickness and the seeming inevitability of death aggravated popular terror. Fourteenth-century medicine was too primitive to isolate the source of the disease, which is carried by vermin from infected rats, but an Italian author, Boccaccio, in the introduction to his *Decameron,* indicates that it was recognized as a natural contagion spreading from place to place and that some attempts were made to control it by quarantine and isolation. In the crowded conditions of medieval towns, however, such efforts were fruitless, and the epidemic ran its course unchecked; Europe is estimated to have lost between a fifth and a third of its population in the latter half of the fourteenth century, a slaughter worse than the effects of any of the human invasions that medieval Europe had suffered.

The immediate effects of the Black Death were many and varied. Those who could afford to do so sought to escape areas where the plague was raging, and some regions were quite depopulated by death and flight; some squandered their resources in revelry, expecting they soon would die; many sought refuge in religion, often with wild devotional excesses such as flagellation—whipping one another viciously to mortify the flesh and free the spirit.

The long-term effects of the epidemic were even more serious. Extensive mortality caused labor shortages with a consequent rise of wages and prices, producing an apparent prosperity, but this was followed by a long and serious recession when the market felt the impact of reduced demand. Groups that exercised political power, aristocrats and wealthy bourgeois, tried to protect their position through governmental and guild regulation which shifted much of the burden of economic problems to the less organized and more vulnerable classes of society—peasants and lesser nobility in the countryside and the working force in the cities. The late fourteenth century saw a number of violent but generally fruitless revolts by these classes and even more violent repression by the dominant classes: the Peasants' Revolt in England, the *Jacquerie* in France and the Ciompi rising in Florence. The turmoil abated only about the middle of the fifteenth century, and even then serious problems remained. Western Europe experienced a widespread recovery, though the economy stabilized at levels of prosperity probably considerably lower than those of the twelfth and thirteenth centuries, and in Germany the economic recovery was limited to urban centers, leaving the peasantry in a very depressed condition.

Thus, chronic economic problems and extensive social change accompanied and probably intensified the religious restiveness of later medieval society. Nobles resented amply financed bourgeois who lived well, had money to lend and even were buying noble lands and titles. Urban populations resented lords who tried to squeeze ever more money from their towns and attempted to impede the growing independence of town life. Peasants resented the exactions of their overlords, which became more onerous as the lords felt the pressure of economic problems, and market controls in the towns, which tended to depress the prices that peasants received for their agricultural produce while maintaining the high prices that they had to pay for the towns' manufactures. The development of Europe certainly cannot be recounted as a steady progress, and there is no doubt that later medieval society witnessed a contraction of population, a shrinking of opportunity and an economic decline that were bewildering to those who experienced them. In such circumstances it ought not to be surprising that religious fanaticism, blind violence and brutal repression flourished.

THE LANCASTRIAN AND YORKIST KINGS

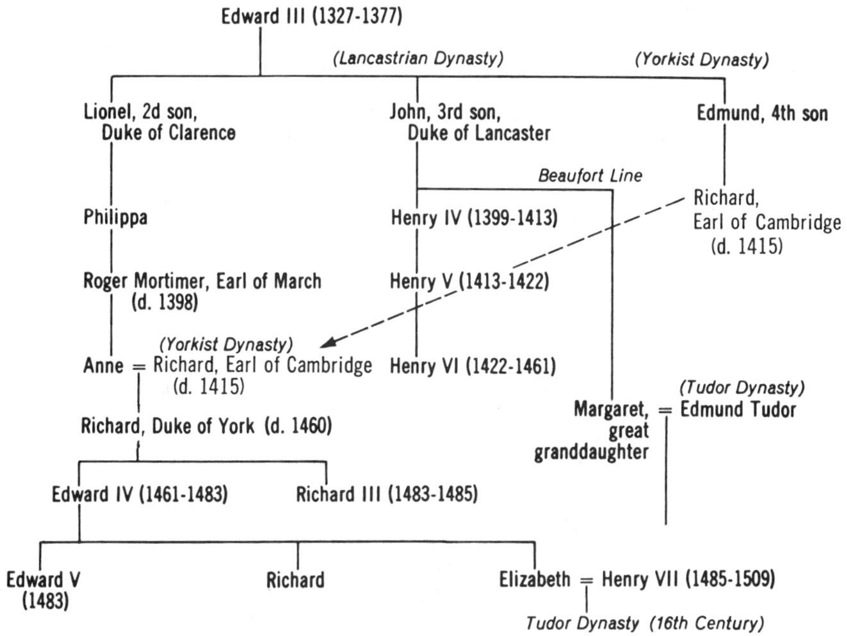

THE LUXEMBURG AND HABSBURG DYNASTIES

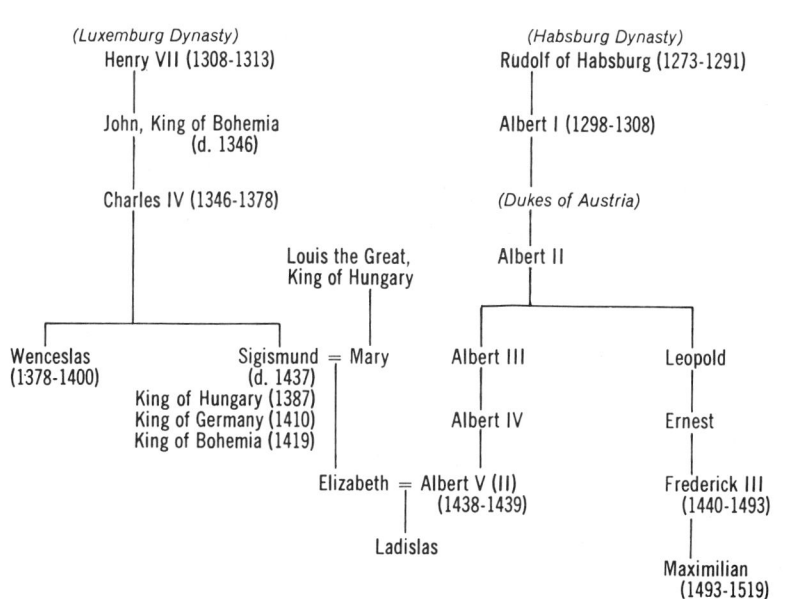

THE HOUSE OF HABSBURG

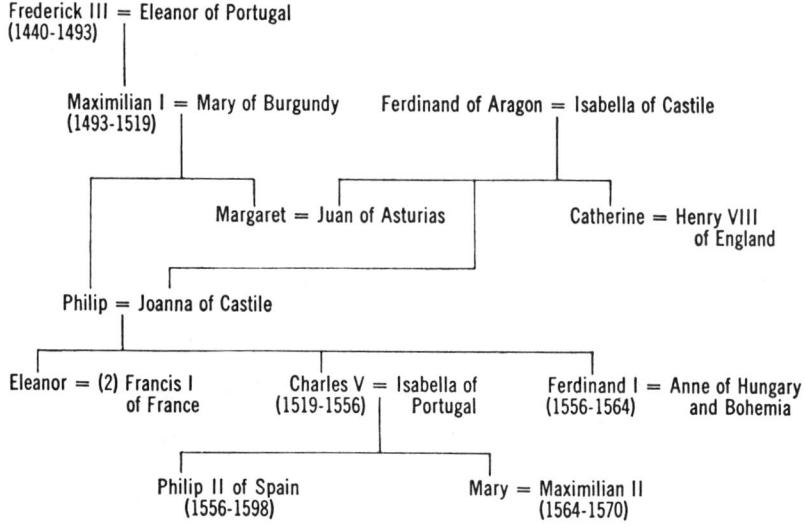

THE HOUSE OF VALOIS

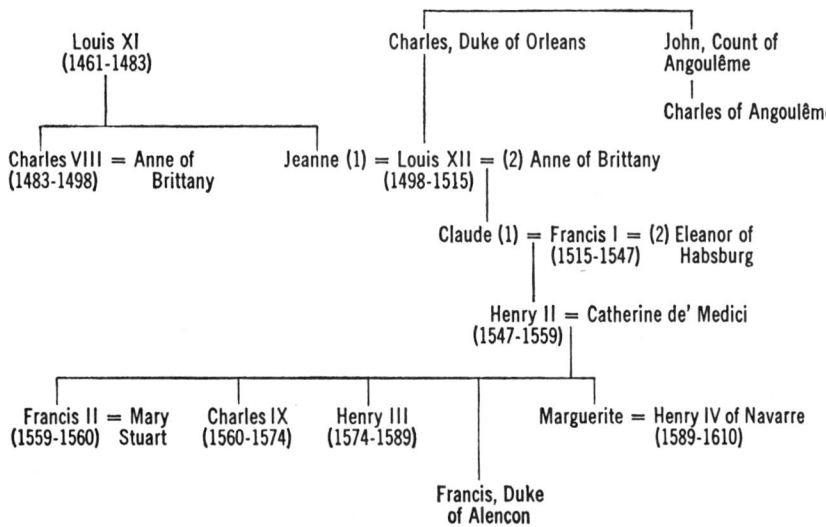

Chapter 16

The Hundred Years War

From the middle of the fourteenth century to the middle of the fifteenth century, while Germany lay fragmented by aristocratic anarchy and Italy was torn by the rivalries of the city states, western Europe was dominated by a great conflict between the French and English crowns. Actually the struggle was a series of wars broken by treaties and truces, which lasted from 1337 to 1455, but usually it is called the Hundred Years War and is treated in its entirety, for issues changed little during its course.

It is difficult to isolate reasons for the outbreak of war in 1337, not because of any lack of causes for conflict but rather because several causes long had existed, and war might have broken out at any time. The French and English crowns had been hostile to one another ever since the Norman conquest of 1066 had made one of the French monarch's vassals a king in his own right; this issue had not been settled by Philip Augustus' conquests from John of England, for the kings of England continued to hold most of France's southwestern coastal region, an area called the duchy of Gascony. The Albigensian crusade, which strengthened the French king's control over much of the south, left the English position in Gascony rather tenuous, and this problem was aggravated further by the rapid development of the judicial authority of the French crown after the middle of the thirteenth century. Not only did the kings accept appeals from their vassals' courts to their own parlement of Paris, which had serious financial repercussions, but the administration of this appellate procedure often involved sending royal agents into the great fiefs. When these practices were applied to the duchy of Gascony, they often caused serious quarrels between the king of France and the king of England, and twice—at the end of the thirteenth century and at the beginning of the fourteenth century—the French crown seized the duchy, though in both instances the disputes were settled and it was restored. Nonetheless, by the second quarter of the fourteenth century precedents had been established for a major confrontation.

Exacerbating this quarrel, which was basically feudal in nature, were a number of lesser issues. By the early fourteenth century Flanders was a highly developed industrial area producing woolen cloth, but there was conflict between the wealthy merchants who controlled the trade in their own interest and the artisans of the craft guilds, who made the cloth. The artisans revolted, and when the count of Flanders proved unable to pacify the situation, the French crown intervened on the side of the merchants, who represented stability and traditional authority in the Flemish towns. But Flanders was the chief market for raw wool from England, that country's primary export, and any increase in the influence of the French monarch in this area posed the threat that he might control an important part of the English king's revenue. Consequently, while the king of France aided the merchants, the king of England aided the artisans.

Another disruptive issue was the problem of piracy in and around the Channel, where the transport of wine and wool and other lesser trade had led to the development of rather heavy shipping. Since English and French ships attacked one another on every occasion, both monarchs were deluged with requests for aid from their seamen; usually these requests were ignored, but the issue was readily at hand if an excuse were needed for military action. In the same category was French aid to the Scots who troubled England's northern borders; generally the matter was ignored, and occasional English protests met only bland excuses, but the issue always was susceptible to escalation.

Finally, another dangerous element was added to the rivalry between the two monarchies when the French succession came into question. In 1316 the tradition of passing the crown from father to son, a practice unbroken since Hugh Capet, ended when Louis X's death was followed within a year by the death of his posthumous son. After some dispute over the claims of Louis' daughter, the crown went first to his brother Philip V (1316–1322) and then to another brother Charles IV (1322–1328). The legal questions involved were complex, but the parlement of Paris appears to have unearthed an old provision of Frankish practice called the Salic Law, which forbade female inheritance and thus justified what had been done.

The matter became more serious in 1328 when Charles IV died without sons, for the senior male line of the Capetians died with him. If the Salic Law were observed, the heir to the throne was Philip, count of Valois, a nephew of Philip IV through the latter's younger brother. But there were no long traditions or strong precedents to support the exclusion of a female, and if a woman's rights could be upheld, Edward III of England (1327–1377) had a claim to the throne through his mother, who was a daughter of Philip IV. However, the issue did not become critical immediately. When the count of Valois was proclaimed Philip VI of France (1328–1350), Edward's mother registered a formal protest, but her son did homage for Gascony, and it appeared that the Valois succession would be accepted. Only a decade later was the arrangement challenged.

With so many contentious issues outstanding between them, it is not surprising that Edward III and Philip VI fought, but the reason for the war having begun in 1337 appears to turn on personal factors. Both monarchs were imbued thoroughly with the knightly desire to win glory through military achievements, and both considered their crowns and their resources personal property to be used as they saw fit. Hence, both were eager for a war and thought they could sustain its costs. As so many times before, Gascony provided the source of a new quarrel, one which Philip VI appears to have manufactured deliberately. The French crown declared that the homage performed for Gascony by Edward III had been faulty and demanded that he renew it as full liege homage; he refused, and Philip declared Gascony forfeit in 1337. Edward's response was to declare war on Philip, addressing him as "the so-called king of France," which implied clearly a revival of Edward's claims to the French throne, an implication later made explicit. In 1338 Edward crossed to the continent with an army, and the war that both kings desired so eagerly was begun.

Despite certain similarities of leadership (leadership which was generally vainglorious, often impractical and sometimes simply incompetent), there were striking differences between the English and French forces. The French army still depended primarily upon the armored knight, a small fraction of the realm's population, and its only infantry support consisted of pikemen from town militia and some hired crossbowmen. Such a force was reasonably effective in a heavy cavalry charge and the melée of hand-to-hand combat that followed, but as the crusades already had demonstrated, it was ill-disciplined and was vulnerable to attack from a distance with missile weapons. By contrast, the English army had developed some quite startling innovations; it was composed chiefly of infantry, commoners who served for pay, and it depended heavily upon an impressive new missile weapon, the longbow, supported by pikes. This new force had developed largely from Edward I's campaigns against the Welsh. In the rough country of Wales he had learned the value of infantry, and after feeling the power of the Welsh bow, his soldiers had copied it. The longbow was six feet in length and fired an arrow three feet long with sufficient velocity to pierce armor at short ranges. Its greatest advantage was its rate of fire, however; in random firing, such as into a densely packed mass of charging cavalry, the longbowman could get off about ten arrows per minute to the crossbowman's two, for the latter had a heavy and complex mechanism to rewind and reload. The pikes used by both sides were long wooden spears with iron points; when a group of pikemen set themselves, with the butts of their weapons braced against the ground, tips angled forward and upward, the resulting wall of points could stop a cavalry charge.

For eight years the war proceeded in a desultory manner, the two kings avoiding large-scale engagements and limiting their activities to skirmishes and sieges of castles. Then, in 1346 a major confrontation occurred, and the new English army proved its worth. Edward III had brought a force of about nine thousand men to Normandy, where he had plundered the city of Caen, but when Philip VI began gathering a large force at Paris, Edward decided to withdraw. Since his fleet had returned to England, leaving him stranded in France, Edward had no choice but to march northward to his allies in Flanders. A sort of race then developed, with the

English moving north by forced marches and the French trying to intersect their line of retreat and cut off their escape. By good luck Edward managed to get his troops across both the Seine and the Somme before the French caught up to him, but since the French cavalry could move faster than the English infantry, at that point he had to fight. On 26 August 1346 he took up a defensive position near the forest of Crécy and awaited the French attack; his position was well chosen, for his flanks were covered somewhat by the forest and a village, and he was at the top of a rise, which the French would have to charge to get at him. Organizing his force into three divisions, he dismounted his knights and set them with his pikemen between large bodies of archers. Then he waited.

What happened next is explicable only in terms of the ill-disciplined independence and vanity of the medieval knight. Philip VI could have moved around the English, and waited for Edward to attack or starve; or he could have concentrated his army and attempted an assault with the massed weight of his heavy cavalry. He did neither. Instead, he sent his crossbowmen forward to harass the English, but as the longbow outranged the crossbow, they could accomplish little. Then he allowed some cavalry to try to charge through the crossbowmen, creating a confused mob into which the English poured volleys of arrows. Finally, as the rest of the French army came up, he sent it forward piecemeal in over a dozen separate assaults, which lasted until midnight and only added to the slaughter wreaked by English arrows. The few who reached the English lines of dismounted knights and pikemen were killed or captured, and those who survived fled south. When morning came, the English realized that they had won a great victory, and instead of continuing his withdrawal to Flanders, Edward marched to the coast and besieged the port of Calais, which surrendered a year later. The English had acquired an invasion port which they were to hold until the middle of the sixteenth century.

Shortly after the capture of Calais, the Black Death swept across Europe and imposed a few years' lull in the fighting; major operations were not resumed until the middle 1350s. By this time Philip VI had been succeeded by his son John the Good (1350–1364), and Edward was being assisted by his son, the Black Prince. In 1355, while John and Edward III sparred inconclusively in and around Normandy, the Black Prince ravaged the south of France; by providing horses to transport his archers, he created a fast-moving column that swept through the countryside, avoiding strongpoints while looting and burning everything else. In 1356 the Black Prince moved north with the same sort of expedition and plundered the rich Loire Valley, but this time King John set forth to meet him and tried to stop his withdrawal toward Bordeaux.

The Black Prince did not want to fight, for his army was tired and was burdened with a long wagon train loaded with booty, but in mid-September he was brought to bay near Poitiers and had to either fight or abandon his plunder. Sending the wagons on, the English took up a defensive position, as they had at Crécy a decade earlier. Their flanks were protected by a ravine on one side and thick woods on the other, and their front was covered better than at Crécy by rough ground and thickets unfavorable for a cavalry charge except along a narrow road that traversed it. In the face of this position, King John, who had even less military ability than his father, devised an incredible plan of attack that seems to have been influenced by the English victory a decade before. The vanity of the French nobles would not allow them to admit that Crécy had been won by commoners, whose arrows had cut to pieces the flower of French chivalry, so they concluded that the decisive factor must have been the dismounted knights. King John therefore ordered most of his knights to dismount and form three divisions to fight on foot, but there was a grave error in his calculations. In a defensive position a dismounted knight was simply an armored pikeman; on the offensive, as at Poitiers, a dismounted knight was a man in heavy armor who had to march a mile over rough country to get within striking distance of the enemy. The difference proved significant.

First, John sent a small body of cavalry charging up the road to smash a hole in the English line; confined to a narrow approach, it was cut up badly by the English archers. Then he sent forward his three divisions of dismounted knights, holding his crossbowmen in the rear where they would not interfere with the nobles and thus depriving his attack of any missile support. Some of the first division reached the English, and there was hard fighting, but the French knights—weary from the march and harassed by the archers—soon were killed or captured. Having observed this, the second division withdrew without attacking. The third division, led by King John himself, then repeated the first division's assault, with the same results. When the Black Prince resumed his withdrawal to Bordeaux, he took along as prisoners the king of France, the king's youngest son, three dozen great nobles and a large number of lesser nobles, all of whom would command valuable ransoms.

With the army destroyed and the king a prisoner, John's eldest son, the Dauphin Charles, had no choice but to negotiate, and in 1360 the Treaty of Brétigny-Calais ended the first phase of the Hundred Years War. England made great gains. France was to pay an enormous ransom for King John, and the king of England was to receive all of the old duchy of Aquitaine and a few other territories. Though most of the provisions of the Treaty of Brétigny-Calais never were carried out, the agreement brought a decade of peace marked by little of note except King John's death in 1364 and the succession of his capable son Charles V (1364–1380). The new king of France was determined to recover what his father had lost, but like his ancestor Philip Augustus he was conscious of the value of legal justifications. For a few years he continued paying instalments on the money owed to England and simply waited; then in 1369 the Black Prince, who was governing Aquitaine for his father, gave Charles the opportunity he sought.

Some Gascon nobles appealed from the Black Prince's harsh rule to the parlement of Paris, and Charles so maneuvered the case as to pronounce the whole duchy of Aquitaine forfeit to the French crown. The war was resumed, though the campaigns of the 1370s were curious in that the two forces pursued different objectives and never met in battle. The English continued their plundering expeditions across open country, but Charles V, who was more practical than chivalrous, simply harassed them from time to time and concentrated on retaking castles. His commanders, of whom the most famous was the Breton Bertran Du Guesclin, were men capable of planning ambushes and midnight assaults and of using bribery. Though such practices scandalized contemporary concepts of knightly honor, they proved effective, and the English position was reduced to a coastal strip between the Garonne River and the Pyrenees, less than Edward III had held before the war began.

Unfortunately, this successful reconquest did not spare France from the depredations of soldiers. Both sides used hired troops, and when fighting slackened they simply dismissed them; many of these unemployed soldiers formed bands of brigands called free companies and continued to live off the land, plundering and killing wherever they went for the next century.

Changes of leadership and internal troubles in both kingdoms caused a stalemate in the war after the French recovery. Between 1376 and 1380 the Black Prince, Edward III and Charles V all died. The English crown passed to the Black Prince's son, Richard II (1377–1399), and then to his cousin, Henry IV (1399–1413), while Charles V of France was succeeded by his son, Charles VI (1380–1422). During most of this period England was preoccupied with baronial revolts, which precluded effective military action in France, but the French were in no better condition; after 1392 Charles VI suffered frequent fits of insanity, and France was divided as the government was disputed by two of his relatives, the duke of Orléans and the duke of Burgundy. Except for a truce signed in the mid-1390s, little happened in the war until 1413, when two important events caused it to take a new turn: in England Henry IV was succeeded by his son Henry V (1413–1422), who possessed real military talent, and in France the Armagnacs (as Orléans' supporters were called) succeeded in expelling the Burgundians from Paris, leaving the court seriously divided.

In the summer of 1415 Henry V led a new army to France, and while attempting to withdraw to Calais after some modest successes, he had to face the French host at Agincourt. Again the English took up a defensive position with their flanks protected and their pikemen and dismounted knights set between formations of archers. Again the French ignored their crossbowmen and sent in a cavalry charge followed by three divisions of dismounted knights, just as at Poitiers. The results were even worse at Agincourt, for since the last confrontation French armor had been made much heavier in an attempt to find some defense against the longbow; by the time the French reached the English lines, across a muddy field, they were too weary to raise their weapons or to rise again if knocked down, and most of the first two divisions were taken prisoner. Unfortunately, at this point in the battle Henry V was told that the rear of his army was under serious attack, and he ordered the prisoners killed; by the time this was discovered to be a false alarm, many of the French nobles had been slaughtered, and the third French division had withdrawn, leaving the English once more masters of the battlefield. Agincourt destroyed the Orléanist party, and in the aftermath of the battle the Burgundians seized Paris again and allied with Henry V. They then imposed upon Charles VI's son, the dauphin, the Treaty of Troyes of 1420, which confirmed the English in Aquitaine and divided all of France north of the Loire between the English and the Burgundians; moreover, in one provision of the treaty the French queen declared that the dauphin was illegitimate, so when Henry V married Charles VI's daughter, English claims to the French throne were strengthened immeasurably. The Treaty of Troyes ended the second phase of the Hundred Years War with the English in an even more extensive position than they had enjoyed under the Treaty of Brétigny-Calais.

In 1422, only two years after the Treaty of Troyes, both Henry V and Charles VI died, and the infant Henry VI (1422–1461) was claimant to both crowns. However, the Dauphin Charles, resident in Bourges, was far from defeated, for most of the English aristocracy had no further interest in France, which had been picked clean of plunder, and the harsh rule of English and Burgundian officials drove many northern French nobles into his camp. What was needed by Charles, who was a colorless young man, was something to add excitement to his cause, and this was provided in 1429 by Joan of Arc. A peasant girl who had visions of saints, Joan managed an interview with the dauphin, and she impressed him by her complete confidence in his destiny to rule France. With his blessing, she went to Orléans, one of the cities being besieged by the English, and her inspiration began a new French recovery.

Joan of Arc's influence lay mostly in the factor of morale. Inspired by her unshakable faith, the French soldiery drove off the besiegers of Orléans, relieved other places threatened by the English and then defeated an English army in the field. Swept along by her confidence, the dauphin allowed himself to be persuaded into a mad dash across enemy territory to Rheims, the traditional site of coronations, where he was crowned King Charles VII (1422–1461) on July 17, 1429. However, Joan's zeal was not accepted as sanctity by her opponents; in 1430, when the Burgundians captured her and sold her to the English, she was treated as a witch, and the next year she was burned at the stake.

For several years the war continued in a desultory fashion, and then in 1435 the duke of Burgundy, whose ambition to control Flanders had resulted in a clash with his English allies, made peace with Charles VII by the Treaty of Arras. After that the French recovery proceeded slowly but surely. Reverting to the strategy of Charles V, the French captured castle after castle, and a last battle in the north in 1450 and one in the south two years later left the English only Calais. At that point the Hundred Years War simply died out, but the strategic impact of the French victory was enormous. With her continental possessions wiped out, England found her first line of defense forced back into the channel, and it is no coincidence that the new Tudor dynasty, established in the late fifteenth century, showed great interest in naval affairs from the outset. With the threat from the west finally resolved, French armies were freed for other ventures, and at the end of the fifteenth century France's kings responded to the lure of Italy, as had the Carolingians several centuries before; in the mid-1490s Charles VIII led across the Alps the first of those armies that were to involve France in a new struggle and, incidentally, were to be so important in bringing the Renaissance to France.

The last stages of the Hundred Years War witnessed some interesting military innovations, especially the development of French artillery. Primitive cannon, called bombards, had been known since the 1320s, but throughout the fourteenth century they remained largely ineffective because they were too ponderous to move readily and too inaccurate and slow to fire to cause much damage. By the mid-fifteenth century there had been some improvements. Cannon were still too clumsy to be much use in the field, and they threw too light a round to have much effect on stone walls, but their concentrated fire could knock down the gates of castles or towns, and they played no small part in the French successes. Also of note was the redevelopment of a permanent professional army. About a decade before the end of the war, Charles VII hired into his service on a year around basis about six thousand of the mercenary soldiery who long had plagued France, using them to fight both the English and the infamous free companies; he also attempted to form a nationwide militia of archers, but nothing much came of this idea.

These mid-century forces differed markedly from those that had fought at Agincourt, and the differences became more pronounced through the second half of the century. Armor tended to grow lighter again, since heavy plate made a soldier slow and clumsy without providing adequate protection against arrows or pikes. Some officers still used full armor, and it was worn for tournaments, but most troopers began to wear only helmet, breastplate and backplate in battle. Nobles still formed an important part of the army as they made up most of the cavalry and the officer corps of the infantry, but as paid soldiers they were more susceptible to discipline than the old feudal levy. And the growing importance of the pike, a cheap weapon capable of stopping cavalry, made infantry recruited from among commoners ever more significant. One far-reaching effect of these developments was that military power came to depend more upon financial resources than upon vast lands for the endowment of vassals. Thus, at the very end of the Hundred Years War some of the elements of modern armies began to appear.

During the century of war political as well as military changes took place, stimulated largely by the demands of the great struggle. In England, Edward III's preoccupation with the French wars had led him to allow certain powers to parliament that it likely would not have obtained otherwise, particularly the right to demand dismissal of officers of the crown for improper acts; this power, which later came to be called impeachment, was an important step in the development of ministerial responsibility to the parliament. Edward's reign also saw the House of Lords begin to take firmer form. The notion that the grand council, ancestor of the upper house, should be determined by feudal tenure as provided in *Magna Carta* clearly was obsolete by the late fourteenth century; Edward's predecessors had invited whomever they thought important, with small regard for the lands they held, and Edward tended to invite men whose fathers had sat. While the hereditary character of the House of Lords was not established definitely until the fifteenth century, it made great progress during Edward III's reign. And at the same time the king tended to meet prelates separately on church questions, so far fewer bishops and abbots came to parliament; a sort of general principle developed that only those ecclesiastical lords attended who also held secular baronies, who were lords temporal as well as lords spiritual.

Finally, Edward summoned the knights and burgesses to parliament with greater frequency and allowed some increase in the scope of their activities. During his reign it became habitual for these men, who were beginning to be called "the Commons," to draft petitions on matters they considered important and then to submit them to the grand council; if this second body endorsed the petition, it was sent on to the king, and petitions that he approved became statutes of the realm. Thus was born a form of parliamentary legislation in England. The king and the lords retained control, but it became customary for most legislation and all money bills to be initiated in the Commons. All of these developments owed something to Edward's involvement in the long and costly wars in France, but none more than parliamentary control of taxation. In order to get parliament to vote him money regularly, Edward promised to take no taxes without its consent and even agreed to allow parliamentary committees some right to audit royal expenditures. The results of all this were that during the reign of Edward III the outlines of the modern parliament became apparent, and parliament became an integral part of royal government, sufficiently important that later kings put considerable effort into manipulating its sessions and the election of its members.

Less a direct result of the war but perhaps influenced by Edward's desire that things run smoothly during his absences from England was the further development of royal justice. On the one hand, the king's chancellor developed a tribunal called chancery court with very wide powers in equity, to provide justice in the king's name in cases where there were no clear laws or precedents. On the other hand, a whole new group of judges was appointed all over the country, called justices of the peace; these men were drawn from that class of lesser nobility and untitled property owners called gentry, the same that provided the knights of the shires to parliament, and though officers of the king's government, they were unpaid. They soon became the chief power in local government.

In France, the unhappy course of the greater part of the war delayed further development of royal government except for the continuous increase in size of the royal bureaucracy. Though at the beginning of the fourteenth century Philip IV's administration was very similar to that of Edward I, by the end of the century the English government was much more sophisticated. The lack of development of the estates general, for reasons of provincialism already noted, made the raising of money by the French crown quite haphazard. A variety of levies was used: sales taxes, a tax on salt called the *gabelle*, a hearth tax, and in addition the crown very frequently debased the coinage so as to pay off its debts in cheap money.

All of these measures bore hard upon the bourgeoisie, and the annoyance of this class was aggravated by the magnificent incompetence demonstrated by the kings and the nobility, especially at Crécy and Poitiers. In the late 1350s, when the dauphin was in desperate straits to raise money for the ransom of King John, several of the towns of France, led by Paris, attempted to use the estates general to win some control of royal government, at least of its tax powers. The dauphin was in a weak position and was inclined to negotiate so long as the bourgeoisie remained moderate in its demands, but impatience led to violence, and the effort to attain political influence soon became a full-scale urban revolt. At the same time, the unrestrained ravages of English plundering expeditions and special war levies by noble lords resulted in a violent peasant rising in the north of France. The Parisian leader of the urban revolt, Etienne Marcel, tried to make common cause with the peasants, but this was their undoing. Troops repressed the peasant revolt savagely, and the conservative upper bourgeoisie, as disturbed as the nobles by the violence and the overtones of social revolution in the peasant movement, abandoned Marcel and the other urban leaders and opened the gates of Paris to the dauphin. The commoners' attempt to win a position of influence over royal policy had failed.

During the 1360s and 1370s the able and effective Charles V restored order and achieved an important gain for royal government; having persuaded the estates general to approve collection of taxes without putting a time limit on the approval, he collected them year after year, establishing a pattern of more or less regular taxation by the king's decision. But during the long reign of the insane Charles VI (1380–1422), the government again was disrupted seriously in the struggle between the Armagnacs and the Burgundians who fought to control the power and the patronage of the crown. Only in the reign of Charles VII (1422–1461), when France was recovering militarily, did governmental development make much progress, and then it was along lines very different from the English pattern. Able ministers developed for the king not only the beginnings of a standing army, already referred to, but also complete independence from the estates general in matters of taxation, so that within the royal domain the king's authority was virtually unlimited. On the other hand, great princes such as the duke of Burgundy and the duke of Brittany were almost independent and many others enjoyed virtual autonomy. Thus, while Charles established in his domain patterns that were to lead to absolutism, at the end of his reign there were still large areas of France that lay outside his effective control, and the consolidation of most of France into an effective national monarchy came only in the latter half of the fifteenth century.

Chapter 17

The Disintegration of Medieval Europe

In addition to the governmental and military changes that took place in the English and French monarchies during the course of the Hundred Years War, the fourteenth and fifteenth centuries also witnessed other significant transformations and innovations. Within these two centuries the medieval papacy collapsed, popular heresies flourished again, the European monarchies underwent important social consolidation and voyages of exploration discovered the New World and opened direct sea routes to the Far East.

When Clement V moved the papacy to the papally owned city of Avignon in the south of France in 1305, the transfer was intended to be temporary, but for seventy years the popes remained exiled from the spiritual capital of the west and dangerously susceptible to the influence of the French monarchy. Philip IV's highhanded treatment of Boniface VIII already had dealt a serious blow to papal prestige, and exile from Rome proved even more damaging. For all Europeans, Rome was a city with special connotations. It had been the capital of the Roman Empire, which continued to be remembered as a sort of golden age of the past; it was the site of the tombs of two Apostles, Peter and Paul; for centuries it had been the seat of the papacy. It was *the* Holy City of the west. The pronouncements of a pope at Avignon simply could not carry the same authority, the same sense of ecclesiastical majesty, as those issued from the ancient See of St. Peter.

On the other hand, the period that the papacy spent at Avignon was not without some notable achievements. Missionary work was expanded considerably, especially in Persia and China. The papal administration, the *curia,* was organized into highly specialized departments and became, probably, the most efficient government in fourteenth century Europe; special sections staffed by experts dealt with such matters as justice, finance, appointments and dogma. At the same time, papal power over churches throughout Europe increased markedly as a consequence of determined efforts at centralization through more vigorous enforcement of papal rights in matters of appointments and clerical discipline and of more efficient papal taxation.

Unfortunately, some of these achievements were very unpopular throughout most of Europe. The expansion of papal control of appointments often resulted in church positions being filled by unknown foreigners who were regarded with suspicion and hostility by governments and populace alike, while papal taxation moved money beyond the control of monarchs and reduced the resources of the rest of the clergy. Normal resentment was aggravated by the fact that the Avignon papacy was infamous for pomp and luxury, expenditures that did not inspire willing contributions from all Christians. As a result of financial issues the clergy became divided against itself; there was no way to increase very substantially the total amount of money that ecclesiastical taxation could extract from the community of the faithful, so the usual result of new fiscal mechanisms was redistribution. One churchman's gain became another's loss, and of course this was resented. When a bishop took more of diocesan revenue, the parish clergy was left with less. When the pope increased his levies upon the dioceses, the bishops lost. Complicating the matter still further was the rivalry between regular and secular clergy, that is, between monastic groups and the parochial organization of priests and bishops; if monks or friars, who often served as papal agents, increased their activities in preaching, hearing confessions and administering sacraments, the offerings they collected escaped from parish and diocesan coffers, for the regular clergy usually answered only to their own superiors and to the pope rather than to bishops. Thus, on the whole the Avignon period was quite damaging to the papacy. Despite positive achievements in administrative efficiency and the expansion of Christian missions, papal prestige declined and wide resentment of the papacy arose.

Some popes were aware that continued residence at Avignon was dangerous, and they made serious efforts to return to Rome. Pope Urban V (1362–1370) did return, but he found the city in such a shambles that he bowed to the pleas of the cardinals and went back to Avignon. Then Pope Gregory XI (1370–1378) visited Rome, possibly with some thought of re-establishing papal residency, and he died there; his death was a catalyst to much of the discontent that surrounded the Avignon papacy, and the consequences soon proved disastrous.

Not only had the papal government been the chief glory of Rome until the transfer to Avignon, it also had been the city's primary source of income through staff salaries, the household expenditures of popes and cardinals and the money spent by tourists and pilgrims. Thus, the Roman citizenry had many reasons to resent the transfer of the papacy to Avignon, and when Gregory XI died, there was a riot, and a mob threatened the cardinals with violence if they did not elect an Italian pope. Under this pressure the cardinals chose Urban VI, in 1378, but he quickly antagonized them by threatening to reduce the luxury in which they lived, and in any case many of them found Rome dismal and dilapidated. Regretting the splendor of Avignon, thirteen rebellious cardinals elected another pope, Clement VII, who returned to Avignon, and for the next four decades Europe was presented with the unedifying spectacle of rival popes in Rome and Avignon, who promptly excommunicated each other. The situation became still worse in 1409 when the pressure of public opinion, and especially the insistence of the king of France, forced the convocation of the Council of Pisa, attended by five hundred prelates. The Council deposed both the Roman and Avignese popes, successors of Urban VI and Clement VII, and recognized the election of Alexander V; however, the reform failed, for the first two refused to admit the council's authority to depose them, and Europe had three popes.

The Great Schism finally was healed a half dozen years later when another council met at Constance from 1414 to 1417. One pope was deposed and held prisoner to assure the effectiveness of the deposition; a second was induced to resign; the third was obstinate, but all of his supporters deserted him, so he could be ignored until his death in 1423. And the Council of Constance chose a new pope, Martin V (1417-1431), whom everyone recognized. The Great Schism was over.

Martin V reestablished a unified papacy in Rome, dissolved the Council of Constance and turned his attention to repossessing the Papal States, which had been usurped to a great extent during the century of troubles. Papal difficulties were not yet at an end, however, for the decline of papal prestige had led some Christians to assert the supremacy of councils over popes, the return to Rome necessitated an extensive and costly renovation of the papal buildings there, and the endeavor to reestablish effective control of the papal states committed the papacy to deep involvement in fifteenth century Italian politics.

The conciliar movement was the most immediate of these problems. The basic idea, that a council of prelates and representatives of the European governments held authority superior to a pope, was expressed by several fourteenth century writers, though there were differences of opinion concerning who could convene and dismiss councils and how they should function. When the papacy was dishonored and the religious affairs of Europe thrown into a turmoil by the schism, the conciliar idea won more support, including first the king of France and then the Holy Roman Emperor. One group at the Council of Pisa sought to impose limitations upon the papacy, but it was a minority, and in any case its proposals were lost in the general failure of the council. However, extreme conciliarists were stronger at Constance, and that council issued two decrees on the subject, one declaring councils superior to popes and the other providing for their frequent convocation.

Martin V took up the struggle against conciliarism as soon as the schism was ended, declaring it impious to appeal to a council against a pope and dissolving the Council of Constance. The conciliarists were not beaten, however, and Martin's successor, Eugenius IV (1431-1447), found that a council which he summoned at Basel was strongly antipapal; it refused to accept his commands, refused to dissolve when he so ordered, and even elected briefly another antipope. Happily for the papacy, the Council of Basel fell to quarreling over questions of heresy and reunion with the Greek

Church and proved ineffective; in 1449 it finally was persuaded to dissolve by Pope Nicholas V (1447–1455), but the question remained to haunt successive popes for another century until it was buried by the Council of Trent in the 1540s.

Throughout the greater part of the fifteenth century and the early sixteenth century, much of the energy and the revenue of the papacy was absorbed by the struggle to rebuild the papal states, and the papacy became just one of several Italian governments vying for power in the peninsula at the expense of its spiritual responsibilities. At the turn of the century Italy was ravaged by armies paid for from the papal treasury and led by a pope's son, Caesar Borgia, while the same pope's daughter had become infamous through implication in murder by poison.

In addition, the papacy faced very high extraordinary costs in that the Vatican complex in Rome was in a state of ruin when the papacy returned from Avignon, and to maintain the prestige of the head of the Church rebuilding had to be done on a grand scale by the best artists. The major item was St. Peter's Church, the mother church of all of western Christendom. Architectural studies showed that the old church had deteriorated to a point where repairs and renovations were impractical, and it was decided to demolish the old structure and build a large domed church in the new renaissance style, the biggest and grandest church in Europe. Like involvement in Italian politics, the new construction work at Rome proved very expensive.

Financial strain all through the church and the long period of weakened papal leadership finally led to serious problems of clerical morality and blatant ecclesiastical corruption. Abuses of position by high clerics had become an open scandal. Bishops and popes kept mistresses and found careers in the church for their illegitimate offspring. There were many instances of laymen being forced to pay for the sacraments they received, of offices in the church being sold, of clerics holding church offices for their revenues but not fulfilling the duties of them. There was little conscientious preaching, few orthodox seminaries for the training of priests, too many instances of clergy who were ignorant and illiterate. Under such circumstances it is not surprising that the church failed to command any great loyalty among the laity.

There was another problem, too, that in the long run proved even more serious. The church had become a formal, highly-structured organization. It offered the possibility of salvation to all who accepted the faith as the church taught it, participated in the rituals that the church presented and took the sacraments that the church provided. In such a pattern there was little room for devotion, for love, for personal religious experience. Rather, the individual Christian was to follow a carefully marked path and trust the church to assure his salvation. But through the late fourteenth and fifteenth centuries, deep-rooted popular piety was growing into a fervent evangelical movement, a Christian revival. In the forefront of the new movement were the Lollards in England and the Hussites in Bohemia, both popular heresies potentially as dangerous as thirteenth century Albigensianism.

The Lollards were led by John Wycliffe, a royal chaplain and Oxford don, who in the 1370s preached and published such ideas as a church without property and a laity in direct communication with God without the intervention of the clergy; he also was a major participant in the first English translation of the Bible. Wycliffe's efforts were so successful that it was said that every fourth man in England was a Lollard by the end of the fourteenth century. The movement declined after Wycliffe's death, though in the sixteenth century it seems still to have had a few adherents who were absorbed into Anglicanism. Wycliffe's doctrines spread to eastern Europe through Lollards in the suite of an English princess who was married to the king of Bohemia, and there they stimulated John Hus, a professor at the university in Prague. Until his death in 1415, Hus preached and wrote tirelessly, demanding reform of the church and asserting the supremacy of the Scriptures. The Hussites soon became involved with Bohemian resentment of German influences, which were strong in the clergy and in the university, and when the Council of Constance burned Hus as a heretic in 1415, in violation of a safe-conduct that had been given him, the identification of religious reform and Bohemian national feeling was complete. Despite a decade and a half of religious wars, including papal proclamation of a Bohemian crusade in imitation of the earlier Albigensian crusade, the Hussites remained unconquered, and in the mid-1430s the Council of Basel finally worked out a compromise that ended the fighting. The Hussite movement remained an important element of Bohemian society and formed a basis for the rapid spread of Calvinism in Bohemia in the sixteenth century.

The Disintegration of Medieval Europe 239

In sum, the fourteenth and fifteenth centuries saw developments dangerous to the unity of western Christendom. Even after the end of the schism, papal prestige was at a low ebb, and papal leadership of the church was practically non-existent. Clerical morality was an open scandal, and the whole church was wracked by financial abuses. And popular piety was generating evangelical movements with strong anti-clerical overtones. To make matters worse, princely governments were growing ever stronger and ever more aggressive, and the policies they were attempting were growing more expensive. As an international institution of considerable wealth and influence, the church often had been regarded by princes as an obstacle, but by the early sixteenth century the problem had become even more serious. All over Europe ambitious princes eyed the wealth of the church greedily and resented the church's support of the *status quo*.

In the second half of the fifteenth century the European monarchies underwent further important development. Shortly after the end of the Hundred Years War, Charles VII of France died and was succeeded by his son Louis XI (1461–1483). A thoroughly unlikeable person—homely, coarse and overbearing—Louis had a keen mind and relentless determination to rebuild the power of the French crown. Only a few years after his accession he faced a great alliance of nobles called the League of the Public Weal, and he immediately set the pattern that he was to follow throughout his reign in dealing with the princes. First he appeared to concede all they asked; then he bribed away their support; then he set them to quarreling with one another so that they were no longer any threat to him and slowly rescinded what he had granted earlier. This notably unchivalrous conduct was politically successful, and it avoided fighting. Partly through calculated efforts and partly through good fortune Louis added immense territory to the possessions of the royal family. Anjou and Provence came to the crown by testament of their last ruler, a tribute to Louis' diplomacy and bribery; Berry and Gascony were acquired by inheritance, simple good fortune.

But Louis XI's most important success in his struggle to reduce the great princes to obedience to the crown was his victory over the duke of Burgundy. One of the most interesting political phenomena of fourteenth and fifteenth century Europe was the brief prominence

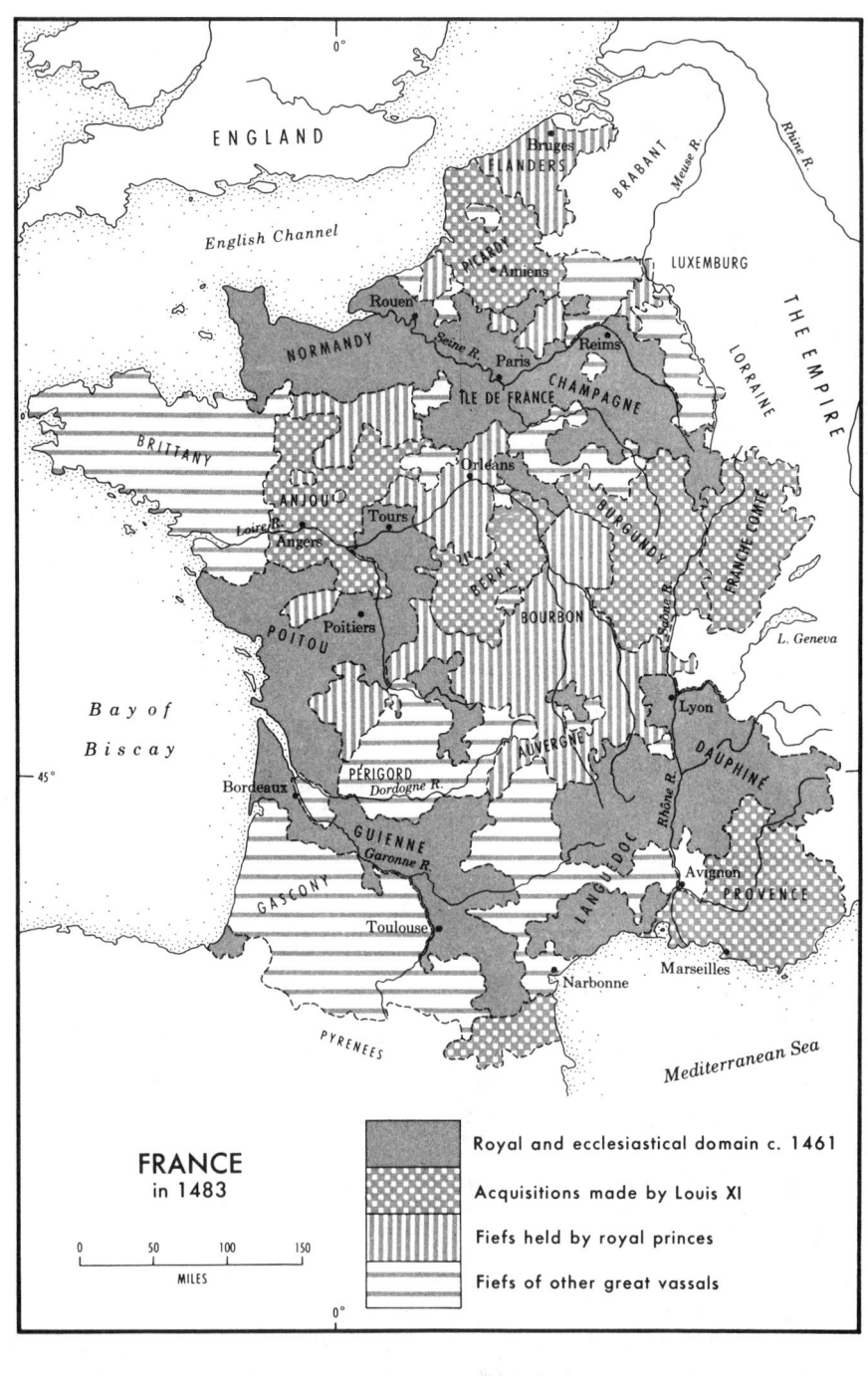

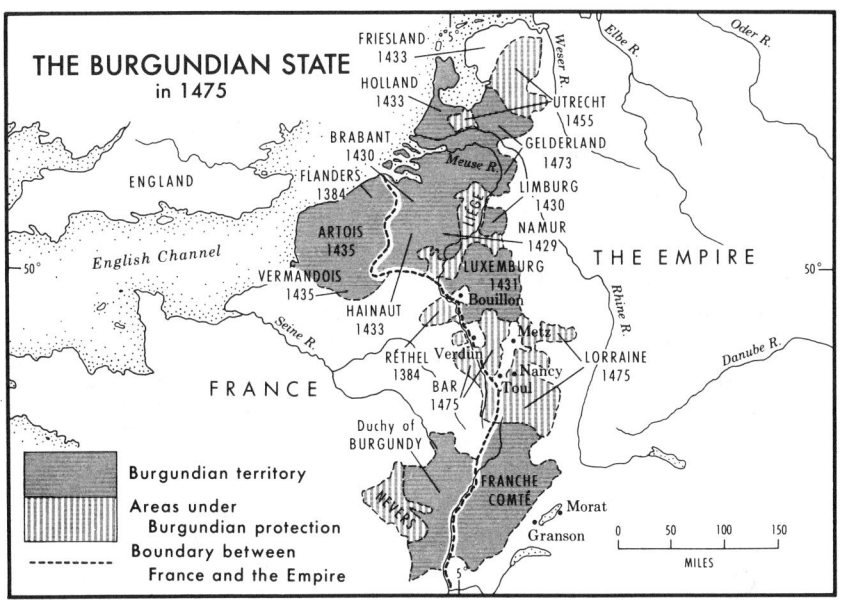

of the collection of territories between France and Germany usually called the Burgundian inheritance. In 1361 the duchy of Burgundy came into the possession of the French crown, and King John "the Good" gave it to his younger son, Philip. Duke Philip married the daughter and heiress of the last count of Flanders, and upon the count's death in 1384, he added to his possessions the extremely wealthy county of Flanders with its textile industry, the imperial fief called the Franche-Comté and numerous lesser territories. Then he pushed his possessions into the Dutch Netherlands through the marriages that he arranged for his children. Thus the duke of Burgundy became one of the greatest princes of France, and during the minority and then the madness of King Charles VI, he disputed control of the whole realm with the House of Orléans. John "the Fearless," who succeeded to the Burgundian titles in 1404, fought the Armagnac (Orléans) faction, allied with the English in the Hundred Years War and saw the French crown humbled before he was assassinated in 1419. Thereafter the Burgundians, under John's son Philip "the Good," supported the English until 1435 when the French king recognized most of the duke's claims in the Treaty of Arras.

By about the middle of the fifteenth century, the Burgundian inheritance had grown to include much of the old Carolingian Kingdom of Lotharingia except Alsace and Lorraine, a great sweep of territories from the Franche-Comté, on the Swiss border, through the duchy of Burgundy in eastern France and down the Rhine to the Dutch Netherlands. It appeared that the end of the Hundred Years War might see the English threat to France from the west replaced by a Burgundian threat from the northeast, but Duke Philip "the Good" was a gentle man and a patron of the arts, not an expansionist. So long as he lived, Burgundy was more notable for its cultural vigor, especially the painting of the Van Eycks, than for any danger it might pose to the French crown. However, in 1467 Duke Philip died and was succeeded by his ambitious son, Charles "the Rash"; it was he whom Louis XI had to confront.

Charles "the Rash" hoped to build his lands into a kingdom between France and Germany, and he constituted a real danger to the French monarchy's recovery from the Hundred Years War. To check him, Louis XI stirred up revolt in his lands and subsidized his enemies, but nonetheless Charles made progress, for in 1473 he managed to seize Alsace and Lorraine. Then three years later Louis XI enjoyed success when a Swiss force in the service of the duke of Lorraine (but paid by Louis) defeated the Burgundians and killed Duke Charles, leaving the whole Burgundian inheritance in the hands of Charles' daughter Mary. Louis XI would have liked to obtain the whole inheritance for the French crown, but Mary refused marriage with his son (who was still a child), and the king had to content himself with seizing the duchy of Burgundy, for which there were legal pretexts. The rest of the inheritance went to the rulers of the Holy Roman Empire when Mary married Maximilian von Habsburg, and once again the old "middle kingdom" became a matter of contention between French and German rulers.

When Louis XI died in 1483, the only French prince who remained largely independent of the king was the duke of Brittany, and Louis' daughter Anne de Beaujeu, acting as regent for her young brother Charles VIII, soon assured that Brittany, too, would come into the possession of the crown. She arranged for young Charles to marry the daughter and heiress of the duke, so that by the close of the fifteenth century French territorial consolidation had made great progress. Except for the large eastern areas of Alsace, Lorraine, Franche-Comté and Savoy, only small border territories would be added in the shaping of the modern French nation.

Social consolidation also progressed considerably in France in the fifteenth century. Resentment against English depredations and the inspiration of leaders like Bertran Du Guesclin and Joan of Arc had built a strong national feeling, though in a realm the size of France regionalism remained strong, and divisions between classes still were to loom large in France's future. The fifteenth century is too early to speak of nationalism, for "isms" imply deep commitment to abstract concepts, and at this time national feeling still was identified with the king. Nonetheless, the French had developed a sense of their own uniqueness and a pride in their culture that might be called national consciousness; as a result of this territorial and social consolidation the government of Louis XI and his successors usually is referred to as national monarchy in contrast to earlier feudal monarchy.

England, too, underwent important political development in the late fifteenth century. After the death of Henry V in 1422, En-

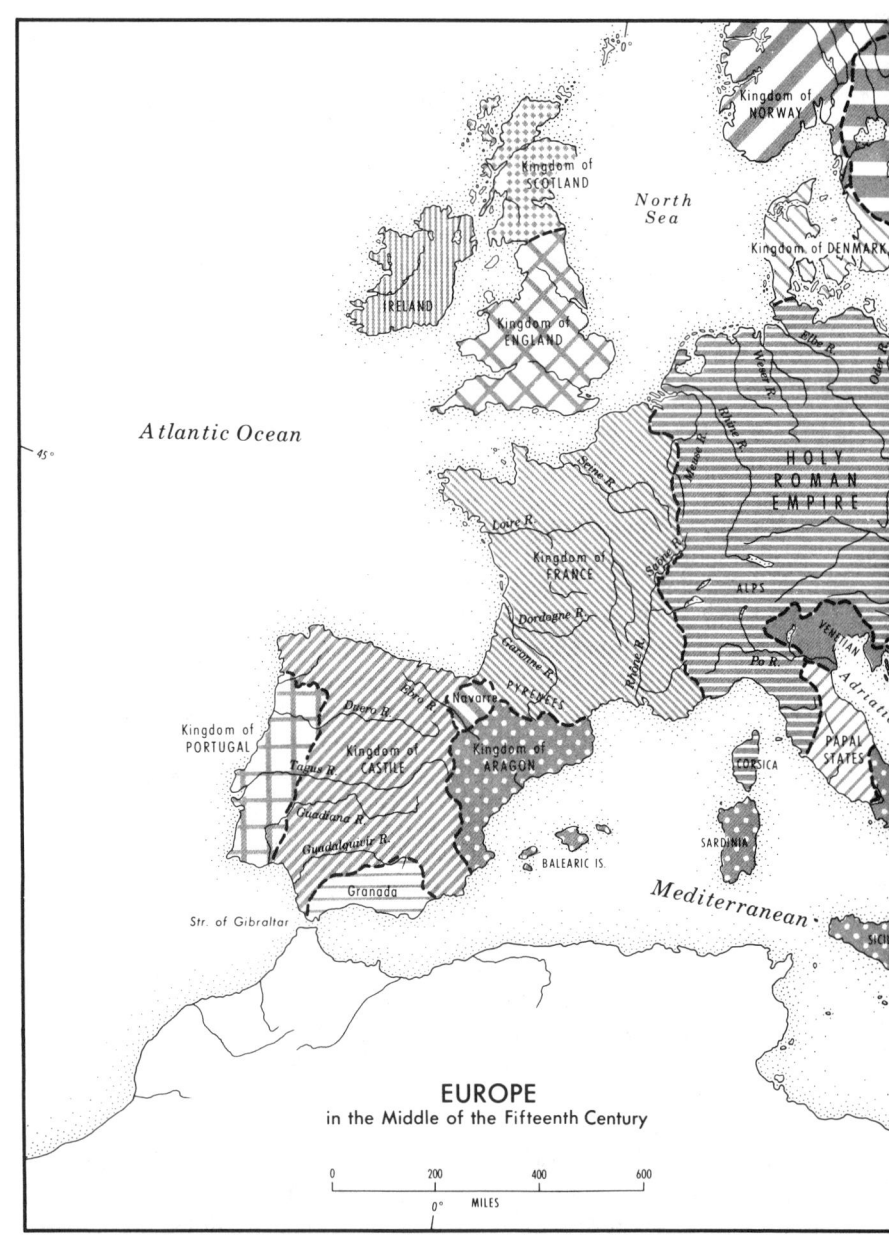

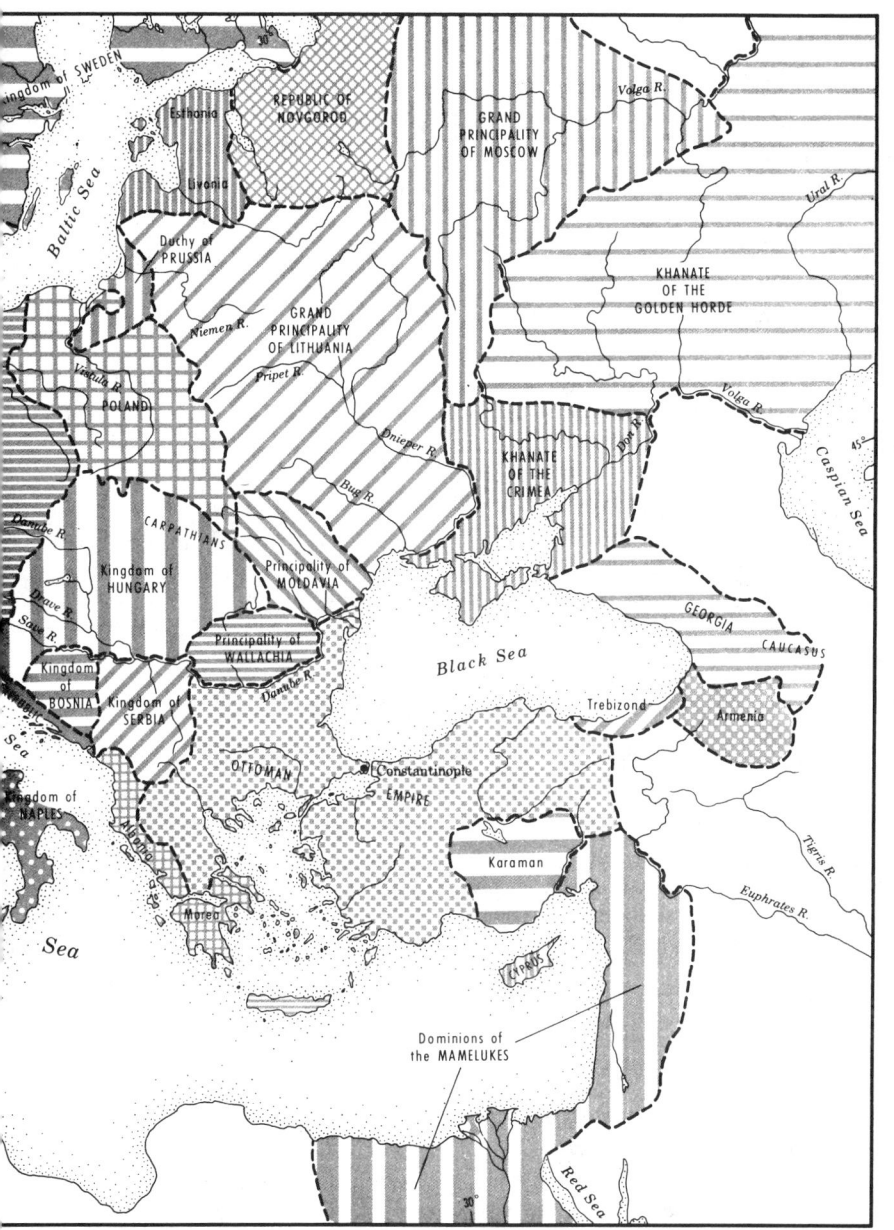

gland's affairs deteriorated rapidly as military reverses in France were paralleled by aristocratic rivalries at home. Henry VI (1422–1461) was first a minor, then a weak young man, and then insane, and civil war soon broke out between his Lancastrian relatives and the house of York; the struggle is known as the Wars of the Roses because of the devices adopted by the contenders—a red rose for Lancaster and a white rose for York. After Henry's death two Yorkists wore the crown, Edward IV (1461–1483) and his brother Richard III (1483–1485), but the civil wars continued unabated. Not until 1485 was stability restored with the victory of a somewhat distant Lancastrian claimant, Henry Tudor, who took the crown as Henry VII (1485–1509) and married the heiress of the house of York, uniting the competing claims.

Henry VII rebuilt the strength of the English crown rapidly, and in the process he both encouraged and drew support from the growing merchant class. Establishing an administrative court called Star Chamber, he levied heavy fines upon many of the great noble families which maintained private military forces in defiance of old statutes; this policy reduced somewhat the political importance of the great families and abolished large feudal armies and private warfare, two results very popular with the business classes that sought stability for peaceful trade and greater political influence for themselves. Henry's most successful effort to strengthen the alliance between the crown and the middle class was his negotiation of a commercial agreement with the Habsburg government of the Netherlands in 1496, the *intercursus magnus*, which regularized the position of English woolen merchants and fixed customs duties. Henry VII's consistent encouragement of the middle classes won their firm support, and when he died, his son Henry VIII (1509–1547) inherited a crown that was both strong and popular.

Taken together, the administrative developments of the late fourteenth century and the popular policies of Henry VII in the late fifteenth century resulted in a growing integration of the various classes of English society. There is no doubt that by the fifteenth century most Englishmen of all social classes thought of themselves as a distinct people, and when they went to Flanders to trade or to France in war, they were conscious of an alien environment in more than language. Given the compactness of England and its insularity, national consciousness had developed even more strongly than in France, and the Tudors quickly built a consolidated national monarchy.

Two other monarchies developed importantly in the late fifteenth century, and a marriage alliance joined them together into a vast new political complex. Maximilian von Habsburg, who married the Burgundian heiress, was the son of Frederick III of the Holy Roman Empire, and though that crown was elective rather than hereditary, the Habsburgs managed the election so that at Frederick's death, his son succeeded him as Maximilian I (1493–1519). Since the middle of the fifteenth century, the Habsburgs had held, in addition to the imperial crown, family lands in southeastern Germany—Austria, Styria, Carinthia and the Tyrol—and the crown of Bohemia. Maximilian's marriage added to these holdings the wealthy and strategically located Burgundian lands of western Germany and the Netherlands. Thus, for the first time in three centuries there appeared the possibility of a Holy Roman Emperor having sufficient resources to control the German princes and to undertake effective monarchical development.

At roughly the same time a territorial consolidation took place that unified all of the Iberian peninsula except Portugal. In 1469 Ferdinand, heir to Aragon, married Isabella, heiress to Castile, and when they ascended their respective thrones in the 1470s, they combined the resources of the two kingdoms to complete the Christian reconquest of Spain; the Moorish kingdom of Granada in the south fell to their armies in 1492. Forced Christian conversions were instituted immediately, thousands of Moors and Jews were expelled from Spain in the decade following the victory, and the Spanish Inquisition (founded in 1478) was expanded greatly. By modern standards these policies are reprehensible on humane grounds, and they had adverse economic effects very quickly, but given the Spanish tradition of seven hundred years of crusade, Catholic uniformity was an important and effective aspect of national consolidation.

Joanna, a daughter of Ferdinand and Isabella, was heiress to all of Spain, and when she married Maximilian I's son, Philip, an enormous collection of territories was brought together. The son of this marriage of Joanna and Philip was named Charles. In 1516 he became king of Spain; in 1519 he became Holy Roman Emperor as Charles V, the title by which he is known most commonly; he held the family lands of the Habsburgs in southeastern Germany and all of the Burgundian inheritance except ducal Burgundy; Spanish armies and Spanish rights of inheritance brought him Naples and Milan, assuring him control of both ends of the Italian peninsula; and rapid Spanish expansion in the New World made him Lord of the Indies and master of the booty of conquered Indian empires of the Americas. Jealous contemporaries were prone to remark: "Oh happy Austria; while other powers fight, Austria marries," and certainly marriage alliances had resulted in unprecedented expansion of Habsburg rule. But Charles V was not spared the necessity of fighting, for his reign witnessed renewed Turkish expansion in the Danube valley and the Mediterranean, intensification of French efforts in Italy and the Lutheran Reformation in Germany.

One of the most far-reaching European achievements at the end of the Middle Ages was the great development of seafaring that resulted in the opening of new routes to the fabulous east and the discovery of new continents to the west. Europeans had traveled and traded fairly extensively in both the Near and Far East in the thirteenth and early fourteenth centuries when the great Mongol Empire maintained stability and security all the way from the China coast to the eastern frontiers of Europe; Marco Polo is only the most famous of many travelers of this period. Then in the middle of the fourteenth century the Mongol Empire collapsed and was succeeded by a number of smaller states. In western Asia this political convulsion was accompanied by a Moslem resurgence which inspired the capture of Constantinople by the Turks in 1453 and much confusion and fighting everywhere; as a result, security of travel declined and the cost of trade increased, which provided increased incentive to seek new routes to the sources of spices and silk. The commercial motive was also reinforced by a religious motive, for the Moslem revival intensified the hostility between Christendom and Islam, and the fall of Constantinople frightened Christians everywhere. A widely believed medieval myth held that there was a Christian kingdom in east Africa, and there was considerable enthusiasm, especially on the part of the papacy and the Iberian gov-

The Disintegration of Medieval Europe 249

ernments, for finding this kingdom and establishing an alliance against the Moslems.

Probably this crusading ideal was the chief motivation of the most organized explanatory work, the expeditions sent out by Portugal's Prince Henry the Navigator in the last years of the fourteenth century and the first half of the fifteenth century. Prince Henry's captains explored the Madeira Islands and the Azores and pushed down the west coast of Africa. By the 1440s they had passed the barren northern reaches of the coast, rounded Cape Verde and established a flourishing trade with west Africa. Though Prince Henry died in 1460, the exploratory work went on; in 1487 Bartolomeu Dias rounded the Cape of Good Hope, the southern tip of Africa, before returning to Portugal, and a decade later Vasco da Gama followed his route and continued on to India. Thus, the Portuguese were the first to develop a direct all-water route to the east.

Voyages westward were much more haphazard affairs. Vikings settled Greenland late in the tenth century and visited the North American coast early in the eleventh century; records of their activities are sparse and inconclusive, but it would appear that the Greenland colony lasted until the mid-fifteenth century with at least sporadic ventures to the mainland. There also is some inferential evidence that European fishermen fished the Grand Banks in the fifteenth century and probably saw the mainland, though this cannot be proved. However, none of these early voyages, known or assumed, had permanent effects or influenced later attempts.

Little is known of the early life of Christopher Columbus save that he was a Genoese who spent several years in Portugal and made some voyages under the Portuguese flag. Since Ptolemy's *Geography* had been translated into Latin in 1410, the idea that the earth was round and the east could be reached by sailing west had gained ever wider acceptance. Columbus wished to try this idea, but he needed financing. Turned down by the king of Portugal, he approached the Spanish rulers, Ferdinand and Isabella, and though he had to await the successful conclusion of the war against Granada, Queen Isabella financed him in 1492. It is not altogether

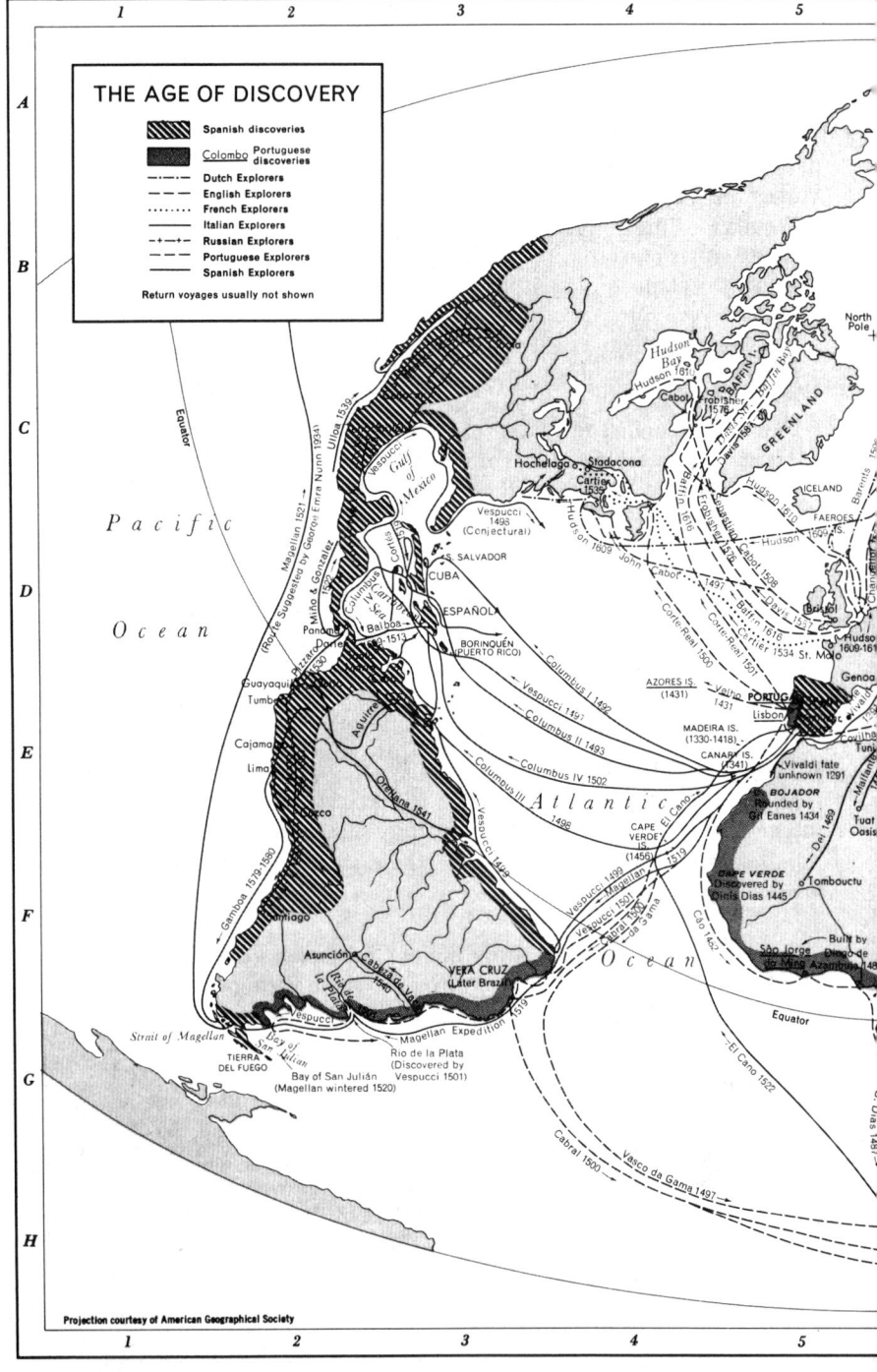

clear just what Columbus' voyage was supposed to achieve, but it would appear that he and his patroness hoped for both the discovery of new lands and the opening of a direct route to China. In any case, Columbus' four voyages in the last decade of the fifteenth century and the first years of the sixteenth century established the Spanish flag firmly in the Caribbean Islands and Central America.

The successes of Da Gama and Columbus sparked a whole series of voyages. In the late 1490s John Cabot, an Italian resident in England, explored some of the North American coast, but since he found neither gold nor spices, the effort was abandoned after two voyages. At the turn of the century, Alonso di Ojeda and Amerigo Vespucci explored some of the South American coast for Spain, discovering the Amazon River, and in 1501–1502 Vespucci returned, this time in the Portuguese service. It was largely in consequence of his account of this second voyage and his insistence that this was a new land, not part of Asia, that geographers began calling the New World America. And after these first voyages, exploration proceeded rapidly. In a three year voyage (1519–1522) only a quarter century after the successes of Da Gama and Columbus, Ferdinand Magellan's expedition circumnavigated the earth.

At the end of the fifteenth century some important elements of medieval society, such as the papacy, clearly had declined in importance, while others, such as the towns, had become more significant; monarchical government was more elaborate than it had been a century or two earlier, and it rested upon different bases; explorations and discoveries had opened wider horizons, but no one about 1500 could have predicted the great growth of colonial empires that was to follow. With hindsight it is relatively easy to indicate that medieval society was dying and that Europe stood upon the threshold of the modern world, but it is doubtful that in most of Europe there was any sense of entering a new era. An exception might be made for Italy, where a very self-conscious cultural revolution had been developing for a century and a half; but since the Italians drew their inspiration from classical sources, they did not call their achievements innovation but rather a rebirth, the Renaissance.

Chapter 18

The Renaissance

Any survey of the development of Europe must take note of cultural changes, and it should be noted, too, that to a large extent the nature of the cultural product of any given period is determined by the interests of the social elite that controls the society's resources. Thus, Greco-Roman culture, in which the social elite was a leisured class of worldly aristocrats, consisted largely of philosophy, literature, and drama which tried to explain man's place in the natural and social world and of plastic arts which idealized the human form and embellished daily life; this culture disintegrated before the impact of economic decline, civil war and barbarian invasions.

The society that emerged after the decline of Rome had to struggle at first for bare subsistence, and the new elite consisted largely of illiterate soldiers. Artistic product seems to have been limited to a few articles of daily life, such as ornaments for clothing and tableware of precious metals, and to finely worked hafts for weapons and accouterments for horses; items of this sort, which survive today as museum pieces, suggest highly skilled craftsmanship, but the scope of such artistry was very limited, and of course it was accomplished by almost no literary product in a primarily illiterate society. Some of the more Romanized Germanic kings supported a weak revival of Latin pagan literature, but with few exceptions it was the church that could provide literate and reflective individuals and only the church that had the resources and willingness to support them. Thus, it is not surprising that Europe's outstanding writers between about A.D. 400 and A.D. 800 were two bishops and a monk: St. Augustine (*Confessions* and *The City of God*), Gregory of Tours (*The History of the Franks*) and Bede (*The Ecclesiastical History of the English People*). This sort of cultural development reached a peak in the Carolingian renaissance and then suffered another decline under the impact of the Magyar and Viking invasions.

During the rapid development of medieval society between the eleventh and thirteenth centuries, a period that produced the monastic and cathedral schools and then the universities, there was a corresponding cultural revival, but again it was largely in the service of the church. One must not ignore the impressive military architecture of medieval castles, the beautifully carved furniture and finely woven tapestry that embellished later medieval households or the intricately developed epics and poems recited and sung for the entertainment of the nobility; but the finest products of medieval culture were the great cathedrals with their rich decoration and the scholastic works of theology and Christian philosophy, all produced under the patronage of the church. Despite contact with highly sophisticated Islamic thought and the recovery of important parts of the classical heritage, medieval culture subsumed all to the Christian interests of its patrons. Thus, though the idea may be repugnant to modern artists and intellectuals, the direction of European cultural development depended upon the interests of the elite that commanded sufficient wealth to support that culture; in medieval Europe the elite meant primarily churchmen, though noble patronage produced a minor counterpoint to the dominant religious culture.

While the Hundred Years War was being fought in western Europe, a cultural revolution was developing in Italy that was to inspire a whole series of transformations of European society. This movement, called the Italian renaissance, began in the fourteenth century, and in the fifteenth century it swept through northern and central Italy. The culture that grew out of the Renaissance differed from medieval culture in that its chief interests were in political and social life, with stress upon the human individual, rather than in religion and eternity with stress upon God. This secular emphasis reflected a new sort of patronage, town governments and wealthy businessmen instead of the church and wealthy ecclesiastics.

Ever since they had attained virtual independence under the Hohenstaufen emperors in the twelfth and thirteenth centuries, the towns of northern and north central Italy had been developing rapidly, both economically and politically, and rivalries among them were fierce. One of the most prominent was Florence, in Tuscany; its industry and commerce grew so successfully that in the mid-thirteenth century it reestablished gold coinage, the florin, and its money quickly was accepted all over Europe. Florence fought wars with its neighbors, especially Pisa and Siena, and its internal politics hardly were less violent, with twenty-one guilds struggling for control of the city government, but despite these vicissitudes the city continued to increase in wealth and strength, and in the fourteenth century it became the cradle of the Italian renaissance.

The Renaissance appeared first as a new human element within the general Christian context of medieval Italian culture. This new interest showed itself in two ways, a greater concern with man and the world he lived in and a growth of a literature in the vernacular, the language of the people, instead of Latin. In the arts it appeared in the form of more realism, especially in the treatment of human subjects. In the birth of this new literature and painting, two Florentines were prominent, Dante (1265–1321) and Giotto (1276–1337).

Dante worked with a Christian subject, but he treated his material in ways that differed from his predecessors. His *Divine Comedy*, still one of the great works of European literature, illustrates well the tentative beginnings of Italian humanism. Presented as a journey through Hell, Purgatory and Paradise, the *Divine Comedy* is fundamentally a synthesis of medieval Christian thought, but in a series of imaginary conversations with and about great historical figures, Dante makes it clear that his judgments are based less on what people believed in hair-splitting theological arguments than on how they behaved toward their fellow man and what they contributed to humanity. Thus, though religious in content, its goals were ethical rather than theological, and the author showed great sympathy for pre-Christian pagans who had contributed humane philosophical ideas to the world. Finally, Dante composed his work, in verse, in the Tuscan vernacular rather than in Latin, making it accessible to educated laymen. In summation, through its concern with human behavior, its sympathetic interest in classical authors and its appeal to a lay audience, the *Divine Comedy* showed in primitive form the most important of the humanist elements that were to dominate early renaissance literature.

In painting Giotto illustrated the same sort of early humanist tendencies shown by Dante in literature. Probably his most famous work is the series of allegorical panels honoring St. Francis, which he painted in the late thirteenth century for the church of the Franciscan Order at Assisi. Again the theme was totally Christian, the life of a simple and pious saint, but Giotto's treatment of it made his work a new departure in painting. Early Christians had turned away from Greco-Roman realism in art in favor of a slightly abstract primitivism which allowed the treatment of spiritual subjects without the appearance of glorification of the flesh; this style had continued to dominate medieval Christian art, offering little differentiation of human figures, so individuals had come to be identified by spiritual symbols associated with them—keys for St. Peter (the keeper of the keys), a gridiron for St. Lawrence and arrow wounds for St. Sebastian (the instruments of their martyrdoms), etc. By contrast, Giotto painted St. Francis as a real person and portrayed incidents in his life which illustrated his piety, his humility and his simple faith; he made his subject a man with whom anyone could identify and explained his life pictorially so that all could understand. Then, in the first years of the fourteenth century, he gave even fuller scope to his new humanist treatment in a beautiful series of frescoes he painted for the arena chapel in Padua, which turned around scenes from the life of Christ.

Another development in early fourteenth-century Florence that was to prove important to the development of the Renaissance was the beginning of large-scale public works. To a considerable extent this reflected another aspect of the competition among Italian towns; the city fathers determined to beautify Florence beyond anything that neighboring towns could rival, and for a first project they decided to build a new cathedral. Again the theme was Christian, but the treatment was new. That the cathedral of Florence would be an episcopal center and a house of worship were secondary considerations; primarily it was to be a monument to the wealth and glory of the city. Moreover, the construction of the cathedral and its ancillary structures, a bell tower and a baptistry, lasted all through the fourteenth century and well into the fifteenth century and provided commissions for many important Renaissance artists.

The enthusiastic reception of vernacular literature and artistic realism and the undertaking of public works all reflected the growth of the Florentine bourgeoisie, worldly men of wealth who had leisure and wished to fill it with interesting and beautiful things. They were Christians, but they were businessmen, not churchmen, and they did not find theological debates or edifying accounts of saints either entertaining or interesting. They were building large comfortable houses, and medieval Christian art did not provide the warmth, the gaiety or the sense of luxury that they sought in the decoration of their new homes. Urban politics, business rivalries and warfare with other towns posed problems for which they found no guides in medieval literature. And their wealth, leisure and local power gave them an enjoyment of daily life for which there was little justification in medieval tradition. This class comprised potential patrons of enormous resources, and scholars and artists soon began producing for it in quantity.

Classical authors had concerned themselves with many of the interests reborn in the Italian cities, and through the fourteenth and fifteenth centuries masses of manuscripts—mostly Roman and some Greek—were unearthed in old libraries, recopied and circulated widely. Here were poems and essays extolling the intrinsic value of man and the joy of life, treatises expounding the purposes and methods of government, speeches and letters on the subject of patriotism, scandalous biographies and racy stories simply for entertainment, a whole literature concerned with man and his place in the world. In addition, the physical remains of classical civilization—triumphal arches, amphitheaters, aqueducts, temples, villas and public baths—provided models of monumental construction for city councils seeking to embellish their towns and for wealthy merchants and princes desirous of building impressive palaces; the larger remains were excavated, measured and studied, while smaller artifacts such as statuary were sought eagerly for private collections.

So vast and exciting was the human content of the classical heritage, that soon *studia humanitatis* came to refer to the study and imitation of classical culture, and both the literary and the artistic remains of classical civilization soon were being emulated.

A generation after Dante and Giotto, Florence produced two more eminent writers important to the development of the Renaissance, Petrarch (1304–1374) and Boccaccio (1313–1375). The revival of interest in Roman literature led to the study of classical Latin, which differed considerably from the Latin commonly used in the fourteenth century, and Petrarch became famous as an outstanding classical Latinist. He also wrote beautiful lyric poetry which contributed to the growing appreciation of man and nature. His friend Boccaccio was a many-faceted scholar and writer, one of the first Italians to read ancient Greek fluently, a collector of classical manuscripts, a lecturer on Dante and the author of the first prose work in Italian, the *Decameron*. In the *Decameron* Boccaccio took as his setting a group of wealthy young men and women who had shut themselves away in a country house to escape the Black Death which was raging in Florence; to pass the time they told one another stories, a schema which allowed the author scope for the use of different styles and for the presentation of themes ranging from social criticism to sexual satire. Not only does the gentle humor of the *Decameron* still make delightful reading, but subsequently its literary device of isolating a group of people and having them recount stories was used frequently; probably the most famous example is the work of Boccaccio's near contemporary, Geoffrey Chaucer, whose *Canterbury Tales* is one of the seminal works in English literature, but the device is timeless and still is used.

During the fifteenth and early sixteenth centuries the Italian renaissance developed rapidly, and Florence remained its center. Under the patronage of the Medici family, especially Cosimo and Lorenzo the Magnificent, the city produced distinguished artists in every field: the painters Fra Angelico and Botticelli, the architects Brunelleschi and Alberti, the sculptors Ghiberti and Donatello, and those two universal artists who defy categories, Leonardo da Vinci and Michelangelo. Humanist scholarship also flourished as Cosimo di Medici founded the Library of San Marco, the Medici

Library and the Platonic Academy for Greek studies, and in the early sixteenth century Florence produced the brilliant and controversial historian and political theorist, Machiavelli.

In the middle of the fifteenth century the Renaissance spread to Rome, Milan and several other Italian cities. Pope Nicolas V (1447-1455) had been a librarian for Cosimo di Medici before his election to the papal throne, and as pope he continued his interest in humanism and the collection of manuscripts by founding the Vatican Library and supporting scholars and artists. His immediate successor opposed the new culture; but most of the late fifteenth century popes supported the Renaissance with varying degrees of enthusiasm. In the early sixteenth century popes of the Borgia, della Rovere and Medici families made the papacy famous for artistic patronage, political intrigue and immorality at the price of religious leadership. In Milan the Renaissance was associated chiefly with the rule of the Sforza family and reached its peak under the patronage of Ludovico "the Moor" (1479-1500). The Sforzas undertook large public works in the city, bringing in Florentine architects and painters, including Leonardo da Vinci, until Milan was established as a cultural center in its own right. Though the Milanese renaissance was short-lived, the city was beautified greatly. By contrast, Venice with her strong eastern orientation toward Constantinople, long remained outside the mainstream of the Renaissance, and older Byzantine and Gothic influences continued dominant. Ironically, the high quality of Venice's printing industry from the late fifteenth century onwards resulted in much of the Renaissance literature of other Italian cities being transmitted through the Venetian presses, but except for the painting of the Bellini family in the second half of the fifteenth century, there was little sign of a Venetian renaissance until after 1500. Then the city suddenly exploded into prominence by producing two of Italy's best Renaissance painters, Tintoretto and Titian.

In the course of the fifteenth and early sixteenth centuries the Italian renaissance developed a philosophical basis that moved far beyond the simple humanism of its early writers and artists. Christian thematic material was used less and less, and admiration of the classical Greeks and Romans grew into adulation, so that the Renaissance became a pagan cultural movement. The Italians conceived a new ideal to replace the medieval Christian, the *uomo universale*, the universal man who did everything well with no apparent effort. This Renaissance individualism was only for the elite, of course, for it assumed wealth and leisure, but it became the goal of many wealthy fifteenth- and sixteenth-century Italians. They not only patronized artists and scholars but also painted and composed Latin songs and verses themselves, designed new palaces and public buildings, laid out gardens and developed elegant and witty society. This adulation of man was reflected in the art works of the period. Portraiture became a major subject in painting as merchants and princes sought a secular immortality; palaces, city halls and gardens replaced cathedrals as the chief subjects of architects; and authors concerned themselves primarily with man and his works as exemplified in Castiglione's *Book of the Courtier* (a handbook of elegant behavior in everything from table manners to seductions), Guicciardini's *History of Italy* and Ariosto's epic poetry.

Perhaps the work that best sums up the purely secular, pragmatic and somewhat cynical intellectual climate of Italy toward the end of the Renaissance, however, is *The Prince*, published in 1514 by Niccolo Machiavelli. Not only was this book one of the last great literary works of the Italian renaissance, it was also one of the most controversial books ever written and may be considered the first step in the establishment of political science as an empirical study rather than as an exercise in moral philosophy. Almost without exception, classical and medieval writers on government had concerned themselves with political theory, reflecting upon the goals that government should seek to attain, the forms of political organization that would assure the fullest social development, the governing apparatus that best would provide justice, or the underlying principles that could legitimatize some men's power over others. Machiavelli cast all of this aside. He had been involved personally in the political life of Florence, and when his party was ousted he was forced to retire to a country house, where he passed his time reflecting upon and writing about politics. All around him he saw strong states swallowing weaker ones, *condottiere* captains of mercenary bands of soldiers seizing control of states they were supposed to serve, political rivals using torture and assassination to defeat each other. He had seen Caesar Borgia, a pope's son, subject most of central Italy to papal rule, using every means no matter how unscrupulous. Thus, the major influence upon Machiavelli's thought was experience of turbulent Renaissance politics. Abandoning moral judgments and philosophical commitments, he attempted in *The Prince* to present a rational and dispassionate analysis of the political process that he had observed. It was largely this amoral position that his critics found scandalous.

In Machiavelli's analysis, politics is the means whereby some men acquire and attempt to retain authority over others. Thus, it has no goal, no moral purpose; it is a mechanism for the exercise of power. Starting from such a postulate, Machiavelli necessarily concluded that the important questions for anyone interested in politics are: what succeeds? what fails? The observations he presented in trying to answer these questions revealed a view of man and society that moralists found as shocking as his basic amorality. He stated that a prince could sustain himself and command respect through fear; if laws were enforced harshly and consistently most people would prefer to avoid trouble and would render obedience. He stated that a prince ought not to be impeded by the moral precepts of religion or philosophy where his self-interest was concerned; if it were advantageous to break his word or violate a treaty, he ought to do so. Implicitly he justified the use of bribery, torture and assassination if they would strengthen a prince against his enemies. Perhaps the most cynical aspect of *The Prince* is the author's judgment of public opinion: however moral and just a ruler might be, he observed, if he be overthrown he soon will be despised and forgotten by the public; but a ruler who succeeds in maintaining himself securely, even if cruel and unjust, will be acclaimed, and his worst deeds will be forgiven, for the public admires nothing so much as success and will judge that the ends have justified the means.

About the beginning of the sixteenth century the influence of the Renaissance began to spread significantly, northward to France and England and westward to Spain, largely as a result of foreign military involvement in Italy. There were five major states in the peninsula at this time: Milan, Venice, Florence, the Papal States, and the kingdom of Naples; they competed viciously with one another in a web of shifting alliances, and at the end of the fifteenth century they began invoking foreign aid. Both the French and the Spanish crowns had some claims in Italy, and the Holy Roman Emperor still possessed at least theoretical rights, so there was no lack of pretext for intervention. The French came first, in 1494, at the invitation of the Sforza ruler of Milan, and by 1500 German and Spanish forces were involved. For the next three and a half centuries Italy was to be a battleground for Europe's great powers, but the most important immediate effects were to expose large numbers of influential foreigners to the culture of the Renaissance and then, through the devastation consequent upon the wars, largely to put an end to the growth of that culture in Italy.

The cultural ferment of the Renaissance already had had some effect outside Italy even before 1500, chiefly in the field of scholarship. News of the study of ancient languages and the recovery of classical manuscripts had attracted students from other countries to northern Italy, and by the middle of the fifteenth century they were there in some numbers. Through their efforts, northern scholars developed a considerable acquaintance with the classics, and studies in Latin, Greek and Hebrew were established firmly, but prior to the great invasions of Italy the impact of the Renaissance upon the north was limited almost wholly to literary activity carried on in scholarly circles. The invasions exposed princes and wealthy noblemen to the opulence of Italian art and architecture and to the elegance of Italian social life, opening the way for the expansion of the Renaissance on a much broader basis.

As it spread outside Italy, Renaissance culture changed considerably, adapting to very different social and political circumstances. In France, Spain and England, for instance, the existence of strong royal governments tended to make Renaissance artists depend primarily upon monarchical patronage, and the courts of the kings became the focal points of the new culture. Moreover, Gothic traditions in art and architecture were much stronger beyond the Alps than in Italy, where the Gothic style never had displaced Byzantine and Romanesque forms; one result was that Renaissance styles were used at first simply as decorative motifs in the north, producing unlikely combinations of columned porticoes, arcaded facades and sweeping staircases on basically Gothic buildings.

Perhaps the most notable adaptation consequent upon the expansion of the Renaissance was the transformation of humanist thought. Lacking the strong pagan backgrounds of Italy, French and English intellectuals tended to be more religious than their Italian counterparts, and the universities with which they often were associated generally were more conservative, more closely linked with church and monarchy. Consequently, while they adopted with enthusiasm the Italian passion for collecting old manuscripts and studying ancient languages, they balanced classical interests with studies of early Christian sources; and while they concerned themselves with man in his world, it was primarily Christian man in a Christian world that they considered. In Spain seven hundred years of war against the Moslems had produced a fervent Christianity that had no tolerance for the pagan elements of Italian humanism, and in consequence the Renaissance was more influential in changing artistic styles than in effecting any basic intellectual re-orientations. Thus, though northern and western Renaissance writers produced secular and satirical literature, as exemplified by the works of Shakespeare, Rabelais and Cervantes, the intellectual climate generally remained less frankly pagan, and Christianity retained a far more important role in scholarly endeavor.

The German experience of the early sixteenth century differed so greatly from that of the rest of Europe that there is a real question whether there are grounds to justify speaking of a German renaissance, though on a scholarly level the impact of humanism was felt strongly. About the middle of the fifteenth century the new learning, particularly ancient languages, began to take root in the universities, largely through the influence of German scholars who had studied in Italy, and these studies evoked enough enthusiasm that some of the German princes founded new universities. In the sixteenth century some Italian art was imported and even copied to a limited extent. But the new learning and the new styles failed to arouse deep interest throughout German society, and the best artists and most able scholars of the Holy Roman Empire tended to come from Flanders, the Netherlands and the Rhineland, where the flourishing culture of the late medieval Burgundian court had established a solid foundation. German intellectual interests remained more religiously oriented than those of either Italy or other northern areas.

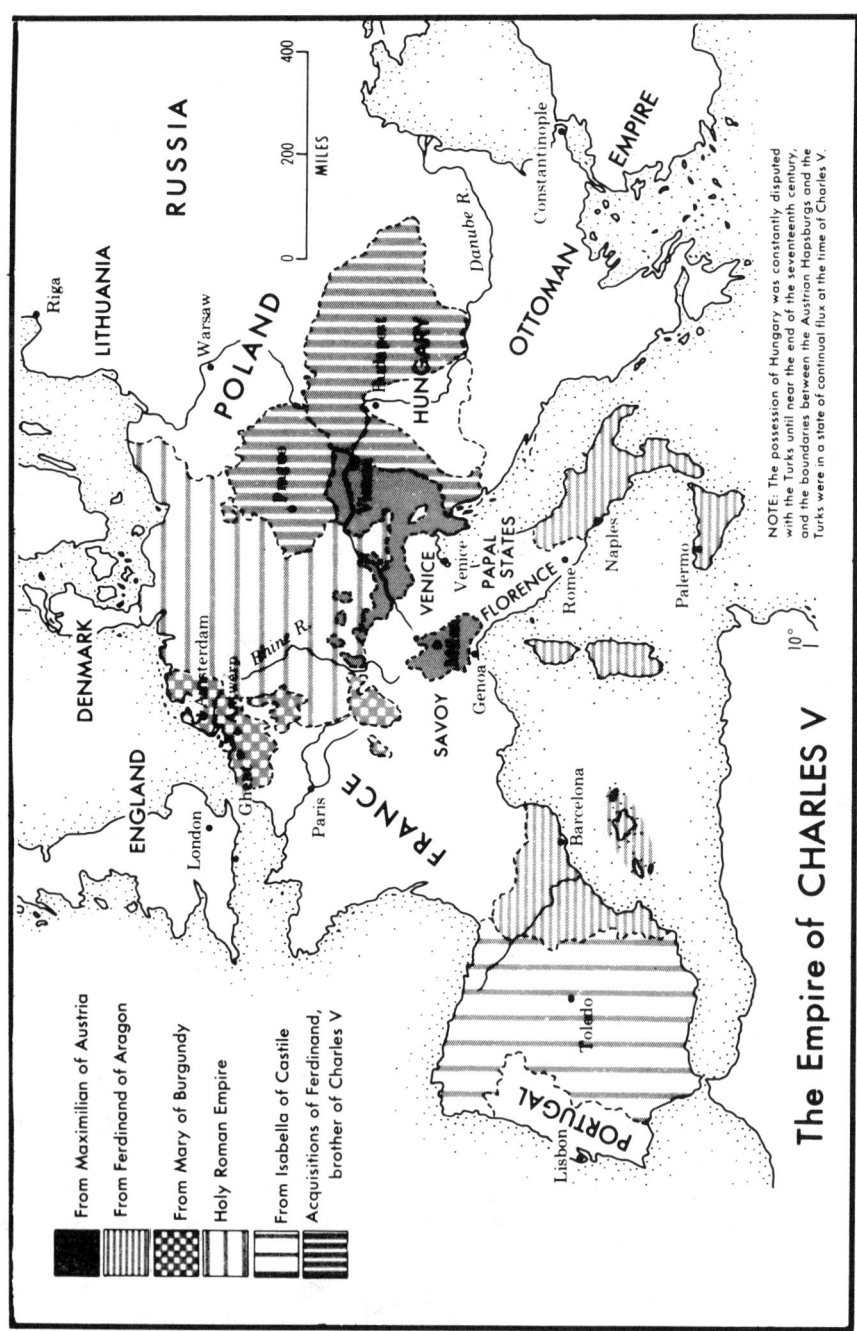

No doubt the deep-rooted pietism for which German Christianity was known had some effect; and perhaps some influence may be attributed to the fact that the beginnings of German civilization east of the Rhine went back to Christian missionary work rather than to Roman experience, with the result that a search for origins led through the medieval church to early Christianity rather than through a Roman conquest to classical culture. In any case, though German humanist scholars were no less able or less learned than the Italians, their interests were very different and their religious commitments far more profound, while Renaissance influence upon German art and architecture remained slight until the seventeenth century, when it penetrated Germany from France.

Outside of Italy the Renaissance made its strongest impact in France. Direct contact between France and Italy was frequent and profound for a quarter of a century after the first Italian expedition of Charles VIII in the mid-1490s, and it continued on a reduced scale throughout the sixteenth century. Generous patronage by Kings Francis I (1515–1547) and Henry II (1547–1559) established Renaissance artistic influence firmly, first as decoration added to older French forms and then as a vigorous new French style, exemplified by the sixteenth century portions of the Louvre in Paris. and by the splendid chateaux of the Loire Valley. Secular humanism found expression in the works of Rabelais, Ronsard and Montaigne, while distinguished religious scholarship developed in a Paris group, of which the most famous members were Lefebvre d'Etaples and John Calvin.

In sum, the Renaissance, which was born in and first flourished in Italy, stimulated a comparable movement in France and to a lesser degree in Spain and England, and while it may be debated whether one can speak of a German renaissance, there is no doubt that there were important specific influences in Germany. Everywhere it spread, the movement released great creative energies, resulting in impressive scholarly achievements and vigorous artistic development which changed profoundly both the content and the style of European culture. The classical and early Christian heritage of Europe was reestablished. Princely residences were transformed from gloomy uncomfortable fortresses into graceful pleasure houses. The entourages of kings developed from bands of crude soldiers into royal courts with highly formalized etiquette, peopled with courtiers who sought to practice elegance and wit.

The creative impulse of the Renaissance continued much modified on into the seventeenth century, when far-reaching religious and political developments demanded symbolic expression. One result of the Reformation was to accentuate the dramatic elements of Christian conceptions of the power of God and of the struggle between good and evil, while at the same time the kings of France developed power undreamed of by their predecessors and indulged in policies that threw all of Europe into turmoil. In an attempt to give expression to these dramatic new developments, Europe's architects and artists combined elements of Renaissance styles in new ways, abandoning earlier commitments to static forms and introducing instead a new plasticity and dynamic line. Drawing upon tentative experiments of Palladio and Michelangelo in mid-sixteenth century Italy, they began designing buildings so that the play of light and shadow upon colonnades and windows would give a sense of movement, and they began incorporating spatial masses in their designs, tying courtyards and gardens to facades by paths and balustrades. Sculptors moved away from figures in repose to subjects in tension, caught in the midst of action, and painters oriented entire canvasses around a single dramatic focal point. The new style, which was called baroque, was well adapted to express the evangelical vigor of seventeenth century Christianity and the aggressive ambition of seventeenth century monarchy, and it flourished, further illustrating the impressive adaptability of the artistic creativity unleashed by the Renaissance.

The considerable cultural development consequent upon the Renaissance ought not to be allowed to obscure the movement's negative aspects, however, for a number of adverse effects upon European society can be identified. The Renaissance certainly was not consciously progressive, and there were some humanists who damned the printing press because they feared it would cheapen knowledge and open the scholar's preserve to a large literate public. The enthusiasm for the classics led to an attempt to purify Latin by reestablishing the language of Cicero and Livy, deleting all the changes of vocabulary and grammar that had developed through fifteen hundred years; the result was that Latin was destroyed as a vibrant living tongue and became a dead language, more and more restricted to the formalities of legal and governmental usage as time passed, and Europe slowly lost the linguistic unity that had characterized its cultural development since the Roman Empire. The adulation of classical authors also had an adverse effect upon natural studies. While the medieval intellectual climate was not conducive to any considerable scientific advances, there had been some progress in the later Middle Ages, exemplified most notably by Friar Roger Bacon, but the great admiration of Greek scientific writers, such as Aristotle and Ptolemy, largely destroyed confidence in modern data and set European science back to the level of the ancient Greeks; for instance, European maps continued for years to show features derived from Ptolemy despite the fact that modern voyages showed some of them to be erroneous, and medical schools continued to teach Greek anatomy although it was contradicted by modern dissections.

Finally, it seems likely that the amorality, the ostentatious luxury and the hostility to religion that were intrinsic to so much of Renaissance culture aggravated the social and political problems that already were assuming serious proportions in fifteenth and sixteenth century Europe, further alienating an elite that accepted these values from a population still largely committed to the medieval ideals of piety, charity and stability. In its negative as well as its positive influences, the Renaissance had far-reaching effects upon Europe.

Chapter 19

Religious Reaction and Reform

The medieval church had experienced many movements of reform, and in fact its history almost could be written in terms of cycles of deformation and reformation. Anticlericalism, heresy and schism had been confronted many times, and national churches were clearly identifiable within the broad framework of medieval European Catholicism. Thus, the real problem in attempting an estimate of the reformation of the sixteenth century is to try to determine what was different in the mixture of problems so that the church was unable to contain the movement within itself.

The woeful condition of the early sixteenth century church inspired frequent criticism of two sorts. There were those who sought to reform and purify the church by improving those who served it, accepting its doctrines and structure; and there were those who believed that not only the clergy but also the doctrine of the church had become corrupt and had to be reformed. The two positions were exemplified best by Erasmus and Luther.

Erasmus has been accused of lacking courage, by comparison with Luther, but such a judgment is unfair, for his purposes were different. As a Christian humanist he was scandalized by the condition of the clergy and wrote biting satires designed to shame the corrupt and provoke a reform of morals, but he never doubted the fundamental truth of the church's doctrines. Confident that God's love and mercy, aided by the sacraments, would bring salvation, his concern was with the Christian life—how laymen might live in greater love and charity and clerics might fulfil their offices in God's church more worthily. If Erasmus' criticisms contributed to Luther's movement, the contribution certainly was inadvertent; he never would have agreed that the corruption of men justified the destruction of the unity of God's church.

By contrast Luther's major concerns were very different. While he certainly shared the horror of clerical abuses and was deeply concerned that the clergy should fulfil a pastoral role in guiding their flocks to a better Christian life, these things were for him secondary considerations. What mattered above all else, the heart and essential core of Christianity, was the fulfilment of Christ's promise of salvation, and it was in this fundamental matter that Luther lost confidence in the church. Like many Christians he found several grounds on which to base criticism, but his intransigence, his refusal of all compromise, is explicable only on the issue of salvation. To imagine that Luther was willing to overturn the traditional church because of the human frailties of some of its clergy is to underestimate him. Rather, he became convinced that the church's teachings regarding the means to salvation were wrong and that, in consequence, many laymen risked damnation. As a responsible priest and theologian he could not compromise on that issue.

Probably too much has been made of the matter of indulgences, but because they are widely supposed to have been at the root of Luther's protest, they must be considered. In fact, they were more a catalyst than a cause. The concept of indulgences is rooted in rather complex doctrines developed by medieval theologians, doctrines which made a clear distinction between the guilt of sin and the penalties of sin. No one ever claimed that any man could forgive sin, wipe away its guilt, for that power belonged only to God, Who presumably would grant forgiveness to those who prayed for it with sincerity and true repentence. God's forgiveness would assure ultimate salvation, but only after the penalties had been paid. Since most men were assumed to accumulate more penalties than could be expiated by good works during a lifetime, the theologians posited the existence of purgatory, a condition between the heaven of the saved and the hell of the damned. In purgatory the soul continued its expiation through suffering, until the penalties had been fulfilled and it was released to heaven. On the basis of the power of the keys, the power of loosing and binding, the pope was asserted to have control over these penalties for sin in the same way that modern civil authorities can grant pardons, which do not eradicate the guilt of an act but do excuse the offender from the fulfilment of the usual penalties. An indulgence was this alleviation of penalties, granted for good cause.

In the medieval period indulgences first were granted for extraordinary personal effort, such as going crusading, which involved enormous cost and risk in the service of the faith. Then they were granted for money payments so that those who were old or crippled could participate in the good work and the benefits of it even if they could not serve personally. Given the financial strains of the early sixteenth century and the corruption of the clergy, probably it was inevitable that indulgences were exploited as a source of revenue, sold at varying prices for different periods of alleviated penalties. The papal agents who handled transactions in indulgences often added poor taste to what was already poor practice and became, in effect, hucksters. One of the worst of these was the monk Tetzel, who was operating in Germany in the early sixteenth century. An evangelistic preacher who painted horrifying word pictures of the torments of purgatory, Tetzel was notably successful as a salesman, but his crass merchandizing of ecclesiastical benefits offended many, including Luther, to whom the whole process was simply blatant extortion and financial exploitation of the faith of simple Christians. It was the indulgence issue that persuaded Luther to pose his first overt challenge to papal authority, but the challenge was the result of years of patient reflection and meditation upon the problem of salvation.

In essence Luther had become convinced that salvation was attainable only through faith, through a personal commitment of love and belief in man's worthlessness and God's mercy. Holding this conviction he could not believe in the efficacy of priests or saints as intermediaries between the individual and God, he could not accept the role of the sacraments as steps to salvation, and he could not accept the formalized role of papal powers in distributing God's mercies to men. In many ways Luther was the revivalist voice of medieval pietism hurled against worldliness and formality, the voice of St. Bernard reborn, protesting both the pagan corruption of the clergy and the genial tolerance of Erasmus' Christian humanism. If in any way Luther represented the Renaissance spirit in religion as often is asserted, it was in the individualism of his belief, his conviction that a man must stand naked and alone before his God, without intermediaries and with nothing but his faith to justify him.

Moved to action by Tetzel's scandalous behavior, Luther offered his first overt challenge in October of 1517 by posting his Ninety-five Theses on the doors of the church in Wittenburg, where he was professor of theology. It was a very modest revolt; the theses were simply theological positions relative to indulgences which he wished to debate, and traditionally the churches were the centers of their towns and their doors the bulletin boards. The posting of the theses was simply an attempt to stimulate interest among other theologians in the hope that ripples would spread with beneficial effect. The rapid and explosive effects of the theses must have astonished their author.

The church's reaction to Luther's challenge followed normal practice, for he was simply another dissenting priest. In 1518 he was summoned before Cardinal Cajetan, the papal legate in Germany, and ordered to retract his statements, but he refused. Then in 1519 a theologian of some eminence, Dr. Eck, undertook to debate with him, and almost immediately the situation took a more serious turn. An experienced debater, Eck maneuvered Luther into extremist positions—denial of the divine right of the papacy, assertion of the supremacy of Scripture, doubt of the authority of councils and defense of some Hussite propositions that had been condemned as heresy. Luther's excommunication followed naturally, in 1520, and in an act of defiance he publicly burned the papal document of excommunication (called a bull from the Latin *bulla,* for the great seal on it). Since heresy was considered a serious offense by civil as well as religious authorities, carrying the penalty of outlawry, the case was reviewed by the emperor at the Diet of Worms in 1521; there Luther maintained the positions he had adopted and consequently the emperor outlawed him. At this point Luther might have been executed, as had happened to Hus, but the emperor honored his safe-conduct and allowed him to go in peace. As he had become a controversial figure, his life was in real danger, but his immediate overlord, the elector of Saxony, soon took him into protective custody, and his movement continued to grow.

Thus far Luther's protest had revealed nothing that the European church had not experienced many times, and the question as to why it succeeded while earlier efforts failed becomes more and more complicated. One new factor which probably was important was the recent invention of reasonably cheap printing. This fifteenth century invention, usually attributed to Johannes Gutenberg, made possible the wide distribution of Luther's statements, first his theses and later the eloquent pamphlets in which he explained and developed his positions. The printing press made available to him a larger audience than earlier preachers of reform had been able to reach, and while recognizing the limitations posed by widespread illiteracy, one must regard the press as important in the rapid and extensive communication of Luther's ideas.

In the successful establishment and expansion of the Lutheran movement, however, as distinct from its origins in Luther's own agony of conscience, the most important factor was its relationship to the secular power structure. In the early 1520s the political and social situation in north Germany was singularly receptive to the sort of movement that Luther launched. Agrarian depression, the decline of the once-prosperous Hanseatic league of trading towns, increased exactions by manorial lords to meet their own rising costs— all of these factors brought hardship to those who were economically vulnerable, among commoners this meant chiefly peasants and urban workmen, while among the nobility it meant that turbulent group known as the free imperial knights, a group of petty lords who were for all practical purposes independent of any higher authority. Luther's teaching that all men were equal before God appealed greatly to these groups, and they extended this spiritual equality to speculation upon social and economic equality. Moreover, Luther's ideas were capable of stimulating greed, for he said that the church was too much drawn into worldly affairs because it was a great landowner; his church, he said, would be maintained by the contributions of believers. The prospect of large tracts of church land available for seizure was attractive even to great princes of the empire.

Luther's movement was launched at a time when many of the German princes were resisting seriously the authority of the church and of the emperor. Many of them were attempting to consolidate territorial states based on Roman and Renaissance concepts of the sovereignty of the prince, and the loose medieval suzerainty claimed by the emperor and supported by the church was international in character and obstructive to this development. Emperor Charles V's position was vulnerable, for not only was he Holy Roman Emperor; he also was king of Spain and its growing colonial dominions and ruler of various Italian and Netherlands territories, and in the Danube valley he was beset by ferocious Turkish attacks which broke the kingdom of Hungary in 1529 and besieged Vienna. In these circumstances the princes sought to increase their power at the emperor's expense, and support of Lutheranism would help finance the effort with confiscated church lands, would eliminate the generally pro-imperial influence of Catholic clergy, and would offer a religious issue on which to rally the populace. German princes began to convert rapidly and to encourage Lutheran preachers. By the mid-1520s most of north Germany down to the Main River was Lutheran.

The spread of German Lutheranism stopped almost as suddenly as it began, however. In 1522 there was a revolt of imperial knights, and in 1524-25 there was a costly and destructive peasant revolt. Both groups claimed inspiration from Lutheranism, and though Luther disclaimed them, the revolts intimidated the princes by suggesting that Lutheranism carried the seeds of social revolution. Princely conversions stopped, and a few princes who had declared for Lutheranism even returned to Catholicism. The revolts were crushed, but Germany was left with a religious division, a Lutheran north and a Catholic south, each group eager to destroy the other in the name of the true faith.

The emperor, who was a dedicated Catholic, sincerely sought compromise. He recognized the validity of much of the criticism levied against the Catholic Church and wanted the pope to convene a council to reform the church and heal the rift, but the pope feared the anti-papal conciliar movement which had survived from the previous century, and he refused. Within the empire, Charles V convened a diet at Speyer in 1526 to try to find a compromise. When this produced no result, a second was called in 1529. The second Diet of Speyer was dominated by Catholics and it resolved that the empire's laws against heresy should be enforced. This meant civil war.

The Lutherans withdrew to Augsburg, where they drew up a confession (basic creed) of their faith and a protest, whence the term Protestant. In their own defense they also formed a military alliance known as the Schmalkaldic League, while their opponents formed a Catholic Union. The Lutherans soon got aid from France, which was willing to help any enemy of the emperor, while Catholic forces were supported by the emperor's Spanish resources. For the next quarter century Germany was torn by religious war that ended only in 1555 with the Peace of Augsburg. Religiously the wars changed little; for the north remained Lutheran and the south Catholic. Politically they had important results, however, for the Peace of Augsburg allowed every prince to choose between Lutheranism and Catholicism for his state, although the ecclesiastical reservation forbade further secularization of church lands; this meant legality for Lutheranism where the prince supported it, and also it meant the transfer of an important area of decision from the emperor to the princes.

Implicit in the German religious wars and the Peace of Augsburg was a general principle: religious protest movements could succeed where they had the support of important elements of the political establishment, but without that support they failed. This general principle also was supported by the experience of Lutheranism outside of Germany. Henry VIII of England opposed religious innovation and wrote a pamphlet attacking the Lutherans (which, ironically, won the papal title "Defender of the Faith" for the man who later was to launch the Reformation in England), while the king of France actually persecuted and burned any Lutherans he caught; in neither England nor France did Lutheranism make significant progress. In fact, after the mid-1520s the only area of notable Lutheran expansion was Scandinavia, and there the religious reformers had political support; in Sweden a new monarchy in revolt against Danish domination supported Lutheranism as an element of national consolidation, and a bit later the Danish crown did the same thing to rally the populace against the Catholic nobility.

Another dissident religious movement of wide influence was launched by John Calvin. At the same time that Luther was taking the first steps toward founding his church in Germany, there was emerging in Paris a reformist group of which the most prominent member was LeFebvre d'Etaples. Calvin, a brilliant young man educated in both theology and law, was influenced strongly by this group and undertook extensive study of early Christian writing, particularly the work of St. Augustine; in 1536, at the age of twenty-nine, he published the first edition of his *Institutes of the Christian Religion*. This highly sophisticated theological tract, which Calvin continued to develop and expand through subsequent editions, became the foundation of a new church. Calvin's doctrines differed radically from both Catholicism and Lutheranism, for Calvin believed that there was nothing an individual could do that would help him to achieve salvation. Both Lutheranism and Catholicism maintained that though man was too degraded by sin to merit salvation through his own efforts, if the efforts were sincere, God's mercy would extend the necessary grace. Calvin argued that if God were all-knowing and all-powerful, as was necessary by definition of God, then He must have known from the day of creation who would be saved and who would be damned, and, moreover, men were saved or damned because God willed it. This doctrine, known as predestination, divided humanity into two groups: those whom God intended to save, called the Elect, and those whom God intended to damn. Instead of evoking fatalism and resignation, as might seem likely, this doctrine proved very dynamic. Though a man could do nothing to improve his chances of salvation, he could seek signs that he was chosen for the Elect. He could never really *know*, but since everything in the world happened by God's will, the individual might hope that if his affairs prospered, it was a sign of God's blessing upon one of His chosen. Thus the followers of Calvin were motivated to live frugally and work hard, not for their own prosperity or comfort but to demonstrate through their activities the power of God's blessing and to find in their success some encouragement for their hopes of salvation.

King Francis I enjoyed good relations with the Catholic Church, and by agreement with the papacy (the Concordat of Boulogne, 1516) he had important patronage powers controlling most high appointments in the French church. Consequently he was hostile to religious innovation, particularly after seeing and encouraging the division and violence it brought to Germany. He launched persecutions which broke up the Paris group and forced Calvin to flee abroad. The brilliant eighteenth century writer Voltaire later observed cynically that Francis I was a good king, burning heretics at home while subsidizing them in Germany, both for the greater glory of France.

After some wanderings, Calvin went to Geneva, in Switzerland, where he had been invited by a group that was attempting a two-fold change in the city: religious reform and overthrow of the authority of the bishop who was the city's overlord. Calvin soon was accepted as the leader of this group, and it was in Geneva that he established the theocratic government that became the model Calvinist community. The city and the church were run by the same people, the laws of the civil government enforced the rules of the church, and church and state together supported an extremely puritanical moral code that sought to force Genevans to be godly.

Because Calvinism was dynamic and sympathetic to worldly success, it appealed strongly, though not exclusively, to middle-class people. Its spread from Geneva can be traced along the trade routes: down the Rhine to the Netherlands, down the Rhone and thence along the great highways of southern France. In neither France nor the Netherlands did it become an important social force, however, until the latter half of the sixteenth century when political circumstances became favorable. In France King Henry II was killed in a sporting accident in 1559, leaving a minor heir, and confronting a weakened royal government Calvinism spread rapidly; in the Netherlands a great revolt broke out in the 1560s against the king of Spain who ruled the area, and Calvinism soon became the unifying force of the revolutionaries. Both of these processes will be considered in more detail later.

Generally it was in the towns that the new church found support at first, though it soon began to recruit noblemen. In fact, one of its greatest successes—Scotland—depended upon the support of nobles. The Reformation in Scotland was enmeshed so deeply with political revolution that it is difficult to separate religious and political motivation. In the middle of the sixteenth century the Scottish crown was held by Mary, Queen of Scots, a woman reared in France and very French in outlook. A Scot, John Knox, was Calvin's most dedicated disciple in Geneva, and when Knox returned to Scotland the new faith he brought soon became the rallying issue for a consolidated aristocratic opposition to the crown which, in 1568, drove Queen Mary to seek refuge in England. The uncompromising new faith found wide support among the Scots, and Scotland soon was predominately Calvinist except for the highlands, which remained Catholic until the mid-eighteenth century.

Luther and Calvin were not alone in launching religious dissidence, however, for there were other important movements. In

Switzerland an independent protest movement was started in 1518 by a priest named Zwingli; though differing from Luther on important doctrinal points, the Zwinglians also insisted upon the unique importance of personal faith and the inefficacy of the clergy as intermediaries. Their movement spread importantly through some of the northern Swiss cantons, but after Zwingli's death it was absorbed by Lutheranism and Calvinism. And much more radical than Lutherans, Calvinists, or Zwinglians were the Anabaptists. These were people who sought to re-create primitive communal Christianity. It is difficult to generalize about them, for they never established any formalized organization. Though their name implies opposition to baptism, what they were against was infant baptism, maintaining that such an initiation into the Christian community should be an adult decision. Some were pacifists who "turned the other cheek" while others had the reputation of fighting like lions. What they shared was a primitive and simple faith in Christ the Redeemer and in the Bible as God's word. They were persecuted by both Catholics and Lutherans and never became a very influential movement, surviving in modern times as Mennonite and Amish communities.

A unique reformation occurred in England, where the movement was directed by the crown and in its origins was clearly political. Henry VIII was only one generation removed from the devastating Wars of the Roses, which had been based chiefly on the lack of a clear line of succession to the throne. Thus the king was terribly aware of the succession issue and was disturbed deeply that in twenty years of marriage the queen had produced only one child, a girl, Mary. Henry desperately desired a male heir to ensure his family's succession, and in 1527 he sought a papal annulment of his first marriage so that he might remarry. There were grounds, and such annulments often were granted to royal families, but in this case the pope was reluctant. In 1527 Rome had been occupied and sacked by the armies of Emperor Charles V; Queen Catherine, whom Henry was seeking to divorce, was Charles' aunt, and the pope feared to give offense in that family. He tried to procrastinate, hoping to find a solution, but Henry became impatient, for his mistress was pregnant and he wanted to marry her before the birth so the child would be legitimate. He used his considerable power over the English church to confiscate church lands, cut papal revenues from England and intimidate the English clergy, and when these attempts at pressure proved unavailing, he had his annulment pronounced by the archbishop of Canterbury. Undaunted by papal excommunication in 1534, the king passed an Act of Supremacy through the English Parliament, cutting off the English Church from Rome and making himself "Supreme Head of the Church of England." Additional benefits of these actions were increased control over the church and increased support for his government from those to whom he had distributed the confiscated church lands.

Henry VIII was a religious conservative, however; in his lifetime few doctrinal changes were made in the English Church, and he resisted the efforts of reformers of Lutheran or Calvinist inclinations, maintaining a sort of Catholic Church that denied the authority of the pope. Henry's bold action had secured him greatly increased political and economic power as well as matrimonial freedom, but England was to suffer religious struggles despite his efforts to control religious change.

Despite several marriages, at his death Henry left only three children: Mary, Elizabeth and Edward. The male took precedence over his older half-sisters and succeeded to the throne as Edward VI (1547–1553), a sickly boy. His government was run by a regency council sympathetic to religious reform, and a number of changes were made in the English Church, moving it far in the direction of Calvinism. But after only six years, young Edward died and was succeeded by his half-sister Mary (1553–1558), an ardent Catholic who was married to Philip II of Spain, the European champion of Catholicism. Persecutions and violence followed as Mary attempted to return England to Roman obedience, and then she too died and was succeeded by her half-sister Elizabeth.

It was during the reign of Queen Elizabeth I (1558–1603) that the English Church was stabilized as a moderate and national reformed church. The queen had no sympathy for extreme Calvinism, and she could not support Catholicism for Catholics considered her illegitimate and hence ineligible for the crown. She chose a middle course, continuing to deny papal authority in England but otherwise adopting deliberately vague positions and avoiding enforcement of laws that required membership in the Church of England, so as to give offense to as few people as possible. The enormous personal prestige she developed in defending England against Spanish aggression combined with her moderation to create a situation most

THE HOUSE OF TUDOR

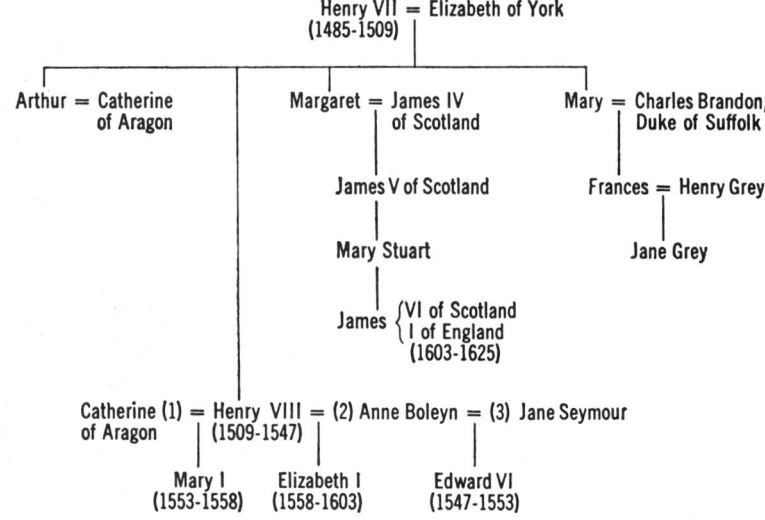

THE HOUSE OF STUART

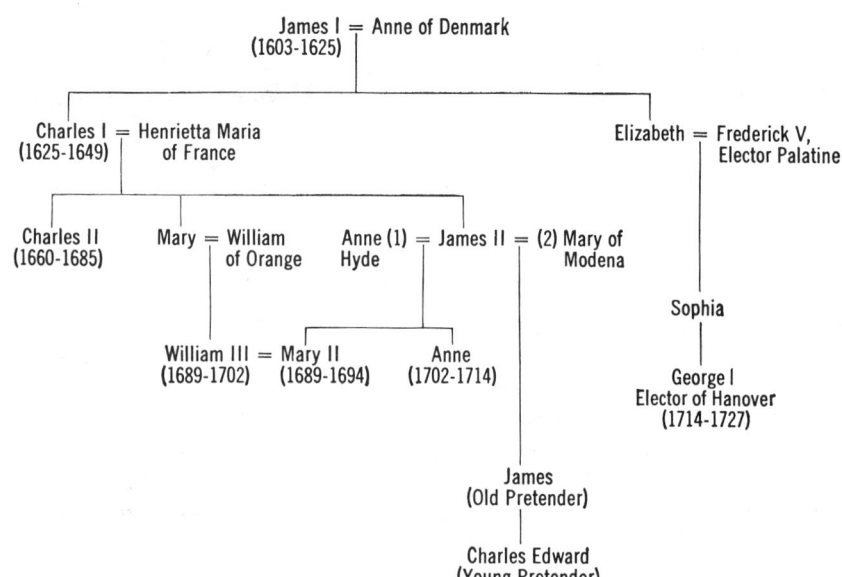

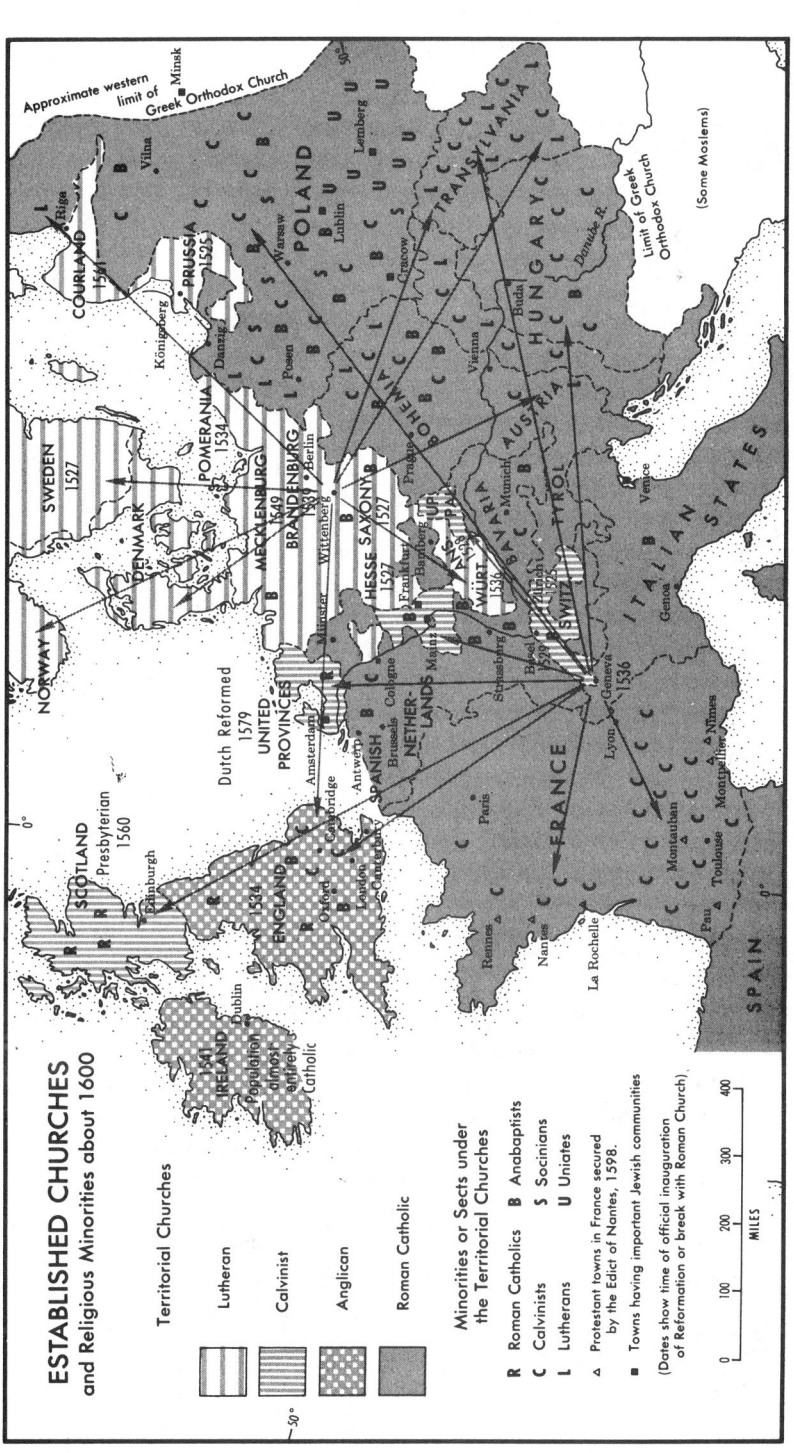

unusual in late sixteenth century Europe—a strong and popular monarchy supported by a stable church.

Finally, the mid-sixteenth century witnessed another important reform movement, the Catholic reformation. Pious and responsible popes rebuilt the dignity and spiritual responsibility of papal government and then led a reform movement within the church along rather Erasmian lines. The chief instrument of this reform was the Council of Trent, which met in three sessions in the middle 1540s, the early 1550s and the early 1560s. The church made no doctrinal compromises with Protestantism, to the great disappointment of the emperor, who long had pressed for this solution, but it achieved a considerable reform program for morals and practices. After confirming the authority of the pope and traditional Catholic doctrine, it forbade financial abuses, plurality of offices and non-residence of clergy; and it provided for the foundation of new seminaries to produce better-educated priests. It took a long time for some of the council's proposals to be effective, and some never were, but the council marked the beginning of an important rejuvenation of the Catholic clergy.

As well as internal reform, the reinvigorated papacy also began a counter-attack upon Protestantism, for which two new instruments were the Roman Inquisition (not to be confused with the corrupt Spanish Inquisition) and the Index of Banned Books. The Roman Inquisition was a special court with jurisdiction over the whole church; it heard questions of faith and tried to establish a little clarity in the sixteenth century confusion of argument and counter-argument. Unfortunately it proved a very conservative body, and in the early seventeenth century, in the Galileo case, it put itself in the ludicrous position of condemning as heresy a scientific hypothesis. The famous Index was an attempt to limit the spread of Protestantism by establishing a list of persuasive but heretical books forbidden to Catholics. In the long run neither of these efforts was very effective.

Without a doubt, the most successful Catholic response to the challenge of Protestantism was the foundation of the Society of Jesus or Jesuits. Authorized by the pope in 1543 the society was the creation of a former Spanish soldier, St. Ignatius Loyola. Setting a very high educational standard for its members, the society dedicated itself especially to preaching, teaching and instructing the conscience in the confessional. By the end of the sixteenth century Jesuit colleges, such as the University of Ingolstadt on the Danube, had won the reputation of being among the best and most progressive schools in Europe. Jesuit scholars had achieved considerable fame as controversialists defending the validity of Catholicism, and the society was developing rapidly the missionary work that with expanding European colonialism was to carry its priests as far as China and the Philippines.

By about the middle of the sixteenth century the first phase of the Reformation had ended. New churches had been founded and the old unity of western Christendom, often more apparent than real, had disappeared. Lutheranism had run its course and dominated Scandinavia and north Germany. The Church of England had left the Roman fold, and though it was still incompletely developed at Elizabeth's accession, it was established solidly as another variety of Protestantism. Calvinism, the dynamic new force in the mid-sixteenth century, had a secure base in Geneva and was reaching out to the south of France, the Netherlands and Scotland. And a reform movement had been launched within Catholicism. The latter half of the sixteenth century witnessed another phase in which the lines of controversy were drawn more sharply as Protestant Europe was put on the defensive by the ambitions and might of King Philip II of Spain.

Chapter 20

Habsburg Hegemony

When Charles V abdicated his many titles in the mid-1550s, he divided his vast holdings between his brother and his son. To his brother, Ferdinand, who already was king of Bohemia and Hungary, he left his central European domains; to his son, Philip II, he left the Spanish crown with its New World dependencies, the Netherlands, the Franche-Comté and the Italian territories of Naples and Milan. Thus the old emperor tried to rationalize somewhat the crushing burdens of governing the far-flung Habsburg lands.

The troubles in Germany had abated after the Peace of Augsburg; if its recognition of Lutheranism was distasteful to the pious emperor and its transfer of religious decisions to the German princes marked some further diminution of imperial authority, at least the settlement brought an end to much of the exhausting military conflict and weakened the excuse for French intervention. In the Danube Valley the Turkish wars had settled to a series of sieges and sporadic peace treaties. Internally and on both the eastern and western borders, German conflicts were dying down, while Spain, with a rapidly expanding colonial empire, seemed to be developing rapidly.

The new Habsburg rulers appeared to be men of great promise. Ferdinand was a central European in his attitudes; his experiences in Bohemia and Hungary involved him in a point of view wholly congenial to the Holy Roman Empire, and as Charles V's deputy for German affairs since 1522 he appeared to have won wide respect among the German princes. Young Philip had been reared mostly in Spain, spoke the tongue naturally, and had the piety and austerity of the Castilian; his obvious intelligence, his capacity for hard work and his serious demeanor all promised well for a man who was by birth one of Christendom's most important princes. Both branches of the house of Habsburg seemed to be in good hands, and at the same time there were possibilities for a further growth of Habsburg influence. In England, there appeared hope for a stronger Spanish alliance and perhaps even for England's return to Catholicism, for Mary Tudor—Catherine of Aragon's daughter—married Philip of Spain in 1554, and England was drawn into Spain's war with France in 1557; even after Mary's death in 1558 the situation was far from irretrievable, for her half-sister and heir, Elizabeth, held forth hope of Catholic conversion and Spanish marriage.

But behind this optimistic facade stirred many troubles. The religious peace in Germany reflected exhaustion more than agreement. The settlement merely extended to Lutherans (if their prince so decided) the position formerly enjoyed only by Catholics; it made no provision for the various groups of Anabaptists nor for the aggressive new Calvinist cult. It accepted things as they were, but it sought to impede further change, and the religious protest movements had not exhausted their dynamics yet. Despite the ecclesiastical reservation of the Peace of Augsburg, church lands continued to be secularized, and Calvinism—quite without legal recognition—became the established faith of the Rhineland state of the Palatinate.

The Spanish branch of the family also ruled over undercurrents of potential trouble. Castile and Aragon were staunchly particularistic, and amalgamation had made little progress under Charles V. The Moorish south was still restive under Spanish Catholic rule, breaking into revolt in 1569. The New World provided some treasure, but its importunities were many, and the sea routes were dangerous. The Netherlands were prosperous but also very particularistic, and the Spanish Philip, so very different from his cosmopolitan father, soon was to fan fires of rebellion with an attempt to impose outside authority. Italy seemed firmly in the Habsburg grip, but the Republic of Venice was hostile, and the papacy never had countenanced quietly a dominating secular power. The Turks, relatively quiet on the Danube, still controlled the Mediterranean and threatened Christian shipping. And no one could guess how long France would be willing to accept a secondary role, ringed in by Habsburg power. The potential of conflict lay on all sides.

Philip II of Spain (1556–1598) long has been the subject of characterizations ranging from fanaticism and bureaucratic rigidity to saintly devotion and impractical idealism. During the nineteenth century he was portrayed often as a king who had sacrificed the national resources of Spain to a religious crusade, much to the disgust of nationalist historians. But modern study has delineated a man of much more persuasive character—pious, austere and unbending but intelligent and hard-working and quite as devoted to the secular ambitions of his dynasty as to religious goals. It was easy for generations of historians still fascinated by the internal divisions of the Christian faith and still reacting to the universal pretensions of Roman Catholicism to portray King Philip as a Catholic crusader; yet, while such an interpretation can be defended, modern research has added broader perspectives, and historians now believe that the king's religious goal should be considered as one among many motivations of his policy. Certainly Philip II saw himself as the champion of the counter-reformation; as the strongest Catholic king in Europe, he felt God had laid upon him a special obligation to defend the church. But this aspect of his character should not be allowed to obscure his other important motives.

Moslem naval power constituted an old threat to European shipping on the Mediterranean, and in fact Moslem raiding of the south coasts of Europe continued into the seventeenth century, but Spain's vigorous efforts under King Philip made European commerce a bit more secure. In 1571, with support from the papacy and Venice, Spain mounted a strong naval expedition led by the king's half-brother, Don Juan, and struck at the main Turkish flotilla. The two fleets, totalling nearly four hundred and fifty galleys, came together off the coast of Greece, and the ensuing engagement took its name from the nearby town of Lepanto. The fighting was bloody, and both sides sustained heavy losses, but in the end the Turkish fleet was destroyed, and though the Turks rebuilt, they remained somewhat weakened in waters west of Sicily. It would be an exaggeration to suggest that the western Mediterranean became safe, for piracy was rife, and expeditions from north Africa still descended upon the European coast to carry off plunder and slaves; but there was a difference between such irregular activity and the constant threat of regular battle squadrons.

King Philip had a long-standing interest in England, and although religion undeniably was a motive, there were important commercial and political considerations, too. He and Mary Tudor had tried to restore English Catholicism, and as the champion of the counter-reformation, Philip hoped to see his task completed. But there also was the fact that England's seamen proved an expensive nuisance and a potential danger to Spain's colonial empire; the great days of the Elizabethan sea-dogs were just beginning, but there was enough harassment to make the Spanish government eager to control English activity at sea. And finally, there were political issues. After 1567 King Philip faced insurrection in the Netherlands, armed resistance to what he believed to be his just authority; England was aiding the rebels, and Philip felt that if he could neutralize England he would be able more easily to pacify the Netherlands. Thus, an important element of Spanish policy all through Philip II's reign was an attempt to dominate England.

Philip began peacefully enough with proposals for a marriage alliance with Elizabeth, but when these efforts met no result he sought alternatives. It was an age when some men still took their religion more seriously than their country, so of course the king of Spain had supporters among English Catholics; intercepted correspondence and often-exaggerated rumors of plots and conspiracies escalated the tension between the two governments, and growing popular animosities resulted from increased English raiding of Spanish colonial interests—activities at which Queen Elizabeth connived, often providing part of the capitalization of such expeditions. A crisis developed only in the 1580s, and by that time religious, commercial and political interests were intertwined thoroughly. The focus of the crisis was the exiled queen of Scotland, Mary Stuart.

In the third quarter of the sixteenth century Scotland underwent a violent religious and political transformation. It was the misfortune of the house of Stuart that the crown became the object of religious and political opposition at the same time. Mary Stuart had succeeded her father while still an infant, had been reared in France and when grown was married to the French King Francis II (1559–1560). During her minority and her absence abroad, her mother, a French princess, ruled as regent of Scotland, and French influence was strong at the Scottish court. But French governmental concepts of monarchs who ruled as well as reigned grated hard upon the stubborn independence of the Scots nobility, and there was trouble even before the frivolous and head-strong Mary Stuart returned from France in 1561 to begin her personal reign; her autocratic views worsened the situation. At this inopportune time John Knox returned to his native Scotland to preach the Calvinist gospel; his detestation of the Stuarts and their French adherents was exceeded only by his hatred for the Church of Rome. Knox's preaching won wide support, and soon the religious and political protests fused. Queen Mary antagonized the nobility by her autocratic behavior and all of her Calvinist subjects by her frivolity, her lovers and her gay court. Knox's fiery attacks upon the queen rallied popular support to the aristocratic opposition, and civil war broke out. Mary was forced to abdicate in favor of her son James in 1567, and the next year she fled to England to seek refuge, despite the fact that Elizabeth had been helping the Scots rebels.

In England Mary Stuart constituted a political danger to Elizabeth. Anne Boleyn's daughter had been born while Henry VIII's first wife, Catherine of Aragon, still lived; she was considered illegitimate by English Catholics who did not recognize Henry's divorce, and they denied her right to the throne. By an unhappy coincidence, if Elizabeth's claims were disallowed, the next heir to the crown of England was Mary Stuart. She was, therefore, the natural rallying point for Catholic opposition in England.

Mary did nothing to make Elizabeth's problems easier, for she intrigued constantly to usurp the throne of her protectress. Legend to the contrary, Elizabeth's treatment of Mary was not ungenerous. She was provided with a residence, and though her movements were restricted, close confinement came only when her subversive activities made it a political necessity. Still she dabbled at conspiracy, attempting to bribe one of the servants whom Elizabeth had assigned to her; but that individual delivered her secret correspondence straight to a member of the royal council. Despite massive provocation, Elizabeth tolerated this sort of behavior for more than eighteen years. If not moved by sympathy, at least she had no desire to continue the unhappy precedent of shedding royal blood.

Meanwhile, Philip of Spain had grown weary of the cat and mouse game that Elizabeth had been playing with him. In 1577 she had made an alliance with the rebels in the Netherlands, and in 1585 she sent troops to their aid; English depredations upon Spanish shipping had grown worse; England was a bastion of heresy and a haven of pirates. Philip conceived a grand plan to make an end to England. In 1580 he had added Portugal to his domains by a combination of inheritance and military force, and in the port of Lisbon, one of the finest in Europe, he began to assemble a great fleet, the proud Armada. It was to sail north, embark the Spanish troops in the Netherlands, then cross the Channel and invade England. Simultaneously, English Catholics were to rise in rebellion, rally to Mary Stuart, and overthrow Elizabeth. The joint operation was to culminate in a Spanish marriage for Mary and reimposition of Spanish influence and Catholicism in England. Probably the English government, which was informed of all these projects, exaggerated the danger of a great Catholic rising, but undeniably Mary had become a serious political threat. Reluctantly, Elizabeth ordered her execution in February of 1587.

In the summer of 1587 Sir Francis Drake struck another damaging blow against Philip's plans. Off the south coast of Spain he caught and burned ships carrying hardwood to make the Armada's water casks; replacement was difficult, and England gained a year. More bad news came; Philip's brilliant commander in the Netherlands, the duke of Parma, insisted that the rebels were so strong in the shallow coastal waters off the Low Countries that the Armada would be unable to embark the troops. Philip prayed, hoped and decided to gamble. The Armada sailed anyway; somehow it would have to manage. Then disasters succeeded one another.

England did not flame with rebellion. English ships harried the Armada, rearming and reprovisioning from English ports while the Spanish ships were far from a friendly base. The Armada was forced into the lee of the European coast, and incompetent command and unfavorable winds wrecked many ships. A storm drove the rest of the fleet north; there was no hope of embarking troops, and the Spanish were without charts for these waters. They tried to round the British Isles to return to Spain, but bad weather continued, supplies ran low, and wrecks multiplied. Only a third of them got home, and England was saved.

Philip took the disaster bravely and decided that God was punishing him for his sins. Begging God not to punish all of Spain for her king's misdeeds, he sent other fleets to comparable fates during the remaining decade of his life, but the defeat of the Great Armada of 1588 had ruined his English policy. England preyed more vigorously upon Spain's shipping, continued to help the Netherlands and opposed Spanish interests in France. It should be obvious from this that a second important pivot of Philip II's policy was his quarrel with his subjects in the Netherlands. The civil war which resulted was carried on by his successors and lasted but for one brief interlude until the middle of the seventeenth century. Religion was only one of many issues, and at the outset it was not even the most important. Rather, the roots of the revolt in the Netherlands lay in the traditions and complex organization of that area.

The Netherlands were part of the old Burgundian inheritance, a loose association of seventeen separate provinces with many differences among them. Particularist traditions were strong, for the fishing and farming population of the north long had been secure behind the marshy barriers of what was almost a wasteland, and the wealth of the great textile cities of the south had made them proudly independent. When the area passed to the Habsburgs, both Maximilian I and Charles V humored local particularism. They used deputy governors in the Netherlands, maintaining a sort of autonomy from other Habsburg holdings, and they recognized the traditional right of local estates to determine grants of taxes and troops, thus allowing a large role to aristocratic and bourgeois interests. Not until 1548 did Charles V formally annex the Netherlands to the empire, and even then he created a Burgundian Circle (military district) which preserved much of the old autonomy. On the whole Charles and the Netherlanders got on well.

Within a decade of Philip II's accession, however, trouble broke out. At first two issues were involved, political authority and religion, but soon an economic consideration complicated matters further. Philip had introduced a Spanish garrison and Spanish clerics to the Netherlands, and religion became a sensitive issue as

Calvinism spread through the poor and restive lower classes of the southern cities, resulting in desecration of some Catholic churches and occasional riots. The government's heavy-handed endeavors to enforce religious uniformity no doubt reflected Philip's sincere convictions, but harsh penal edicts against heretics, the threat of the use of Spanish troops and a rumor that the dreaded Spanish Inquisition would be introduced seemed to violate the Netherlands' jealously guarded autonomy. There were sporadic outbreaks of popular violence, but the first organized resistance came not from a popular religious movement but from a league of three hundred nobles who protested the imposition of foreign authority.

Philip reacted with even harsher repression, sending from Spain the duke of Alva with twenty thousand troops. Alva created a special tribunal, soon called the Council of Blood for the many executions it prescribed, and prominent local aristocrats as well as many humbler folk were sent to their deaths.

Thus far the resistance to Philip had come chiefly from two sources: popular religious protest and aristocratic political protest. The persecutions gave rise to a much more general resentment, however, and Alva added a third force to his opposition, the urban oligarchies, those proud merchants and manufacturers who formed the wealthy backbone of the Netherlands' economy. The policies that Alva was attempting to implement were both unpopular and costly, and, certain that the estates would not support him, he sought financial independence by imposing a sales tax of ten percent on all transactions. Such an imposition would have ended all local restraint upon government and probably would have meant ruin to the area's important commerce. There was a new revolt. Alva had drawn into alliance against himself and his master the most disparate elements—urban magnates and their workmen, who usually detested one another, and the old nobility, who generally scorned both. Religious, political and economic issues melted together, inflaming the entire population to armed resistance. His policy a failure, Alva was recalled in 1573 at his own request.

Thereafter command changed rapidly: Requesen from 1573 to his death in 1576; Don Juan of Austria (the victor of Lepanto) from 1576 to his death in 1578. Neither could suppress the revolt, but the ferocity of the Spanish armies led in 1576 to the short-lived Pacification of Ghent, a compact wherein the seventeen provinces agreed to overlook their own rivalries and to unite to drive out the Spaniards. Philip II had achieved the greatest unity the Netherlands had ever known, but it was unity in opposition to him rather than in the service of his crown.

At the end of the 1570s the war settled into the patterns that were to mark its course until 1648, with the seven northern provinces in revolt and the ten southern provinces loyal to Spain. The catalyst of this change was the appointment of a new Spanish commander, Alexander Farnese, duke of Parma. A man as able in negotiations as he was brilliant in command of armies, Parma quickly exploited the conflicting interests that divided his opponents. The great bourgeoisie of the southern cities was Catholic in faith and conservative in politics; the merchants and manufacturers found the Calvinism and social radicalism of the urban lower classes frightening, and they resisted Philip chiefly in defense of traditional privileges and through fear of the sort of taxation that Alva had attempted. Parma persuaded King Philip to allow him to compromise. He confirmed ancient privileges, especially with regard to taxation, and he had the troops to guarantee social stability; the southern oligarchies agreed to return to obedience, to enforce religious conformity and to provide financial support for Parma's forces. At the price of some sacrifice of his personal political authority, Philip achieved his religious goals in half of the Netherlands and secured for his forces a base of operations against those who remained rebellious.

The seven northern provinces were a different matter. In contrast to the urbanized and industrialized south, this was a land of small towns, farms and fishing villages, a population of stubborn peasant stock. At first Calvinism had grown slowly in this conservative peasant society, but once it became the rallying standard of the revolt, it had spread rapidly. The northern provinces had offered refuge and men to aristocratic resistance leaders such as William of Nassau-Orange, called the Silent, and their men had gained some of the first victories over the Spaniards when their light fishing craft were armed to harass Spanish ships and raid Spanish positions. In the course of the war some of the northern towns, especially Amsterdam, grew in importance and wealth as they became centers of rebel shipping and the bases from which the Dutch raided Spanish commerce. After 1580, when Portugal became part of Philip's domains and hence fair game, Portuguese shipping began to suffer, and at the end of the sixteenth century a Dutch fleet sailed to the East Indies and cracked the Portuguese monopoly of the affluent eastern trade.

These stubborn northerners did not abate their resistance in the slightest when the southerners made their peace with Spain. In 1579 they bound themselves into the Union of Utrecht, and in 1581 they declared their total independence. It seemed a futile if brave gesture, for Parma appeared unbeatable, and in 1584 he captured the port of Antwerp, the last of the great cities that had not made terms with Philip. But the English sent aid in 1585, and Philip's attempt to bring the war to a quick conclusion ended with the disastrous loss of the Armada in 1588. Then in 1592 Parma died from an infected wound, and thereafter the fighting was intermittent and inconclusive. To the year of his death in 1598, Philip never abandoned hope of crushing the rebels, and his successor Philip III was equally determined to make no peace recognizing independence. Sheer exhaustion finally produced a twelve years' truce in 1609, and when hostilities were resumed early in the 1620s the Dutch war was subsumed in the larger struggle known as the Thirty Years War. Peace did not come to the Netherlands until 1648.

In all fairness to Philip II it should be noted that he attempted little that was not being done by his contemporaries. Toleration was foreign to the thought and spirit of the sixteenth century, and most governments sought religious uniformity; most governments also were trying to increase taxation sharply, for rising prices and increasing military costs made more money essential. But it is particularly ironic that Philip should be damned for his efforts to suppress particularism in the Netherlands, for similar efforts in the next century by the French government of Louis XIII and Richelieu, by the Prussian Hohenzollerns and by the Swedish Vasas are praised, and nationalist historians long have lamented the failure of Germany to achieve such a result until the late nineteenth century. Much of Philip II's policy in the Netherlands was a failure, but there was nothing unique or particularly wicked about his efforts, and in the south he managed to hold a strategically and economically important area for his crown and his church.

One other great effort was important to Philip II's reign, his attempt to establish dominant Spanish influence in France and perhaps even to secure the French crown for his family after disaster struck France in the middle of the sixteenth century. The Peace of Cateau-Cambrésis, which brought peace between the Valois and the Habsburgs in 1559, was the occasion of celebrations. One of the events was the old noble sport of jousting, and through a freak accident King Henry II was killed when a lance broke, and a splinter passed through his visor and penetrated his eye. Henry's oldest son, the sickly young Francis II (husband of Mary, queen of Scots), succeeded to the throne until his death in 1560; then he was succeeded by Henry's second son, Charles IX (1560–1574), who was only ten years old. The deaths of two kings and the succession of a minor removed the stabilizing influence of royal authority, and France was thrown into turmoil.

France had escaped serious religious trouble during the first half of the sixteenth century, for the French Church was largely in the king's hands, and no strong secular power was ready to offer the sort of support that the princes had given Lutheranism in Germany. But Calvinism won some adherents toward the middle of the century, and by then the political climate was more congenial to religious dissent. The long wars which France fought against Charles V largely had pauperized the lesser nobles, and they had tended to seek the support and patronage of a few wealthy aristocratic houses, creating a client system often called bastard feudalism. By the middle of the century, four great cliques existed: the royal house of Valois; the house of Bourbon, related by blood to the Valois; the house of Guise, a French branch of the important imperial house of Lorraine, related by marriage to the Valois; and the house of Montmorency, a proud old family with vast lands and great wealth. Until Henry II's death the Valois had maintained control, and the conservative Montmorencys usually had supported the crown, while the Guises and Bourbons had fought and quarreled for offices and patronage. But upon the death of Henry II the fortunes of the royal family passed into the hands of his widow, Catherine de Medici, and though clever and unscrupulous, she faced a difficult task in the scramble for power that marked the last half of the sixteenth century.

The succession of Francis II gave great influence to his uncles by marriage, the Guises. The Bourbons opposed this favor, and soon the Montmorencys also went into opposition. Younger members of both houses espoused Calvinism, and religious dissent took on strong political overtones. Under persecution French Calvinists took up arms and formed a political organization, and soon the cult had grown to impressive proportions. Called Huguenots (probably from a German word meaning "covenanters"), the French Calvinists at their peak claimed something near to half of the French nobility as well as many townsmen in the south and west, Montmorency and Bourbon territory; few peasants were attracted to the movement, however, and generally the north and northeast were little penetrated by the new doctrines. For both religious and political reasons the government tried to suppress the Huguenots, and fighting broke out which was to continue sporadically until the mid-1590s. Generally the Huguenot cavalry (drawn from the ranks of the nobility) was the best on the field, while royal armies fielded better infantry (peasants) and had the financial resources to support more artillery. The wars were savage.

In 1574 Charles IX was succeeded by his brother Henry III (1574–1589), a well-meaning but weak and vacillating man who sought peace with the Huguenots. To oppose Henry III's attempt at compromise, the fanatical Guises formed a Catholic League in 1576 and sought help from Philip of Spain, who thus was drawn into the French civil wars. Then France's troubles were aggravated further as a succession crisis loomed. Two of Henry II's sons had sat upon the throne and died childless. The third, who then reigned, was childless and was expected to remain so as he appears to have been homosexual. A fourth brother, known as the duke of Anjou, was the dynasty's last hope, but he died—also childless—in 1584. Under the old Salic Law, which governed the French succession according to male blood lines only, the next heir to the throne was Henry of Bourbon; but he was a heretic, the leader of the Huguenots and unacceptable to French Catholics. The Guises hoped to set aside the Salic Law and probably aspired to the throne themselves, arguing with some justice that the religious requirement of Catholicism went back to Clovis and was as old as the principle of heredity by male blood lines. Philip II of Spain hoped to have the Salic Law set aside in favor of his daughter, who was a granddaughter of Henry II.

When Henry III was murdered in 1589, the fighting became even more intense, and the pattern of the struggle clarified. Bourbon claimed the crown with the support of his Huguenots and of some Catholics called *politiques,* who set civil peace above religious uniformity; he was opposed by the Catholic League, which had the support of Philip of Spain. In the early 1590s, Bourbon managed to conquer most of France, but Paris was too strong for him to take, and after long negotiations he was persuaded that most of France would accept him if he were Catholic while Paris would accept him on no other terms. With many reassurances to his Huguenot supporters, he converted to Catholicism in 1593 and reunited the country as King Henry IV (by royalist tradition reigning from Henry III's death in 1589 until his own assassination in 1610). Everywhere opposition collapsed, and another of Philip II's policies was bankrupt.

In 1598 Henry IV fulfilled his pledges to his former coreligionists with the proclamation of the Edict of Nantes. By this edict he guaranteed freedom of conscience to all Frenchmen, extensive freedom of public and private worship to the Calvinist minority, equal access to governmental offices to people of both faiths and special mixed courts to avoid religious prejudice in judicial processes. In addition, he granted the Huguenots the right to fortify a number of cities for protection against the Catholic majority, and he agreed to help defray the costs of their fortifications and their garrisons. Thus France achieved internal peace again, and during the remainder of Henry's reign the country recuperated rapidly from the ravages of the civil wars. Despite Philip II's efforts, France—like the Dutch Netherlands—survived to become a major opponent of the Habsburgs in the seventeenth century.

THE AUSTRIAN HABSBURGS

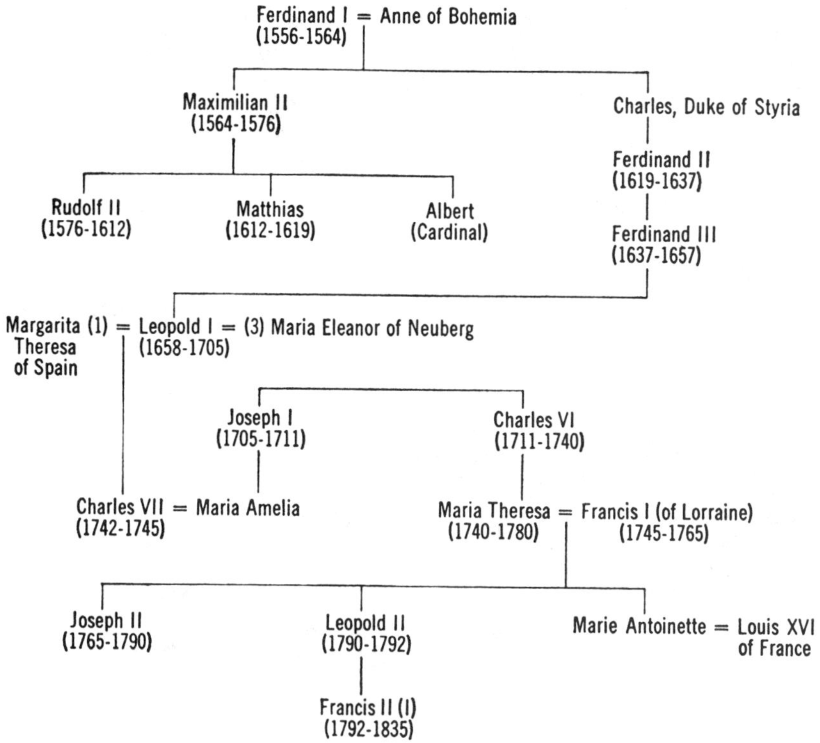

Ferdinand I = Anne of Bohemia
(1556-1564)

- Maximilian II (1564-1576)
  - Rudolf II (1576-1612)
  - Matthias (1612-1619)
  - Albert (Cardinal)
- Charles, Duke of Styria
  - Ferdinand II (1619-1637)
    - Ferdinand III (1637-1657)
      - Margarita (1) Theresa of Spain = Leopold I = (3) Maria Eleanor of Neuberg (1658-1705)
        - Joseph I (1705-1711)
          - Charles VII = Maria Amelia (1742-1745)
        - Charles VI (1711-1740)
          - Maria Theresa = Francis I (of Lorraine) (1740-1780) (1745-1765)
            - Joseph II (1765-1790)
            - Leopold II (1790-1792)
              - Francis II (I) (1792-1835)
            - Marie Antoinette = Louis XVI of France

THE SPANISH HABSBURGS

Philip II = (3) Isabelle of Valois
(1556-1598)

- Philip III (1598-1621)
  - Philip IV (1621-1665)
    - Maria Theresa = Louis XIV of France
      - Louis
        - Philip of Anjou (Philip V) (1700-1746)
    - Charles II (1665-1700)
    - Margarita Theresa = Leopold I of Austria
      - Maria Antoinette
        - Joseph Ferdinand of Bavaria

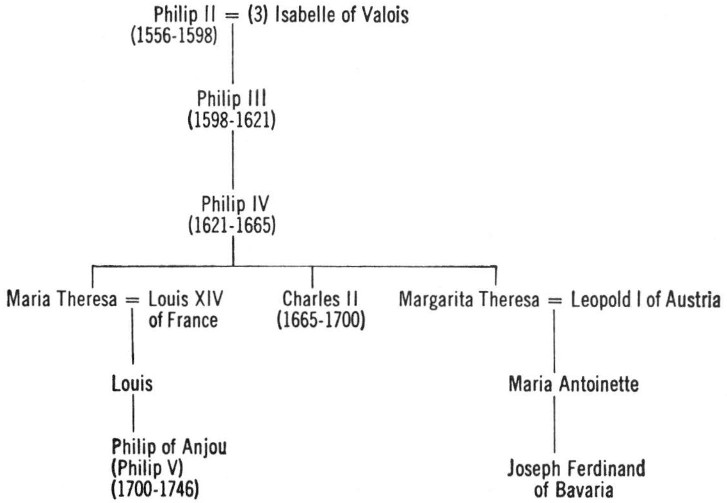

THE HOUSE OF BOURBON

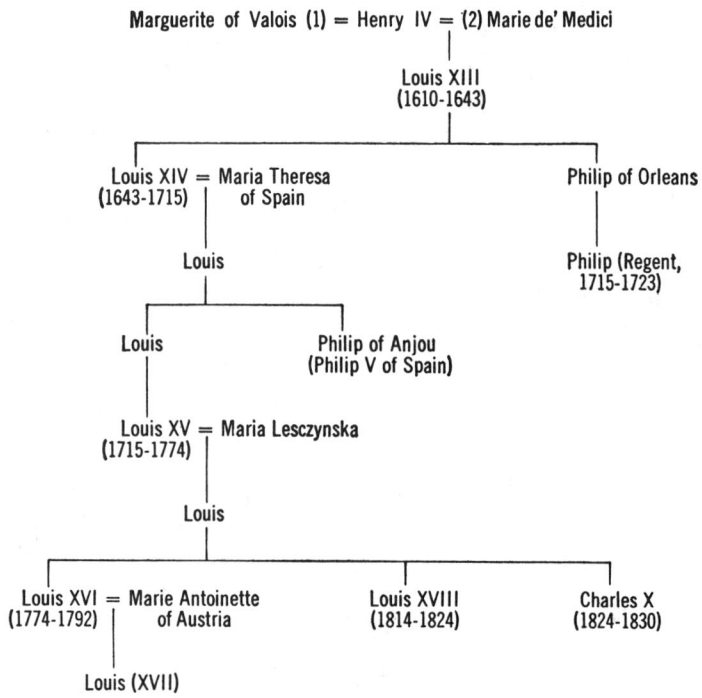

Chapter 21

The Scientific Revolution

About the middle of the sixteenth century western man's traditional assumptions about his physical environment were challenged seriously by the growth of a critical movement usually called the scientific revolution. In the course of approximately two hundred years, from the mid-sixteenth century to the mid-eighteenth century, basically modern conceptions of astronomy, mechanics and anatomy were established, and perhaps most important of all this period saw the development of that critical and quantitative approach to natural studies which is called the scientific method.

To understand the problems and the achievements of the scientific revolution, it is necessary first to consider the broad framework of scientific theories that constituted earlier accepted opinion. These theories were outlined under the title of natural philosophy by the Greek thinker Aristotle in the fourth century B.C., for which reason this older body of thought is termed Aristotelianism. Though modern science has discredited most of Aristotle's ideas, he should not be underestimated. His brilliant mind conceived theories that integrated all branches of natural studies into a coherent whole, explaining persuasively the varied natural phenomena of man's environment.

Though Aristotelian natural philosophy was extremely complex, it rested upon a few relatively simple assumptions. Aristotle assumed, with many of his contemporaries, that there were four basic elements in the universe—earth, air, fire and water—and that each of these elements had inherent properties such as warmth or coldness, wetness or dryness. Since all material objects comprised some combination of these elements, physical differences could be explained.

The four elements also had natural positions in the universe, places where they would come to rest were they not prevented from doing so by mixture with other elements. Freed from constraint, the elements had a natural motion toward their places of rest. The natural position of earth, the heaviest of the elements, was at the center of the universe; water, the next heaviest element, found its place around the earth; and two successive layers formed the blankets of air and fire. Thus Aristotelians conceived of the terrestrial environment as a series of concentric spheres and believed that only a fortunate imbalance allowed some earth to stand above the level of the waters, forming a home for mankind. (One interesting result of this idea was the theory almost two thousand years before Columbus' voyage that another continent must exist on the other side of the world, the antipodes or counterbalance of the Eurasian land mass.)

The concept of natural position and its related theory of natural motion permitted a whole system of mechanics. An object was heavy, and fell when dropped, because its major element was earth, which sought to move to the center of the universe. Flames leaped upward because burning something released the fire that was entrapped, and, freed from restraint, the fire sought its position farthest from the center of the universe. Unnatural motion could be imparted to an object, but it required the application of an outside force, and such motion stopped when the force wore out. Hence an arrow, with a large proportion of earth in it, could be made to fly perpendicular to the direction of its natural motion by the force the bow imparted to it; but as the external force was used up, natural motion would reassert itself, and the arrow would fall.

A theory of astronomy was made possible by the addition of the assumption that natural motion could be inherent to form as well as to matter, particularly that it was a natural motion for a sphere to rotate. Aristotle theorized that beyond the terrestrial environment lay concentric spheres of heavenly crystal—a substance that was colorless, weightless and frictionless by definition. These spheres rotated because it was natural for them to do so, and planets imbedded in their walls were carried around with them. Separately these notions might appear superficial and even amusing to the modern student, but if one remembers that Aristotle was forced to depend only upon naked eye observation and his power of reason, his achievement is impressive. His system could explain coherently the appearance and behavior of the everyday phenomena of life.

Over years and centuries fundamental Aristotelian ideas were elaborated in detail. A basically physical theory of the human body developed in which health was dependent upon a happy balance of four humors—blood, phlegm, yellow bile and black bile; these humors were various combinations of the four basic elements. For instance, blood was the hot humor because it contained a large proportion of the element fire. Hence, fever was diagnosed as an excess of blood, and the standard remedy was bleeding. (It should be recognized that this theory appeared sound; bleeding lowers blood pressure and temporarily reduces fever. This was, of course, treatment of symptoms rather than of causes, but it had some temporary effectiveness.)

The growth of Christianity reinforced Aristotelian thought. Aristotle's science placed the earth in the center of the universe. Christians assumed that the universe existed only as a stage-set for the drama of the struggle for man's salvation, and naturally they expected to find the drama set center-stage. Moreover, popular preachers could derive many useful analogies from the Aristotelian universe. The outer sphere, nearest to the purity of God's heaven, held the fixed stars, which sparkled with the white of purity; the planets, closer to the corruption of earth, shone in softer colors; and of course poor dross earth, corrupted by man's sin, did not shine at all. Thus, on both theoretical and practical levels Christianity found Aristotelianism congenial, and with appropriate modifications to make room for God's creation and God's will as a motive force the medieval church adopted the Aristotelian world view. In consequence of this adoption, Aristotelianism remained the basis of "establishment" opinion for over fourteen hundred years.

One of the fascinating questions posed by the scientific revolution of the early modern period is why it succeeded with relative rapidity after so many centuries of Aristotelian predominance. An attempt to answer this question must consider several different subjects: the accumulation of challenges, the development of better mathematical tools, the invention of instruments and the growth of improved communications. The combination of these developments rather than any one of them ultimately overturned Aristotle.

Challenges to Aristotelian science had existed from the beginning—some sound and some foolish. There were some who maintained that the world was flat, not round. (This idea has been exaggerated greatly in popular lore; anyone who lived by the sea saw the curve of the horizon, and those who watched a ship disappear into the distance—hull down, then sail down, then masthead down— could not doubt the curvature of the earth.) Others asserted that the sun, not the earth, was the center of the universe. But generally these challenges posed too many problems. For instance, if one displaced the earth from the center of the universe, the whole structure of physics would collapse. Why would heavy objects fall if the element earth were not seeking its natural position at the center of the universe? Why would flames leap if the element fire were not seeking to move to the outer ring? An old Greek experiment had attempted to determine whether the earth moved by measuring angles to fixed stars at different times. The experiment was well-conceived, but it failed to produce valid results, for the Greeks vastly underestimated the distance to the stars, and their instruments were too primitive to detect the differentials of angle that such a measurement produces. They concluded that the earth did not move.

Yet by the later middle ages serious criticisms had accumulated, particularly in the areas of astronomy and medicine. The great vogue for astrology which entered Europe from the Arab world stimulated astronomical observation considerably. The scientific studies of the Franciscans, of whom Roger Bacon probably was the most notable, raised problems. And Renaissance experiments in medicine, clandestine dissections and attempts to treat illnesses with herbs and minerals, refuted some traditional medical views.

The greatest interpreter of Aristotelian astronomy was the Alexandrian geographer Ptolemy. In the second century A.D. he had translated complex Aristotelian natural philosophy into astronomical charts on plane surfaces, showing planets revolving around the earth in concentric orbits. Even Aristotle had recognized, however, that planetary orbits were not perfect circles around the earth, and he had theorized that the spheres which carried the planets around turned on eccentric centers (that is, that they did not share the same focus), which made their revolutions appear irregular to an observer on earth. As a device to transfer this conception to plane surfaces,

Ptolemy had devised the epicycle; a planet followed an orbit around an imaginary point, which point revolved in an orbit around the earth. Accumulating astronomical data made Ptolemy's device more and more necessary, for astronomers were attempting the impossible task of describing elliptical movement around the sun in terms of complex circular movements around the earth.

By the sixteenth century, accepted charts of the solar system included one hundred and forty epicycles, a complexity that raised serious doubts in the minds of some astronomers. Copernicus, a Polish astronomer-mathematician, saw the problem in its starkest terms. He came to believe that such complexity defied reason and that he must assume either that the observational work of his predecessors over several centuries was sloppy and inaccurate or that the theory was wrong. He chose the latter assumption and tried to fit the observations to a theory that the sun rather than the earth was the center, resolutely ignoring the problems this would create in physics and mechanics. The results were promising but inconclusive. Because Copernicus continued to assume that planetary orbits were circular, he could not achieve total harmony of data and theory, but he was able to cut the number of epicycles by about half. His conclusions were published in 1543, after his death, in a work titled, *The Revolutions of Heavenly Spheres,* and aroused violent controversy.

In the same year, 1543, another book challenged Aristotelian conceptions in the medical field. A young Italian, Vesalius, produced a book called *The Structure of the Human Body.* In this work the challenge lay not so much in any theory in the text but rather in the illustrations. For centuries the great medical authority had been Galen, a Greco-Roman doctor of the third century A.D., who had codified medical knowledge on an Aristotelian basis. However, Galenic medicine faced even more serious problems than Ptolemaic astronomy. Many early societies have strong taboos against desecration of the human body, and Greco-Roman society was no exception. Consequently, most of Galen's dissections seem to have been practiced upon apes and pigs, whose anatomy differs importantly from that of humanity. Moreover, Galen's treatises survived into the middle ages only in condensations, with many of his explanations drastically cut or abbreviated, and the Christian church of medieval Europe reaffirmed the traditional opposition to dissections, so his descriptions rarely were checked or criticized. In consequence, for centuries the teaching of basic anatomy was derived from animal analogies.

In the later middle ages, however, human dissection began to be practiced again, especially in Italy. It was mostly clandestine, depending upon grave robbers and sympathetic rulers who would give medical schools the bodies of condemned criminals, but it was sufficient to cause serious unease among anatomists who found results at variance with those described by Galen. Vesalius' book exemplifies the conflict well. His text is conservative, repeating a lot of Galenic error, but his illustrations showed what he actually saw, and new techniques of reproduction—engravings and woodcuts—quickly spread his sharply detailed illustrations throughout European medical circles, encouraging those who otherwise might have faulted their own methodology rather than Galen's theories.

Thus, in the mid-sixteenth century two important challenges were posed to traditional science. Yet this simple fact does not explain why these challenges launched a successful scientific revolution while other challenges had been discounted. The greater body of conflicting evidence that the new challengers could muster represents a difference of degree rather than of kind. And vague statements about a Renaissance spirit of inquiry are not satisfactory either, for the Renaissance was not an unmixed blessing to scientific investigation. The adulation of classical writers—very much a part of any definition of Renaissance spirit—tended to make challenges to Ptolemy and Galen and especially to Aristotle all the more scandalous. Recognition of the very real achievements of these men, especially Aristotle's logic and Ptolemy's geography, tended by analogy to lend authority to all of their theories, many of which simply were erroneous, such as Ptolemy's astronomy. In fact, the intellectual establishment offered enormous opposition to the new challenges. Classicists damned those who dared to criticize the ancient Greeks and Romans. Universities, which have a tendency to structure and formalize knowledge, opposed the radicals who would overturn traditional teaching. The church condemned the desecration of the human body and damned those who would assert that the divine drama of good and evil was played upon a stage that was but a speck of dirt spinning at dizzying speed through the universe.

Luther, who often is taken to represent the Renaissance spirit in religion, characterized Copernicus as a damned fool who would turn the universe upside down.

Nor can the traditionalists be faulted seriously for failing to adopt the new theories with enthusiasm. Copernicus could not offer an integrated and unified astronomy, only some simplification. Vesalius could not explain the mysteries of disease and death, only some structural errors of Galen. And to have accepted the theories of these men would have meant discarding all that was known of astronomy, physics, mechanics and medicine, to begin again fumbling into the vast unknown.

Nonetheless, the challenge was established successfully, and it did prove revolutionary. The printing press was one important factor, for it allowed dissemination of the new ideas not as ill-copied manuscripts with multiplying errors but as consistent treatises with careful illustrations. And the printing press was but one of several new tools, both physical and intellectual, that were developed about this time.

The ancient Greeks had not progressed beyond geometry, no mean achievement but only a first step in the development of mathematics, and they had instruments no more sophisticated than the astrolabe, a primitive device for measuring elevations above the horizon. The medieval period saw important additions to the mathematical tools known in Europe as well as some improvement in physical aids to research. From the Arab world had come arabic numerals (the advantage of which will be recognized readily by anyone who ever has tried to multiply or divide with Roman numerals) as well as the mathematics known as algebra. In addition, the Arab world had transmitted to Europe the Indian concept of zero, a concept terribly important to the continued development of mathematics. The most important new instrument to appear in medieval Europe was the compass, probably an import from China, and this was accompanied by a slow but steady increase in the availability of research data, such as compendia of astronomical observations. The early modern period saw both of these kinds of tools, intellectual and mechanical, proliferated further. By the end of the seventeenth century, mathematics had progressed to calculus, and laboratories and observatories were equipped with lens systems and all sorts of devices for measuring time, temperature and pressure.

Finally, the early modern period inaugurated a much fuller communication among experimenters. Sir Isaac Newton, originator of the hypothesis of universal gravitation, was to remark that he felt like a pygmy standing on the shoulders of giants, and although perhaps overmodest, the comment illustrates another important achievement. In Paris and London, in Naples and Salerno and as far away as Philadelphia and Warsaw, scientific investigators of the seventeenth and eighteenth centuries formed societies that began to publish papers and proceedings. No longer did the investigator work in a vacuum or from the basis of bits of other peoples' results that came to him by chance, but rather he could read of earlier experiments and could submit his own results for learned criticism.

In consequence of all these developments, the revolution launched by Copernicus and Vesalius progressed relatively rapidly despite opposition. There were those who tried to absorb the new theories into older ideas, such as the Danish astronomer Tycho Brahe (1546–1601), who postulated a universe in which the earth circled the sun while all of the other planets circled the earth. (Of greater long-range significance were the vastly improved astronomical instruments that he designed.) But there also were a few men who struck out boldly to substantiate the new ideas. In the late sixteenth and early seventeenth centuries, two men in particular contributed to the Copernican hypothesis, Galileo Galilei (1564–1642) and Johannes Kepler (1571–1630).

Galileo really was more important to mechanics than to astronomy, his experiments such as those with projectiles and with falling bodies providing some viable alternatives to Aristotelian notions. But probably he is most famous for his demonstrations with telescopes. It appears that he learned of experiments with lens systems that had been carried out in the Netherlands and that he undertook to duplicate them. In any case, he built telescopes, and with them he succeeded in giving visual refutation of the old astronomy. From observation of the phases of the inner planets, Venus and Mercury, he could show that they circled the sun, not the earth. With telescopic magnification he also could show that other planets, particularly Jupiter, had satellites, a serious blow to the defenders of Aristotelian astronomy. Over the course of a long life, he built hundreds of telescopes, progressing from early three-power models to something over thirty-power before his death. His dramatic descriptions of the universe revealed to him by his telescopes and his defense of the new astronomy attracted much attention and made him one of the foremost popularizers of the new astronomy.

Kepler, on the other hand, worked out the mathematics that established the sun-centered hypothesis beyond dispute. Discarding the Copernican theory of circular orbits, he tried and rejected other regular forms such as the oval, and he discovered ultimately that if orbits were assumed to be elliptical, the observational data could be fitted to the sun-centered theory without need for epicycles to explain discrepancies. A further problem remained in that planets moved at varying speeds along their elliptical orbits, and Kepler sought a regular and calculable basis for the variation. He found this basis in a relationship that linked the variations in a planet's speed with its distance from the sun. The results of these successes were Kepler's laws.

The latter seventeenth century saw continued scientific progress. Mathematics was advanced by the French philosopher René Descartes (1596–1650), who invented analytical geometry, a mathematical system that made it possible to express curves in algebraic equations and conversely to translate formulae back into curves on graphs, and by Blaise Pascal (1623–1662), whose work in combinations and permutations opened the whole field of number theory. A bit later, in independent but contemporary developments, the Englishman Sir Isaac Newton (1642–1727) and the German Baron Gottfried von Leibniz (1646–1716) invented calculus, a shorthand system of calculation and annotation to handle varying speeds and curves of movement.

In astronomy, these developments came to a sort of fruition in other works of Sir Isaac Newton, whose world view remained fundamental to science until whole new areas of consideration were opened up by Albert Einstein early in the twentieth century. That the sun-centered hypothesis was valid was obvious after Kepler, but Newton was intrigued to discover how it worked. The results of his investigations were the hypothesis of universal gravitation, which stated that all matter exercised an attractive force upon all other matter, and Newton's laws, which expressed the force of attraction between two bodies in terms of relationships between their masses and the square of the distance between their centers.

About the same time, the challenges posed by Vesalius were producing fruitful results. William Harvey (1578–1657), an English doctor who had studied in Italy, denied the old theory of two separate blood systems, venous and arterial, and propounded the circulation of the blood. He could advance his theory only inferentially, however, for he could not show the connection between the two systems; it remained for an Italian, Marcello Malpighi (1628–1694), using a microscope, to show the capillaries that passed the blood from the arteries to the veins for return to the heart.

By the early eighteenth century, Aristotelian science clearly was dying. Its greatest strength, overall unity, also was its greatest weakness. A challenge to part of it opened enormous problems, but if the challenge to part of it could be substantiated, then the whole structure had to be doubted. Vestiges of Aristotelianism lingered long. Aristotle's dictum that nature abhors a vacuum resulted in all sorts of imaginary substances filling outer space long after his crystalline spheres had been abandoned; Descartes spoke of celestial fluids, and as late as the early twentieth century many people found some sort of ether a notion more congenial than vacuum. Popular parlance still carries echoes of Aristotle in such phrases as "the sun is trying to shine." But by and large the scientific revolution was an established fact by the eighteenth century. Copernicus and Vesalius had posed challenges which men such as Galileo, Kepler and Newton, Harvey and Malpighi had substantiated. Not surprisingly, the new and radical scientific thought spilled over into other fields.

The late seventeenth century saw new speculation stimulated by patterns of stratification, such as those exhibited by the famous cliffs of Dover, by fossils unearthed in the Netherlands and by what appeared to be sharks' teeth found on mountain tops in Italy. These phenomena had disturbing implications; it appeared the earth was older than the Bible suggested and, moreover, that life forms had disappeared and new ones had appeared in ways not accounted for in Biblical accounts of Genesis and the Flood. Already in the eighteenth century, concepts of evolution were being suggested, though no one could advance any very persuasive arguments of how evolution might have worked until the mid-nineteenth century when Charles Darwin (1809–1882) published his *Origin of the Species* (1859), which suggested that natural selection by environment could transform species over the course of many generations. And the eighteenth century saw a variety of advances in a whole range of scientific studies: electricity (Galvani and Volta), chemistry (Lavoisier), botany (Buffon and Linnaeus), geology and paleontology (Hutton and Lamarck) and composition and behavior of gases (Boyle and Cavendish). Obviously a new and very productive approach to natural studies had evolved.

Inevitably there were those who tried to sum up and explain the new approach that had proved so fruitful, the discipline eventually called the scientific method. Most prominent among the explainers were the English Francis Bacon (1561–1626) and the French René Descartes. Neither described the whole of the scientific method, but each described a part of it in a way probably important to the continued progress of early modern science. Bacon stressed observation and careful recording of observed data, though it may be said in criticism that he seems to have assumed that explanations would pop into the head of the observer and that he probably was convinced that there existed a relatively limited set of general principles that would explain all scientific phenomena. Descartes, on the other hand, stressed the subdivision of problems into component parts that could be subjected to individual study and the casting of hypotheses susceptible to testing; he may be criticized for giving too little weight to careful and critical observation, for seeming to assume that once a part of the natural world had been studied, a great deal more could be explored by pure reason. Yet taken together, these two men caught the essence of the new science: an attempt at detachment from *a priori* assumptions, careful observation of quantitative data, construction of hypotheses to explain data, and exhaustive testing of the hypotheses to substantiate or refute them.

It is almost impossible to overestimate the impact of the new science, and especially of the scientific method, upon the mentality of early modern Europe's intellectual elite; for the new science destroyed age-old beliefs and set intellectuals to speculating in wholly new directions about the nature of the universe. In accord with Descartes's and Newton's basically mechanical conceptions, the European intellectual came to view his world—socially, politically, and physically—as a great machine in which understanding depended upon mathematics and quantitative data rather than upon theology and speculation. Descartes's method of analysis, blocking out separate problems within larger ones and using the solutions of these as building-blocks of a larger understanding, grew to be the dominant methodology of European thought. This geometric spirit, as it was called, was believed to hold the key to all fields of knowledge, and the French even coined a verb meaning "to Cartesianate" to express this mode of analysis that depended upon observation, experiment and reason. Explicit in this new intellectual methodology was the rejection of traditional authority unless that authority could bear the scrutiny of experimental analysis. In his *Discourse on Method*, Descartes specifically endorsed the value of skepticism, demanding that the researcher should doubt everything until he saw persuasive proof. Soon ethics, theology and politics also were adjusted to the new scientific and mechanical view of the world by Spinoza, Malebranche and Locke, and their followers were numerous. The eighteenth century English poet, Alexander Pope, summed up the universality of the impact of the new science in his couplet:

Nature and Nature's laws lay hid in night: God said,
Let Newton be! and all was light.

In a long perspective, the world view established by the scientific revolution, as distinct from the skepticism and the methodology that evolved from it, probably has been exaggerated in importance, for the twentieth century is overturning the conclusions of the seventeenth and eighteenth centuries with great rapidity, and acceptance for two or three hundred years is not nearly so good a record as Aristotle could claim. It is possible that relativity theory and investigations of sub-atomic structure, psychedelic drugs and genetic experiments with DNA and RNA, may leave Copernicus and Newton, Vesalius and Harvey, as antiquated as Aristotle and Ptolemy. But future investigators, however startling their discoveries, also should admit that they stand upon the shoulders of giants.

Chapter 22

The Rise of the National State

When Philip II of Spain died in 1598, the Habsburg hegemony in Europe was far from ended. Despite the loss of the Great Armada and the rise of English naval strength, the reconsolidation of hostile royal authority in France and the *de facto* autonomy of Switzerland and the Dutch Netherlands, the two branches of the house of Habsburg still controlled vast territories. Spain remained the greatest military power in Europe, and though the Holy Roman Empire appeared still prostrate from the religious wars and the emperor weakened in relation to the princes, imperial claims to extensive authority throughout Germany never had been relinquished. Habsburg pretensions to universal monarchy still seemed a real threat, and England, France and the Netherlands were still very much on the defensive.

The beginning of the seventeenth century saw a few years of uneasy peace, but the situation remained far from stable. France was at peace officially after 1598, but King Henry IV continued to aid the Dutch in their war against Spain and to encourage the German Protestant princes in their political opposition to the emperor. In 1609 the Dutch signed a twelve years truce with Spain, but it seemed to be regarded by both sides as a pause to rearm and re-

The Rise of the National State 313

equip rather than as an opportunity to negotiate a peaceful settlement. Imperial claims in a succession dispute over Cleves-Jülich, a group of small territories on the lower Rhine, evoked the threat of French intervention in 1609. Revived religious quarrels in Germany led to the foundation of new armed alliances, the Protestant Union in 1608 and the Catholic League in 1609, and there were comparable difficulties in Bohemia. In 1606 the Austrians and the Ottoman Turks signed an inconclusive peace, but the Danube frontier remained insecure. The war between England and Spain was ended officially in 1604 by Queen Elizabeth's successor, James I, but beyond European waters, in the colonies and on the high seas, sporadic hostilities hardly were diminished. In sum, about 1610 none of Europe's major powers was at war officially, but old hostilities were still powerful forces, and many issues from colonial rivalries to religious clashes had the potential of precipitating great conflict.

The massive war that dominated the first half of the seventeenth century was triggered finally by religious incidents in Bohemia and by Habsburg reactions to them. This struggle usually is called the Thirty Years War (1618–1648) and often is designated the last of the religious wars, but neither of these appellations should be applied too rigorously. The Dutch long have talked of the Eighty Years War, considering the fighting in the early seventeenth century as part of their long effort to break Habsburg power, and a case can be made for considering the fighting of the whole period from the 1530s to the 1640s a second Hundred Years War, a struggle by non-Habsburg Europe to break the Habsburg encirclement. The designation "last of the religious wars" also must be considered carefully, for the implication that the war can be explained satisfactorily by religious motivation simply will not bear scrutiny. Religious factors were an important though not exclusive cause of the outbreak of the war, and they often complicated its course, but the conflict between Catholic France and the Catholic Habsburgs cannot be treated in terms of religious factors.

The Thirty Years War began with a Protestant revolt in Bohemia in the spring of 1618, over a combination of religious issues and a Habsburg succession question. Emperor Matthias (1612–1619), who also was king of Bohemia, was childless, and toward the end of his life he arranged to be succeeded by his cousin

Ferdinand of Styria. Ferdinand, however, was a strict Catholic and a leading exponent of the Counter-Reformation, so his accession was much feared in Bohemia, where Protestantism was well established, with roots going back to the fifteenth century Hussities. The Bohemian Protestants rose in revolt, and with help from German Protestants they drove Habsburg forces from Bohemia in 1619. At this juncture Emperor Matthias died.

The imperial electors awarded Ferdinand of Styria the crown of the Holy Roman Empire as Emperor Ferdinand II (1619-1637), which strengthened his position, but the Bohemian Protestants sought to prevent his accession to the Bohemian crown. Unfortunately the Bohemian estates once had elected Ferdinand successor to Matthias, but they reassembled, declared him deposed and offered the crown to Frederick Count Palatine; they hoped he could rally the Protestant forces of Europe to their defense, for he was one of the seven electors of the Holy Roman Empire, the leader of the Protestant Union and the son-in-law of King James I of England. Meanwhile, Emperor Ferdinand sought help from his Habsburg cousins in Spain and from Duke Maximilian of Bavaria, leader of the Catholic League.

The Protestant Union was divided internally by discord between Lutherans and Calvinists and by disagreement whether the Bohemian war was properly a religious or a political struggle, and in mid-1620 it abandoned Frederick. A few months later Bohemian forces were crushed by the army of the Catholic League at the Battle of White Mountain, and Frederick's Palatinate lands were invaded by troops from the Spanish Netherlands. By 1623 the Bohemian revolt was over, and Ferdinand's agents were eradicating Protestantism and political liberties.

The war that had begun in Bohemia spread quickly to Germany, however, largely as a result of Ferdinand's actions in the aftermath of the revolt. In addition to the repression in Bohemia, which frightened German Protestants by its display of the new emperor's fanaticism, Ferdinand also outlawed Count Frederick and other German princes who had supported the revolt and awarded part of Frederick's lands and his electoral vote to Maximilian of Bavaria. These actions raised a sort of constitutional issue, for traditionally, in the case of a prince, outlawry and confiscation could be decided only by the emperor and the other princes together, not by the emperor alone. Even those princes who had felt that

Ferdinand was justified in his policy in Bohemia had to fear the absolutist ambitions implicit in his unilateral action in Germany.

Christian IV, king of Denmark (1588–1648), was a prince of the Holy Roman Empire in his capacity as duke of Holstein. As a Lutheran he opposed the Counter-Reformation; as a German prince he opposed the emperor's political ambitions; as a dynast he aspired to secularized church lands as principalities for his sons. In 1625 he rallied some of the northern princes to oppose the emperor militarily, and in the summer of 1626 he marched south, opening what usually is called the Danish phase of the war. His campaign was supported by Bethlen Gabor, the Protestant prince of Transylvania (in Hungary) who attacked Austria from the east.

The emperor had new resources too, the army of Albrecht von Wallenstein. An adventurer who had made a fortune in land speculation in Bohemia during the repression, Wallenstein had offered to raise a force of twenty-five thousand men at his own expense if he might be allowed to command it. The emperor was delighted to accept the offer, for not only did it give him new resources in the spreading conflict but also a force which was not dependent upon the princes of the Catholic League, who were no more eager than Protestant princes to see a notable increase in the emperor's political strength. Wallenstein's army soon became infamous for living off the land, devastating any area it moved through like a swarm of locusts, but it was effective militarily. Part of this force turned back Bethlen Gabor, while the rest supported the armies of the Catholic League. Christian of Denmark was defeated at the Battle of Lütter am Barenberge in 1626.

Though Christian was forced to retreat, his army was still intact, and fighting continued for another two and a half years. Then Wallenstein thought he saw a new threat developing elsewhere and persuaded the emperor to make a moderate peace, the Treaty of Lübeck of 1629. By this treaty Christian got his lands back in return for a promise not to interfere further in German affairs; in addition, he abandoned his German allies, some of whom were outlawed and their lands given to Wallenstein.

The Treaty of Lübeck appeared to mark the collapse of opposition to the emperor's growing power. That Ferdinand II was determined to use this new power was made clear a few months before the treaty, when in March of 1629 he issued the Edict of Restitution. The Peace of Augsburg of 1555 had prohibited the confiscation of any more church lands, but this provision had proved unenforceable. During the succeeding three quarters of a century, Protestants had seized two archbishoprics, twelve bishoprics, and about one hundred and twenty monasteries. The Edict of Restitution proposed to restore all of these lands to the church and to break up all Protestant sects except Lutheranism, since only it had been given legal status with Catholicism by the Peace of Augsburg.

Concern over the emperor's growing power was not limited to German Protestants and princes, for a Germany firmly under the control of the Habsburgs also would have been a dangerous threat to France. During the 1620s the French crown was occupied with internal Protestant rebellions, but in 1629 the last of them was crushed, and the government at last could undertake a more aggressive foreign policy; having just concluded a costly civil war, it was not yet ready to send French armies across the Rhine, but French diplomacy and French gold were committed freely to persuade the king of Sweden, Gustavus Adolphus (1611–1632) to intervene in Germany. It was this threat which Wallenstein had seen when he advised the emperor to make a generous peace with Denmark.

Gustavus Adolphus was attracted by the role of Protestant champion, and he liked war and the command of armies; moreover, control of the German Baltic coast would have made the Baltic almost wholly a Swedish sea. He concluded a subsidy treaty with France, and in the summer of 1630 he landed an army in north Germany, beginning the Swedish phase of the war. The north German princes did not rally to Gustavus with enthusiasm, however, and a year was spent in negotiations to secure his base of operations and his supply line; but when his campaign began in the late summer of 1631, Gustavus Adolphus proved to be a military genius, and his army cut through Germany like a hot knife through butter. Wallenstein managed to cover the Danube Valley and protect Vienna, but for a year Gustavus Adolphus dominated the battlefields of the empire. Then at Lutzen, in November of 1632, the Swedish king was killed, and fighting was desultory for the next two years.

In 1634 the nature of the war changed again, when imperial forces with Spanish reinforcements won a great battle at Nördlingen which drove the Swedes and their Protestant German allies back almost to the Baltic. As in 1629, the emperor appeared again the military master of Germany, and in the spring of 1635 he consolidated his position by making peace with most of the German princes. The Peace of Prague granted amnesties and suspended most of the provisions of the Edict of Restitution. The emperor still refused to recognize Calvinism, but most of the German princes were satisfied.

As a result of the Peace of Prague, France increased her intervention, and the fighting continued, but this last phase of the war was fought by a new generation. Gustavus Adolphus had been killed in 1632 and Wallenstein in 1634. Emperor Ferdinand died in 1637, the French First Minister, Richelieu, in 1642 and the king of France, Louis XIII, in 1643. The new generation was less committed to the old issues of the early war years, and peace became possible at last.

The Peace of Westphalia of 1648 resolved a number of issues. The German princes gained effective independence from imperial control, and Calvinism was granted the same legal status as Lutheranism in the empire. The family of the Count Palatine got part of its lands back, and a new electoral vote was created for it (the eighth) so that Bavaria could retain the vote given to it in the 1620s. The independence of the Dutch and of the Swiss was recognized. Imperial hopes of Counter-Reformation and political consolidation were ruined, for the new Germany was a land of princely states and religious diversity. The peace also provided gains for the intervening foreign powers: Sweden obtained control of great stretches of Baltic coast and three commercially important river mouths as well as a financial indemnity, while France received the greater part of Alsace, which brought her frontiers to the Rhine. Perhaps the most significant aspect of the settlement was the division of the house of Habsburg. France refused to make peace with Spain, but the German Habsburgs settled nonetheless, abandoning their Spanish cousins to a solitary war with France that dragged on until 1659.

Within Habsburg Spain, the long years of war proved costly, and at the same time court favoritism and the crown's religious policy led to an enormous growth of noble estates and church foundations, largely tax-exempt, which reduced the government's resources. When Spain first joined the war in central Europe in the 1620s, she was still the greatest power in Europe, but about 1640 she began to experience serious problems. King Philip IV (1621–1665) had placed his government in the hands of the Count-Duke Olivarez, an able and loyal administrator who sought to increase royal power at home while maintaining Spain's hegemony abroad, but the program proved too ambitious. Olivarez' policy required heavy taxation at the same time that the crown was restricting the traditional privileges of local authorities, and revolts in Portugal and Catalonia resulted. With France supporting the rebels, the revolts became serious enough to cause Olivarez' dismissal and to win Portugal's independence, though Catalonia eventually accepted a compromise settlement. Moreover, these domestic disturbances were paralleled by reverses abroad: a French victory at Rocroy in May of 1643, a revolt in Naples in 1647, Spain's abandonment by the German Habsburgs in 1648. For another eleven years the war with France dragged on, but after another French victory in 1658, the Battle of the Dunes, Spain had to accept the costly Peace of the Pyrenees in 1659. She made important border concessions to France, both on the French frontier with the Spanish Netherlands and on the Pyrenees frontier, and she gave the king of Spain's eldest daughter as a bride to the young king of France, Louis XIV, which drew French interest more deeply into the troubled affairs of the Habsburg family. The Peace of Westphalia and the Peace of the Pyrenees marked the end of the Habsburg hegemony.

In France the war years, though costly, produced much more positive results. After the assassination of Henry IV in 1610 and the succession of his nine-year-old son, Louis XIII, the French crown was weakened at first by noble factions competing for favor, but in the mid-1620s, when the king put his confidence in the brilliant and dedicated Cardinal Richelieu, the French crown's policies of national consolidation and the overthrow of Habsburg domination were resumed. Richelieu often has been portrayed as unrestrainedly ambitious, threatening the authority of the king himself, and as a dictatorial tyrant seeking the destruction of the French nobility and the Huguenots, but such assertions are groundless. The king and his cardinal-minister worked in close harmony to promote the interests of the crown, and they sought not to destroy but to compel obedience. Richelieu, like Wallenstein or Olivarez, was a royal servant. All three appeared innovators to their contemporaries, and all three made many enemies, but Richelieu never lost the confidence of his royal master. That the work of national consolidation proved more effective and more enduring in France than in neighboring countries reflects the continuing importance of the person of the king in these nascent national states; without the intelligent and consistent support of royal authority, even able and dedicated ministers proved ineffective.

The increase of royal authority in France faced two major obstacles, the Protestants and the nobility. Despite Henry IV's Edict of Nantes of 1598, which had granted freedom of conscience and widespread toleration of Protestant public worship, extremist elements among the French Huguenots remained restive, still aspiring to destroy French Catholicism completely. These extremist elements involved the Protestants in several rebellions in the 1620s, but the key city of La Rochelle fell to the king's forces in 1628, and with it fell the political and military power of the Huguenots. Yet Louis XIII and Richelieu showed moderation in victory. The Protestants lost their private armies and their fortified towns, the special status that set them apart from other Frenchmen, but they kept their freedom of religion. The crown would allow diversity if coupled with obedience.

The same general policy governed Louis XIII's and Richelieu's treatment of the nobility. They had no desire to destroy it as a class; Richelieu himself was of the nobility, and the king depended upon noble families to supply personnel for his cavalry and the officer corps of his infantry. It was not the nobility but the endemic rebellions fomented by some noblemen that the king and his cardinal-minister attempted to control, and in this endeavor they were largely successful. The most dramatic incidents of their policy were the executions of the duke of Montmorency-Bouteville in 1630 and of the duke of Montmorency in 1632, two members of a family so great that it always had been considered beyond the reach of justice; the execution of the two dukes frightened the nobility into recognition of the fact that the king meant to be obeyed. Minor punishments for lesser offenders drove the lesson home; some were fined, some were imprisoned and others were compelled to destroy the fortifications of their chateaux at considerable expense. The nobility continued to be an important class, but it learned the meaning of obedience.

Both Richelieu and Louis XIII died in the midst of the Thirty Years War, and France again faced a long regency as Louis XIV (1643–1715) was only five years old. Direction of the regency government passed to the queen mother, Anne, and to her minister, Cardinal Mazarin, who brought the foreign wars to a successful conclusion but had to confront another internal upheaval before the accomplishments of the preceding reign were secure. This rebellion, known as the Fronde (1648–1652), was partly a protest against continuing the costly war against Spain after peace had been made with the Holy Roman Empire and partly an attempt to reverse the centralizing tendencies of the crown. The many disparate elements that participated in the revolt could never coordinate their efforts, however, and the government managed to defeat them completely. Subsequently, though there were occasional regional uprisings against royal officers or royal tax policy, there were no more rebellions aimed at forceful revision of the central government until the great French revolution of 1789.

When Cardinal Mazarin died in 1661, Louis XIV took personal control of his government. On the basis of earlier innovations by Richelieu, he created an extensive bureaucracy of officials called intendants to administer the provinces; with the advice of his finance minister, Colbert, he inaugurated tariff and subsidy policies designed to promote trade and encourage economic expansion; with the assistance of his war minister, Louvois, he raised the French army to a half million men, uniformed and better trained and equipped than any large army that Europe had seen since the Roman legions. Such consolidation did not proceed without setbacks, however: a new series of long and costly wars necessitated high taxation that negated some of the efforts at economic development; the construction of a new capital outside of Paris, at Versailles, largely isolated the king from the mainstream of French life and made the court a world in itself; and the revocation of the Edict of Nantes, in 1685, cost France tens of thousands of productive citizens, who fled abroad to escape religious persecution, and the sympathy of Protestant Europe. Nonetheless, by the end of the seventeenth century France was a national state, centralized and served by a fairly controllable modern army and an extensive bureaucracy.

In the aftermath of the Thirty Years War, the Dutch Netherlands also emerged as a powerful modern state. During the long war with Spain the Dutch fleets had expanded remarkably, and commerce ranging from the Baltic to Japan had brought fabulous wealth, so that though small in both population and area, the Netherlands was able to hire troops and play the role of a great power through the latter half of the seventeenth century. But the Dutch failed to solve political issues despite their commercial sophistication. Centralizing and aristocratic tendencies were represented by the house of Orange, which held the stadtholdership of the republic, a title that subsumed a number of military offices. The ambitions of the house of Orange were opposed by the seven provinces, which were fanatically jealous of states' rights; this opposition was expressed chiefly through the states-general, the republic's elected assembly, and through the office of the grand pensionary of Holland. Through the third quarter of the seventeenth century, the extreme youth of the heir of the house of Orange left power in the hands of the decentralizing party, and the able grand pensionary, John de Witt, piloted the Netherlands successfully through two trade wars with England. In the 1670s, however, war with France broke out, and in consequence of a French invasion, de Witt was murdered by a mob which called the now grown William III of Orange to power. The Netherlands then engaged in several wars with France, but their high cost and growing commercial competition from other states eroded the strong economic position that the Dutch had enjoyed in the middle of the century. An alliance with England appeared very advantageous to the Netherlands when William III secured the English crown in 1688, but as the Dutch economy weakened and the role of the central government remained unresolved, the republic became more and more a satellite of the English system. Nonetheless, by the end of the seventeenth century the Dutch Netherlands clearly was a modern national state if no longer a great power; the grim wars over more than a century had developed a sense of national consciousness in the populace, and despite political instability the republic had developed a modern fiscal administration and modern military and naval forces.

After some years of recuperation from the devastation of the Thirty Years War, signs of political revival began to appear in central and northern Europe in the late seventeenth century. With the Holy Roman Empire shattered, the government in Vienna focussed upon consolidation of the Habsburg family lands and achieved impressive results. Governmental reform in the late 1680s was effective, especially in financial administration. War with the Turks succeeded in freeing most of Hungary by the end of the century, and an extensive program of colonization began the revival of that country. In renewed wars with France, Austrian forces acquitted themselves well, and shortly after the turn of the century Austria replaced Spain as the controlling power in Italy and the southern Netherlands. While the multi-racial character of the population of the Habsburg lands impeded the sort of national consolidation that was developing elsewhere, the Vienna government did make some progress in developing the political and military apparatus of the modern state.

In north Germany, too,. a modern state was beginning to appear on the foundation of the old Electorate of Brandenburg. In the middle of the seventeenth century, the electoral family of Hohenzollern held land all across north Germany from the Rhineland to Prussia, and in the chaos that followed the Thirty Years War, Frederick William the Great Elector (1640–1688) began hammering these scattered territories into some semblance of an effective power. He broke down local particularist privileges, established productive tax policies and rebuilt his army. He subsidized economic expansion, and when the Huguenots fled from France after 1685 he welcomed thousands of them to help repopulate his lands. His son Frederick (1688–1713), by using his armies wisely, obtained the emperor's consent to a royal crown in 1701, and proclaimed himself Frederick I, king in Prussia. As in the lands of the German Habsburgs, whether there was a national basis for the emerging new government remained uncertain, but it appeared to be developing rapidly the administrative and military components of a modern state.

Sweden also underwent an important transformation in the late seventeenth century. Domestic instability resulted from the abdication of Gustavus Adolphus' daughter Christina (1632–1654) and from the rivalry of aristocratic factions, while foreign policy was most notable for unsuccessful wars with Poland and Brandenburg. Toward the end of the seventeenth century, however, King Charles XI (1660–1697) succeeded in breaking the aristocracy's economic power by widespread confiscation of estates and its political power through limitation of the noble council's role. He established a strongly centralized royal government that was supported by highly developed popular national consciousness, and at his death in 1697, Sweden was a nascent modern national state. The royal victory was short-lived, however. Charles XII (1697–1718) had to fight to preserve Swedish control of the Baltic, but Sweden's resources were limited, and the series of wars he engaged in proved disastrous. Early in the eighteenth century Sweden's military power was broken, and an aristocratic resurgence undid the political achievements of Charles XI, so that Sweden declined to the level of a second rank power like the Dutch republic.

England experienced unique national development in the seventeenth century, moving from nascent absolutism through revolution and radical political experiment to restrained and responsible monarchy. When Elizabeth I died in 1603, she left a very delicate political balance to her Scottish cousin James I (1603–1625). The crown's frequent use of parliament had given that body the habit of regular assembly and a sense of institutional importance, especially in matters of money and religion. While it is certainly true that James I did not understand English political practice and that he lacked the Tudor's political skill, in all fairness it must be noted that England's peculiar interaction of king and parliament was without parallel anywhere and that the new king inherited difficult religious and financial problems from his predecessors. Further aggravating matters was the fact that James I, like most monarchs of his time, believed in the divine right of kings and sought to increase royal absolutism at the very time that the maturing parliament was seeking to increase the parliamentary role in government. Quarrels arose quickly, some over taxes and some over the demands of religious radicals called puritans, and these issues were aggravated by James's unpopular effort to achieve a Spanish alliance. In the early 1620s, tension reached a breaking point when parliament impeached some of the king's officers, criticized the proposed Spanish alliance and drafted the Great Protestation defending the parliament's right to debate any matter of government policy. In a rage, James destroyed the protestation and dismissed parliament.

Charles I (1625–1649) got on no better with parliament than had his father, and it presented him with the Petition of Right, a statement of parliamentary authority even more outspoken than the Great Protestation. Through the 1630s Charles attempted to govern without parliament, but severe religious troubles and shortage of money forced him to reconvene it in 1640, and the angry parliamentarians forced surrender after surrender upon him; he sacrificed counselors, agreed to summon parliament every three years, abolished unpopular courts and compromised on religious issues. Still the parliamentarians were not satisfied, and in 1641 when Charles refused further concessions, they raised troops and civil war broke out. After the war ended in victory for parliamentary forces in 1648, extremists wrested control from moderates, enacted radical religious reform and executed the king (January, 1649).

After the execution of Charles I, England attempted a Commonwealth (1649–1660), in theory a republic but in practice a military government run by Oliver Cromwell, a situation recognized in 1653 when Cromwell created a nominated parliament and adopted the title of Lord Protector. But despite almost dictatorial powers, even Cromwell had difficulties with parliamentary ambitions and continuing religious radicalism; when he died in 1658 English government was on no more stable basis than it had been in 1640, and a series of military *coups* led to the restoration of the Stuart monarchy in 1660.

The new king, Charles II (1660–1685), honestly sought compromise at first, but the old royal-parliamentary struggle soon flared again. The king tried financial expedients, including a subsidy treaty with Catholic France, to avoid dependence upon the parliament for money; he showed sympathy for Catholicism, and his brother and heir, James, joined that faith openly and married an Italian Catholic princess. These quarrels resulted in the emergence of two loose political factions, called Tories and Whigs; the former was strongly royalist and the latter generally parliamentarian, but both supported the English religious settlement. Hence, both groups were disturbed when Charles died and was succeeded by his Catholic brother. James II (1685–1688) was unpopular from the outset for his overt Catholicism, and when the queen bore him a son in 1688 it appeared that a Catholic royal line would be perpetuated. Consequently, the opposition invited William III of the Netherlands, who was married to James' daughter Mary (child of an earlier Protestant marriage) to save England from Catholic tyranny, and William accepted. Crossing to England with an army, he soon held the country, and James fled to France. Early in 1689 parliament declared James's flight to be an abdication and bestowed the crown jointly upon William and Mary. The Glorious Revolution had been accomplished quickly and with little bloodshed.

The settlement of the crown by parliament completed the emergence of England as a modern national state, for it established a stable centralized government composed of the king *and* parliament upon the basis of strong national consciousness. William and Mary agreed that laws and taxes needed the consent of parliament and that parliament should be convened frequently. Further, parliament excluded the Catholic Stuarts from the English throne and provided for a Protestant succession. The king retained extensive prerogatives, but parliament had achieved a secure place in the concept of crown government.

Hence, at the end of the seventeenth century Europe presented a political aspect very different from that of a century before. The Habsburg hegemony was broken; France and England were modern national states; the Dutch Republic and Sweden, though declining as great powers, seemed to be evolving in the same direction, and something comparable could be descried in Prussia and Austria. Not surprisingly, the emergence of a number of competing states changed the pattern of international affairs quite as much as those nations had changed internally.

Chapter 23

The Birth of the Balance of Power

In the last quarter of the seventeenth century a new pattern of international relations began to emerge in Europe, stimulated chiefly by the ambitions of Louis XIV of France, for the collapse of the Holy Roman Empire and the decline of Spain had created a power vacuum which the French king sought to fill. Louis XIV's foreign policy is extremely complicated, for it was based upon both national and dynastic goals; but his ambitions, whatever their bases, threatened neighboring states. A changing pattern of coalitions developed to limit Louis XIV, and from the wars that resulted emerged the balance of power.

Louis XIV assumed personal control of his government at Mazarin's death in 1661, two years after the Peace of the Pyrenees. He was young, vigorous and eager to prove himself. Though his contemporaries sometimes thought him ill-educated because he was weak in the classics, Mazarin had trained him well for his responsibilities. That he would engage in war was almost certain; the tradition of the king as a military leader still was strong, and besides he had to provide honorable employment for his nobility. Within a few years France was involved in the first of the wars that were to dominate his reign.

Alleging rather obscure rights of inheritance called devolution, Louis tried to seize the Spanish Netherlands in his wife's name in 1667–1668, and Spain was too weakened to mount a very effective resistance. However, Europe had learned the effectiveness of cooperative resistance during the long struggle against the Habsburgs, and Louis soon found himself faced with a hostile coalition called the Triple Alliance: the Dutch, who feared to have France as a neighbor and commercial rival; the English, who feared the competition their trade might face if the port of Antwerp were in French hands; and the Swedes, whose commercial interests tied them to the Dutch and English. The French king was forced to content himself with a dozen fortified towns that strengthened France's northern borders.

Hardly was the War of Devolution ended when Louis XIV prepared an onslaught against the Dutch. He recognized them as the instigators of the alliance that had frustrated his first efforts and the chief opponents of French northern expansion; he resented their protection of French dissidents who published masses of hostile political tracts in the Netherlands; and he realized that Dutch commercial strength was one of the chief obstacles to French economic growth. By diplomacy and bribery he dismantled the Triple Alliance, concluding treaties with England in 1670 and Sweden in 1672, which drew them into co-operation with France. Then in the summer of 1672 he launched an army of 100,000 men against the Dutch while the English attacked them by sea. The Dutch war went well for France at first, and the southern Dutch provinces were overrun, but again Louis failed to achieve total success. The Dutch flooded their lands, stopping the progress of the French armies, and rallied around William III of Orange. Then France's allies abandoned her or were defeated. Again Louis XIV had to accept a negotiated peace. The Peace of Nimwegen of 1678 restored to the Dutch their conquered territories but allowed France some gains at the expense of Spain: border towns and the whole of the Franche-Comté.

In the 1660s and 1670s Louis XIV had aimed north and had met stiff opposition; about 1680 he began to aim eastward toward Germany. The Peace of Westphalia and subsequent treaties had given Alsace and other Rhineland positions to France, but the boundaries of these concessions were unclear. Louis established special courts, called chambers of reunion, to decide disputed cases and used his troops to enforce decisions. Naturally, French courts deciding

French claims on German lands tended to be prejudiced, and the result was a steady advance which the Germans called peaceful aggression. When the French seized Strasbourg in 1681, war seemed imminent, but the Empire was still weak, and negotiations resulted in a settlement in 1684. Louis kept most of what he had seized, and much of Germany was antagonized.

In the mid-1680s Louis XIV was at the height of his power. He had made significant territorial advances to the north and east, and he was respected and feared throughout Europe. But his neighbors were concerned to check his expansion, and the English and Dutch were fearful of the growth of French commercial power. Louis' policies were evoking general opposition such as had destroyed the Habsburgs. The hatred of Protestant Europe was increased further in 1685 when he revoked the Edict of Nantes; soon Protestant lands were flooded with Huguenot refugees who spread tales of the atrocities that had been committed in the king's name.

In 1686 the emperor, the kings of Spain and Sweden and some German princes concluded the League of Augsburg, aimed at containing Louis XIV. In 1687 the duke of Savoy joined. In 1688 William III of the Netherlands became king of England, and both the Dutch and the English joined the league, which then was called the Grand Alliance. Nine years of fighting resulted in a stalemate, however; Louis could not break the ring formed around him by his enemies, but neither could they crack his defenses and invade France. Peace was made finally at Ryswick in 1697, but it changed little except that France recognized William III as king of England, and the Dutch were permitted to garrison some towns in the Spanish Netherlands as a barrier against France.

The major powers agreed in 1697 to a settlement that settled almost nothing because of the growing crisis of the Spanish succession. The king of Spain was childless, and the Spanish branch of the house of Habsburg was about to die out. The French Bourbons and the Austrian Habsburgs had more or less equally good claims to the inheritance, though both faced legal complications. Because of the trade resources of Spain's colonies as well as possible effects upon the military situation in Europe, both the English and the Dutch felt their interests were involved and wished to prevent the union of Spain with either France or Austria. Thus, in the late 1690s all the powers sought to disengage so as to be free for whatever action their interests dictated when the king of Spain died.

The years immediately following the Peace of Ryswick saw a flurry of diplomatic activity in all the European courts, and the English and Dutch seem to have pursued the concept of a balance of power in which no one state could dominate Europe. Louis XIV understood this desire of the naval powers and was sympathetic to it; he was willing to forego the major inheritance, so long as it did not pass into Austrian hands, if that were the price of peace. For awhile it appeared that the issue might be settled peacefully, for though the Austrians were unwilling to accept a partial inheritance, they would have been helpless before a Franco-Anglo-Dutch agreement. Then a series of disasters befell the negotiators. In 1699 a Bavarian prince who had been chosen as a compromise candidate for the Spanish crown died, and hardly had new partition agreements been reached when the king of Spain died in 1700, leaving a will that prohibited partitions and left the entire inheritance to Louis XIV's grandson, Philip. When Louis XIV, as head of the Bourbon family, accepted the legacy, war with Austria was almost certain, but the English and Dutch were undecided at first. However, rapid French moves to exploit Philip's accession in Spain soon antagonized the naval powers, and in the autumn of 1701 the Grand Alliance was reestablished.

The War of the Spanish Succession was almost a replay of the War of the League of Augsburg except that Spain was allied with embattled France. Again France could not defeat her enemies and they could not invade France, though the brilliant English commander, Marlborough, won the Spanish Netherlands for the allies. Eventually the cost of the war forced the participants to the conference table, and the struggle ended in the Treaties of Utrecht in 1713 and Rastatt in 1714. The Spanish crown and its overseas colonies remained with the new Bourbon king, Philip V (1700–1746), but with the agreement that the Spanish and French crowns never would be joined. The Spanish Netherlands and most of Spain's possessions in Italy went to the Austrian Habsburgs. England made major gains: Newfoundland, Nova Scotia and the Hudsons Bay Territory from France and Gibraltar, Minorca and colonial trading privileges from Spain. The treaties also gave international recognition to the Protestant succession in England and to the royal crowns awarded to the duke of Savoy (Sicily, later exchanged with Spain for Sardinia) and the elector of Brandenburg (Prussia).

Most of all, the Treaties of Utrecht and Rastatt established the balance of power as the new pattern of European international relations. France remained the greatest power in Europe, but no longer could she threaten the security of the entire continent, for it had been proved that alliances could contain her. England had emerged as Europe's greatest naval power, but the Dutch, the French and the Spanish remained important in colonial affairs. Both Austria and Prussia had shown renewed vitality, and both had become significant politically and militarily. In the early eighteenth century western and central Europe counted England, France, Prussia and Austria as major powers with Spain and the Dutch Netherlands as secondary powers, but no one of them was strong enough to establish hegemony in Europe.

About the same time as the War of Spanish Succession, another struggle known as the Great Northern War was effecting equally significant changes in northern and eastern Europe. The basis of this war was the opposition of Russia, Saxony-Poland and Denmark to the Swedish hegemony in the Baltic area; the three powers allied in 1699 and attacked Sweden in 1700. However, the new Swedish king, Charles XII, proved to be a military genius, and he knocked Denmark out of the war, inflicted a humiliating defeat upon the Russians and then subjected the Poles and Saxons to a six-year struggle that ended in their defeat. But Peter the Great of Russia (1689–1725) was determined to continue the struggle until he held a secure harbor on the Baltic, giving access to the west, and during the half-dozen years that Charles was occupied in Poland the Russian armies were improved greatly. Thus, when Charles turned against Russia again, Peter was able to inflict a crushing defeat upon him in 1709, and the Swedish king had to flee southward into Turkey, where he spent several years in exile before returning to Sweden in 1714. Meanwhile, the Russians continued their conquests in the east, while in the west Denmark and Saxony-Poland revived and were joined by Hanover and Prussia. When Charles returned, he fought until his death in 1718, trying to restore the Swedish position, but without success. The war dragged on desultorily for a few more years until peace was made with the western allies in 1720 and with Russia in 1721. The Treaties of Stockholm and Nystadt dismembered the Swedish empire on the Baltic, giving Prussia and Hanover most of the north German lands formerly held by Sweden, while Russia secured most of the eastern Baltic coastal lands except Finland. Thereafter, Sweden was of secondary importance, while Russia became significant in Europe and a factor in the balance of power.

The first few decades of the eighteenth century were years of relative tranquillity, partly because the new balance of power brought international stability and partly because some of the major European powers were distracted by internal developments. In England, William and Mary died without children and were succeeded in 1702 by Mary's sister Anne (1702–1714). As Queen Anne also was without direct heirs, parliament passed a new Act of Settlement conferring the crown upon the related family of Hanover, excluding James Edward, the son of James II. Thus, when Queen Anne died, she was succeeded by the Hanoverian prince, George I (1714–1727), and England faced difficult adjustments. George I, who spoke little English and knew little of the laws and customs of England, was not a popular figure. Moreover, his succession caused a political reversal, for it was the Whigs who most strongly had favored transfer of the crown to him, while many of the Tories were Jacobites (from the Latin *Jacobus*, James) sympathetic to the claims of the Stuarts. Thus, in the new reign the Whigs formed the government instead of the Tories whom Queen Anne had favored. In addition, England was indebted heavily from the recent wars. Finally, the new government met serious crises at the very outset: in 1715 there was an armed rebellion in Scotland in support of the Stuarts, and in 1720 there was a financial crash and a scandal concerning illicit profiteering by members of the government. Out of this turmoil emerged a Whig government headed by Sir Robert Walpole, England's first real prime minister (who governed 1726–1742). Walpole concentrated upon pacification of the Tories and Jacobites, economic expansion, exploitation of colonial resources and retirement of war debts; the death of George I and the accession of George II (1727–1760) made little difference to these policies, so for many years foreign affairs held a subordinate place in English government.

At the same time France faced similar problems. Louis XIV died in 1715, at the age of seventy-seven, having outlived both his son and his grandson; he was succeeded by his five-year-old great-grandson, Louis XV (1715–1774), and France faced another long regency. Like England, the French government suffered financial strain from the wars, and a crash and scandal soon followed when a speculative financial scheme failed in 1720. As in England, the new government was insecure; young Louis XV's health was uncertain, and it was feared that if he should die Philip V of Spain might claim the French throne in defiance of the Peace of Utrecht and catapult Europe into another major war. Thus the regent, the duke of Orléans (governed 1715–1723), and after him Louis XV's first minister, Cardinal Fleury (governed 1726–1743), were inclined toward an unaggressive foreign policy and agreement with France's former enemies while encouraging economic development.

These programs of peace and economic growth also had their parallels in Prussia and Russia. In Prussia King Frederick William I (1713–1740) ran his state with what amounted to military discipline, rebuilt his treasury, and expanded his army to 83,000 men, an impressive force for a country with only two and a half million people. In Russia, Peter the Great launched a vast scheme of reforms that included breaking the power of the nobility in government and substituting a centralized and bureaucratized administration dependent upon the Czar, reduction of the independence of the Russian Church, and encouragement of commerce, manufacturing and education along western lines. Many of the Czar's reforms were superficial, and some proved impractical, but at his death in 1725 Russia had a modern army and navy, a revitalized economy, and a much stronger government than she had known previously. Peter's immediate successors were undistinguished rulers, but the effects of Peter's reforms and the influence of imported German advisors continued the modernization and strengthening of Russia as a great European power.

While the early eighteenth century was more tranquil than the seventeenth century, it was not unmarked by war. In 1717 and 1718 an attempt by Spain to seize Sardinia and Sicily resulted in joint military action by England, Holland, France and Austria to maintain the Treaties of Utrecht and Rastatt; but the affair was negotiated in 1720, and with a few territorial exchanges in Italy, peace was restored. Another conflict arose in the mid-1730s, the War of the Polish Succession, which set Austria and Russia against France, Spain and Sardinia. The war began in a conflict between French and Austro-Russian interests in Poland, but Russia quickly occupied Poland, and most of the later fighting took place in Italy between French and Austrian forces. Consequently, the treaty that ended the war not only left Austro-Russian influence dominant in Poland but also confirmed the Austrians in much of north Italy while recognizing a Spanish prince as king of the Two Sicilies (the island of Sicily and southern Italy up to Naples). But these struggles of the early eighteenth century did not spread to engulf all Europe as had earlier wars; the balance of power appeared to have established an equilibrium.

Toward the middle of the eighteenth century the issue of colonial supremacy emerged as one of the paramount questions in Europe. The Peace of Utrecht had given the English important trading privileges in Spain's American colonies, of which the most profitable was the *Asiento*, a thirty-year contract for the supply of slaves. In the late 1730s two factors made the situation explosive: as the *Asiento* neared expiration, a growing rapprochement between France and Spain seemed to threaten that France might replace England as a licensed supplier to the Spanish colonies, and the development of a more effective Spanish colonial coast guard threatened the illicit but very profitable smuggling that the English had built up around their legitimate trade. These threats evoked in England a faction within the Whig party that clamored for war with Spain and France, and in 1739 Walpole lost control of the situation. An English captain named Jenkins was caught smuggling by the colonial coast guard, and he and his crew were handled very roughly. At some point in the fray the Spaniards cut off Jenkins' ear, and he brought it back to England pickled. This atrocity story spread rapidly and provided the war party the issue it needed to overcome Walpole's objections. In 1739 parliament voted for war, and the ensuing struggle, which lasted until 1748, was known as the War of Jenkins' Ear.

About the same time, an equally serious issue was developing in central Europe around the question of the Austrian succession. Emperor Charles VI (1711–1740), who had no sons, hoped to see his lands pass intact to his daughter, Maria Theresa (1740–1780). This arrangement was set forth in a document called the Pragmatic Sanction, and the emperor succeeded in obtaining endorsement of it from several European governments. Despite the Pragmatic Sanction, however, there were many diverse legal traditions in the Habsburg lands, and a female succession was likely to be disputed in at least some areas. In fact, no sooner was the emperor dead than the king of Prussia, Frederick II (1740–1786), claimed and occupied the rich province of Silesia, triggering the War of the Austrian Succession.

The two wars became linked when France, already engaged against England at sea, joined Prussia against Austria in 1741, and a year later England allied with Austria. In central Europe the war raged for eight years, interrupted by numerous truces and short-lived treaties, but by 1745 a pattern was clear: Prussia held Silesia and could not be pried out, but Austria was able to fend off her other enemies; this was the basis of the Treaty of Aix-la-Chapelle of 1748. The colonial war went badly for England except in North America, where colonial forces took the great French fortress of Louisbourg at the mouth of the St. Lawrence, and military reverses forced Walpole's retirement in 1742. Then in 1745 another great rebellion broke out in Scotland in favor of the Stuart pretender, Charles Edward, son of James Edward, and for nearly a year badly needed English forces were tied down. At the Peace of Aix-la-Chapelle England had to give up even her small gains in North America to get back the important town of Madras that France had taken from her in India, so the war had accomplished nothing. Probably the only power satisfied with the Peace of Aix-la-Chapelle was Prussia, which retained Silesia. Both Austria and England were humiliated while France remained eager to rebuild the colonial position she had enjoyed before the Peace of Utrecht. Consequently, the years immediately following 1748 were not so much a time of peace as a time of preparation for renewed war.

The chief area of colonial rivalry had shifted to North America, where vigorous French expansion threatened the future of the English colonies. Solidly established on the St. Lawrence and the lower Mississippi, the French were moving into the Ohio and upper Mississippi valleys, building forts and trading posts. The chief routes of communication in North America were the river valleys, and west of the Appalachian Mountains everything drained toward the Mississippi; hence, a French line following the St. Lawrence, the Ohio and the Mississippi threatened to limit the English colonies to the narrow coastal plain between the mountains and the Atlantic. Clashes were frequent, and in 1755 war broke out between the French and the English in North America, providing a catalyst to the plans of Maria Theresa's brilliant chancellor, Count Kaunitz.

Having concluded that Austria was not strong enough to defeat Prussia alone, Kaunitz had proposed an encircling alliance, and agreements had been reached with Czarina Elizabeth of Russia (1741–1762) and some of the German princes. However, Kaunitz also desired to reverse traditional patterns and bring France into the coalition against Prussia, and this proved more difficult. Kaunitz knew the French court, and he succeeded in building a pro-Austrian party that included the king's mistress, Madame de Pompadour, but the French government was hesitant. However, the undeclared Anglo-French war that had begun in North America brought Kaunitz' plans to fruition. Fearful of a French attack upon Hanover, King George II signed a neutrality treaty with Frederick II of Prussia in January of 1756, and this apparent abandonment by Prussia caused great indignation at Versailles; in May France signed the alliance Kaunitz had been seeking, and a month later fighting between France and England broke out in Europe. Frederick II followed these moves carefully, and in 1756 he seized the initiative with a late summer campaign that occupied Saxony and defeated an Austrian army. Thus, in the mid-1750s a diplomatic revolution had taken place, and in an effort to break the stalemate of the old balance of power the Seven Years War was begun with changed partners: France, Austria and Russia against England and Prussia.

On the continent Frederick II again won brilliant victories, but he also suffered defeats, and in the long run his resources could not match those of his enemies. When the new king of England, George III (1760–1820), decided to stop English subsidies in 1760, Frederick was in serious trouble, and only luck saved him from disaster. In January of 1762 Czarina Elizabeth died, and her successor, Peter III (January to July, 1762), was a great admirer of Frederick. Though he was deposed a few months later, Peter reigned long enough to pull Russia out of the war, and freed of the Russian threat, Frederick again defeated the Austrians in the summer of 1762. As negotiations between the English and the French made it likely that France, too, soon would quit the war, Austria was forced to accept failure. By the Treaty of Hubertusburg (1763) Prussia kept Silesia, an area that increased her size and population between a third and a half.

In the colonial war the English, under the brilliant political leadership of William Pitt, soon established their superiority. English command of the sea left French colonial forces isolated, and in both North America and India they were defeated; the Battle of Quebec delivered all of French Canada to the English, and the capture of Pondichéry destroyed the French position in India. By the Treaty of Paris of 1763, France ceded to England all of Canada, the eastern side of the Mississippi basin and positions in the West Indies and Africa. Spain ceded Florida to England, in return for which she received Louisiana from France and the restoration of the positions in Cuba that the English had conquered. Almost wiped out of North America and Africa, France was in little better condition in India; she was allowed to retain only two unfortified trading stations. England took the rest.

Despite the mid-eighteenth century wars, the balance of power had survived. Although England and Prussia emerged somewhat strengthened, Austria and France somewhat weakened and Russia somewhat more involved in European affairs, after 1763 there appeared no greater danger than there had been in 1713 of the domination of the entire continent by a single power. That the value of the balance of power was recognized by the European governments was demonstrated in eastern Europe early in the 1770s. The once great monarchy of Poland had been in a state of decline for a century, a pawn in the schemes of its neighbors; after the Seven Years War the dominant influences were Russia and Prussia, alleging protection of Greek Orthodox and Protestant minorities against the Catholic majority. A fanatically Catholic anti-Russian group, the Confederation of Bar, soon emerged and won French support, and civil war broke out. The Turks, with French encouragement, chose this moment to attack Russia, and there appeared a real danger that the Polish-Turkish question might embroil the great powers in a new general war; this danger increased when Russian victories over the Turks threatened Russian occupation of the lower Danube to the detriment of Austrian interests, and Austria seemed about to intervene. At this point Frederick the Great, fearful that a general conflict would destroy Prussia, proposed a compromise to preserve the peace and maintain the balance of power. Russia would abandon her Turkish conquests and be compensated with Polish lands, gains not objectionable to Austria; to compensate for the increased Russian strength and westward advance, Austria and Prussia also would take slices of Poland. Thus, a sacrifice to the balance of power, Poland lost about a third of her territory and half her inhabitants. This unhappy solution to eastern European rivalries set a precedent; in 1792 Poland was partitioned a second time, and in a third partition in 1795 she disappeared altogether.

The late 1770s and early 1780s witnessed a sort of epilogue to the eighteenth century colonial struggles, the American War of Independence. Questions of political authority and powers of taxation that long had been irritants in Britain's relations with her North American colonies became serious issues after 1763. The territories that Britain had won in the Seven Years War had lengthened enormously the colonial frontiers that had to be defended against Indian attacks and the shipping lanes that had to be protected. Not unreasonably, the British government expected the colonies to bear some of the costs. The colonists, while happy to be relieved of the French menace, had economic problems of their own, for some of which they blamed crown policy, and they had seen enough blundering of the colonial administration that they were unwilling to accept further taxes without some voice in their expenditure. Ever more violent colonial protests and British attempts at compulsion grew into open fighting in 1775, which led a year later to a declaration of independence by the colonies. Almost immediately France took an interest in the affair.

France's position was delicate. Her resources strained by the costly mid-century wars, she could not afford to plunge recklessly into a new struggle with England. On the other hand, a colonial rebellion that might humiliate the British, weaken their Atlantic position and transfer important colonial trade to France could not fail to interest the government of Louis XVI (1774–1792). The French crown chose to remain neutral officially while giving the colonies large amounts of covert aid. A dummy company was set up, which sold arms to the rebels (the weapons actually financed by the French treasury), while the French government waited to see what the colonists could do against the British. It was not a long wait.

The British plan for 1777 called for dividing the colonies; General Burgoyne was to move down the Hudson Valley from Canada while Lord Howe was to ascend the valley from New York, a campaign that would have isolated New England. But inexplicably Howe turned aside for an attack upon Philadelphia and the Delaware Valley instead. Meanwhile, the colonial General Gates used his Indian allies to annihilate Burgoyne's scouts, and Burgoyne's army, alone and blinded, was left stumbling in near wilderness; after two engagements Burgoyne surrendered at Saratoga in October of 1777. That winter the colonies signed the Articles of Confederation creating the United States of America, and in February of 1778 France signed treaties of alliance and commerce with the new government. Of course this meant war between France and England, and the following year Spain joined in on the basis of a French promise to help retake Gibraltar and Florida.

Aside from such famous volunteers as Lafayette and de Kalb, Franco-Spanish overt assistance to the colonialists was chiefly in the form of naval support until Rochambeau arrived with six thousand French troops in 1780, but even the naval support was very significant. It helped assure the safe arrival of essential supplies, and it played a crucial role in the last campaign of the war. British strategy was founded upon command of the coasts, her fleets embarking and disembarking troops where they wished while colonial forces had to march great distances overland. After the disaster at Saratoga, the British attempted to overpower the southern states; Clinton took Charleston in 1780, and in 1781 Cornwallis fortified himself in Yorktown while awaiting support from the British fleet, preparing to hold off the forces of Washington, Lafayette and Rochambeau, which were concentrating around him. The arrival of Admiral de Grasse with a French fleet upset the British plans, for de Grasse blocked the seaward approaches to Yorktown, and Cornwallis was bottled up so that the British fleet could neither reinforce his army nor evacuate it. In October of 1781 Cornwallis surrendered with seven thousand men, and in the Treaty of Paris of 1783 Britain recognized the independence of the United States.

It is surprising how little immediate effect the success of the American War of Independence had upon the balance of power. The stability that had developed in Europe in the eighteenth century had spread around the shores of the Atlantic and was not upset by an armed conflict and a political readjustment. Trade with England, interrupted by the war, soon picked up again, and French hopes for a revival of French influence on the Atlantic came to nothing. The new nation, beset with economic and political problems in the aftermath of independence, exerted no great force on the international scene. Calm returned and the eighteenth century balance of power appeared secure for another decade until it was swept away by the new forces unleashed in the French revolution.

Chapter 24

Man, God, and Reason

During the eighteenth century, Europe experienced an intellectual revolution, the twin bases of which were skepticism toward accepted beliefs and a mechanical interpretation of both natural and human phenomena. Drawing heavily upon the discoveries and speculations of their immediate predecessors, eighteenth century intellectuals undertook to reexamine critically the very foundations of European society. Newton's description of a mechanistic universe was a major influence in this revolution, as was Descartes' skepticism, the doubting attitude which he advocated as essential to scientific inquiry; but in addition to the scientific revolution, eighteenth century Europe also had to assimilate the impact of foreign cultures and the discrediting of many of its beliefs concerning its own history.

Europeans traveled widely in the seventeenth century, often writing accounts of their travels which posed disturbing contradictions to Europe's ethnocentric confidence and sense of superiority, and after 1700 these were supplemented by fictitious voyages in which imaginary peoples and societies further challenged western values. Europeans tended to become self-critical, and eighteenth century literature became studded with idealized types, of which the simplest was the noble savage, derived from the American Indian; the idealizations exemplified the virtues of simplicity, honesty and loyalty which European writers found lacking in their own culture, and it was a short step from such idealized accounts of real people and societies to the invention of peoples and societies whose governments and morals made the Christian monarchies of Europe appear barbarous.

Religion also was challenged by the impact of foreign cultures and by European speculation stimulated by that impact. In the seventeenth century most Europeans were convinced, on the basis of Biblical chronology, that the world had been created about 4000 B.C., and it came as a shock to find that the Egyptians, the Babylonians and the Chinese traced their history back beyond that date; despite the tendency to discount the reliability of such "heathen" traditions, by 1700 confidence in Biblical chronology had weakened greatly. Moreover, study of Egyptian records revealed the striking similarity of Egyptian and Hebrew beliefs and raised the disturbing possibility that the Jewish prophets had derived many of their ideas from Egypt rather than from direct divine inspiration. Since early modern Christians of all varieties tended to take their Bible literally, the implications of derivative prophecy were distressing, and such problems were compounded by studies of fossils which made it clear that early life-forms had disappeared and new ones had appeared during the earth's history, neither phenomenon accounted for in the Bible.

Scholars as well as travelers and scientists contributed to the growing skepticism concerning the historical accuracy of Scripture. In the last years of the seventeenth century, Pierre Bayle's *Historical and Critical Dictionary* demonstrated the implausibility of some Biblical tales, ridiculed the moral examples in others and generally treated religious doctrine as ludicrous superstition. At the same time, Catholic scholars were preparing massive editions of the lives of the saints, trying to sift truth from myth and to establish the authenticity of texts; inevitably, the textual criticism of documents that they developed, summed up in Jean Mabilon's *De Re Diplomatica* (1681), soon were applied to Scripture itself. By 1679 Richard Simon, a Catholic priest and Biblical scholar, published *A Critical History of the Old Testament*, and this was followed in the 1680s and 1690s by his *Critical History of the Text of the New Testament* and comparable works on other versions of and commentaries upon the New Testament. With the best of intentions, a desire to establish a reliable text, he proved transpositions, interpolations and omissions, and skeptics used his work to deny the value of the Bible as revealed truth.

Under the impact of such challenges, large numbers of the European intelligentsia lost their belief in the traditional doctrines of Christianity, and many who tried to defend the old faith, such as John Locke in England and Malebranche and Fénélon in France, did so on the basis of the reasonableness of God as the architect of the Newtonian world-machine rather than on the basis of dogmatic theology; even Christianity's supporters were finding it difficult to accept their faith's revelation and miracles as more than superstitions or symbolic tales for the instruction of the ignorant and were trying to justify themselves on rational and secular grounds. This intellectual revolution had enormous implications, for rationalism and secularism left no possibility of justifying governments on religious grounds, and such attitudes set the intellectuals ever farther apart from the great mass of the population, which was reacting to the formality and coldness of the state churches with popular pietistic and revivalist movements.

Another basis for novel opinions developed out of seventeenth century England, where tumultuous political development inspired new reflections upon society and politics. In 1651 Thomas Hobbes' *Leviathan* sketched a purely secular and naturalistic basis for ethics and politics, proposing the theory that in a state of nature anarchy would prevail and life would be "nasty, brutish and short." Hobbes suggested that government was originated by men seeking security of life and property. Hobbes' idea that government was initiated by men through a social contract rather than instituted by God was not as shocking as his conclusions that the state must have complete domination over churches and, with few exceptions, over all aspects of the subjects' lives if the society were not to revert to the anarchy of the state of nature. Obviously Hobbes' thought was conditioned by the political troubles of England in his day, but it remains notable for its purely secular postulates, and his conceptions of the state of nature and the social contract were very influential.

Secular and rational approaches to man and society were continued by John Locke, who was convinced that all understanding derives of experience. Rejecting theories of innate ideas, he asserted that a child was born with its mind blank and that experience wrote upon it, a conception that demanded new analyses of man as a social and moral animal. In considering politics Locke also posited the idea of a state of nature, but because of his concept of human psychology it was a different condition than that suggested by Hobbes. Locke felt that even in the state of nature man was bound by natural law interpreted by reason and experience and that men always established general principles for the safeguard of life and property, conventions that created society; this idea introduced an intermediate step in the agreement between subject and monarch, and repudiation of the monarch did not dissolve the social contract but only left society to make new arrangements for its governance. Because Locke's *Two Treatises on Government* appeared in 1690, because it was an easy step to interpret parliament as the voice of society and because he lauded William III, the author has been accused of acting as apologist for the Glorious Revolution, but his political ideas seem to have been worked out well before that event and to have proceeded from his basic philosophy.

Locke was read widely in the eighteenth century, and translations made both his *Two Treatises on Government* and his *Essay Concerning Human Understanding* accessible to continental readers; he became for psychology and philosophy what Newton was to physical science, a guide to fruitful areas of investigation and the architect of new conceptions. Though always moderate himself, he provided potent intellectual weapons to those who mounted an ever more aggressive attack upon tradition, and those who sought only security and stability were drawn into this attack. Locke's summation of the bases of social order as security of life, liberty and property is a fair outline of what many articulate men were concerned to protect in the early eighteenth century, and threats seemed to come less from a few intellectual innovators than from old institutions. For two centuries, sectarian quarrels and dynastic struggles had kept Europe immersed in civil conflict and international war; if life, liberty and property were to be protected by reasonable laws, it appeared that the claims of the theologians and the ambitions of dynastic monarchs would have to be restrained.

The leadership of England in the development of secular, rational and humane thought was founded on Newton and Locke, and it was reinforced by writers on both sides of the channel during the second quarter of the eighteenth century, but by the middle of the century intellectual supremacy had passed to France. The early writers of the French Enlightenment acknowledged their debt to the English, as in Voltaire's *Elements of the Philosophy of Newton*, but Paris quickly became the center of the new philosophy. The scope of the Enlightenment and the range of individual variation from one writer to another make generalizations difficult, but some common positions can be sketched briefly. At the foundation of most Enlightenment thought was a mechanistic view of a world governed by natural law that was discoverable by reason. Such an assumption implied that not only natural science but all aspects of life were integrated in a vast mechanical scheme such as Newton's laws of gravitation. Skepticism toward traditional beliefs and authorities was reinforced by the rapid advances in natural studies produced by the scientific method and by contemplation of exciting new possibilities in human and social studies; by comparison with the natural sciences, the social sciences were still primitive, but they had become empirical and inductive, and they had developed methods that could be used to judge traditional institutions and authorities by new standards.

Most writers of the Enlightenment shared the expectation that great discoveries would continue to be made, that reason would uncover further natural laws and that much that remained mysterious would become explicable. In this context, mysteries were but natural phenomena as yet unexplained, and miracles were fanciful explanations of natural phenomena, not only inaccurate but also an offense to human intelligence. The confidence in right reason and experience as tools leading ultimately to complete understanding was almost limitless. Few figures of the Enlightenment asserted atheism, however, for they still required a creator for their worldmachine, an architect or engineer whose designs were the foundation of natural law, but their rejection of the miraculous generally meant a denial of concepts of an afterlife of salvation or damnation. Life no longer was a mere preparation, the world a vale of tears; life was reality, the world the place where fulfilment or frustration had to be found, and it began to be perceived that happiness in itself might be a valid goal in life.

Reluctant to affirm a thoroughgoing atheism, most eighteenth century intellectuals adopted a religious creed called deism, characterized as natural religion. Deists accepted a God, usually impersonal, who had fabricated the universe, and they accepted a set of morals that God had engraved on the hearts of all men. To some extent deism was a reaction against the arid arguments of Christian theologians and the horrors of persecution and religious wars that had resulted from Christian dissension; to some extent it was the outgrowth of the impact of foreign cultures which showed common religious tenets in many faiths and of the new science which stressed the orderliness of the physical universe and the unity of mankind. God was assumed to be rational, not capricious, so the deists had no patience with miracles, which would require the suspension of natural law, or with metaphysical revelation, which claimed knowledge of God other than through understanding His natural laws. Comparative religious studies convinced the deists that their tenets were the core of all the world's religions and that the varieties of religious belief were but superstitious error derived from false claims of particular revelation.

It was not angry Christian theologians but the Scotch skeptic, David Hume, who challenged these opinions most effectively; his *Natural History of Religion,* published in the late 1750s, attacked the fundamental assumption of the advocates of natural religion by denying that men allowed themselves to be guided by reason or that there was any universality of human motivation. Hume contended that reason was not and could not be a guide to principles but only a tool for devising the means of gratifying irrational impulses and desires which varied among individuals and societies; thus he negated, to his own satisfaction at least, the whole concept of rational natural religion and, incidentally, challenged the very basis of Enlightenment rationalism and its derivative structure of universal morality and self-evident truths.

Another common element of Enlightenment thought was optimism. This attitude was encouraged by the great scientific progress that had resulted from the new methodology, but its roots ran much deeper. On the one hand, the great German scientist, Leibnitz, was convinced of the existence of a beneficent deity, and his endorsement of optimism had some influence through his popularizer, Christian Wolff. But in a broader sense, the general optimism of eighteenth century intellectuals derived from their convictions about the nature of the universe. They believed firmly that all phenomena were explicable through natural law, and they were convinced that in reason they had found the key to understanding natural law; hence, they fully anticipated that further application of reason would make both the physical and social world more explicable and more predictable and that men would be able to plan their lives and their societies to avoid catastrophes. Some of the more superficial aspects of this optimism, especially the idea of a beneficent deity, were satirized brilliantly by Voltaire in his *Candide*, but general confidence in human progress continued to be characteristic of most eighteenth century intellectuals.

It was in specific applications to man and society that Enlightenment thought had its most far-reaching effects, in such concepts as the theory of natural rights. Grounded originally in principles of natural law, as time passed the theory of natural rights was justified more and more on the basis of empiricism, on the conviction that history showed that security of life, liberty and property was essential to the stability of society and the development of the potential of humanity. Fused with the older theories of the state of nature and the social contract, the doctrine of natural rights provided a standard against which to measure the performance of governments. To the extent that a government contributed to the greater security of life, liberty and property, it was fulfilling its function; when corruption of its purposes, as through subservience to dynastic ambition, for instance, weakened the security in which these basic rights were held, to that extent it failed to fulfill its purpose. Implicit, of course, was a notion of the right of revolution.

An important corollary of these ideas was the conception of society based on individuals who were born free and equal, in contrast to older notions of society based upon family units enmeshed in a web of divinely ordained social inequality and obligations to church and king. By born free and equal, the eighteenth century writers understood free to mean the individual's right to choose his own goals and equal to mean that all started life with minds the blank slate on which experience wrote; they quite accepted that qualitative differences of experience would produce human inequality, and they were not disturbed much by that so long as inequality was not institutionalized in law. Perhaps the best summation of the socio-political thought of the Enlightenment, natural rights and social contract with vague deistic overtones, is provided by the American Declaration of Independence of 1776:

> We hold these truths to be self-evident, that all men are created equal, that they are endowed by their Creator with certain unalienable Rights, that among these are Life, Liberty and the pursuit of Happiness.—That to secure these rights, Governments are instituted among Men, deriving their just powers from the consent of the governed,—That whenever any Form of Government becomes destructive of these ends, it is the Right of the People to alter or abolish it....

The substitution of "pursuit of happiness" for Locke's "property" usually is attributed to the existence among the Americans of radical elements who were seeking to weaken property rights and would not agree to any endorsement of them in the declaration, but the idea that the "pursuit of happiness" was a natural right certainly was deep-rooted in Enlightenment philosophy and existed independent of the political maneuvers surrounding the framing of the Declaration of Independence.

Perhaps the most effective demonstration of the scope and variety of Enlightenment thought is provided by a brief survey of some of its leading advocates. In France, one of the earliest of these was Baron Montesquieu. As a young man, Montesquieu embarked upon the judicial career traditional in his family, but he soon turned to writing, and in 1721 he published his *Persian Letters;* the literary device of letters purporting to be written by two refined Persians traveling in Europe provided an opportunity for amusing but merciless satire of church, state and society in France, and the book became very popular. It was the first of the devastatingly witty works of social satire that were to typify the eighteenth century French rationalist critics who called themselves *philosophes*. In the 1730s he published some reflections upon Roman history, and then in 1748 appeared his greatest work, *The Spirit of the Laws;* a comparison of various constitutional patterns, this work demonstrated the sociological and anthropological relativism that was to transform the study of history and social science in the eighteenth century. The concepts of the separation of powers and checks and balances that Montesquieu presented in his idealized analysis of English practices proved very influential upon later writers of constitutions.

Of the same generation as Montesquieu was Voltaire, a notary's son who produced his first successful play in his mid-20s. A penchant for writing political satires resulted in occasional arrests and frequent exile from Paris; three years spent in England during his early 30s had a strong influence upon him, for he came to admire England's toleration of free thought and general absence of censorship. This influence showed itself in 1733, when he published his *Philosophical Letters on the English* and behind the pretense of comments on English society attacked the church and government of France. Official reaction to the *Philosophical Letters* was violent; the work was seized and burned, and the author escaped arrest only by another flight out of the country.

The continued development of Voltaire's critical spirit was marked in the late 1730s by the appearance of the *Elements of the Philosophy of Newton* and a *Treatise on Metaphysics,* which endorsed the value of experience and reason and renewed the attack upon religion. In 1751 he had to leave Paris again, and after sojourning for two years with Frederick the Great of Prussia, he settled near Geneva in a house that was in France but very near the Swiss border, in case escape should prove necessary. There he spent the last quarter century of his life, entertaining friends and writing voluminously, except for a final visit to Paris, where he died in 1778 at the age of eighty-four. During these last years he produced masses of letters, essays and lampoons attacking the establishment in church and state with bitter sarcasm, denouncing oppression and ridiculing the extremes of other rationalists. Some of the best of these efforts were his many contributions to the *Great Encyclopedia,* which involved him with the next generation of Enlightenment writers, who dominated the third quarter of the eighteenth century, and especially with the encyclopedia's general editor, Diderot.

Denis Diderot, a craftsman's son, first appeared on the literary scene in the mid-1740s with a translation of Shaftesbury's *Inquiry Concerning Virtue and Merit;* this was followed by his own *Philosophical Thoughts, The Promenade of a Sceptic* and a *Letter on the Blind*, the latter an assertion of man's total dependence upon his senses. The vigor of his skeptical criticism cost him three months in prison, but after his release he undertook a massive and even more daring work, the *Great Encyclopedia*. A Parisian publisher, André-François LeBreton, had conceived the idea of publishing a translation of the popular Chambers' *Cyclopedia*, but the project quickly grew into an original multivolume collection surveying the whole range of human knowledge, and as Diderot had some reputation as a translator and author, he was drawn into the venture, first as a staff writer and then as general editor. The series eventually comprised seventeen volumes of text and eleven volumes of illustrations, and most of France's great eighteenth century writers contributed to it. This encyclopedia reflected the unorthodox views of the *philosophes,* and it soon became a center of controversy; there were two attempts at governmental suppression in the 1750s, and in the 1760s Diderot discovered that the worried publisher, LeBreton, was censoring some of his more extreme articles. Nonetheless, the *Great Encyclopedia* emerged as a statement of faith of eighteenth century rationalism; more than a compendium of information, it was an arsenal of weapons and ammunition for the critics of eighteenth century society. Its explanations of science, its easy assumption of universally valid, simple mechanical laws of nature and its brilliant list of contributors offered reason, optimism and confidence to critics of the world as it was, and it became an enormous success. Published by subscription in advance, the work was issued first in fifteen hundred, then two thousand and finally four thousand copies, and hardly was it completed in 1772 than reissues and pirated editions began to appear; despite the protests of the establishment, the publisher and his associates made something in the range of four million dollars profit from the venture, for the spirit and the content of the *Great Encyclopedia* had caught the cosmopolitan and iconoclastic temper of the eighteenth century literate public.

One of the most direct influences of the Enlightenment was its impact upon progressive rulers who admired the *philosophes.* Few exponents of the Enlightenment had enough confidence in the common man to advocate a democratic society; most, like Voltaire, were supporters of enlightened despotism and aspired only to persuade the governing powers of Europe that rational law guaranteeing "natural rights" was the best basis of the state. They found some audience among Europe's crowned heads, and though enlightened despotism generally remained more theory than practice, it deserves notice. Most notable among governing powers who endorsed the idea were the sovereigns of Prussia, Russia and Austria, though there were others.

Frederick the Great of Prussia (1740–1788) was a cultured man as well as an able administrator and a distinguished soldier. Despite the mid-eighteenth century wars, he was the most effective of the enlightened despots, rationalizing and codifying Prussian law, adopting policies designed to improve the economic condition of his subjects and reforming the judicial system in an effort to assure equal justice; his attitude toward government was summed up best in his famous comment, "I am the first servant of the state." Catherine the Great of Russia (1762–1796) is more difficult to evaluate. She endorsed the *philosophes,* admired Voltaire greatly and entertained Diderot; but as she depended upon the conservative Russian nobility both for the maintenance of her domestic authority and for the support of her aggressive foreign policy, her avowed intention of governmental reform, such as codification of Russian law, produced no results. The most dramatic attempt to establish enlightened despotism was that of the Emperor Joseph II (1780–1790). When the death of his mother, Maria Theresa, delivered power into his hands, he plunged into rapid and radical legislative experimentation aimed at breaking the power of the church and the nobility and destroying provincial privileges. Joseph II achieved impressive results on paper, but in practice he aroused a storm of opposition that blocked the effective implementation of his intentions, and his brother and successor, Leopold II (1790–1792), had to revoke most of the radical decrees in order to undertake more moderate and more practical reforms. Probably even Louis XVI of France (1774–1792) thought of himself as an enlightened despot, at least in the early part of his reign, when he encouraged his minister Turgot to undertake reforms in justice, taxation and economic regulation; and other governments in Portugal, Italy and the German states were influenced by the principles of enlightened despotism.

Despite the Enlightenment, however, there were many people who supported different values and denied that the *philosophes* had discovered great new truths. Often their feelings were expressed through an emotional religious revival. In the late seventeenth century, France had the earliest experience of this movement, with a group called Quietists, whose faith was so mystical as to be dangerously close to a rejection of clerical authority, and another called Jansenists, who sought to introduce into Catholicism a puritanical and predestinarian doctrine reminiscent of Calvinism; the Quietists were suppressed quickly, and early in the eighteenth century the Jansenists were condemned, but the currents of emotional commitment to a more personal Christianity that they stirred flowed strongly among the common people in France while the intellectuals were debating reason and natural religion. The religious revival in Germany occurred in the middle of the eighteenth century, led by the Moravian Brethren who sought to find personal religious experience and preached a religion of the heart; genuinely tolerant on an individual basis, they condemned both rationalist deism and the dogmatic theology of the established Christian churches. The movement had a strong influence through many German states, encouraging the abandonment of an artificial French culture, and contributed importantly to the richness of the German language and the emotional sensitivity that marked Germany's late eighteenth century literary blossoming with Herder and Goethe.

Probably the most influential of the eighteenth century pietistic movements was English Methodism, organized by the devout and energetic John Wesley and inspired by the emotional evangelism of George Whitefield. Throughout England the Methodists preached and published the love of God, the assurance of salvation and the horror of sin; unfortunately, in their reaction against the cold rationalism of the elite they also were rather anti-intellectual, condemning science and critical study of Scripture as paths to atheism. Their meetings often aroused emotional hysteria repugnant to the fastidious upper classes, but whatever their shortcomings, the emotional preaching and the simple fundamentalism of the Methodists communicated to the horribly depressed masses of the eighteenth century and began their integration into modern English society.

Eventually distrust of the doctrine that reason and the senses were man's only reliable faculties penetrated even the intellectual elite. Dissenting voices were a minor counterpoint in the thundering acclamation of rational empiricism, but some of them spoke too forcefully to be ignored. As noted already, Hume, though no antirationalist, had challenged the psychological assumptions of his contemporaries in the 1750s, and another dissident of formidable reputation appeared in the person of Jean-Jacques Rousseau. A member for awhile of the Paris circle of *philosophes* and a contributor to the *Great Encyclopedia*, he broke with his associates in the mid-1750s over differences of principle, for the *philosophes* were reformers and Rousseau was a true radical who sought the overthrow and replacement of contemporary society. In his search for the nature of man, upon which a moral regeneration might be based, Rousseau reached conclusions radically different from those of Locke. He asserted that natural man was neither corrupted by original sin nor simply blank but filled with good impulses which society negated. Alienated from the world and the people he would have liked to have claimed as friends, Rousseau found himself committing actions he disapproved, and he concluded that he had been corrupted and degraded by society. With lashing invective, he damned the social order and pleaded for a return to nature, which he sought within himself; sweeping aside all of the sociological and anthropological inquiry of his contemporaries, he asserted the sole validity of his own experience and intuition. Proceeding from such tenuous foundations and susceptible to his own changing perceptions, Rousseau's philosophy often is contradictory, for at times he endorses unrestrained individualism, and at other times he projects a stringent collectivism. The unifying rationale is his passion for simple, unspoiled humanity at the same time exercising freedom and associating harmoniously, and these general ideas are more important than his specific theories. His love of nature and the beauty he discovered in it found a wide audience; his passion and his sensitivity offered a valuable counterpoise to the chill rationality of the *philosophes;* and his endorsement of human values provided a glow of warmth in the impersonal mechanistic universe of the Enlightenment.

The negation of the Enlightenment was a strong current by the late eighteenth century, revealed by English poets such as Gray and by a growing enthusiasm for things medieval, such as a revival of gothic styles and a fondness for old castles and abbeys in contrast to the classical enthusiasm of the mainstream of eighteenth century culture. A cult of sentimentality was growing that found the sterile intellectualism of the Enlightenment as much a prison for humanity as the metaphysical otherworldliness of the medieval churchmen.

Chapter 25

A Harvest of Violence

All over Europe the eighteenth century ended in a cataclysm of social upheaval and political innovation that began in France in the late 1780s. The French revolution developed from many factors: arbitrary government which, though not tyrannical, was unresponsive to important interests in the kingdom; the unpopularity of the royal family, which weakened traditional loyalty to the crown; the discredit of the government in consequence of military failures and its inability to relieve economic distress; and political awareness intensified by the critical literature of the Enlightenment. All of these problems were aggravated by inequitable taxation, which generated particular grievances as focal points for discontent and left the government tottering on the verge of bankruptcy in a prosperous nation. By the 1780s some sort of far-reaching reform probably was unavoidable, but there was nothing inevitable about the revolution that grew out of efforts at reform.

In the late eighteenth century France had a population of about twenty-six million and a complex social structure. At the top of the society stood the church and the aristocracy, both groups closely linked to the monarchy and both enjoying privileged positions with regard to taxation. The church depended heavily upon the king, for most of its high offices were filled by royal nomination, and it was exempt from direct royal taxes paid by commoners, for each year it made a free gift to the government. While this sum was less proportionately than that paid by the peasantry, it should be remembered that the church supported at its own expense most of the educational, charitable and hospital services of the society as well as its religious obligations. The princes of the church, archbishops, bishops and abbots, often were wealthy, powerful and urbane members of aristocratic families, active in politics, while parish priests and simple monks were commoners, usually impoverished and often ill-educated. Though all were considered together as the first estate—the church—the social and economic gulf between the worldly bishop at the king's court and the simple priest in a country parish was enormous.

The aristocracy held a position comparable to that of the church, both in its dependence upon the king and in its privileged exemption from most direct taxation. Honorific and remunerative positions at the court, commissions in the army, and offices in the administration and the church depended upon the king's will, and royal pensions formed an important part of aristocratic income. The aristocracy was variegated, its common feudal and military character long lost. The distinction between nobility of the robe, with titles earned in the royal administration, and nobility of the sword, with older feudal origins, that had divided the aristocracy in the seventeenth century had been blurred through marriage by the late eighteenth century, but another equally divisive distinction had grown up with the development of the court: the courtier nobility that lived near the king and the country nobility that lived on its estates. Generally the courtiers depended heavily upon the king; they drew rents from their lands as absentee landlords, but their chief income derived from royal appointments and royal pensions. They lived in some luxury, and vast sums of money passed through their hands to meet the high expenses of court life, but most were deeply in debt and would have been ruined financially as well as socially by loss of the king's favor. By contrast country noblemen lived upon their estates and generally depended upon them for their income, but even the country nobility was not homogeneous. Some were modestly prosperous and lived as comfortable country gentlemen, renting out their lands on relatively short-term leases that allowed them to raise rents from time to time to keep pace with inflationary costs. Most of these country gentlemen were important figures in the life of their districts, experimenting with new crops and livestock, adjudicating disputes among peasants, and articulating local grievances or needs to the government; generally they were regarded with respect and often with affection. By contrast, there was another class of country noblemen that was impoverished, frequently because family lands had been divided too often or because the lands were rented on perpetual or near-perpetual leases, leaving the owners defenseless against inflation. Often these impoverished noblemen, called *hobereaux*, were distinguishable from the peasantry only by their right to wear a sword and by the traditional dues they could collect from their tenants.

By the late eighteenth century the urban middle classes formed an important group in French society. At the top of the urban social structure was the *grande bourgeoisie*, wealthy bankers and large-scale merchants. Beneath them was the *petite bourgeoisie*—shopkeepers, artisans and small tradesmen, a class which had grown large with the urban and commercial development of the eighteenth century. And beneath these classes was the urban working force, not a vast modern proletariat, but a considerable group, nonetheless. These groups did not enjoy the general tax privileges of the clergy and the aristocracy, but many of them were privileged. Wealthy bourgeois often achieved exemption on a personal basis by buying royal offices which carried such privilege. Whole towns often enjoyed partial privilege, having negotiated special tax rates with the crown in return for extraordinary contributions or some other service. Thus, in the upper levels of the third estate the incidence of taxation was quite uneven.

At the base of the society were about twenty million peasant farmers, most of them free of any vestiges of personal servitude and many of them small landowners. The peasants paid rents, dues and tithes to landlords and to the church and heavy taxes to the government, but probably they were freer and economically better off than anywhere else in Europe; their participation in the revolution certainly was not a blind rebellion motivated by hopeless conditions. But upon the peasantry fell the major burden of taxation, and even at this level there were great differences in the burdens imposed. About two-thirds of the French provinces, the older ones, were called *pays d'élection;* there the crown's authority was great, and the *taille,* the major direct tax, depended largely upon the assessments of the tax collector. By contrast, the newer provinces, called *pays d'états,* had maintained local assemblies, and the *taille* was negotiated between royal and local officials.

Given this vast web of privilege—by class, by region and by person—it should not be surprising that the government faced bankruptcy in a prosperous country; the wealthy usually escaped taxation, and the government was left in the awkward position of taxing primarily the poor. Moreover, the mechanism of collection was costly and inefficient; the *taille* was collected by government personnel, but indirect taxes, such as the hated *gabelle* on salt, were contracted to private collectors called tax-farmers, and their charges often were exorbitant. Generally rising costs and the military expenses of the eighteenth century wars had forced the government to borrow heavily, and by the 1780s about fifty per cent of the crown's expenditure went to interest charges on the debt; another twenty-five per cent went to military expenditures, leaving only twenty-five per cent for all the costs of administration, public services and the court. Thus, the expenses of the court, while undeniably extravagant, were less significant than angry critics believed. The root of the fiscal difficulties was privilege, which protected France's wealth from governmental exactions; for political reasons it was not possible to reduce governmental expenditures significantly, and because of traditional privileges it was not possible to increase income to meet expenses without the consent of the groups that would have to pay. In the 1780s a number of finance ministers attempted various expedients to relieve the fiscal crisis, but the best of them always came to the same conclusion: those who were privileged would have to be persuaded to accept taxation. The question was how.

Early in 1787 the crown convened an assembly of notables, a hand-picked group of prominent people, and submitted new tax proposals to it, but this group refused to accept the responsibility and was dismissed without results. Then new tax edicts were submitted to the parlement of Paris, the high court that registered royal laws and provided the judicial machinery for their enforcement, but the parlement refused to accept them. Though a nonelective and nonrepresentative body, the parlement had become spokesman of the opposition to royal absolutism, and when the crown tried to put pressure upon the court, the parlementarians became public heroes for their resistance. They claimed that neither they nor the assembly of notables had the authority to approve what the crown asked and insisted that for such momentous decisions the estates general had to be revived.

France's privileged classes did not refuse adamantly to consider assuming some of the national burden, but they aspired to political power as the price of their support. The French admired England greatly, and though English government often was ill-understood, the French privileged classes understood clearly enough that in England royal power had been limited through parliamentary control of governmental finance; what they sought in the 1780s was to force the crown's officers to negotiate with a large and representative body dominated by the aristocracy and to concede some measure of political authority to that body in return for new taxes. They scored a victory when the crown agreed that an estates general should be convened in the spring of 1789, the first such assembly since 1614.

Unfortunately for the intentions of the aristocrats, they did not constitute the only politically ambitious group in France. The large middle class—prosperous, vocal and influenced by the *philosophes*—also desired a political voice as the price of their taxes, and their influence persuaded the government to authorize for the estates general as many representatives for the third estate as for the first two estates combined. The aristocracy quickly countered this maneuver by having the king declare that the estates would vote separately upon all resolutions. This was a desperately important issue, for if votes were taken by head the commoners could expect that with double representation and a little support from sympathetic lower clergy and country noblemen they could dominate the assembly; but if the estates voted separately, it could be anticipated that the two upper estates would stand together to evoke concessions from the crown in their own interest while blocking the ambitions of the third estate. Thus, when the estates general assembled in May of 1789 the commoners already were restless and angry, and there was an atmosphere of tension.

The royal financial position was worse than ever, and bad harvests had caused widespread economic distress. In the countryside there was violence, and rumors spread that the food shortages were the result of an aristocratic conspiracy to starve the commons into submission. The third estate was in an ugly mood. In June of 1789, in defiance of the king's order, it assumed the title of the National Assembly and invited the representatives of the other two estates to join it, and several of the clergy and some nobles did. Uncertain what to do, the king suspended the assembly and closed its meeting hall, but the delegates gathered in a nearby indoor tennis court and took an oath not to disband until they had given France a constitution; the king capitulated, ordering the remaining members of the upper estates to join the National Assembly, and the reform movement launched by the aristocracy had slipped from its control.

Despite this victory, the third estate remained distrustful of the vacillating king, for royal troops were concentrating around Versailles and Paris, and there were rumors that the government would break up the assembly; these rumors acquired more force early in July when the king dismissed the popular minister, Necker, who had convened the estates general, and violence erupted in Paris. On July 14, 1789 a crowd stormed the Bastille, a royal fortress, massacred the garrison and seized the arms stored there, ready to fight if the king should try to use troops to suppress the National Assembly and its Parisian support. About the same time, peasant uprisings broke out all over France against the exactions of aristocratic landlords. In this revolutionary atmosphere a number of great nobles began to leave France, rioting spread, and popular militias and provisional governments were formed.

In August the pace of change accelerated. Liberal aristocrats began a voluntary surrender of feudal rights, and the National Assembly abolished titles and adopted a Declaration of the Rights of Man. Hunger and fear of repression caused more popular demonstrations in Paris, and a mob marched to Versailles and forced the royal family and the National Assembly to transfer to the city. A liberal monarchical constitution was adopted under which legislative power resided in a unicameral assembly, and the king's power was limited to a suspensory veto which could delay legislation for two terms of the assembly. Declarations of war and foreign treaties also required the consent of the assembly. In the summer of 1790 regional privileges were destroyed as the old provinces were abolished and France was redivided into eighty-three departments. The assembly then moved to the establishment of a new currency, a national reorganization of the clergy and the establishment of new political mechanisms (which included financial qualifications for voting). The revolution appeared to have been accomplished with the victory falling not to the aristocrats who had begun it but to the middle class.

There were groups that wanted the revolution to continue, however, most notably the radical political clubs of which the Jacobins, under the leadership of Robespierre, was most prominent. These groups tended to be republican and to favor abolition of the monarchy. Shortly before the elections that were to establish a legislative assembly under the new constitution, an attempted flight by the king and his family strengthened these radical groups by demonstrating the king's implicit hostility to the new limited monarchy, and the Legislative Assembly of 1791–1792, though still primarily representative of the bourgeoisie, had a republican majority. War with Austria and Prussia, which broke out in the spring of 1792, further stimulated republican and national extremism, and new elections in the fall of 1792 produced an assembly, called the National Convention, that was composed entirely of republicans elected by universal manhood suffrage. The new assembly was more radical than either of its predecessors; one of its first acts was to abolish the monarchy under mob pressure, and in July of 1793 Louis XVI was executed.

In the midst of foreign war, political activity in the capital became more and more radical, and by mid-summer of 1793 Robespierre and the Jacobins dominated the government through its Committee of Public Safety, backed by the revolutionary Commune of Paris. Alleging the dangers of counterrevolutionary activity, Robespierre inaugurated a reign of terror, with mass arrests, trials by revolutionary tribunals and summary executions, which lasted until his enemies overthrew and killed him in the summer of 1794.

The overthrow of the Jacobins and French victories in the foreign war brought more moderate policies, and in the summer of 1795 a new constitution provided for a two-house legislature with executive authority vested in a committee of five called the Directory. Radical Paris objected to the new arrangements, but in October a young Corsican general, Napoleon Bonaparte, protected the government by firing artillery into a mob, and the projected elections took place.

The foreign powers reacted with indifference to the first stages of the French Revolution, for they were distracted by other problems. Britain had just gone through a governmental crisis concerning her interests in India, she faced rising unrest in Ireland, and in 1788 King George suffered the first of his fits of insanity. English opinion generally was hostile to the rising tide of violence in France and shocked by the execution of Louis XVI, but the British held aloof until the French Republic declared war on them in 1793. Similarly the interests of the eastern monarchies (Austria, Prussia and Russia) were committed elsewhere, to traditional involvements in Poland and to new rivalries consequent upon the decline of the Turks. After 1789, however, refugee aristocrats from France began to pour into foreign capitals, particularly Vienna and Berlin, where they begged foreign intervention to restore their positions and the authority of Louis XVI. In August of 1791 the Austrian emperor and the king of Prussia met at Pillnitz to discuss various issues, and with reference to the French situation they announced that they would intervene only with the unanimous consent of all the great powers. Since such agreement was quite unlikely, the declaration of Pillnitz was not a very dangerous statement, but in France it appeared a serious threat, particularly as it came only two months after Louis XVI's attempted flight abroad.

Developments early in 1792 made war almost certain. In Austria the new Emperor Francis II (1792–1835) was sympathetic to the war party, and an Austro-Prussian alliance against France was signed in February. In France the republicans wanted a war which they anticipated would intensify national and revolutionary sentiment. Both sides were eager for the conflict when the French Republic began it in April of 1792.

At first the war went badly for the French, but about the same time that the Convention proclaimed the republic, they managed to stabilize the military situation by winning an artillery duel at Valmy, and then one French army swept the Prussians back over the Rhine while another conquered the Austrian Netherlands. These victories were followed by a French offer of assistance to any people that wished to overthrow its government, by the reopening of the Scheldt to commerce and by the execution of Louis XVI. This series of events brought Britain, Holland, Spain and the Holy Roman Empire into alliance against France, and in the summer of 1793 the republic was in real danger, for the allies overran the southern Netherlands (which France had annexed) and invaded northern France, while internally a number of revolts threatened political chaos. However, the war had the political effects that the republicans had sought. They were able to intensify the terror against their political enemies and to institute radical measures of price controls and rationing, and in August of 1793 they called to military service all males capable of bearing arms, putting fourteen armies into the field. In the autumn the French began achieving military success, and in 1794 and 1795 they were victorious everywhere. Both the Austrian and Dutch Netherlands were conquered and turned into a Batavian republic under French influence; Prussia and the lesser north German states were forced out of the war, and France annexed the left bank of the Rhine. In the summer of 1795 British troops and emigrant French royalists attempted a landing in Brittany, but they were defeated quickly. Thus, when the Directory took office the situation appeared quite favorable.

The successes of the rapidly levied and ill-trained French armies astonished their enemies. Part of the credit belongs to the splendid artillery and sound officer training of the eighteenth century royal army and part to Carnot, the brilliant member of the Committee of Public Safety who undertook the organization and logistical support of the armies of the republic, but the greatest credit belongs to the revolution itself. The abolition of privilege and the political reorganization of the country enabled the republic to mobilize the vast resources that had been beyond the reach of the royal government. Popular participation in political processes, the terror and a campaign of hatred against royalists and foreigners who would undo the revolution all contributed to a wave of unprecedented national and patriotic sentiment.

The crucial factor in the new armies was morale, which enabled them to survive reverses and withstand casualty rates that destroyed the professional forces of the eighteenth century, but though morale was crucial, it should not be overlooked that France rapidly developed new methods and tactics adapted to the large but raw armies she was putting into the field. The exodus of masses of aristocrats deprived the French army of many of its senior officers, some of them competent professionals but many of them titled bunglers who held their rank through favor; thus rapid promotion was open to talented junior officers, such as Bonaparte, and the battlefield quickly sorted the talented from the merely competent. New junior officers were chosen from among sergeants with experience in the old royal forces, and new recruits were organized around cadres of old professionals. The most startling innovation, however, was in tactics. The French lacked the time to train masses of new recruits in the complex drill of rapid fire musketry and swift field maneuver that was the basis of eighteenth century tactics, so they relied upon the bayonet charge after artillery bombardment had softened enemy ranks. In early encounters, casualties were very high, but in the new French forces casualties were replaced more easily than in the professional armies of Austria or Prussia, and as the new French armies acquired experience, their casualties decreased while their victories increased. Though a few precedents might be found in the Dutch forces that fought Spain in the sixteenth century, in Cromwell's army in the seventeenth century, or in the American colonial forces in the eighteenth century, Europe had never seen anything like the new French armies of the republic for sheer size and dedication. The revolution had mobilized both the economic and human resources of the wealthiest and most populous nation in Europe, and it soon reestablished French military domination of the continent.

The Directory, which lasted from 1795 to 1799, faced acute financial crises, and accusations of corruption swirled around its members, but it provided an effective war government. In 1795 the only great powers still in the field against France were Austria and Britain, with the support of the south German states. After some initial successes, two French armies invading Germany were checked by the Austrians in 1796, but a third army under Bonaparte swept the Austrians from north Italy and established two republics there under French domination; in 1797 Austria accepted a peace that recognized the new Italian states and ceded the Austrian Netherlands to France. The next year the French invaded both the Papal States and Switzerland, setting up two more republics. Thus, already by 1798 the French had altered the political organization of Europe greatly, and of all the great powers only Britain remained in the war.

Desirous of forcing Britain to terms and convinced that an invasion of England was not feasible, Bonaparte proposed the seizure of Egypt, from which position the French could threaten the British empire in India. Early in the summer of 1798, Egypt was occupied easily, but in August the British destroyed the French Mediterranean fleet, which negated the strategic value of the success. French forces remained in Egypt until 1801, but Bonaparte returned to France in the summer of 1799. The Directory never had won popular support, while military success had made a hero of Bonaparte, and in November of 1799 the general overthrew the constitution and seized control of the government. A consulate of three men was established (1799–1804) which was dominated by Napoleon Bonaparte as First Consul.

During the course of the fruitless Egyptian campaign, a second European coalition had been formed against France, this time including Russia. Early campaigns of Russian and Austrian forces drove the French out of south Germany, Switzerland and north Italy, but a British invasion of the Netherlands failed, co-operation among the allies broke down, and the Russians quit the war. The French then inflicted crushing defeats upon the Austrians in 1800, both in Germany and Italy, and in 1801 Austria had to sign the Treaty of Lunéville, which conceded to France everything west of the Rhine and recognized the client princes and the satellite republics that France had established. In the same year, long negotiations with the pope produced a concordat by which part of the Papal States was restored in return for papal acceptance of the situation of the church in France: high clergy appointed by the government, all clergy paid by the government, confiscated church lands in

France not to be restored and all education to be controlled by the state. Finally, in March of 1802, England also made peace with France by the Treaty of Amiens.

In 1804 Bonaparte abolished the Consulate, proclaimed the French empire with himself as Emperor Napoleon I and established a brilliant court with an aristocracy based on talent and service. The Corsican general had succeeded in establishing the absolute monarchy that the Bourbon kings had sought, and he appeared secure. War with England had broken out again in 1803, but the rest of Europe was at peace, and France was the strongest nation on the continent. The situation remained basically unstable, however, for the English felt that their security was threatened by French control of the southern Netherlands, and Austria was humiliated and determined upon vengeance.

In 1805 a third anti-French coalition was formed, including England, Austria, Russia and Sweden, and Europe plunged into war again. At sea the English victory at Trafalgar in October of 1805 broke French naval power definitively, but on land a series of French successes, culminating in the victory over the Austrians and Russians at Austerlitz in December, quickly knocked Austria out of the war again. In the aftermath, the greater part of west Germany was organized into a Confederation of the Rhine under French "protection," the Holy Roman Empire was dissolved, Austria confirmed earlier territorial concessions, and Napoleon made one of his brothers king of Naples while establishing another as king of Holland (the former Batavian republic). The war was far from over, however, for Russia was still in the field, and Napoleon's new arrangements in Germany brought Prussia into the war against him. In 1806 he broke the Prussians completely at Jena and Auerstädt, and in 1807 he defeated the Russians at the Battle of Friedland, which left the French in control of all of Europe to the Nieman River. By the Treaties of Tilsit, signed in July of 1807, Prussia was reduced to half of her former size, and Russia accepted the French reorganization of Europe. A few months later Russia joined France in the war against England.

Napoleon's policy at this time was dominated by the war with England and by new provisions for his family. In 1806 he had proclaimed the Continental Blockade, banning English goods from all the ports of Europe to break the economy of the nation of shopkeepers, and the desire to make the blockade effective led him to occupy Portugal and Spain, areas that he was never to succeed in pacifying. At the same time, he created a new kingdom of Westphalia in northwest Germany for another of his brothers and moved his elder brother from Naples to Spain, giving Naples to a brother-in-law. In 1809 Austria once again tried to raise Germany against Napoleon, but again she suffered defeat, at Wagram, and had to accept another humiliating peace that cost her much territory and three and a half million subjects.

About 1810 Napoleon was at the height of his power, but there were many signs of discontent. An English expeditionary force in Portugal received strong local support, and the French were unable to complete their conquest of that country; though the French occupied Spain, guerilla resistance never ceased, and large French forces were tied down; in Germany there were a number of uprisings against French domination; and in new quarrels with the pope, French armies reoccupied the Papal States in 1809, whereupon the pope excommunicated Napoleon and the pope himself was taken as a prisoner to France. All over Europe Napoleon's creation and dissolution of new states were resented, and all governments were strained by the large levies of men and money that Napoleon constantly demanded of them. But the greatest danger was the growing tension with Russia. Personal rivalry between Napoleon and Czar Alexander I (1801–1825) was reinforced by a conflict over a number of issues, such as the Continental Blockade, the future of Polish lands and Russian ambitions for expansion in the Balkans. As Franco-Russian relations deteriorated, Napoleon assembled the Grand Army, a multinational force of about six hundred thousand men, and in June of 1812 if advanced into Russia. The Russians fell back, forcing Napoleon to depend upon very long supply lines; then at Borodino they stood and fought a bloody engagement with heavy losses on both sides. After Borodino the Russians had to fall back again, and the road to Moscow was open, but the French could claim no great victory; the Russian army was still intact and dangerous. When Napoleon's army occupied Moscow, the Russians burned the city, leaving the French with neither shelter nor provisions, and Napoleon had no choice but to withdraw. He was caught by the Russian winter, while cold and hungry men and horses were harassed by Cossacks and armed peasants and sometimes had to fight the pursuing Russian

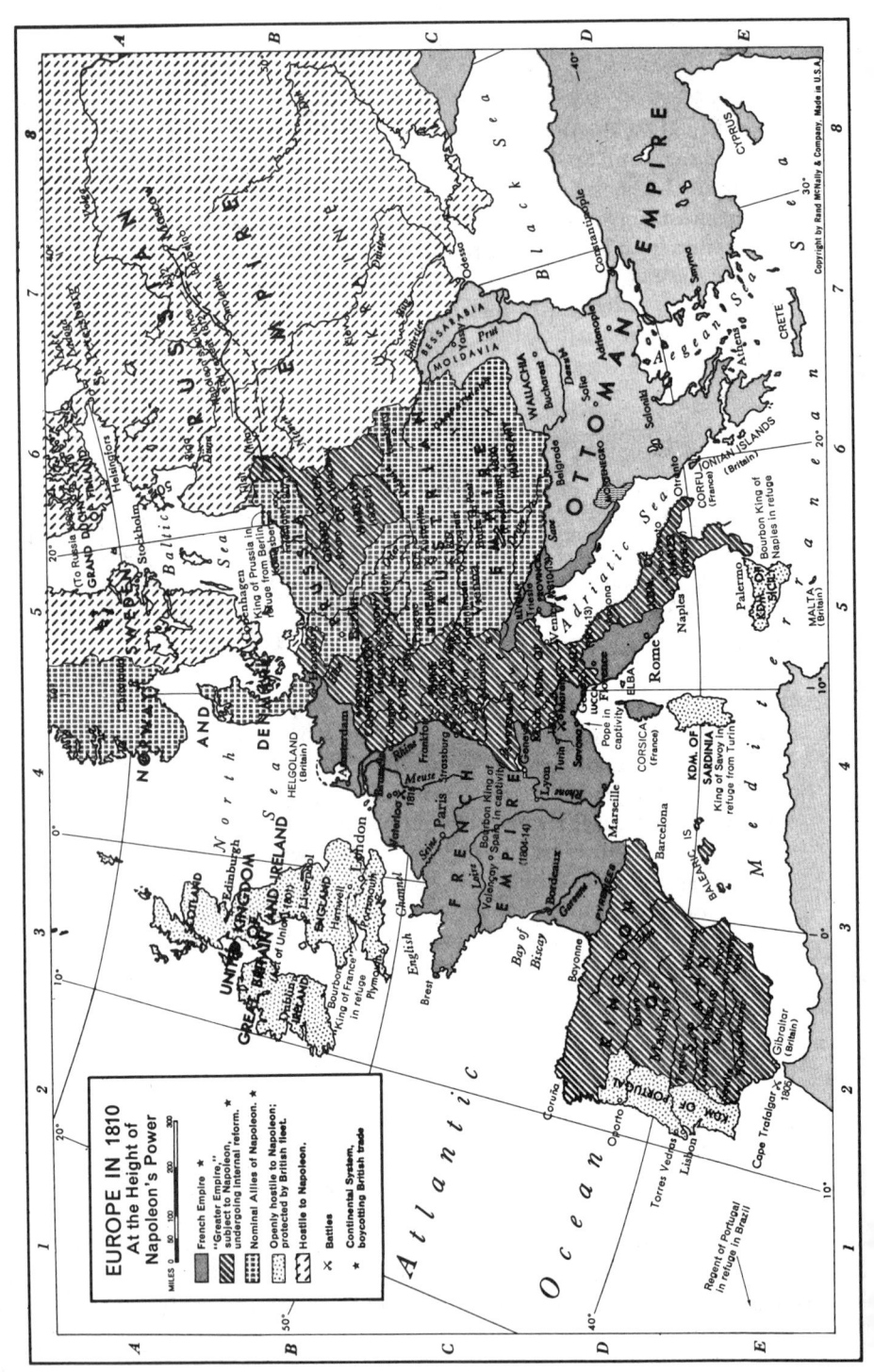

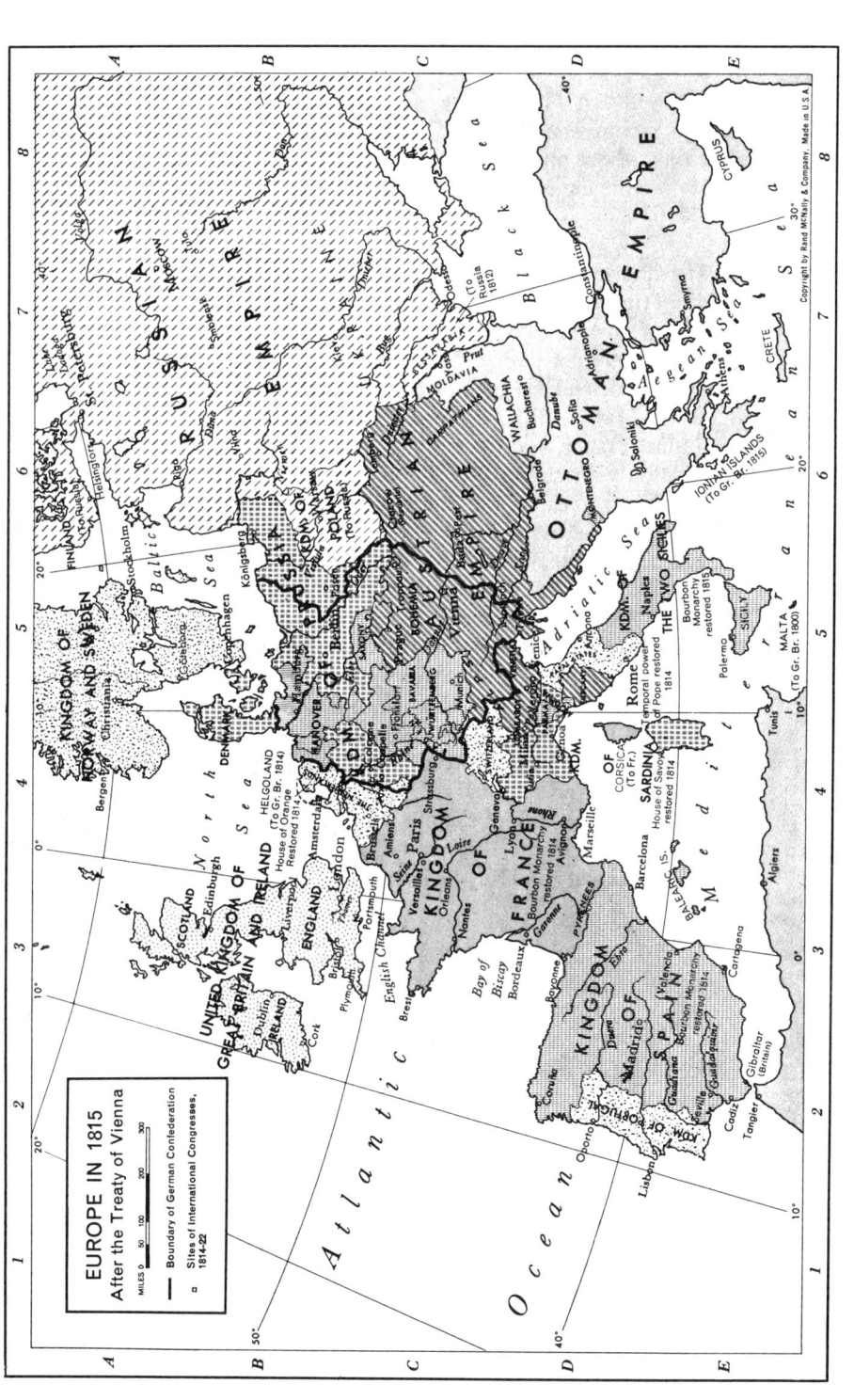

army; only about one hundred thousand men of the Grand Army lived to recross the Niemen. Napoleon hurried back to Paris.

The disaster in Russia encouraged France's other enemies. In 1813 the Prussians allied with the Russians; England was already in the war, of course, with forces in Portugal and Spain. As Russian and Prussian forces gathered, Napoleon raised another army and prepared to defend his control of Germany, winning the first encounters in May of 1813. Then in August Austria once more declared war against France, and the ensuing conflict became a German war of liberation with strong Russian support. In October of 1813 the Battle of Leipzig, called the Battle of the Nations, was fought, and Napoleon was defeated decisively by the combined allied forces. The war in Germany had forced the recall of French troops from Spain, and the English army under Wellington soon crossed the Pyrenees and besieged Bayonne. The allies made steady progress in Germany, and in December of 1813 they crossed the Rhine into France; despite some brilliant defensive actions against superior numbers, Napoleon could not halt the allies, and on March 31, 1814 they entered Paris. The imperial senate declared that Napoleon had forfeited the throne, and on April 11 he abdicated, being granted by the allies the island of Elba and a pension. The victorious powers then settled to the task of shaping the peace, a major problem because the Europe of the 1790s had disappeared during two decades of the revolutionary and Napoleonic wars.

Suggestions for Further Reading

The following lists include books of considerable variety—source material, monographs, and interpretive essays. Some are new studies, others classics in their fields. Obviously, so short a list cannot be exhaustive, but it is hoped that this one at least will provide some introduction to the varieties of history and of historical writing. Naturally some works are applicable to more than one chapter, but they have been listed only once, with the chapters to which they seem most appropriate.

The student seeking more detail of subjects touched here only briefly also would be well advised to consult the great compendia published by Cambridge University, as they treat an enormous range of topics. Examples are *The Cambridge Medieval History*, 8 vols.; *The Cambridge Modern History*, 14 vols., and *The New Cambridge Modern History*, 14 vols.; *The Cambridge History of the British Empire*, 8 vols.; and *The Cambridge History of Islam*, 2 vols.

Introduction

Cahnman, W., and Baskoff, A., eds. *Sociology and History: Theory and Research.* New York, 1964.
Collingwood, R. G. *The Idea of History.* Oxford, 1946.
Dray, W. H. *Philosophy of History.* Englewood Cliffs, N.J., 1964.
Gardiner, P. *The Nature of Historical Explanation.* London, 1961.
Gooch, G. P. *History and Historians in the Nineteenth Century.* Boston, 1959.
Gottshalk, L. *Understanding History.* New York, 1963.
Jones, T. B. *Paths to the Ancient Past.* New York, 1967.
Meyerhoff, H., ed. *The Philosophy of History in Our Time.* New York, 1959.
Muller, H. *The Uses of the Past.* New York, 1954.
Thompson, J. W. *A History of Historical Writing*, 2 vols., New York, 1942.

Chapter 1. Historians, History, and Prehistory

Braidwood, R. J. *Prehistoric Men*, 7th ed. New York, 1967.
Clark, G. *The Stone Age Hunters.* New York, 1967.
Gabel, C. ed. *Men Before History.* New York, 1964.
Mallowan, M. *Early Mesopotamia and Iran.* New York, 1965.
Mellaart, J. *The Earliest Civilizations of the Near East.* New York, 1965.
Palmer, R. R. *Atlas of World History.* Chicago, 1957.
Piggott, S. *Approach to Archaeology.* New York, 1965.
Streuver, S., ed. *Prehistoric Agriculture.* New York, 1971.
Shepherd, W. R. *Shepherd's Historical Atlas*, 9th ed. New York, 1964.

Chapter 2. The First Civilizations

Chiera, E. *They Wrote on Clay.* Chicago, 1956.
Edwards, I. E. S. *The Pyramids of Egypt.* Harmondsworth, 1952.
Frankfort, H. *The Art and Architecture of the Ancient Orient.* Baltimore, 1959.
Glanville, S. R. K., ed. *The Legacy of Egypt.* Oxford, 1942.
Kramer, S. N. *The Sumerians.* Chicago, 1963.
Oppenheim, A. L. *Ancient Mesopotamia.* Chicago, 1964.

Pritchard, J. B. *Ancient Near Eastern Texts Relating to the Old Testament.* Princeton, 1950.
Roux, G. *Ancient Iraq.* Harmondsworth, 1966.
Saggs, H. W. F. *The Greatness that Was Babylon.* New York, 1962.
Wilson, J. A. *The Culture of Egypt.* Chicago, 1956.

Chapter 3. The First Empires

Chadwick, J. *The Decipherment of Linear B.* New York, 1958.
Graham, J. W. *The Palaces of Crete.* Princeton, 1962.
Gurney, O. R. *The Hittites.* Harmondsworth, 1961.
Harden, D. B. *The Phoenicians.* New York, 1962.
Hutchinson, R. W. *Prehistoric Crete.* Harmondsworth, 1962.
Laessoe, J. *The People of Ancient Assyria.* New York, 1963.
Mylonas, G. *Ancient Mycenae.* Princeton, 1957.
Samuel, A. *Mycenaeans in History.* New York, 1965.
Steindorff, G., and Seele, K. C. *When Egypt Ruled the East.* Chicago, 1963.
Vermeule, E. *Greece in the Bronze Age.* Chicago, 1964.

Chapter 4. The Greek City States

Andrewes, A. *The Greek Tyrants.* New York, 1963.
Boardman, J. *Greek Art.* New York, 1964.
Cook, R. M. *Greek Painted Pottery.* Chicago, 1960.
Desborough, V. R. *The Greek Dark Ages.* New York, 1972.
Hignett, C. *The Athenian Constitution.* Oxford, 1952.
Hill, I. T. *The Ancient City of Athens.* Cambridge, Mass., 1953.
Jones, A. H. M. *Athenian Democracy.* New York, 1958.
Kitto, H. D. F. *Greek Tragedy.* New York, 1954.
Richter, G. M. A. *Archaic Greek Art.* New York, 1949.
Zimmern, A. E. *The Greek Commonwealth.* Oxford, 1961.

Chapter 5. The Great Empires

Adcock, F. E. *The Greek and Macedonian Art of War.* Berkeley, 1957.
Brown, T. S. *The Greek Historians.* Lexington, Mass., 1973.
Bury, J. B., ed. *The Hellenistic Age.* London, 1923.

Cary, M. *The Legacy of Alexander.* London, 1932.
Colledge, M. A. R. *The Parthians.* New York, 1967.
Heurgon, J. *Daily Life of the Etruscans.* New York, 1964.
Hill, H. *The Roman Middle Class.* New York, 1952.
Johnson, A. C. *Ancient Roman Statutes.* Austin, 1961.
More, P. E. *Hellenistic Philosophies.* Princeton, 1923.
Tarn, W. W. *Hellenistic Civilization.* Cleveland, 1961.

Chapter 6. The Decline and Fall of the Roman Republic

Boren, H. C. *The Gracchi.* New York, 1968.
Carcopino, J. *Daily Life in Ancient Rome.* New Haven, 1960.
Cowell, F. R. *Cicero and the Roman Republic.* Harmondsworth, 1956.
Hadas, M. *History of Latin Literature.* New York, 1952.
Kildahl, P. E. *Caius Marius.* New York, 1968.
Laistner, M. L. W. *The Greater Roman Historians.* Berkeley, 1963.
Lewis, N. and Reinhold, M. *Roman Civilization,* 2 vols. New York, 1966.
Syme, R. *The Roman Revolution.* Oxford, 1956.
Taylor, L. R. *Party Politics in the Age of Caesar.* Berkeley, 1961.
Wheeler, J. M. *Roman Art and Architecture.* New York, 1965.

Chapter 7. Imperial Rome

Charlesworth, M. P. *The Roman Empire.* Oxford, 1968.
Dill, S. *Roman Society from Nero to Marcus Aurelius.* New York, 1956.
Grant, M. *Roman History from Coins.* Cambridge, England, 1968.
———. *The Climax of Rome.* Boston, 1968.
Jones, A. H. M. *Augustus.* New York, 1970.
Jones, T. B. *The Silver-Plated Age.* Lawrence, Kansas, 1962.
Rostovtzeff, M. I. *Social and Economic History of the Roman Empire.* Oxford, 1956.
Starr, C. G. *Civilization and the Caesars.* New York, 1965.
Schultz, O. *History of Roman Legal Science.* Oxford, 1946.
Watson, G. R. *The Roman Soldier.* Ithaca, N.Y., 1969.

Chapter 8. The Twilight of the Roman Empire

Chambers, M. *The Fall of Rome: Can It Be Explained?* New York, 1963.

Dill, S. *Roman Society in the Last Century of the Western Empire,* 2nd. rev. ed. New York, 1958.
Gibbon, E. *The Portable Gibbon: The Decline and Fall of the Roman Empire,* ed. D. A. Saunders. New York, 1952.
Havighurst, A. F., ed. *The Pirenne Thesis: Analysis, Criticism and Revision.* Boston, 1958.
Lot, F. *The End of the Ancient World and the Beginnings of the Middle Ages.* London, 1931.
MacMullen, R. *Soldier & Civilian in the Later Roman Empire.* Cambridge, Mass., 1963.
Mattingly, H. *Roman Imperial Civilization.* London, 1957.
Nilsson, M. P. *Imperial Rome.* New York, 1962.
Pirenne, H. *Mohammed and Charlemagne.* New York, 1939.
Wheeler, M. *Rome Beyond the Imperial Frontiers.* Harmondsworth, 1955.

Chapter 9. The Heirs of Rome

Cochrane, C. N. *Christianity and Classical Culture.* New York, 1944.
Dawson, C. *The Making of Europe.* London, 1932.
Dill, S. *Roman Society in Gaul in the Merovingian Age.* London, 1926.
Gregory of Tours, *The History of the Franks,* trans. E. Bréhaut. New York, 1968.
Lewis, A. R. *Emerging Medieval Europe, A.D. 400–1000.* New York, 1967.
Runciman, S. *Byzantine Civilization.* London, 1933.
Van der Meer, F. *Augustine the Bishop: Church and Society at the Dawn of the Middle Ages.* London, 1961.
Vryonis, S. *Byzantium and Europe.* New York, 1967.
Wallace-Hadrill, M. *The Barbarian West, 400–1000.* London, 1952.
———. *The Long-Haired Kings.* New York, 1962.

Chapter 10. Early Carolingian Europe

Andrae, T. J. E. *Mohammed, the Man and His Faith.* London, 1936.
Boussard, J. *The Civilization of Charlemagne.* New York, 1968.
Brentano, R. *The Early Middle Ages, 500–1000.* New York, 1964.
Easton, S. C., and Wieruszowski, H. *The Era of Charlemagne.* New York, 1961.

Einhard. *The Life of Charlemagne.* Ann Arbor, 1960.
Fichtenau, H. *The Carolingian Empire.* Oxford, 1957.
Ganshof, F. L. *Feudalism.* London, 1952.
Laistner, M. L. W. *Thought and Letters in Western Europe, 500 to 900 A.D.* Ithaca, N.Y., 1957.
Rand, E. K. *Founders of the Middle Ages.* Cambridge, 1928.
Strayer, J. B., ed. *Feudalism.* Princeton, 1965.

Chapter 11. A Time of Trial

Bede. *A History of the English Church and People,* trans. J. Sherley-Price. Harmondsworth, 1955.
Brøndsted, J. *The Vikings.* Harmondsworth, 1960.
Daniel-Rops, H. *The Church and the Dark Ages.* 2 vols. New York, 1960.
Duckett, E. *The Wandering Saints of the Early Middle Ages.* New York, 1959.
Hoyt, R. S., ed. *Feudal Institutions: Cause or Consequence of Decentralization?* New York, 1961.
Lewis, B., *The Arabs in History,* 4th ed. London, 1958.
Lopez, R. S., ed. *The Tenth Century: How Dark the Dark Ages?* New York, 1965.
Magnusson, M., and Palsson, H., eds. *The Vinland Sagas.* Harmondsworth, 1965.
Whitelock, D. *The Beginnings of English Society.* Harmondsworth, 1952.
―――, et al. *The Norman Conquest: Its Setting and Impact.* London, 1966.

Chapter 12. The Birth of Feudal Monarchy

Barraclough, G. *The Origins of Modern Germany.* New York, 1948.
Fawtier, R. *The Capetian Kings of France.* London, 1960.
Haskins, C. H. *The Normans in European History.* Boston, 1915.
Herzstein, R. E. *The Holy Roman Empire in the Middle Ages: Universal State or German Catastrophe?* Boston, 1966.
Kelley, A. *Eleanor of Aquitaine.* Cambridge, 1950.
Lyon, B. *The Middle Ages in Recent Historical Thought, Selected Topics,* 2nd ed. Washington, 1965.
Painter, S. *The Rise of the Feudal Monarchies.* Ithaca, N.Y., 1951.

Suggestions for Further Reading 375

Petit-Dutaillis, C. *The Feudal Monarchy in France and England.* London, 1936.
Stenton, D. M. *English Society in the Early Middle Ages.* Harmondsworth, 1952.
Tellenbach, G. *Church, State and Christian Society at the Time of the Investiture Controversy.* New York, 1970.

Chapter 13. Merchants, Money, and Social Change

Adelson, H. L. *Medieval Commerce.* Princeton, 1962.
Bennett, H. S. *Life on the English Manor: a Study of Peasant Conditions, 1150–1400.* Cambridge, England, 1948.
Bloch, M. *Feudal Society.* Chicago, 1961.
Luchaire, A. *Social France at the Time of Philip Augustus.* New York, 1912.
Mundy, J. H., and Riesenberg, P. *The Medieval Town.* Princeton, 1958.
Pirenne, H. *Economic and Social History of Medieval Europe.* New York, 1937.
———. *Medieval Cities.* Princeton, 1925.
Power, E. *Medieval People.* London, 1924.
Schevill, F. *Siena, the History of a Medieval Commune.* New York, 1909.
Thrupp, S. L. *Medieval Industry, 1000–1500.* London, 1964.

Chapter 14. The Apogee of Medieval Christianity

Adams, H. *Mont-Saint-Michel and Chartres.* Boston, 1933.
Copleston, F. C. *Medieval Philosophy.* London, 1952.
Haskins, C. H. *The Renaissance of the Twelfth Century.* Cambridge, Mass., 1927.
———. *The Rise of the Universities.* New York, 1923.
Joinville, J. de, and Villehardouin, G. de. *Memoirs of the Crusades,* trans. Sir F. T. Marzials. New York, 1958.
Kern, F. *Kingship and Law in the Middle Ages.* New York, 1970.
Leff, G. *Medieval Thought.* Harmondsworth, 1958.
Runciman, S. *A History of the Crusades,* 3 vols. Cambridge, 1951–54.
Southern, R. W. *The Making of the Middle Ages.* New Haven, 1953.
Tierney, B. *The Medieval Mind.* New York, 1955.

Chapter 15. Challenge and Conflict in Later Medieval Society

Bryce, J. *The Holy Roman Empire.* London, 1904.
Cheyney, E. P. *The Dawn of a New Era, 1250–1453.* New York, 1956.
Huizinga, J. *The Waning of the Middle Ages.* New York, 1956.
Lea, H. C. *The Inquisition of the Middle Ages.* New York, 1956.
Madaule, J. *The Albigensian Crusades.* London, 1967.
Myers, A. R. *England in the Late Middle Ages.* Harmondsworth, 1952.
Otto of Freising. *Deeds of Frederick Barbarossa.* New York, 1953.
Runciman, S. *The Medieval Manichee.* New York, 1961.
―――. *The Sicilian Vespers: a History of the Mediterranean World in the Later Thirteenth Century.* Cambridge, England, 1958.
Tierney, B. *The Crisis of Church and State, 1050–1300.* New York, 1964.

Chapter 16. The Hundred Years War

Coulton, G. G. *Medieval Panorama: The English Scene from Conquest to Reformation.* New York, 1955.
Figgis, J. *Studies in Political Thought from Gerson to Grotius.* Cambridge, 1931.
Froissart, J. *Chronicles of England, France, Spain and the Adjoining Countries.* New York, 1961.
Jacob, E. F. *Henry V and the Invasion of France.* London, 1947.
Jewkes, W., and Landfield, J. B. *Joan of Arc.* New York, 1964.
Michelet, J. *Joan of Arc.* Ann Arbor, 1957.
Oman, C. *The Art of War in the Middle Ages.* Ithaca, N.Y., 1953.
Painter, S. *French Chivalry.* Ithaca, 1957.
Perroy, E. *The Hundred Years War.* New York, 1951.
Pollard, A. F. *The Evolution of Parliament,* 2nd ed. London, 1926.

Chapter 17. The Disintegration of Medieval Europe

Cipolla, C. M. *Guns, Sails and Empires.* London, 1965.
Elton, G. R. *The Tudor Revolution in Government.* Cambridge, England, 1953.
Gilmore, M. P. *The World of Humanism, 1453–1517.* New York, 1952.

Kendall, P. M. *The Yorkist Age: Daily Life During the War of Roses.* New York, 1962.
———. *Louis XI.* New York, 1971.
Morison, S. E. *Christopher Columbus: Mariner.* New York, 1955.
Parry, J. H. *The Establishment of the European Hegemony, 1415–1715.* London, 1949.
Penrose, B. *Travel and Discovery in the Renaissance, 1420–1620.* New York, 1962.
Runciman, S. *The Fall of Constantinople, 1453.* Cambridge, England, 1969.
Wood, C. T., ed. *Philip the Fair and Boniface VIII.* New York, 1967.

Chapter 18. The Renaissance

Ady, C. M. *Lorenzo de' Medici and Renaissance Italy.* London, 1955.
Burckhardt, J. *The Civilization of the Renaissance in Italy.* New York, 1958.
Ferguson, W. K., et al. *The Renaissance, Six Essays.* New York, 1953.
Hay, D. *The Italian Renaissance in Its Historical Background.* Cambridge, England, 1961.
Helton, T., ed. *The Renaissance: A Reconsideration of the Theories and Interpretations of the Age.* Madison, 1961.
Kristeller, P. *Renaissance Thought.* New York, 1961.
Mattingly, G. *Renaissance Diplomacy.* Boston, 1955.
Schevill, F. *The Medici.* New York, 1949.
Sypher, W. *Four Stages of Renaissance Style.* Garden City, 1955.
Von Martin, A. *Sociology of the Renaissance.* New York, 1945.

Chapter 19. Religious Reaction and Reform

Bainton, R. *Here I Stand: a Life of Martin Luther.* New York, 1955.
Bindoff, S. T. *Tudor England.* Harmondsworth, 1950.
Brandi, K. *Emperor Charles V.* New York, 1940.
Dickens, A. G. *Reformation and Society in Sixteenth Century Europe.* London, 1966.
Elton, G. R. *Reformation Europe, 1517–1559.* Cleveland, 1963.

Hillerbrand, H. J. *Men and Ideas in the Sixteenth Century.* Chicago, 1969.
Hughes, P. *A Popular History of the Reformation.* Garden City, 1957.
Mattingly, G. *Catherine of Aragon.* Boston, 1941.
Tawney, R. H. *Religion and the Rise of Capitalism.* New York, 1955.
Weber, M. *The Protestant Ethic and the Spirit of Capitalism.* New York, 1948.

Chapter 20. Habsburg Hegemony

Elliott, J. H. *Europe Divided, 1559–1598.* New York, 1969.
———. *Imperial Spain, 1469–1716.* London, 1963.
Franklin, J. H., ed. *Constitutionalism and Resistance in the Sixteenth Century: Three Treatises by Hotman, Beza and Mornay.* New York, 1969.
Lewis, M. *The Spanish Armada.* London, 1966.
Mattingly, G. *The Armada.* Boston, 1959.
Neale, J. E. *The Age of Catherine de Medici.* London, 1943.
———. *Queen Elizabeth I.* London, 1957.
Oman, Sir C. *A History of the Art of War in the Sixteenth Century.* New York, 1937.
Roth, C. *The Spanish Inquisition.* New York, 1964.
Trevor-Davies, R. *The Golden Century of Spain, 1501–1621.* London, 1937.

Chapter 21. The Scientific Revolution

Andrade, E. N. *Isaac Newton.* London, 1954.
Butterfield, H. *The Origins of Modern Science*, rev. ed. New York, 1957.
Caspar, M. *Kepler.* London, 1959.
Farrington, B. *Francis Bacon: Philosopher of the New Science.* New York, 1961.
Fermi, L. *Galileo and the Scientific Revolution.* New York, 1961.
Hall, A. R. *From Galileo to Newton, 1630–1730.* New York, 1963.
———. *The Scientific Revolution, 1500–1800*, 2nd ed. Boston, 1962.
Koyré, A. *From the Closed World to the Infinite Universe.* New York, 1957.

Kuhn, T. S. *The Copernican Revolution.* Cambridge, Mass., 1956.
Tillyard, E. M. W. *The Elizabethan World Picture.* London, 1961.

Chapter 22. The Rise of the National State

Aston, T. ed. *Crisis in Europe, 1560–1660.* London, 1965.
Barbour, V. *Capitalism in Amsterdam in the Seventeenth Century.* Baltimore, 1950.
Cronin, V. *Louis XIV.* London, 1969.
Geyl, P. *The Netherlands in the Seventeenth Century.* London, 1961.
Nussbaum, F. L. *The Triumph of Science and Reason, 1660–1685.* New York, 1953.
Steinberg, S. H. *The Thirty Years' War.* London, 1966.
Wedgwood, C. V. *Richelieu and the French Monarchy.* New York, 1949.
———. *The Thirty Years' War.* London, 1938.
Willson, D. H. *King James VI and I.* London, 1956.
Wolf, J. B. *Louis XIV.* New York, 1967.

Chapter 23. The Birth of the Balance of Power

Bruford, W. H. *Germany in the Eighteenth Century.* Cambridge, 1935.
Cobban, A. *A History of Modern France,* 2nd ed., vol. 1. Baltimore, 1962.
Dorn, W. L. *Competition for Empire, 1740–1763.* New York, 1940.
Fay, S. B., and Epstein, K. *The Rise of Brandenburg-Prussia to 1786.* New York, 1964.
Goubert, P. *Louis XIV and Twenty Million Frenchmen.* New York, 1970.
Klyuchevsky, V. *Peter the Great.* New York, 1959.
Moote, A. L. *The Seventeenth Century.* Lexington, Mass., 1970.
Plumb, J. H. *England in the Eighteenth Century.* Harmondsworth, 1950.
Roberts, P. *The Quest for Security, 1715–1740.* New York, 1947.
Wolf, J. B. *The Emergence of the Great Powers, 1685–1715.* New York, 1951.

Chapter 24. Man, God and Reason

Barber, E. *The Bourgeoisie in Eighteenth Century France.* Princeton, 1955.
Becker, C. *The Heavenly City of the Eighteenth Century Philosophers.* New Haven, 1932.
Cassirer, E. *The Philosophy of the Enlightenment.* Boston, 1951.
Cobban, A. *Rousseau and the Modern State.* London, 1964.
Ford, F. *Robe and Sword: the Regrouping of the French Aristocracy after Louis XIV.* Cambridge, Mass., 1953.
Hazard, P. *The European Mind, 1680–1715.* London, 1953.
———. *European Thought in the Eighteenth Century.* New Haven, 1954.
Lanson, G. *Voltaire.* New York, 1966.
Martin, K. *French Liberal Thought in the Eighteenth Century,* 2nd ed. London, 1954.
Talmon, J. L. *The Origins of Totalitarian Democracy.* New York, 1961.

Chapter 25. A Harvest of Violence

Beik, P. H., ed. *The French Revolution.* New York, 1970.
Brinton, C. *A Decade of Revolution, 1789–1799.* New York, 1934.
Brunn, G. *Europe and the French Imperium, 1799–1814.* New York, 1938.
Gershoy, L. *From Despotism to Revolution, 1763–1789.* New York, 1944.
Geyl, P. *Napoleon: For and Against.* New Haven, 1949.
Lefebvre, G. *The Coming of the French Revolution, 1789.* Princeton, 1947.
Palmer, R. R. *Twelve Who Ruled.* Princeton, 1941.
Rudé, G. *The Crowd in History, 1730–1848.* New York, 1964.
———. *Revolutionary Europe, 1783–1815.* Cleveland, 1964.
Tocqueville, A. de. *The Old Regime and the French Revolution.* Garden City, 1955.

Index

Abélard, Peter (1079–1142), 193
Absolutism: origins, 232; early modern, 314, 315, 319, 320, 323, 324, 357; Napoleon, 364
Achaean League, 60, 66, 71, 73
Achaemenes, 38
Acre, Siege of (1189–1191), 199, 200
Actium, Battle of (31 B.C.), 85, 90
Act of Settlement (1714), 331
Act of Supremacy (1534), 279
Adrianople, Battle of (378), 120, 121
Aëtius (d.454), 121, 122
Aediles, 69
Aetolian League, 60, 66, 71, 73
Africa: Vandals, 121, 123, 125; explorations, 249
Agincourt, Battle of (1415), 226–228
Agricultural revolution, 10–12
Agrippa, Roman general (d. 12 B.C.), 92
Ahmose, pharaoh (1570–1546 B.C.), 30
Aix-la-Chapelle: Treaty of (1748), 334
Akkadian language, 19, 23, 33
Alberti, Leone Battista (1404–1472), 258
Albigensian Crusade (1209–1229), 212–214, 219, 238
Alcuin of York (c.735–804), 140
Alexander the Great (336–323 B.C.), 56–59, 73 64–65,
Alexander I, czar of Russia (1801–1825), 365
Alexander V, pope (1409–1410), 235

Alexius Comnenus, Byzantine emperor (1081–1118), 196, 197
Alfred the Great, king of Wessex, then king of England (871–899), 152, 163, 164
Algebra, 21, 26
Alphabets, 36
Alsace, 242, 317, 328
Alva, duke of (1508–1582), 291
American War of Independence (1775–1783), 337, 339, 362
Amiens, Treaty of (1802), 364
Amorites, 19–20
Anabaptists, 278, 285
Angevins, 158, 166–168. See also Henry II; Richard the Lionhearted; John, king of England
Anglicanism, 238, 281. See also Act of Supremacy; Church of England; Henry VIII
Anglo-Saxons, 121
Anjou, 239. See also Angevins
Anjou, duke of (1554–1584), 295
Anne, queen of England (1702–1714), 331
Anne de Beaujeu (1450–1522), 243
Anne of Austria (1601–1666), 320
Antigonids, 59–61
Antioch, 118; and Crusades, 197, 198
Antiochus III, Seleucid king (223–187 B.C.), 60, 71
Anti-Semitism: medieval, 187, 197, 247

Antoninus Pius, Roman emperor (138–161), 93
Antony, Mark, Roman general (d. 30 B.C.), 85, 88, 89
Apollonius of Rhodes (3rd century B.C.), 63
Appanages, 170
Aquitaine, 166, 225, 227
Aquitaine, William I "the Pious," duke of (886–918), 192
Aquitania, 131
Arabs, 155, 305. *See also* Islam; Moslems
Aragon, 247, 285
Arameans, 35, 41
Archimedes (287–212 B.C.), 63
Areopagus, 51
Archon, 51, 52
Arian Christianity, 119, 123
Ariosto, Ludovico (1474–1533), 260
Aristarchus (220–150 B.C.), 62–63
Aristophanes (448–380 B.C.), 54
Aristotelianism, 301–303; challenged, 302–308
Aristotle (384–321 B.C.), 62, 203, 268; scientific theories, 299, 301, 303, 304, 307
Armada of Spain, 289, 290, 312
Armagnacs, 226, 231, 242
Armored knight, 222–226, 228, 229
Arras, Treaty of (1435), 227, 228, 242
Articles of Confederation (1777), 338
Aryans, 32
Ascalon, Battle of (1098), 198
Ashurbanipal, king of Assyria (663–626 B.C.), 37
Asiento (1713), 333
Assembly of Notables (1787), 356, 357
Assyria, 30, 36–37, 41
Astrology, 4, 203
Astronomy, Aristotelian, 300, 308
Athanasians, 119
Athens, history of, 45–53
Attalus, king of Pergamum (d. 133 B.C.), 72
Attila, king of the Huns (445–453), 121
Aüerstadt, Battle of (1806), 364
Augsburg: Confession of (1530), 274; League of (1688–1697), 328, 329; Peace of (1555), 275, 284, 285, 316
Augustine, Saint (354–430), 254, 275
Augustinians, 194
Augustus, Roman emperor (27 B.C.–14 A.D.), 89–92, 94

Austerlitz, Battle of (1805), 364
Austrasia, 131, 132
Austria, 247, 313, 315, 322; in eighteenth century, 329–337; French Revolutionary Wars, 359–368
Austrian Netherlands. *See* Netherlands
Austrian Succession, War of the (1740–1748), 333, 334
Autocracy, 89, 94, 101
Avignon, 209, 233, 235

Babylonians, 17–18, 37–39
Bacon, Francis (1561–1626), 309, 310
Bacon, Roger (c. 1214–1294), 268, 302
Baillis, 168
Balance of Power (early modern), 326–337
Balkans: settlement, 155; Russian ambitions, 365. *See also* Bulgaria; Hungary
Balliol (or Baliol), John (d.1269), 202
Banking (medieval), 186–187
Barbarians, 105–109. *See also* Celts; Germanic peoples
Baroque, 267
Basel, Council of (1431–1449), 236, 238
Bastille, 186, 348
Batavian Republic, 361, 364
Bavaria: electorate, 314, 317; Stem Duchy, 161, 162
Bayle, Pierre (1647–1706), 341
Bede, "the Venerable" (673–735), 254
Bellini family, 259
Benedict of Nursia, Saint (c.480–553), 135
Benedict XI, pope (1303–1304), 209
Benedictine Rule, 135, 136; Cluniacs, 192; Cistercians, 194
Benefice, 142
Bernard, Saint (1116–1153), 194, 199, 272
Bethlen Gabor, prince of Transylvania (1580–1629), 315
Black Death, 186, 214–216, 223, 258
Black Prince, Edward (1330–1376), 158, 223, 226
Boccaccio, Giovanni (1313–1375), 215, 258
Bohemia: Bohemian Crusade, 238; Thirty Years War, 313, 315
Boleyn, Anne (1507–1536), 280, 288

Bologna, 201; Concordat of (1516), 276
Boniface, saint (c.680–755), 133, 134, 136, 148
Boniface VIII, pope (1294–1303), 209, 233
Bordeaux, 180
Borgia, Caesar (1475–1507), 237
Borodino, Battle of (1812), 365
Botticelli, Sandro (1444–1510), 258
Boule (Council of the 500), 51–52
Bourbon, House of: gains French crown, 294–296. See also Henry IV; Louis XIII; Louis XIV; Louis XV; Louis XVI; and Philip V of Spain
Bouvines, Battle of (1214), 167
Boyle, Robert (1627–1691), 309
Brahe, Tycho (1546–1601), 306
Brandenburg, 322, 323, 330
Brétigny-Calais, Treaty of (1360), 225, 227
Britain: early, 95, 121, 147, 154. See also England, Scotland
Brittany, Duchy of, 232, 243
Brunelleschi, Filippo (1377–1446), 258
Buffon, Georges (1707–1788), 309
Bulgaria, 155
Burgundian Circle, 290
Burgundian inheritance, 239–243, 247, 248, 290
Burgundian Party, 226–231, 242, 243
Burgundians (Germanic tribe), 109, 121
Burgundy, 119, 162, 165, 192; Duchy of, 239–243
Byzantine empire, 125, 154, 156, 178; artistic influences, 259–262; crusades, 196–200

Cabot, John (1450–1498), 252
Caesar, Julius (100–44 B.C.), 81–88, 92; *Commentaries*, 105, 106
Caesaropapism, 119, 139
Cajetan, cardinal (1469–1534), 272
Calais, 223, 226, 228
Calendar (Julian), 85
Caligula, Roman emperor (37–41), 92
Caliphate, 127, 130, 196
Calvin, John (1509–1564), 266, 275–277
Calvinism: early spread of, 238, 277–279, 281, 283, 285, 288; in France, 294–296, 319, 321, 322; in the Netherlands, 291, 292; in Peace of Westphalia, 317; compared with Jansenism, 351; Thirty Years War, 314
Cambyses, Persian king (530–522 B.C.), 38
Canada, 336
Canon law, 193, 195, 204
Canons (semi-monastic priests), 194
Capet, Hugh, West Frankish king (987–996), 160, 161, 170, 172, 220
Capetians: founded, 160, 172; end of, 221. See also Robert the Strong, Odo, Hugh Capet, Louis VII, Philip Augustus, Louis IX, Philip III, Philip IV
Carloman, king of the Franks (768–771), 136, 157
Carloman, mayor of Austrasia (d.754), 133, 134, 157
Carnot, Lazare (1753–1823), 361, 362
Carolingian Empire, 144–145, 147–150, 157, 179
Carolingian Renaissance. See Renaissance
Carolingians, 132–150, 159–161; and Italy, 228. See also Charles Martel, Pepin, Charlemagne, Louis the Pious, Charles the Bald, Louis the German, Lothar
Carthage, 70–72
Carthusian Order of France, 193, 210
Castiglione, count Baldassare (1478–1529), 260
Castile, 195, 247, 285
Catalonia, 318
Cateau-Cambrésis, Peace of (1559), 294
Cathari. See Albigensian Crusade
Cathedral schools, 254
Catherine of Aragon (1485–1536), 278, 280, 285, 288
Catherine "the Great," czarina of Russia (1762–1796), 350
Catholic League (French), 295, 296
Catholic League (German, 1609), 313–315
Catholic Reformation, 282, 283, 351
Catholic Union (German), 274, 275
Catullus (c. 84–54 B.C.), 88
Cavendish, Henry (1731–1810), 309
Celestine I, pope (422–432), 123, 124
Celts, 105–109, 146, 147, 151
Centuries, Roman Assembly of, 70
Cervantes, Miguel de (1547–1616), 263

Chaeronea, Battle of (338 B.C.), 58
Chambers of Reunion, 327
Chambre des comptes, 169
Champagne (medieval fairs), 181, 182
Chancery court, 230
Charlemagne, Frankish king, then Holy Roman emperor (768–814), 136–141, 144, 157; government, 147–150; defenses, 152, 155
Charles Martel ("the Hammer"), mayor of Austrasia, then duke of the Franks (714–741), 132–134, 136, 144, 157; and basis of feudalism, 133, 142, 148, 156
Charles II "the Bald," West Frankish king (843–877), 150, 157
Charles III "the Simple," West Frankish king (893–923), 154
Charles IV, king of France (1322–1328), 172, 221
Charles V, king of France (1364–1380), 173, 225, 226, 228, 231
Charles VI, king of France (1380–1422), 173, 226, 227, 231, 242
Charles VII, king of France (1422–1461), 173, 227, 228, 231, 232, 239
Charles VIII, king of France (1483–1498), 173, 228, 243, 266
Charles IX, king of France (1560–1574), 294, 295
Charles V, Holy Roman emperor (1519–1556), 247, 248, 264; divides lands, 284; in Netherlands, 290; wars with France, 294; religious wars, 272–275; sacks Rome, 278; in Spain, 285
Charles VI, Holy Roman emperor (1711–1740), 297, 333, 334
Charles XI, king of Sweden (1660–1697), 323
Charles XII, king of Sweden (1697–1718), 323, 330, 331
Charles I, king of England (1625–1649), 284, 324
Charles II, king of England (1660–1685), 280, 324, 325
Charles "the Rash," duke of Burgundy (1433–1477), 173, 242, 243
Charters: towns, 183–185, 190; of emancipation, to serfs, 188
Chaucer, Geoffrey (c.1340–1400), 258
China: explorations for, 248, 252; missionaries in, 214, 234, 283
Chivalry, 204, 205

Christian IV, king of Denmark (1588–1648), 315
Christianity, 4, 105, 116–119, 137, 154; apogee, 204–214; challenged by Enlightenment, 342; conflict with Moslems, 195, 196, 198–200, 248; medieval scholars, 202, 203; reinforces Aristotelianism, 301; Renaissance, 255–257, 263–265. *See also* Church; Papacy
Christina, queen of Sweden (1632–1654), 323
Church: early modern, 281, 294, 304, 315, 316, 332, 353, 354; in later Roman empire, 115, 116–119; medieval, 133–139, 160–163, 171, 186, 187, 191–202, 204–214, 233–239, 254; nineteenth century, 363, 364; Peace of Augsburg, 275, 285, 311; sixteenth century reform, 269–271. *See also* Christianity; Monasticism; Papacy; *names of popes and monastic orders*
Church of England, 279, 281, 283. *See also* Anglicanism
Cicero, Marcus Tullius (106–43 B.C.), 81–83, 89, 91
Cimbri, 89
Ciompi uprising, 216
Cistercian Order, 194, 195, 210
City states (medieval Italy), 219, 265
Civilization, defined, 8; primary phase, 15–26
Classical heritage, 202; natural sciences, 268, 304, 305; Renaissance, 257–258
Claudius, Roman emperor (41–54), 92, 94
Clement V, pope (1305–1314), 209, 233
Clement VII, Avignon pope (1378–1394), 235
Cleopatra, Egyptian queen (d.30 B.C.), 84, 85, 89
Clermont, Council of (1095), 196
Cleves-Jülich, 313
Clovis, king of the Franks (481–511), 122–125, 129, 131, 144, 145
Cluniac Reform, 162, 191–194, 210
Coinage: Carolingian, 141, 148; debased in medieval France, 231; and medieval commerce, 181, 186, 255
Colbert, Jean-Baptiste (1619–1683), 320

Index

College of Cardinals, 192
Colonies: ancient, 45; European beginnings, 248, 250–252; eighteenth century rivalries, 333, 334, 336
Columbus, Christopher (c.1451–1506), 249, 250–252, 300
Commercial law (medieval), 183
Committee of Public Safety (French Revolution), 359, 361
Commodus, Roman emperor (180–193), 93
Commonwealth (England, 1649–1660), 324
Commune of Paris: French Revolution, 359
Communes (medieval), 184, 185
Conciliar movement, 236, 237, 274
Concordat of Bologna (1516), 276
Condottiere, 260, 261
Confederation of Bar (Poland), 336
Confederation of the Rhine, 364
Conrad II "the Salian," Holy Roman emperor (1024–1039), 157, 162
Consolamentum, 213
Constance, Council of (1414–1417), 235, 236, 238
Constantine "the Great," Roman emperor (306–337), 99, 101, 102, 116–119
Constantinople, 129, 178, 179, 197–200, 259
Consulate (France, 1799–1804), 363, 364
Consulship, 68–69
Continental Blockade, 364, 365
Copernicus, Nicolas (1473–1543), 303–308
Council of Blood (Netherlands), 291
Counter-Reformation, 281, 282, 286, 287, 314, 317
Crassus, Roman general (d.53 B.C.), 81, 83
Crécy, Battle of (1346), 223, 224, 231
Croesus, king of Lydia (560–547 B.C.), 37–38, 46
Cromwell, Oliver, Lord Protector of England (1649–1658), 324, 362
Crossbow, 222–224
Crusades: expeditions, 175, 195–200; Christian endeavor, 204, 208; socioeconomic effects, 180, 189, 190
Cuba, 336
Cult of the Virgin, 207, 208, 210
Curia, 205, 234. See also Papacy

Cursus honorum, 76, 78
Cyrus "the Great," Persian king (556–530 B.C.), 38, 39, 48

Dacia, 95
da Gama, Vasco (c. 1469–1524), 249–252
Dagobert, king of the Franks (623–638), 131
Danegeld, 164
Danes, 138, 153, 154
Dante Alighieri (1265–1321), 255, 256, 258
Darius "the Great," Persian king (522–486 B.C.), 38–39, 48
Darius III, Persian king (d.330 B.C.), 58
Dark age, in Greece, 44
Darwin, Charles (1809–1882), 309
David, king of Hebrews (10th century, B.C.), 35
Declaration of Independence, 337, 347
Deism, 345, 351
DeKalb, Baron Johann, 338
della Rovere popes, 259
Delian League, 48
Democracy: Athenian, 50–53; Roman, 81
Demosthenes, 57
Denmark, 150, 151, 275; Great Northern War, 330; Thirty Years War, 315–316
Descartes, René (1596–1650), 307, 310, 340
Determinism and free will, 4, 5
Devolution, War of (1667–1668), 327
Dias, Bartholomeu (c.1450–1500), 249–251
Dictatorship: Roman, 81, 84
Diderot, Denis (1713–1784), 348–350
Dikasteria (Athenian jury courts), 52
Diocletian, Roman emperor (284–305), 89, 94, 101–103
Directory (France, 1795–1799), 360–363
Divine right of kings, 323, 324
Domainal policy, 160, 161
Domesday Book, 164
Domestication of plants and animals, 10–11
Dominican Order, 214
Domitian, Roman emperor (81–96), 93
Dominate, 89

Don Juan of Austria (1545–1578), 286, 287, 291
Donation of Pepin (756), 136–137
Donatello, Donato (1386–1466), 258
Dorylaeum, Battle of (1097), 197, 198
Drake, Sir Francis (c.1540–1596), 289
Druids, 107
Du Guesclin, Bertran (c.1320–1380), 225, 243
Dunes, Battle of the (1658), 318
Dutch, in East Indies, 293. *See also* Netherlands
Dutch War (1672–1678), 327

East Frankish Kingdom, 145, 150, 155
Ecclesiastical courts, 205, 206
Eck, Johann Mayer von (1486–1543), 272
Edessa (Syria), 175, 198, 199
Edict of Nantes (1598), 296, 319; revocation, 321, 328
Edict of Restitution (1629), 316, 317
Edward "the Confessor," king of England (1035–1066), 164
Edward I, king of England (1271–1307), 158, 168, 169, 209, 222, 230
Edward III, king of England (1327–1377), 221, 226, 229, 230
Edward IV, king of England (1461–1483), 217, 246
Edward VI, king of England (1547–1553), 279
Egbert, king of Wessex (802–839), 147
Egypt, 13; primary civilization of, 16–26, 198–200, 363. *See also* Old Kingdom, Middle Kingdom, New Kingdom, Saites, Ptolemies
Einhard (c.770–840), 139, 140
Einstein, Albert (1879–1955), 308
Elamites, 20, 21
Elba, Island of, 368
Eleanor of Aquitaine (1122–1204), 166
Elizabeth, czarina of Russia (1741–1762), 335
Elizabeth I, queen of England (1558–1603), 279, 283, 285, 287–289, 323
Emigré nobility, 360, 361
England: American colonies, 333–336; early modern, 293, 321–325, 327–330; Enlightenment, 342, 343; French Revolution and Napoleon, 357, 360–368; Hanoverian succession, 331; medieval, 163, 171, 179, 182, 189, 194, 195, 216–231, 243–247; Methodists, 351; Reformation, 278–279; Renaissance, 261–263; and Spain, 285, 287, 289, 290. *See also* Britain; Parliament
Enlightened Despotism, 349, 350
Enlightenment: 340–350; political influence, 347, 349, 350, 353, 357, 358; reaction against, 350–352
Enlil, 24
Epaminondas (418–362 B.C.), 50, 56
Epicureanism, 62
Equestrian class, 73–76, 78, 91
Erasmus, Desiderius (c.1466–1536), 269, 270, 272; and Catholic Reformation, 282
Eratosthenes (3rd century, B.C.), 62
Estates General, 169, 171, 229, 231, 232; in 1788, 357, 358
d'Etaples, Lefebvre (c.1450–1537), 266, 275
Etruscans, 66–68
Euclid (3rd century, B.C.), 62
Eugenius IV, pope (1431–1447), 236
Euripides (480–406 B.C.), 54
Evans, Sir Arthur, 34
Evolution, 309
Excommunication, 206; Luther, 272; Henry VIII, 278; Napoleon, 365
Exploration, 233, 248–252

Farnese, Alexander, duke of Parma (1545–1592), 289, 292, 293
Fénélon, François de (1651–1715), 342
Ferdinand of Aragon (1452–1516), 247, 249
Ferdinand of Styria. *See* Ferdinand II
Ferdinand I, Holy Roman emperor (1556–1564), 218, 284, 297
Ferdinand II, Holy Roman emperor (1619–1637), 297, 314–317
Feudal monarchy, 190, 191, 243
Feudalism, 133, 142, 143; and commerce, 189, 190; England, 164; East Frankish kingdom, 145, 161, 163, 165; West Frankish kingdom, 160, 161
Flagellants, 215
Flanders, 166, 220, 227, 242, 266; as commercial center, 151, 179–182, 246
Flavians, 93

Fleury, cardinal (1726–1743), 332
Florence, 187, 216; Renaissance, 255–260, 265
Foederati, 121
Foix, Raymond Roger, count of (d. 1223), 213
Food gatherers, 9–10
Fourth Lateran Council (1215), 205, 206
Fra Angelico (1387–1455), 258
France: Calvinism, 277, 283; civil wars, 294–296; Consulate and Empire, 363–368; early monarchy, 168–171; eighteenth century foreign affairs, 332–339; eighteenth century social order, 353–357; Enlightenment, 344, 347–349, 351, 352; fifteenth century monarchy, 239–243; and Habsburg hegemony, 286, 290, 294, 296; heresies, 211–214; Hundred Years War, 219–232; *Jacquerie*, 216; reconsolidation, 312; religious dissent, 274–276; Renaissance, 262–263, 266; the Revolution of 1789, 357–363; seventeenth century, 318, 321, 325; Thirty Years War, 316–318; wars of Louis XIV, 326–330. *See also* West Frankish Kingdom
Franche-Comté, 242, 284, 327
Francis, Saint (c. 1182–1226), 214
Francis I, king of France (1515–1547), 218, 266, 275, 276
Francis II, king of France (1559–1560), 218, 287, 288, 294, 295
Francis II, Holy Roman emperor (1792–1806), then emperor of Austria (1806–1835), 297, 360
Franciscan Order, 214, 302
Franconia, 161, 162, 174
Franconians. *See* Salians
Frankish kingdom, 125, 127, 129, 131
Frankish Middle kingdom, 162
Franks, 122–125
Frederick I "Barbarossa," Holy Roman emperor (1152–1190), 165, 173, 199
Frederick II, Holy Roman emperor (1215–1250), 165–167, 173, 200, 208, 209
Frederick III, Holy Roman emperor (1440–1493), 217, 218, 247
Frederick V, Elector count Palatine (1596–1632), 314, 317
Frederick, Elector of Brandenburg (1688–1701), then Frederick I, king of Prussia (1701–1713), 323, 324
Frederick II "the Great," king of Prussia (1740–1786), 334, 335, 337, 348, 350
Frederick William "the Great Elector" of Brandenburg (1640–1688), 322
Frederick William I, king of Prussia (1713–1740), 332
Free Companies (Hundred Years War), 225, 226, 228
Free Imperial Knights, 273, 274
Free will and determinism, 4, 5
French Revolution: (1789), background, 353–357; course of, 357–360; wars, 360–363
Freud, Sigmund (1856–1939), 2
Friedland, Battle of (1807), 364
Frisians, 144, 151. *See also* Flanders
Fronde (1648–1652), 320

Gabelle (French salt tax), 231, 356
Galen (c.130–c.210), 97, 203, 303, 304
Galileo Galilei (1564–1642), 282, 306, 307
Galvani, Luigi (1737–1798), 309
Gascony, duchy of, 167, 219–221, 225, 239
Gaugamela, Battle of (331 B.C.), 58
Gauls, 60, 68, 78
Gelasian Doctrine, 124
Gelasius I, pope (492–496), 124
Geneva, 276, 277, 283
George I, king of England (1714–1727), 280, 331
George II, king of England (1727–1760), 331, 335
George III, king of England (1760–1820), 335, 360
German Renaissance, 263, 266
Germanic peoples, 103–104, 106–108, 120, 121, 150
Germany: early, 161–163. *See also* East Frankish Kingdom, Holy Roman Empire, Prussia
Ghiberti, Lorenzo (1378–1455), 258
Gibbon, Edward (1737–1794), 110–111
Gibraltar, 154, 180
Gilgamesh, Epic of, 20
Giotto di Bondone (1266–1337), 255, 256, 258
Glorious Revolution (1688), 325, 343

Goethe, Wolfgang von (1749–1832), 351
"Good emperors," 93
Gothic style, 207, 259, 262
Gracchus, Gaius (153–121 B.C.), 75–78, 81
Gracchus, Tiberius (163–133 B.C.), 75–77
Granada, Moorish kingdom of, 247, 249
Grand Alliance (1688, 1701), 328, 329
Grand Army (Napoleonic), 365, 368
Gratian (twelfth century theologian), 193
Gray, Thomas (1716–1771), 352
Great Encyclopedia, 348, 349, 352
Great Northern War (1700–1721), 330, 331
Great Protestation (1621), 324
Great Schism (1378–1417), 235, 236
Greco-Roman culture, 95, 105, 253
Greeks, 33, 37, 43; civilization of, 43–44, 53–54
Gregory I "the Great," pope (590–604), 126
Gregory VII (Hildebrand), pope (1073–1085), 162, 163, 193, 196, 208. *See also* Investiture Controversy
Gregory XI, pope (1370–1378), 235
Gregory of Tours (538–594), 185, 254
Guicciardini, Francesco (1483–1540), 260
Guilds, 183, 184, 200, 216, 220
Guise, House of, 294, 295
Gustavus II Adolphus, king of Sweden (1611–1632), 316, 317, 323
Gutenberg, Johann (c.1400–1468), 273

Habsburg, House of, 218, 247, 248; decline, 364; sixteenth century hegemony, 284–296, 312, 327, 328; Thirty Years War, 313–318, 325. *See also* Maximilian I, Charles V, Ferdinand I, Ferdinand II, Joseph II, Leopold II, Francis II (Holy Roman Emperors); Philip II, Philip III, Philip IV (Kings of Spain); Holy Roman Empire; Austria; Spain
Hadrian, Roman emperor (117–138), 93, 95
Hammurabi (c.2000 B.C.), 20–21
Hannibal, Carthaginian general (247–183 B.C.), 71, 75
Hanover, 330, 331, 335; House of, 331

Hansa (league of towns), 182, 188, 273
Harold Godwin, king of England (1066), 164
Harvey, William (1578–1657), 308
Hellenistic Age, 61–65
Helots, 46
Henry the Navigator, prince of Portugal (1394–1460), 249
Henry Tudor. *See* Henry VII
Henry I, king of England (1100–1135), 158, 165, 168
Henry II, king of England (1154–1189), also Duke of Normandy, Count of Anjou, 158, 166, 167, 180
Henry III, king of England (1216–1272), 158, 168
Henry IV, king of England (1399–1413), 217, 226
Henry V, king of England (1413–1422), 217, 226, 227, 243, 246
Henry VI, king of England (1422–1461), 217, 227, 246
Henry VII, king of England (1485–1509), 217, 246, 280
Henry VIII, king of England (1509–1547), 246, 275, 278, 279, 280, 288
Henry I "the Fowler," Duke of Saxony, East Frankish king (919–936), 157, 163
Henry III, Holy Roman emperor (1039–1056), 157, 162
Henry IV, Holy Roman emperor (1056–1106), 157, 162, 163
Henry VI, Holy Roman emperor (1190–1197), 165, 173
Henry II, king of France (1190–1197), 218, 266, 277, 294, 295
Henry III, king of France (1574–1589), 218, 295, 296
Henry IV, king of France (1589–1610), 218, 295, 296, 312, 318
Herder, Johann G. von (1744–1803), 127
Heresies: early Christianity, 119, 120, 123, 125; medieval, 210–214, 233, 238, 239. *See also* Albigensians; Hussites; Lutherans; Calvinists; Anabaptists; Anglicanism
Herodotus (5th century B.C.), 37
Hildebrand. *See* Gregory VII
Historical sources, 6–7; historical period defined, 7
Hittites, 21, 27, 28, 29, 30–33

Hobbes, Thomas (1588–1679), 342, 343
Hobéreaux, 355
Hohenstaufen, House of, 165, 173. *See also* Frederick, Frederick William (Electors of Brandenburg); Frederick II, Frederick William I (kings of Prussia)
Holland, 365. *See also* Netherlands
Holstein, 315
Holy Roman emperors, 156, 184, 193, 196, 199; French Revolutionary wars, 361; Habsburgs, 217–218, 244–245, 247; failure, 322, 326; in sixteenth century Italy, 262; Thirty Years War, 312–318
Holy Roman Empire, 364–365. *See also* Holy Roman emperors; *names of emperors* and *names of imperial families*
Homo sapiens, 9
Horace (65–8 B.C.), 88, 100
Hubertusburg, Treaty of (1763), 336
Hudson's Bay Territory, 329
Huguenots, 295, 296, 316, 321, 322, 328
Humanism: and Erasmus, 269, 270, 272; in Italian Renaissance, 255, 256, 259, 263, 266
Hume, David (1711–1766), 345, 351, 352
Hungary, 155, 274, 315, 322
Huns, 107, 121
Hurrians, 27, 33
Hus, John (c.1369–1415), 238, 272
Hussites, 214, 238, 272, 314
Hutton, James (1726–1797), 309
Hyksos, 18, 27, 33

Iberian peninsula, unified, 247, 248
Ignatius Loyola, Saint (1491–1556), 282
Ikhnaton, Egyptian pharaoh (c. 1375–1358 B.C.), 32
Impeachment, right of, 229
Index of Banned Books, 282
India, 214, 249, 252, 305, 336, 360
Indo-Europeans, 32, 39, 50–51, 66
Indulgences, 270, 271
Indus civilization, 16
Innocent I, pope (402–417), 124
Innocent III, pope (1198–1216), 199, 200, 205–208, 213

Innocent IV, pope (1243–1254), 208, 209
Inquisition, 214, 247, 282, 291
Intendents, 320
Intercursus magnus, 246
Interdict, 206
Investiture Controversy, 162, 163
Ionian revolt, 47
Ireland, 360
Isabella I "the Catholic," queen of Spain (1474–1504), 247, 249, 252
Islam: and Christianity, 195, 248; origins, 112, 126, 127, 155, 156. *See also* Crusades; Moors; Moslems
Israel, 35, 41
Issus, Battle of (333 B.C.), 58, 73
Italian allies of Roman republic, 77, 79
Italy: Enlightenment, 350; Habsburg domination, 285, 286, 322, 329; medieval, 156, 162, 165–167, 179–181, 184, 198, 219, 228, 237, 248; Renaissance, 254–268; Revolutionary Wars in, 363

Jacobins, 359, 360
Jacobites, 33
Jacquerie, 216
James I, king of England (1603–1625), 280, 288, 314, 323, 324
James II, king of England (1685–1688), 280, 325, 331
Jansenists, 350
Japan, 321
Jefferson, Thomas (1743–1826), 110
Jena, Battle of (1806), 364
Jenkins' Ear, War of (1739–1748), 333
Jerusalem, 116, 118; Kingdom of, 175, 198–200
Jesuits, 282, 283
Jesus, 101, 117
Jews, 35–36, 39, 116; anti-Semitism, 187, 197, 247
Joan of Arc (1412–1431), 227, 243
Joanna of Spain (1479–1555), 218, 247
Joffre, Marshal Joseph (1852–1931), 334
John, king of England (1199–1216), 158, 167, 213, 219
John "the Good," king of France (1350–1364), 173, 223, 231, 242
John "the Fearless," duke of Burgundy (1404–1419), 173, 226, 227, 242

Joseph II, Holy Roman emperor (1780–1790), 297, 350
Judah, 35, 41
Judaism, 35, 39, 101
Jugurtha, king of Numidia (d.104 B.C.), 77–79
Julio-Claudians, 92
Justices of the peace, 230
Justinian I, Roman and Byzantine emperor (527–565), 94, 125, 129
Justinian Code, 85, 94, 125, 193, 201

Kassites, 27, 28, 30
Kaunitz, Wenzel Anton von (1711–1794), 335
Kepler, Johannes (1571–1630), 306, 307, 308
Kiev, 153, 154
Knights Hospitaler, Knights Templar, 186, 188
Knox, John (1505–1572), 277, 288

Laboring class, 188, 215, 216
Lafayette, Marquis de (1757–1834), 338
Lamarck, Chevalier de (1744–1829), 309
Lancaster, House of, 217, 246
Langton, Stephen (1150–1228), 168
La Rochelle, siege of (1627–1628), 319
Latifundia (Roman estates), 74, 140
Latin League, 68
Lavoisier, Antoine-Laurent de (1743–1794), 309
League of the Public Weal (1465), 239
LeBreton, André-François (1708–1779), 349
Legates (papal), 192, 205
Legislative Assembly (France, 1791–1792), 359
Leibnitz, Gottfried von (1646–1716), 307, 345
Leipzig, Battle of (1813), 368
Leo I "the Great," pope (440–461), 124
Leòn, 195
Leopold II, Holy Roman emperor (1790–1792), 297, 350
Lepanto, Battle of (1571), 286, 287
Lepidus, Roman triumvir (d.13 B.C.), 85
Le Puy, Adémar de Monteil, bishop of (d. 1098), 196
Leuctra, Battle of (371 B.C.), 50

Ligurians, 105
Linnaeus, Carolus (1707–1778), 309
Linear A script, 34
Linear B script, 33
Locke, John (1632–1704), 310, 324, 325, 352
Lollards, 214, 238
Lombard League, 184, 188
Lombards, 126, 129, 136, 139
Lombardy, 144, 162
Longbow, 222, 223
Lorraine, 242, 243; House of, 294
Lot, Ferdinand, 111
Lothar, king of Italy, Holy Roman emperor (840–855), 150, 157
Lotharingia, 145, 150, 242
Louis "the German," East Frankish king (843–876), 150, 157
Louis "the Pious," Holy Roman emperor (814–840), 148–150, 157
Louis VII, king of France (1137–1180), 166, 172
Louis IX (Saint Louis), king of France (1226–1270), 169, 172, 200
Louis X, king of France (1314–1316), 172, 221
Louis XI, king of France (1461–1483), 173, 239–243
Louis XIII, king of France (1610–1643), 298, 316–320
Louis XIV, king of France, (1643–1715), 318–321, 326–329, 332
Louis XV, king of France (1715–1774), 298, 332
Louis XVI, king of France (1774–1792), 298, 337, 338, 350, 357–361
Louvois, Michel Le Tellier, marquis de (1641–1691), 320
Lübeck, Treaty of (1629), 315
Lucretius (96–55 B.C.), 88
Lucullus (79–57 B.C.), 82, 83
Ludovico "the Moor" (1425–1508), 259
Lunéville, Treaty of (1801), 363
Luther, Martin (1483–1546), 269–273, 277, 278, 305
Lutheranism, 248, 271–276, 278–285, 294, 314, 316, 317
Lütter am Barenberge, Battle of (1626), 315
Lutzen, Battle of (1632), 316
Lydians, 30, 38, 41, 42
Lyons: Poor Men of, 211, 212

Mabilon, Jean (1632–1707), 341

Macedonians, 56–60, 64–65
Machiavelli, Niccolo (1469–1527), 259–261
Magellan, Ferdinand (1480–1521), 250–252
Magna Carta (1215), 168, 169, 229
Magyars: raids, 155–162, 254
Malebranche, Nicolas de (1638–1715), 310, 342
Malpighi, Marcello (1628–1694), 308
Manichaeanism, 212
Manorialism, 140–142, 163, 164
Mantinea, Battle of (362 B.C.), 50, 56, 57
Manzikert, Battle of (1071), 196
Marathon, Battle of (490 B.C.), 48
Marcel, Etienne (d.1358), 231
Marches (Marks), 137, 138
Marco Polo (c.1254–c.1324), 248
Marcus Aurelius, Roman emperor (161–180), 93
Marduk, 24
Margrave (Mark Graf), 138
Maria Theresa, empress of Austria (1740–1780), 297, 334, 335, 350
Marius, Gaius, Roman general (155–86 B.C.), 78–80
Marlborough, John Churchill, first duke of (1650–1722), 329
Marriage regulations (medieval), 206–208
Marseilles, 181
Martin V, pope (1417–1431), 236
Marxism, 2
Mary I, queen of England (1552–1558), 278, 279, 280, 285
Mary II, queen of England (1689–1694), 280, 325, 331
Mary of Burgundy (1457–1482), 218, 243, 247
Mary Stuart, queen of Scots (1542–1587), 218, 277, 280, 287–289
Mathematics, development of, 203, 305, 306, 310
Matthias, king of Bohemia and Holy Roman emperor (1612–1619), 297, 313, 314
Maximilian I, Holy Roman emperor (1493–1519), 218, 243, 247, 290
Maximilian I, duke of Bavaria (1573–1651), 314
Mayors of the Palace, 132, 157
Mazarin, cardinal (1602–1661), 320, 326
Medes, 30, 38, 41

Medici: House of, 187, 258, 259; Catherine de (1519–1589), 294; Cosimo di (1434–1464), 258, 259; Lorenzo "the Magnificent" (1449–1492), 258
Medicine, in scientific revolution, 301–305, 308, 311
Mediterranean basin, 102, 248, 286; Sea, 154, 156, 179, 180, 195, 196, 286
Menander (343–291 B.C.), 63
Mendicant Friars, 214
Mennonites, 278
Mercenaries: in Hundred Years War, 225, 228; in Renaissance Italy, 261; in Roman army, 103, 109
Merovingians, 131–134, 182. See also Clovis; Dagobert
Merton, Walter (fl.1264), 202
Mesopotamia, 14, 16–26
Methodism, 351
Michelangelo Buonarroti (1475–1564), 258, 267
Middle Kingdom, 17–18, 27
Milan, 248, 259, 262, 265, 284
Ministerial responsibility, 229
Ministeriales, 162
Minoans, 27, 30, 33–34
Missi dominici, 138, 147
Mittani, 27, 28, 29–31, 33
Mithridates, king of Pontus (121–63 B.C.), 79, 82
Mithras, cult of, 117, 118
Mohammed (570–632), 126, 127
Monasticism: criticism of secular clergy, 210; education, 200, 254; and Franks, 132–136; in Ireland, 147; medieval reforms, 191–195; military orders, 198; mendicant friars, 214; trade, 179
Money fief, 182
Money-lending (medieval), 187
Mongols, 200, 248
Montaigne, Michel de (1533–1592), 266
Montesquieu, Charles de Secondat, baron de (1689–1755), 347, 348
Montfort, Simon de (c.1150–1218), 213
Montmorency, House of, 294, 295, 319
Moors, 247, 285. See also Moslems; Islam
Moravian brethren, 351
Moscow, 365
Moslems: 126, 127; Caliphate, 130;

clashes with Christians before Crusades, 127, 132, 156, 179; Crusades, 197–200; in fifteenth century, 248; and scholarship, 203; war with Spain, 263, 286, 287. *See also* Islam; Moors

Myceneans, 27, 30, 32–34

Nantes, 153; Edict of, *see* Edict of Nantes
Naples, 156, 248, 262, 265, 284, 318, 364
Napoleon Bonaparte: General, 360, 362, 363; Emperor Napoleon I (1804–1814), 364–368; First Consul (1799–1804), 363, 364
National Assembly (France, 1789–1791), 358, 359
National consciousness: Bohemian, 238; English, 246, 247, 325; French, 243; Sweden, 323
National consolidations: religion in, 247, 275, 277, 280; in seventeenth century, 318, 323, 325
National Convention (France, 1792–1795), 359–361
National monarchy, development of, 243, 246–247
Nationalism, 3
Nations, Battle of the (1813), 368
Natural Law, 343, 344, 346
Natural philosophy, 299–302
Natural religion, 345
Natural rights, 346, 347, 350
Near East, ancient: chronology, 27, 29–30, 41
Nebuchadnezzar, Babylonian king (605–562 B.C.), 37–39
Necker, Jacques (1732–1804), 358
Negotiatores, 179
Neo-Babylonian kingdom, 30, 37–38, 41
Nero, Roman emperor (54–68), 92
Netherlands, 246, 277, 283, 290, 306; Austrian, 329, 361, 363; Dutch, 242, 291–293, 312, 317, 321, 322, 325, 327–330, 361, 362; and Spain, 277, 284, 285, 287, 290–293; Spanish, 314, 318, 322, 327–329
Neustria, 129, 131
Nerva, Roman emperor (96–98), 93, 94
New Kingdom, 27, 29–32
Newton, Sir Isaac (1642–1727), 306, 308, 310, 340, 342, 343

Nicaea: Council of (325), 119; during first crusade, 197
Nicholas V, pope (1447–1455), 237, 259
Nimwegen, Peace of (1678), 327
Ninety-five Theses (Luther, 1517), 272
Nineveh, 14, 28, 37, 42
Nobility: in early modern France, 319, 320, 354, 355; exodus in French Revolution, 358, 360, 361; medieval, 159–161, 181, 184, 188–190, 204, 216, 229, 231
Nördlingen, Battle of (1634), 317
Norman conquest of England, 164, 165, 219
Normandy: in Hundred Years War, 222, 223, 226, 227; origins, 154
Northmen. *See* Vikings
Norway, 150, 151
Nystadt, Treaty of (1721), 331

Obelisks, 32
Octavian, 85, 88, 89–90. *See also* Augustus
Odo, West Frankish king (888–898), 160
Offa II, king of Mercia (757–796), 147
Ojeda, Alonzo di (c. 1470–1515), 252
Old Babylonian period, 21, 27
Old Kingdom, 17–18, 27
Olivarez, Gaspar de Guzman, count duke (1587–1645), 318, 319
Opposable thumb, 8
Optimates, 81
Optimism (Enlightenment), 345, 346
Orange, House of, 321
Oratory, 54
Orléans, 153, 227; dukes of, late medieval, 226–231; duke Philippe III (1674–1723), regent of France, 332
Ostracism, 51
Ostrogothic kingdom, 122, 125, 129
Otto I "the Great," East Frankish king (936–962), then Holy Roman emperor (962–973), 157, 161, 162
Otto IV of Brunswick (c.1175–1216), 167
Ottoman Turks. *See* Turks
Ottonians. *See* Henry the Fowler; Otto I
Oxford University, 201, 238

Pacification of Ghent (1576), 291, 292

Palace School (Charlemagne), 140, 148
Palatinate (in Thirty Years War), 314, 317
Palestine, 101, 102, 200
Palladio, Andrea (1508–1580), 267
Papacy: apogee, 205–208; Conciliar Movement, 236, 237, 274; decline, 209, 233; and early exploration, 248, 249; early growth, 123, 124; early medieval problems, 191, 192; and Franks, 136–138; Great Schism, 209, 233–236; and Habsburgs, 286; Investiture Controversy, 162, 163; late medieval heresies, 211–213; mendicant friars, 214; Renaissance, 237–239; repudiated by Eastern church, 196, 210; sixteenth century reformation, 272, 276, 282. *See also* Christianity; Church; *names of popes*
Papal States, 136, 205, 236, 237, 244–245, 262, 265, 363, 365
Paris: early modern, 275, 276, 296, 320; Enlightenment, 344, 352; medieval, 153, 160, 185, 186, 201, 216, 227, 231; Revolution (1789), 358, 359
Paris, Treaty of: American War of Independence (1783), 338; Seven Years War (1763), 336
Parlement of Paris, 169, 219–221, 225, 357
Parliament (English): development, 168, 171, 229, 230, 323–325; establishes Church of England, 279
Parthenon, 53
Parthians, 60, 64–65, 86–87, 90, 95, 98–99, 100
Pascal, Blaise (1623–1662), 307
Paul, Saint (d. 67), 118, 233
Patricians, 68, 70, 73
Paul the Deacon (740–801), 140
Pays d'élection, Pays d'états, 356
Peasants: eighteenth century French, 355, 356, 358; medieval, 188–190, 216, 231
Peasants' Crusade, 197
Peloponnesian League, 46
Peloponnesian War, 47, 50
Pepin, king of the Franks (741–768), 133–136, 144, 148, 157
Pergamum, 64–65, 72, 86–87, 98–99
Pericles, Athenian statesman (d.429 B.C.), 48, 50–53
Persepolis, 39, 58

Persia, 29, 30, 38–41, 46, 49, 50, 58–59, 121, 234
Persian Wars, 47–48
Peter I "the Great," czar of Russia (1689–1725), 330–332
Peter III, czar of Russia (1762), 335, 336
Petition of Right (1628), 324
Petrarch, Francesco (1304–1374), 258
Pharsalus, Battle of (48 B.C.), 84
Philip II, Macedonian king (359–336 B.C.), 56–58
Philip V, Macedonian king (221–179 B.C.), 60, 71
Philip "the Good," duke of Burgundy (1419–1467), 173, 227, 228, 242
Philip II "Augustus," king of France (1180–1223), 166–170, 172, 199, 213, 219, 225
Philip III, king of France (1270–1285), 169, 172
Philip IV "the Fair," king of France (1285–1314), 169, 172, 209, 221, 230, 233
Philip V, king of France (1316–1322), 221
Philip VI, king of France (1328–1350), 173, 221, 223
Philip I von Habsburg (1478–1506), 218, 247
Philip II, king of Spain (1556–1598), 218, 279, 283–297
Philip III, king of Spain (1598–1621), 293, 297, 312
Philip IV, king of Spain (1621–1665), 297, 318
Philip V, king of Spain (1700–1746), 297, 329, 332
Philippi, Battle of (42 B.C.), 85
Philippines, 283
Philistines, 35
Philosophes, 347, 349, 352, 357
Philosophy, 54, 62
Phoenicians, 35–36, 39, 41, 46
Pietism, 266, 271, 272, 351
Pillnitz, Declaration of (1791), 360
Pirenne, Henri (1862–1935), 114
Pisa, 179, 195, 255; Council of, 235, 236
Pitt, William (1708–1778), 336
Plantagenets, Angevin kings of England, 158, 166–168. *See also* Henry II; Richard the Lionhearted; John; Henry III; Edward I

Plataea, Battle of (479 B.C.), 48
Plato (428–347 B.C.), 55, 203
Plebeians, 68, 70, 73
Poitiers, Battle of (1356), 224–226, 231
Poland: early modern, 323, 333, 336, 337
Polis (city state), 44, 56
Polish Succession, War of the (1733–1735), 333
Politiques, 296
Polybius (204–122 B.C.), 63, 72
Pompadour, Antoinette de Poisson, marquise de (1721–1764), 335
Pompey, Gnaeus, Roman general (106–48 B.C.), 81–84
Pontifex Maximus, 84, 90
Pontius Pilate, Procurator of Judea (c.26–c.36), 102
Pope, popes. See Papacy; *names of popes*
Populares, 81, 84
Popular piety: eighteenth century, 350, 351; fifteenth century, 238, 239; thirteenth century, 210, 211, 214
Portugal, 195, 244, 247, 249, 252, 289, 292, 318, 350, 365, 368
Power of the keys, 271
Praetor, 69
Praetorian prefect, 91–92
Pragmatic Sanction (Austrian), 334
Prague: Hussites, 238; Peace of (1635), 317
Predestination, 276
Prehistoric period, 7–10
Premonstratensians, 194
Primary civilizations, 15–16
Primogeniture, 151
Principate, 89–90, 94
Princeps, 90–91
Princeps Senatus, 90, 93
Printing press, 267, 273, 305
Proletarians, 73–78
Protestant Reformation. See Reformation of the sixteenth century
Protestant Union (1608), 313, 314
Prussia: eighteenth century, 330–337; Revolutionary and Napoleonic Wars, 359, 361, 364, 366–368; royal crown acquired, 322, 323, 330
Ptolemies (Egyptian dynasty), 59–61, 63
Ptolemy, Claudius (2nd century B.C.), 249, 268, 302–304
Punic Wars, 70–71, 73–74
Purgatory, 271

Puritans, 324
Pyramid Age, 17
Pyrenees, Peace of the (1659), 318, 326

Quaestiones (Roman juries), 76, 80
Quaestor, 69
Québec, Battle of (1759), 336
Quietists, 351

Rabelais, François (c.1494–1553), 263, 266
Rameses II, Egyptian pharaoh (c.1292–1225 B.C.), 31
Rameses III, Egyptian pharaoh (c.1198–1166 B.C.), 35
Rastatt, Treaty of (1714), 329, 330, 332
Rationalism, 342, 345
Ravenna, 122, 126
Raymond VI, count of Toulouse (1194–1222), 213
Realist-nominalist controversy, 203
Reformation, sixteenth century. See Anabaptists; Anglicanism; Calvin; Calvinism; Catholic Reformation; Charles V; Council of Trent; Edward V; Elizabeth I; Henry IV; Henry VIII; Jesuits; Knox; Luther; Lutheranism; Mary I; Mary Stuart; Philip II; Zwinglians
Reign of Terror, 359, 361
Religious Wars: France, 295, 296, 316, 319; Germany, 273–275; Thirty Years War, 313–317
Renaissance: 202, 272, 273, 304, 305; Carolingian, 140, 147, 254; Italian, 110, 237, 252, 254–261; northern, 228, 261–268, 273
Republicanism: in France, 359
Requesens, Luis de Zuñiga y (1528–1576), 291
Revolts: medieval, 216, 220, 226, 231, 242; in sixteenth century Germany, 274
Revolutions: France, 353–363
Rheims, 155, 227
Richard I "the Lionhearted," king of England (1189–1199), 158, 166, 167, 199
Richard II, king of England (1377–1399), 158, 226

Richard III, king of England (1483–1485), 217, 246
Richelieu, Armand Jean du Plesis, cardinal de (1585–1642), 223, 317–320
Robert the Strong, count of Paris (d.866), 159, 160, 172
Robespierre, Maximilien de (1758–1794), 359
Rochambeau, J. B. Donatien, comte de (1725–1807), 338
Rocroy, Battle of (1643), 318
Rollo, Viking chieftain, baptized Robert, first duke of Normandy (911–931), 154
Roman Empire, 89–100, 102–103, 112–113; legacy, 114, 115; becomes Byzantine Empire, 125. *See also* names of Roman emperors
Roman Inquisition, 282
Roman Republic: ancient, 67–71, 75–87
Romanesque style, 195, 262
Rome, 121, 122, 228; and Avignon papacy, 233, 235, 236; as Christian center, 118, 233, 234; Renaissance, 259
Romulus Augustus, Roman emperor (475–476), 109, 122
Ronsard, Pierre de (1524–1585), 266
Rouen, 153, 180
Rousseau, Jean-Jacques (1712–1778), 110, 352
Russia, 150–155, 330–333, 335–337, 363–368
Ryswick, Peace of (1697), 328

Saites, 30, 41
Saladin (Salah Al-din) (1137–1193), 199
Salamis, Battle of (480 B.C.), 48
Salians (Franconians), 162, 163, 174
Salic Law, 221, 295
Saratoga, Battle of (1777), 338
Sardinia, 179, 195, 330, 333
Sargon of Akkad (c.2350–2300 B.C.), 19
Sassanians, 100, 108, 112–113
Savoy, duke of, 328, 330
Saxons, 137, 153, 163, 164
Saxony, 144, 161, 272, 330, 335
Scabini, 138, 147
Scandinavia, 2, 150–154, 275, 283. *See also* Denmark; Sweden

Schmalkaldic League, 274
Science, Hellenistic, 62–63
Scientific method, 299, 309, 310
Scientific Revolution, 299, 301–311, 340, 342
Scotland, 220, 277, 283, 287, 288, 313, 334
Scripture, 212, 238, 272; in Enlightenment, 341, 342; Methodists, 351
Sea Raiders, 31, 34–35
Seleucids, 64–65, 70–71
Seljuk Turks. *See* Turks
Semites, 19, 35
Senatorial class, 73–78
Senechals, 168
Serfs, 46, 141, 142, 183, 188, 189
Seven Years War (1756–1763), 335–337
Sforza, House of, 259, 262
Shakespeare, William (1564–1616), 263
Shamash, 24
Shield money, 189
Sicily, 156, 165, 166, 179, 191, 196, 199, 333
Silesia, 334, 336
Simon, Richard (1638–1712), 341, 342
Slave trade, 333
Slavs, 153–155
Social Contract, 342, 343, 347
Social War, 79–80
Society of Jesus. *See* Jesuits
Socrates (470–399 B.C.), 55
Solomon, king of Hebrews (10th century B.C.), 35
Solon (638–559 B.C.), 46
Song of Roland, 137, 149
Sophists, 54–55
Sophocles (496–406 B.C.), 54
Sorbon, Robert de (1201–1274), 202
South America, 250–252
Spain, 121, 125, 127, 154, 156, 195, 247, 252; eighteenth century, 332, 333, 336; end of hegemony, 312, 320, 322, 326–329; French Revolutionary and Napoleonic Wars, 361, 365, 368; Philip II, 284, 287, 289–294, 296; Renaissance, 261–263
Spanish Inquisition, 247, 282, 291
Spanish Netherlands. *See* Netherlands
Spanish Succession, War of the (1701–1714), 329
Sparta, 45–50, 56, 82
Speyer, Diets of (1526, 1529), 274
Spinoza, Baruch (1632–1677), 310

Spiritual Franciscans, 214
Star Chamber, Court of, 246
Stem Duchies, 161, 162
Stephen I, king of Hungary, Saint (c.975–1038), 155
Stilicho the Vandal (c.360–408), 109
Stockholm, Treaty of (1720–1721), 331
Stoicism, 62
Strasbourg, 328
Stuart, House of, 280, 287, 324, 325; Charles Edward, 280, 334; James Edward, 280, 331. *See also* James I; Charles I; Charles II; James II
Subinfeudination, 142
Sulla, Roman general (d.78 B.C.), 79–81
Sumerians, 19–20, 26, 27
Swabia, 161, 162, 165, 174
Sweden, 150, 151, 275; eighteenth century, 323, 325, 330, 331; Napoleonic Wars, 364; Thirty Years War, 316, 317. *See also* Gustavus Adolphus; Charles XI; Charles XII; Christina; Varangians
Switzerland, 276–278, 312, 317, 363
Syria, 30, 31, 35, 36, 198, 199

Taille (French tax), 356
Tarentum, 69–71
Tax-farmers, 356
Tetzel, Johannes (1465–1519), 271, 272
Teutones, 78
Teutonic Knights, 198
Thebes, 50, 56
Theocracy, 16
Theodoric I, king of the Visigoths (419–451), 109
Theodoric "the Great," king of the Ostrogoths (489–526), 122, 124, 129
Theophrastus (371–287 B.C.), 62
Thirty Years War, 293, 313, 317, 321, 322
Thomas Aquinas, Saint (1225–1274), 193
Thucydides (471–400 B.C.), 54
Tiberius, Roman emperor (14–37), 92
Tilsit, Treaties of (1807), 364
Timocracy, 45–46
Tintoretto, Jacopo Robusti (1518–1594), 259
Titian, Tiziano Vecelli (1477–1576), 259
Titus, Roman emperor (79–81), 93

Tools, 8
Tories, 325, 331
Tostig, earl of Northumbria (d.1066), 163
Tournaments, 204, 205, 229
Tours, Battle of (732), 127, 132
Towns: Celtic, 107; Church as center, 210, 211, 272; medieval, 165, 182, 186, 188, 190, 252, 255, 256
Trafalgar, Battle of (1805), 364
Trajan, Roman emperor (98–117), 93, 95, 97
Transylvania, 315
Trent, Council of (1545–1563), 237, 282
Tribes, Assembly of, 70, 81
Tribunes, 69, 70, 76
Tripoli, 198
Triumvirate: First, 83; Second, 85
Troyes: medieval fairs, 181; Treaty of (1420), 227
Tudor, House of, 228, 246, 247. *See also* Edward V; Elizabeth I; Henry VII; Henry VIII; Mary I
Turgot, Anne Robert (1727–1781), 350
Turks: Ottoman, 248, 274, 284, 286, 313, 322, 330, 336, 360; Seljuk, 196, 197, 199, 200
Tuscany, 255, 265
Twelve Years' Truce (1609–1621), 293, 312

Union of Utrecht (1579), 293
United Netherlands. *See* Netherlands
United States of America: founded (1777), 338
Universal manhood suffrage, 359
Universities: medieval, 200–203, 214, 254; and renaissance, 263; and scientific revolution, 304
Uomo universale, 260
Ur, Third Dynasty of, 19–20, 22
Urban II, pope (1088–1099), 196, 197
Urban V, pope (1362–1370), 235
Urban VI, pope (1378–1389), 235
Usufruct, 142, 178
Usury, 187
Utrecht, Treaty of (1713), 329–333

Valens, Roman emperor (364–378), 121
Valmy, Battle of (1792), 361
Valois, House of, 173, 218, 221. *See also* Charles V; Charles VI; Charles

VII; John "the Good"; Louis XI; Charles VIII; Francis I; Henry III; Philip VI
Vandals, 109, 121, 122, 125, 129
Varangians, 150, 153–155
Vasa, House of, 293
Vassalage, 142, 163, 206
Vassi dominici, 138
Vatican, 237; Library, 259; State, 136
Venice, 156, 178, 182; crusades, 199, 200; Habsburgs in, 286; Renaissance, 259, 265
Ventris, Michael, 33
Vesalius, Andreas (1514–1564), 303–306, 308
Vespasian, Roman emperor (69–79), 93
Vespucci, Amerigo (1451–1512), 250–252
Vienna, 274, 316
Vikings, 150–155, 179, 249, 254
Vinci, Leonardo da (1452–1519), 258, 259
Virgil (70–19 B.C.), 88, 100
Visigoths, 109, 120, 121, 125–127, 156
Volta, count Alessandro (1745–1827), 309
Voltaire, François-Marie Arouet (1694–1778), 110, 276, 344, 346, 348, 350

Wagram, Battle of (1809), 365
Waldensians, 211, 214
Wallenstein, Albrecht von (1583–1634), 315–317, 319
Walpole, Sir Robert (1726–1742), 331, 333, 334
Wars of the Roses (1455–1485), 246, 278
Washington, George (1732–1799), 338
Wellington, Arthur Wellesley, duke of (1769–1852), 368

Wesley, John (1703–1791), 351
Wessex, kings of, 154, 164
Western civilization, components of, 15–16
West Frankish Kingdom, 145, 150, 153, 154, 159, 161
Westphalia: kingdom of, 365; Peace of (1648), 318, 327
Whigs, 325, 331, 333
White Mountain, Battle of (1620), 314
Whitefield, George (1714–1770), 351
William I "the Conquerer," king of England (1066–1087), 158, 164, 165
William I of Nassau-Orange, "the Silent" (1533–1584), 292
William III of Orange (1650–1702), Stadtholder of Dutch Netherlands, then king of England (1689–1702), 280, 321, 325, 327, 328, 331, 343
Witt, John de (1625–1672), 321
Wolff, Christian (1679–1754), 346
Women, 205, 207, 208, 221
Worms, Diet of (1521), 272
Writing, 7, 25
Wycliffe, John (c.1320–1384), 238

Xenophon (434–355 B.C.), 54
Xerxes, Persian king (486–464 B.C.), 48

York, House of, 217, 246
Yorktown, Battle of (1781), 338

Zara, 200
Zeno, Roman emperor (474–491), 109
Zero, mathematical concept, 305
Ziggurat, 23
Zoroaster (6th century B.C.), 39–40
Zwinglians, 277, 278

PRINTED IN U.S.A.